ADVANCES IN

EXPERIMENTAL
SOCIAL PSYCHOLOGY

VOLUME 10

CONTRIBUTORS TO VOLUME 10

Leonard Berkowitz

Russell G. Geen

R. Harré

Albert A. Harrison

Martin L. Hoffman

Jacques P. Leyens

Ross D. Parke

Michael B. Quanty

Lee Ross

Barry R. Schlenker

Shalom H. Schwartz

Richard J. Sebastian

Stephen G. West

ADVANCES IN

Experimental
Social Psychology

EDITED BY

Leonard Berkowitz

DEPARTMENT OF PSYCHOLOGY
UNIVERSITY OF WISCONSIN
MADISON, WISCONSIN

VOLUME 10

ACADEMIC PRESS
New York San Francisco London 1977
A Subsidiary of Harcourt Brace Jovanovich, Publishers

ACADEMIC PRESS, INC.
111 Fifth Avenue, New York, New York 10003

United Kingdom Edition published by
ACADEMIC PRESS, INC. (LONDON) LTD.
24/28 Oval Road, London NW1

LIBRARY OF CONGRESS CATALOG CARD NUMBER: 64-23452

ISBN 0–12–015210–X

PRINTED IN THE UNITED STATES OF AMERICA

CONTENTS

Some Effects of Violent and Nonviolent Movies on the Behavior of Juvenile Delinquents

Ross D. Parke, Leonard Berkowitz, Jacques P. Leyens, Stephen G. West, and Richard J. Sebastian

The Intuitive Psychologist and His Shortcomings: Distortions in the Attribution Process

Lee Ross

Normative Influences on Altruism

Shalom H. Schwartz

A Discussion of the Domain and Methods of Social Psychology: Two Papers by Rom Harré and Barry R. Schlenker

Leonard Berkowitz

The Ethogenic Approach: Theory and Practice

R. Harré

On the Ethogenic Approach: Etiquette and Revolution

Barry R. Schlenker

Automatisms and Autonomies: In Reply to Professor Schlenker

R. Harré

CONTRIBUTORS

Numbers in parentheses indicate the pages on which the authors' contributions begin.

Leonard Berkowitz, *Department of Psychology, University of Wisconsin, Madison, Wisconsin* (135)

Russell G. Geen, *Department of Psychology, University of Missouri, Columbia, Missouri* (1)

R. Harré, *Linacre College, Oxford University, Oxford, England, and State University of New York, Binghamton, New York* (283, 331)

Albert A. Harrison, *Department of Psychology, University of California, Davis, California* (39)

Martin L. Hoffman, *Department of Psychology, University of Michigan, Ann Arbor, Michigan* (85)

Jacques P. Leyens, *Department of Psychology, University of Louvain, Louvain, Belgium* (135)

Ross D. Parke, *Department of Psychology, University of Illinois, Urbana, Illinois* (135)

Michael B. Quanty, *Department of Psychology, University of Missouri, Columbia, Missouri* (1)

Lee Ross, *Department of Psychology, Stanford University, Stanford, California* (173)

Barry R. Schlenker, *Department of Psychology, University of Florida, Gainesville, Florida* (315)

Shalom H. Schwartz, *Department of Sociology, University of Wisconsin, Madison, Wisconsin* (221)

Richard J. Sebastian, *Department of Psychology, University of Notre Dame, Notre Dame, Indiana* (135)

Stephen G. West, *Department of Psychology, Florida State University, Tallahassee, Florida* (135)

THE CATHARSIS OF AGGRESSION: AN EVALUATION OF A HYPOTHESIS[1]

Russell G. Geen

and

Michael B. Quanty

UNIVERSITY OF MISSOURI
COLUMBIA, MISSOURI

[1] The authors' research reported in this paper was supported by grants from the National Science Foundation. We are grateful to Stephen West for comments on an earlier draft.

1

I. Introduction

The idea that one can purge emotions by experiencing them intensely goes back at least to Aristotle (*Poetics,* Book 6). He had taught that classic tragedy, by arousing feelings of pity and fear, allows the observer to achieve catharsis of those affective states. Over the years many psychologists have accepted the idea that feelings of anger and hostility may also be drained off through intense participation in behavior related to these emotions. Experimental studies of catharsis generally have been of two types. In one the subject is exposed to aggression carried out by others, as in drama and violent sports. The studies along these lines, which embody the essence of the Aristotelian view of catharsis, have been discussed in several recent reviews (e.g., Bandura, 1973; Geen, in press), most of which have failed to support the Aristotelian position. These investigations will not be covered in the present review. Instead, we shall concentrate chiefly on studies involving the other type of catharsis—that in which a subject who has been aroused to aggress is allowed to attack either his antagonist or some substitute target. We shall attempt to answer two questions: First, does such aggression reduce the attacker's emotional arousal? And second, does this aggression make the attacker less likely to behave aggressively afterwards?

A. PSYCHOANALYTIC AND RELATED VIEWPOINTS

Much of the current thinking on catharsis of aggression originated with Sigmund Freud, who first used the idea in connection with the treatment of hysteria. Proposing that therapy for hysterical symptoms requires the abreaction of an affective state previously associated with trauma, Breuer and Freud (1961), held that the optimal abreaction for interpersonal traumas, such as insults, is obtained through direct aggression: "The reaction of an injured person to a trauma has really only . . . a 'cathartic' effect if it is expressed in an adequate reaction like revenge" (p. 5). The form in which retaliation is expressed may be either physical or verbal. Whatever the mode, the expression of hostility is preferable to no aggressive reaction at all:

> An insult retaliated, be it only in words, is differently recalled from one that had to be taken in silence.... [M]an finds a substitute for . . . [direct aggression] . . . in speech through which help the affect can well-nigh be abreacted. [Breuer & Freud, 1961, p. 5]

In relating catharsis to hysteria Freud therefore originally stressed its importance in the treatment (and, by implication, possible prevention) of symptoms, an idea that is still reflected in the belief that expressing anger is better for the person than holding it in, and that suppression of hostility may lead to hypertension or other psychosomatic disorders.

The idea of catharsis was also implicit in Freud's later writing, especially in his principle of the death wish. In much of his thinking on motivation, Freud was guided by an assumption that he carried over from his early training in neurophysiology—the notion that the nervous system operates as a whole to keep itself free of stimulation (Holt, 1965). Because the organism strives constantly to reduce tension, Freud (1959, p. 70) reasoned that "the aim of all life is death" and that the death wish in which this aim is manifested is ultimately self-destructive. The expression of aggression toward others is the alternative available to the organism, by which it turns the death wish outward away from itself. In his famous letter to Albert Einstein on the inevitability of war, Freud articulated the principle that the reduction of aggressive drive through aggressive behavior is necessary to self-preservation:

> The death instinct turns into the destructive instinct if . . . it is directed outwards, on to objects. The living creature preserves its own life, so to say, by destroying an extraneous one. . . . [I]f these forces are turned to destruction in the external world, *the living creature will be relieved* and the effect must be beneficial. This would serve as biological justification for all the ugly and dangerous impulses against which we are struggling. [Italics added (Freud, 1963, p. 143)]

In essence, then, the Freudian position may be summarized by saying that psychic energy arising from the death instinct creates a tension that must be relieved either through self-aggression or aggression toward others. Aggression reduces aggressive motivation and decreases the likelihood of further violence until such a time as tensions again build to an intolerable level. It must be noted that this point of view is hardly exclusive to psychoanalysis. It underlies, in one way or another, many current statements on hostility and aggression that assume an aggressiveness instinct in man (e.g., Eibl-Eibesfeldt, 1970; Lorenz, 1966). It is also implicit in "primal therapy" (Janov, 1970), according to which the expression of aggressive urges has the general effect of lowering aggressive tensions and hostilities. Aggression is therefore regarded as a basically useful activity that provides a catharsis of aversive and potentially harmful feelings and drives.

B. THE LINEAR CAUSE–EFFECT HYPOTHESIS

One need not accept Freud's theory of the innate determinants of behavior to espouse a form of the catharsis hypothesis, however. A more commonly held viewpoint among contemporary psychologists is that aggression elicited by provocation from the environment may reduce tensions produced by such provocations (e.g., Doob, 1970; Konecni, 1975). Dollard and his Yale colleagues

(Dollard, Doob, Miller, Mowrer, & Sears, 1939) added a corollary on catharsis to their version of the frustration–aggression hypothesis that has stimulated much of the research on catharsis over the past thirty years[2] : "The expression of any act of aggression is a catharsis that reduces the instigation to all other acts of aggression" (p. 53). Formulations such as this propose a simple cause–effect model: frustration leads to a hypothetical state of instigation to aggress, which, in turn, produces aggression. Aggressive behavior, by reducing the instigation, renders further violence less probable. In short, it is thoroughly consistent with the Freudian idea relating tension reduction to reduction of aggression.

Part of the popularity of this cause–effect model among some psychologists may be due to the widely held belief, already noted, that it is somehow better for one's mental health not to repress aggressive desires but to express them openly (Holt, 1970). Certainly it makes sense to argue that "letting off steam" through aggression makes a person feel less distressed than he would have felt if he had kept everything inside. Such an argument is also consistent with medical evidence of a connection between repressed hostility and a number of psychosomatic ailments (Alexander, 1950). As we shall see, even this idea may be an oversimplication of the relationship between aggression and somatic states. Even if it were true, however, it would still not lead to any obvious conclusion that a reduction in aggressive *behavior* should be the ultimate outcome of the expression of aggression.

C. AN OVERVIEW OF THE CRITICISM

A great deal of confusion surrounds the notion of aggression catharsis. In part, this confusion arises from the fact that much of the data fails to support the hypothesis outlined in the previous section. This lack of support for the hypothesis will be dealt with in greater detail in the substantive portions of this review. Furthermore, many of the findings that have been offered in support for the catharsis hypothesis are not, as we shall see, invulnerable to explanation in terms of other constructs. The general lack of support to be found for the catharsis hypothesis in the literature at the present time has led to two developments. One is Bandura's (1973) call for a moratorium on use of the hypothesis. The other is Konecni's (1975) more recent reduction of the term *catharsis* to little more than a label describing a reduction in aggressive behavior brought about by prior aggression, whatever the intervening process might be.

---

[2] It is perhaps well to point out that the frustration–aggression hypothesis is a statement relating an antecedent condition (frustration) to a response (aggression) and not one describing the outcomes of aggression. There is nothing in the frustration–aggression relationship described by the Yale group that necessitates the postulation of a catharsis process, even though Dollard and his colleagues did append such a corollary to their hypothesis.

In this review we will attempt to avoid some of the confusion that might otherwise befall us by adopting some fairly narrow definitions of terms. One term that we shall use frequently is *aggressive arousal* or, more commonly, simply *arousal.* By this we refer to a hypothetical state of excitement or activation that results from provocation. This state consists of increased physiological activation associated primarily with the autonomic nervous system, together with emotions such as anger as well as cognitions concerning the provoked person, his provocateur, the relationship between them, and their place in the environment at large. We are not concerned in this review with discussing arousal as an intervening variable and analyzing its several possible physiological, cognitive, and emotional-motivational components, but merely with delineating it as a condition that allows us to relate the antecedent of provocation to the response of aggression.[3]

Having defined arousal as a hypothetical construct, we define *aggression catharsis,* or more often simply *catharsis,* in terms consistent with those of the cause–effect hypothesis described earlier and which, we believe, embody the notion of catharsis most generally employed by psychologists. To us, catharsis is *a reduction in aggressive arousal brought about through the performance of aggressive acts.* This definition does not treat catharsis as *any* lessening of aggressiveness that follows aggressive behavior, but only as a reduction that is produced by a weakening of aggressive arousal. Lowered aggressiveness may be the result not only of reduced arousal but of other processes as well, such as the creation of active restraints against aggressing. Moreover, we do not define catharsis solely in terms of reduced arousal. Aggressive arousal may decrease for reasons other than aggression. The simple passage of time, for example, may produce a cooling off following provocation that would be attended by decreased tendencies to aggress. Aggression catharsis is, therefore, a hypothesized process that occurs following aggression and leads to a postulated reduction in subsequent aggressiveness.

It should also be emphasized that by arousal we do not mean simply physiological activation. The condition to which we have referred as arousal may have a physiological component associated with the autonomic nervous system and manifested in such indicators as blood pressure, heart rate, and localized blood volume. However, much of the confusion that currently characterizes the investigation of aggression catharsis arises from a common tendency to think of aggressive arousal primarily, or even solely, in physiological terms. Hence, the

---

[3] Occasionally we shall refer to arousal that is associated with antecedents other than provocation, such as stimuli for conditioned fear or anxiety. While such a condition differs from aggressive arousal in terms of the emotions, the cognitions, and perhaps also the physiological reactions involved, we assume that they are also excitatory states having some of the same functional properties as arousal produced by provocation.

mistake is sometimes made of defining aggression catharsis as reduced physiological activity following an earlier elevation in activity due to provocation. However, autonomic recovery is only a physiological event that does not necessarily indicate reduced tendencies to aggress. As we shall see, autonomic recovery may, under some circumstances, be produced by behaviors other than aggression. Furthermore, as we shall also see, there is strong evidence that autonomic recovery following aggression is accompanied by more intense, and not weaker, subsequent violence.

In this review we shall attempt to evaluate the evidence pertaining to the catharsis hypothesis as we have defined it. The gist of the argument that we present may be summarized as follows:

1. The cause–effect hypothesis that we have already described is not supported by the data. Little evidence for catharsis, as we have defined it, exists and much of the evidence that has been adduced in its favor is susceptible to alternative explanations that are at least as parsimonious. In fact, when conditions that give rise to such alternative explanations are removed from the experimental setting, the *reverse* of what the catharsis hypothesis predicts is usually found, i.e., aggression begets more, not less, aggression.

2. Data from studies of physiological concomitants of aggression do show in general that activation levels previously elevated by provocation do tend to drop after aggression. The process, however, is moderated by other variables. When conditions are such that aggression is likely to produce feelings of guilt or anxiety, either because of environmental constraints or previous socialization, autonomic recovery is either retarded or prevented. Furthermore, whether or not physiological recovery follows aggression is related to some extent to the person's social learning history; reactions to provocation appear to promote physiological recovery insofar as they have been associated with reward, whether these responses are aggressive or nonaggressive in nature.

3. Several theoretical explanations have been given for the finding that aggression facilitates subsequent aggression. The act of aggressing may stimulate further aggression by providing powerful stimuli for aggressive responses (e.g., Berkowitz, 1962). The person may, in other words, observe himself aggress and thereby receive cues for further violence. In addition, committing one act of aggression may facilitate the weakening of socialized restraints against violence. Finally, aggression may have long-range consequences for behavior in addition to the short-range ones described here. Conceivably a person's aggressiveness could decrease in the immediate situation by allowing him to reach a goal, such as punishing his provocateur. At the same time, however, the aggressive act is being reinforced through goal attainment, so that the probability of aggression occurring later on under similar circumstances is increased (Berkowitz, 1970).

II. Aggression and Autonomic Recovery

A. EARLY INVESTIGATIONS

Two early experiments often cited as demonstrations of catharsis of hostility are those of Worchel (1957) and Hokanson (1961). Neither provided unassailable evidence of reduced arousal following aggression. In Worchel's study, arousal was inferred from performance decrements on two learning measures. All subjects were insulted by an experimenter as they worked at a task in large groups. Some subjects were then allowed to express hostility directly to the experimenter, and others to verbalize their feelings in various indirect ways. Subjects in a third condition were given no chance to voice their animosity. The data revealed three important findings: (1) subjects who verbalized their feelings directly to the experimenter expressed less hostility afterwards than did those who gave indirect utterance to theirs; (2) performance on a digit–symbol substitution task was better in those conditions where either direct or indirect expression of hostility was allowed than in those where neither was allowed; (3) incidental learning among subjects who expressed hostility directly was poorer than that shown by subjects who expressed it indirectly, even though subjects in all three conditions showed more incidental learning than did nonexpressive subjects.

The results of this study are somewhat ambiguous. First, the incidental learning measure appears in part to confirm the idea of arousal reduction and in part to disconfirm it. Presumably, high levels of arousal should hinder incidental learning by restricting the range of cues utilized by the subject (Easterbrook, 1959). Thus, the finding that subjects in the three groups in which hostility was expressed showed better incidental learning than nonexpressive subjects does suggest that the latter were more aroused than the former. However, if we assume that direct expression of hostility to the instigator produces greater arousal reduction than does less direct expression (Dollard et al., 1939), subjects in the direct-expression condition should have shown the best incidental learning of all. They did not. Instead, with incidental learning as the criterion, these subjects appeared to be *more* aroused than those who expressed hostility indirectly. Perhaps expressing hostility to a high status experimenter makes a subject anxious, as the relatively low level of hostility expressed in this condition would indicate.

Downey (1973) has observed that Worchel's (1957) data on the substitution task may be explained as a simple manifestation of an interaction between arousal and habit strength. Making the assumption that a moderate increase in drive facilitates performance on a simple task (Doob & Climie, 1972; Spence, 1958), and further assuming that the digit–symbol substitution task used by

Worchel was relatively easy, Downey concluded that subjects who expressed hostility may have performed at a superior level because their aggressiveness had a slightly *arousing* effect on them. "It would appear," Downey (1973) concluded, ". . . that . . . Worchel's subjects who had aggressed may have performed differently (from nonaggressive subjects) not because they had undergone a 'tension release,' but quite possibly because they had not" (p. 7).

The Hokanson study, which utilized a psychophysiological indicator of arousal, reported a negative correlation between level of systolic blood pressure (SBP) immediately after an attack upon a frustrator and the intensity with which the attack was made. Subjects who pressed vigorously on a button that supposedly delivered an electric shock to the subject's antagonist experienced sharper declines in SBP (from levels elevated by the frustrator's behavior) than did subjects who pressed the button more gently. Unfortunately, the experiment did not contain a condition in which subjects did not give shocks, so that we do not know whether a drop in SBP would have occurred simply as a result of the passage of time.

Furthermore, Hokanson did not report whether subjects actually perceived any relationship between the pressure they exerted on the button and amount of shock felt by the victim. Perhaps simple vigorous physical activity leads to increased SBP (the data show a positive correlation between blood pressure increase and intensity of the pressing response *during* the attack), followed by a homeostatic return in the direction of basal SBP levels, independent of whether the activity represents "aggression." Obviously, the amount of systolic decrease necessary for homeostatic regulation would be greater in subjects who experience a large increase during the attack than among those who do not. It should also be noted that SBP of the two groups showing the strongest pressure on the button was made up of subjects who had not been frustrated and who, moreover, had been told to expect possible retaliation from their victims. It makes little sense to interpret the button pressure manifested by this group as aggression. It does make sense, however, to think of it as a product of arousal produced by anxiety over retaliation.

Although the results of these early investigations into the catharsis hypothesis failed to yield unequivocal evidence for the hypothesis, the general conclusion to be drawn from later research has been that aggression following provocation does facilitate autonomic recovery. Certain qualifications to such a conclusion must be noted, however. These qualifications involve the characteristics of the target of aggression, the social learning history of the aggressor, and any tendencies on the part of the aggressor to react to his aggression with feelings of guilt. To summarize briefly, autonomic recovery following aggression against a tormentor is relatively unlikely to occur when the target appears to be a powerful (and implicitly threatening) person, when the subject perceives aggression to be situationally inappropriate, or when the aggressor has propensities toward the experience of guilt following acts of aggression.

B. STATUS OF THE VICTIM

Hokanson and Shetler (1961) conducted an experiment in which subjects were exposed to harassment and verbal badgering by the experimenter. Afterward some of the subjects were required to shock the experimenter whereas others were not. The experimenter, always a male, presented himself as either a professor or an undergraduate research assistant. Measurement of subjects' SBP indicated that frustrated subjects experienced a greater increase following the frustration treatment than did nonfrustrated controls. Frustrated subjects who were then able to aggress against a low-status experimenter (the "undergraduate") revealed a sharp decline in blood pressure almost to the baseline prefrustration level, whereas those who could not aggress against the same target showed only a negligible decrease. Thus, when the target of aggression was a person of relatively low status, retaliatory aggression reduced arousal. However, when the victim of aggression was a high-status professor, aggression was associated with a slight tendency for blood pressure to *increase* relative to that of nonattacking subjects.

The slight increase in arousal that accompanied an attack on a person of high status could have been the product of anxiety over committing a mandatory aggressive act against a prestigious figure. It must be noted that the subject was, presumably, not free to refrain from giving shocks: the experimental instructions quite clearly demanded that the subject shock the other person each time the latter made a certain response. Aggression against a prestigious person may have seemed inappropriate to the subject. The authors interpret their data in much the same way by concluding that after frustration

(and its concomitant elevation of physiological processes), "tension" reduction may take place when the subject makes a response which he perceives to be appropriate to the situation—i.e., overt aggression towards a frustrator of lower or equal status or withdrawal (or some other nonaggressive behavior) with a high status frustrator. [Hokanson & Shetler, 1961, p. 448]

In a subsequent experiment, Hokanson and Burgess (1962a) found further evidence that aggression against a high-status frustrator does not bring about autonomic recovery. With frustration defined as either verbal harassment or nonpayment of a promised reward, it was shown that the SBP of frustrated subjects returned to levels equal to those of nonfrustrated controls after shock had been given to low-status targets. Once again, however, shocking high-status targets resulted in maintenance of blood pressure at levels equal to those of frustrated, nonaggressing subjects and significantly higher than those of aggressors against low-status victims. Changes in heart rate tended to parallel those in SBP but to be less affected, in general, by the treatments. Still further evidence that aggression against a relatively low-status frustrator leads to tension reduction was found by Hokanson and Burgess (1962b).

To summarize, reductions in arousal following aggression consistent with the catharsis hypothesis appear to be limited to cases in which the target is of relatively low status. The sustained high levels of physiological activation characteristic of those who attack persons of high status are probably due to anxiety resulting either from expectations of retribution that the powerful other may exact or, as Hokanson and Shetler suggest, from the perception that a socially inappropriate response has been made. Regardless of the reason, anxiety arising from aggression prevents autonomic recovery from taking place.

C. AGGRESSION GUILT AND ANXIETY

People who for some reason have learned to feel guilty over behaving aggressively may also fail to experience physiological recovery after aggressing. Meyer (1966) suggested such a conclusion in a study of prison inmates incarcerated for crimes involving physical violence. Men who had been relatively highly aggressive for the 18 months preceding the study (during which time they were behind bars) were found to have lower diastolic blood pressure (DBP) than men classified as relatively nonaggressive over the same period of time. In other words, men who continued to behave aggressively after imprisonment tended to have lower blood pressure than those who did not. Moreover, within the group defined as highly aggressive, those who scored relatively low in guilt on the Mosher Incomplete Sentences Test (MIST) also showed lower DBP than those who scored higher on the same test.

Experimental evidence that supports Meyer's findings has been reported by Schill (1972). Female subjects were divided into high and low scorers on the hostility-guilt subscale of the Mosher Forced-Choiced Guilt Inventory (Mosher, 1968) and then were frustrated by being denied a reward previously promised by the experimenter. Later, each subject was allowed to aggress verbally against the experimenter—frustrator by criticizing him on a questionnaire. Frustrated subjects showed a greater increase in DBP prior to verbal aggression than did nonfrustrated controls, regardless of hostility guilt. Subjects low in guilt not only expressed greater hostility toward the experimenter than did subjects high in guilt but also manifested a greater decrease in DBP following their expression of hostility. Subjects who were prone to feel guilty over aggressing therefore not only inhibited expression of hostility but also, no doubt in part because of that inhibition, tended to remain relatively highly aroused. In a further analysis of his data, Schill isolated the subjects who expressed hostility greater than the mean amount verbalized by all subjects and divided these "highly hostile" subjects into those high and low in guilt. Of the six high-guilt subjects thus identified, only one manifested a decrease in DBP: of the eight low-guilt subjects, seven showed a decrease. This difference in proportions is statistically significant and further corroborates the finding that the display of aggression by highly guilty subjects produces not autonomic recovery but sustained activation.

Gambaro and Rabin (1969), unlike Schill, failed to find that hostility guilt influenced blood pressure following an attack upon a frustrator. In their experiment subjects who scored high on the hostility-guilt scale of the MIST and who gave electric shocks to an experimental confederate after the latter had verbally annoyed them experienced as great a decrease in DBP as did low-guilt subjects given the same treatment. However, among subjects who shocked not the annoying confederate but rather the experimenter himself, guilt played an important role: subjects low in hostility guilt experienced a greater DBP decrease than high-guilt subjects. Thus, the change in DBP following displaced aggression was affected by guilt, but direct aggression did not have a similar effect.

These findings bear closer inspection, especially since they follow experimental operations that are quite different from those used by Schill. First, Gambaro and Rabin's confederate—frustrator was ostensibly a student and thus of approximately the same status as the subject, whereas their experimenter probably had a somewhat higher status than that of the subject. We are unable to judge, therefore, whether the failure of high-guilt subjects to manifest reduced arousal after shocking the experimenter was due to their perceptions that such aggression against an innocent person was unfair and inappropriate or because of the experimenter's perceived status and implicit power. Second, the behavior of the frustrator in the Gambaro—Rabin study was probably more likely to evoke anger and hostility in the subject than was Schill's relatively mild withholding of reward. The confederate in the Gambaro—Rabin experiment barged into the laboratory, growled at the experimenter, yelled at the subject, and interrupted the subject at his task several times. This person may thus have made himself a prime target for thoroughly justified aggression from all subjects, so that the effects of differences in guilt were simply overpowered.

D. NATURE OF THE RESPONSE

Although experiments on catharsis usually involve only one form of aggression, some investigators have compared various aggressive responses for their efficacy in reducing arousal. The evidence, while sparse, nevertheless seems consistent in indicating that either physical or verbal attack upon a frustrator promotes physiological recovery but that covert or fantasy aggression does not.[4] In an experiment already cited, Hokanson and Burgess (1962b) allowed some subjects to give shocks to their antagonist and others to rate the latter on a questionnaire. A third group of subjects could not express either physical or verbal hostility but instead wrote a story in response to a Thematic Apperception Test (TAT) card that had a moderate pull toward aggressive themes. For both SBP and heart rate the subjects who had either shocked or answered the questionnaire showed a greater return toward baseline than did subjects who fantasized violence. Furthermore, both the physically and verbally aggressive subjects showed a larger decrease in SBP than did nonaggressing controls, whereas the aggressive fantasizers did not. Baker and Schaie (1969) subsequently replicated these findings by showing that subjects who either shocked or "orally attacked" a frustrator showed a significant reduction in SBP toward their prefrustration levels, whereas subjects who created fantasy in response to the TAT card did not. The authors did not specify the exact nature of the oral aggression used.

The nature of aggressive responses that do—or do not—facilitate physiological recovery is a matter of some importance and merits further research. One investigation that might be of some value would be an examination of interactions among various types of instigation to aggression and different forms of aggressive response.[5] For example, if the subject is required to deliver a strong electric shock to a victim following a mild and harmless frustration, we might expect very little physiological recovery, and possibly even increased activation due to anxiety. Similarly, a weak aggressive response following a strong provocation would also not be expected, on intuitive grounds at least, to produce much autonomic change. Some experiments have included different types of provocation (e.g., Hokanson & Burgess, 1962a), and others have included different forms of aggressive responses (Hokanson, Burgess, & Cohen, 1963), but none have treated both mode of instigation and mode of aggression as independent variables.

The importance of comparing the means of instigation to aggression with the mode of retaliation available to the subject can be seen in a comparison of two studies that involved "vicarious" attacks on a frustrator. One possible means of aggressing is to procure the services of another person—a "hit man," so to speak—who carries out the attack. Whether witnessing someone else aggress

---

[4] However, Feshbach (1955) showed that fantasy aggression may promote a reduction of verbal hostility against an insulter.

[5] Recent studies by Foa and his associates (Donnenwerth & Foa, 1974; Foa, Turner, & Foa, 1972) suggest that certain forms of aggression tend to elicit some types of retaliatory response more readily than others. Possibly such "preferred" responses are more likely to be cathartic, given the antecedents, than others.

against an enemy allows the frustrated person to experience physiological recovery is a question that has not been satisfactorily answered. Baker and Schaie (1969) found that subjects who merely observed a vicar shock an instigator revealed as substantial a drop in SBP as did subjects who personally attacked their antagonist. However, Geen, Stonner, and Shope (1975) found that subjects' DBP remained at postinstigation level as the subjects observed the experimenter shock their antagonist.

The two experiments are difficult to contrast for more than one reason. Diastolic and systolic blood pressures may not be indicators of the same processes (Ax, 1953), raising a problem to which we shall return later. More important for our present discussion, however, is the fact that the instigation to aggression in the Baker–Schaie study was a relatively innocuous verbal harrassment, whereas in the Geen *et al.* study it was a physical attack perpetrated on the subject by means of electric shock. Perhaps in the latter study subjects were physiologically so highly aroused by the shock that simply watching another person aggress was not sufficient to produce a significant decrease in arousal. Systematic investigation of how various types and intensities of instigation interact with different modes of attack might help us integrate the results of studies such as these.

The importance of preferred response style for the study of physiological recovery has been pointed out by Hokanson and his colleagues in a series of recent experiments. In the studies that we have reviewed so far, the methodology constrained subjects either to deliver some noxious physical or verbal stimuli to a target or to withhold such aggression, depending on whether the subject was assigned to an experimental or control condition. Hokanson's more recent research utilizes a different procedure in which subjects interact with a punitive experimental confederate and are free to ignore the latter's assaults, to retaliate, or to make a prosocial rewarding response. Using this methodology, Hokanson and Edelman (1966) found that male subjects experienced the speediest return to baseline SBP levels after making aggressive counterresponses, and that males who reacted with ignoring or rewarding responses showed a return to baseline levels no more rapid than that shown by controls who made no response at all to the attacks. Female subjects, on the other hand, showed a rate of cardiovascular return following counterattacks that was not different from the rate following ignoring or friendly responses. In general, females experienced more rapid return rates in *any* condition that allowed a response to the provocation than in the condition that did not.

A subsequent study by Hokanson, Willers, and Koropsak (1968) suggests that autonomic recovery is maximal following responses that are associated with a history of reward. These investigators showed that if males are rewarded for nonaggressive responses to provocation they ultimately exhibit a greater decline in their levels of digital blood volume after making such responses than they do after aggressive ones, which are otherwise associated with optimal physiological recovery. The reverse was found to be true of females. Whereas females show greater amounts of decline in digital blood volume following prosocial reactions to provocation than they do after aggressive responses during a baseline period, they display a reverse response pattern after a session of being rewarded for reacting to provocation with retaliatory attacks.

Hokanson *et al.* therefore demonstrated that physiological recovery, in the form of digital vasodilation, can be learned as a concomitant of responses other than aggressive ones. In an extension of this finding, Stone and Hokanson (1969) repeated the general procedure of the study just described with the difference that during phase 2 rewards were given for self-punitive responses, while punishment was given for both shocking and rewarding another person. Whereas vascular recovery was quite slow on those infrequent occasions that subjects shocked themselves during the first phase of the study, it became more rapid following self-punitive acts during the second phase and exceeded the return rate following either rewarding or shocking responses. Self-punishment may therefore be a means to arousal reduction if this behavior is rewarded.

The discussion of Hokanson's recent work was prefaced by our remark that the study of physiological recovery following aggression might profit by an analysis of individual response styles in reaction to frustration. One hypothesis that we might now offer is that physiological recovery will be greatest when an individual responds to provocation with behavior that has generally been highly rewarded in similar situations in the past. Insofar as individual idiosyncracies in responding to provocation are a product of reinforcement histories, we could predict, more generally, that the greatest reduction in physiological arousal following provocation will be achieved through commission of a response that is customary for the person. An unpublished study by Sosa (1968) is relevant to this speculation. Male prison inmates were first classified, on the basis of an analysis of case histories and prison records, into those whose characteristic reaction to threat was direct aggression and those who tended to respond passively. Subjects from each group were exposed to a deliberate provocation (an interpersonal threat) in a laboratory setting. The data revealed that men who characteristically reacted to threat in a passive way showed relatively rapid vascular reduction when they were allowed to respond to the laboratory instigation in a passive way. Vascular recovery was excessively slow when these same subjects were required to respond to threat with an aggressive act.

Two processes may be involved in cases where a response to frustration other than a favorite one fails to facilitate autonomic recovery. As Hokanson has argued, such a response, because it is likely not to have been associated with reinforcement in the past, is relatively unlikely to have the status of an instrumental act. Being relatively ineffective in bringing about either a rewarding state of affairs or the "completion" of a response series set in motion by the original provocation (Berkowitz, 1965), such a response does not promote reduction in tension. But it may have another outcome as well. Because such a nonfavored response is, for the subject, relatively inappropriate to the situation, it may bring about a state of uneasiness that is itself associated with a high level of activation. The person who has a history of being rewarded for nonviolence may therefore feel anxious when he aggresses. Thus, the process here is similar to one we have already reviewed; whenever aggression has a high probability of eliciting anxiety in the aggressor, it does not lead to reduction of bodily tension.

Another experimental investigation that might prove to be revealing would therefore involve the study of individual differences in styles of response to provocation. For example, people who customarily shun physical violence in favor of some verbal means of expressing hostility may exhibit more arousal reduction after verbal aggression than after physical. People who ordinarily utilize indirect and devious methods of retaliation may also achieve reduction in arousal by such means but fail to experience it after aggressing openly.

E. NATURE OF THE TARGET

As has already been noted, in their discussion of the frustration–aggression hypothesis Dollard et al. (1939) proposed that an act of aggression serves as a catharsis, lowering the instigation to all other acts of aggression. Berkowitz (1962, 1965) has raised the question of the equivalence of various targets and aggressive acts. Is it possible that *any* aggressive act upon any victim produces reduced tension? We have already reviewed evidence concerning the nature of the aggressive response, and while tending to agree with Berkowitz (1965) that "there can be a fairly wide range of satisfactory aggressive actions" (p. 325), we also emphasized the need for further study of the ways in which aggressive actions interact with various types of frustration and also of the role of individual differences in aggressive response style.

Studies in which the target of aggression has been a variable do not support the idea that aggression against victims other than the frustrator leads to a reduction in physiological activation. Hokanson et al. (1963) carried out a study in which subjects, after having been frustrated by the experimenter, delivered electric shocks to the experimenter himself, an experimental assistant, a student said to be majoring in psychology, or a student unrelated to psychology or to the experiment. Compared to control subjects who were not allowed to aggress against anybody, only those subjects who attacked the experimenter manifested a reduction in SBP in the direction of the prefrustration baseline. Aggression against substitute targets, even those bearing an ostensible relationship to the experimenter, left SBP at the level it had attained following frustration. More recently, Gambaro and Rabin (1969) have also shown that whereas subjects who shocked a frustrating experimenter's assistant experienced reduced DBP, those who attacked the experimenter did not. Thus, neither this experiment nor the study of Hokanson *et al.* provides any evidence that aggression displaced to substitute targets promotes physiological recovery.

F. MEASUREMENT OF PSYCHOPHYSIOLOGICAL AROUSAL

In the research reviewed so far in this section four different measures, all purportedly indicators of arousal, have been reported: systolic blood pressure, diastolic blood pressure, heart rate, and digital blood volume. Little agreement exists as to the relationship of these measures to each other or, perhaps more importantly, to hostility and aggression. In three well-known studies in which physiological measures were taken from subjects exposed to situations designed to create various emotional states, DBP appeared to be the most clearly established correlate of anger (Ax, 1953; Funkenstein, King, & Drolette, 1957; J. Schachter, 1957). In research on the catharsis hypothesis, Hokanson and his associates have consistently found SBP to be a stable correlate of conditions that presumably create annoyance and hostility. Other investigators, however, (e.g., Gambaro & Rabin, 1969; Geen et al., 1975), have reported that whereas SBP was insensitive to both anger-inducing treatments and to aggression by the subject, DBP was raised by instigation and lowered in a cathartic-like way by retaliation. Conversely, Hokanson and Edelman (1966), while finding significant catharsis effects among males when SBP was measured, found no effects on DBP. Meanwhile, Holmes (1966) found that both SBP and DBP were reliable indicators of aggressive arousal.

In the only study to date that included more than a few indicators of arousal during an aggressive interchange, Kahn (1966) reported some conflicting findings. Male subjects were insulted by an experimental assistant, after which some of the subjects were encouraged to express hostility and resentment against the insulter by the experimenter, or were given no such encouragement. Repeated measures of blood pressure, skin temperature, skin conductance, and muscle tension were taken throughout the study. Analysis of the rate of recovery for each measure during the period in which the subject either did or did not express hostility showed that the recovery rate was faster for the expressing group than for the nonexpressing group only when the two blood pressure measures were considered. Both SBP and DBP, in other words, revealed a catharsis-like effect. A *slower* rate of recovery among expressive subjects was found on four measures: skin temperature, specific GSRs (galvanic skin reflexes), average conductance, and muscle tension. Heart rate revealed no appreciable effects. Thus, both SBP and DBP indicated recovery, but several other measures revealed the very opposite process. Such lack of correlation among psychophysiological measures comes, of course, as no surprise to anyone familiar with the work of Lacey (1967).

In another analysis of his data Kahn found somewhat different evidence for autonomic recovery. Prior to the insulting treatment, all subjects had participated in a cold pressor test, and measurement had been made of their speeds of recovery on the various indices used. Extending Lacey's argument that individuals manifest specific patterns of autonomic response to various stressors, Kahn reasoned that *recovery* from stress should reveal similar patterning. Thus, if expressing hostility promotes recovery from the autonomic activity produced by a provocation, the rank order of recovery rates among the several autonomic measures should be approximately the same following the cold pressor as following the expression of hostility. Kahn did find, as predicted, that subjects who expressed hostility revealed a recovery pattern that was more highly correlated with the recovery pattern after the cold pressor than that shown by nonexpressive subjects. He concluded that possibly "the function of catharsis might be to permit the autonomic nervous system to adopt a recovery pattern" (Kahn, 1966, p. 286) rather than to influence the absolute level of any particular measure. Future research on the psychosomatic aspects of catharsis should allow tests of patterning of functions in an attempt to explore this idea further.

In view of the conflicting evidence on the relationship of the various measures of arousal to experimental conditions associated with frustration and aggression, and lacking any clear theory of the psychophysiological significance of the various measures, we would perhaps be well advised not to generalize too liberally across experiments in which a catharsis-like physiological recovery, or its absence, is reported. Some differences in procedures as yet unexplained could possibly account for diastolic differences but not systolic in one study, and systolic changes in the absence of diastolic in another. The systolic–diastolic difference might be relatively unimportant, and simply blood pressure, quantified in either way, could perhaps be the best indicator of the sort of hypertension customarily associated with aggressive arousal (cf. McGinn, Harburg, Julius, & McLeod, 1964).

G. CONCLUSIONS

The linear cause–effect hypothesis (relating aggression arousal to provocation and subsequent aggressive behavior) assumes that arousal produced by the provocation is reduced by aggression. In the preceding paragraphs we have seen that on the whole the evidence for physiological recovery following aggression i, fairly good. Exceptions to this general finding usually involve situations in which aggressive behavior is likely to create anxiety, either because of the individual's habitual tendencies to become anxious when he aggresses or because of the threat of possible retaliation by the victim. Moreover, in order to be tension reducing, aggression must be directed against the provocateur; aggression displaced to substitute targets apparently does not facilitate autonomic recovery. Furthermore, when provocation is serious, aggression probably promotes recovery only when it is performed by the aggrieved person himself. The reduction of physiological tension through aggression must therefore be regarded as something that occurs only under specific circumstances. The question to which we must now turn is: given that autonomic recovery does sometimes follow aggression, does this recovery necessarily make the person experiencing it less likely to aggress within the given situation?

III. Behavior Following Aggression

A. VERBAL EXPRESSION OF HOSTILITY

Some of the studies reviewed in the preceding section showed that the verbal expression of hostility to a frustrator often promoted a reduction in physiological arousal from the immediate postfrustration level. Experiments in which the dependent measure has been aggressive behavior, on the other hand, have generally shown that aggressive activity typically does not lead to a lessening of subsequent aggressiveness. Even in the few studies that have reported some support for the catharsis hypothesis (in this case dealing with lessened aggressiveness), the evidence is sketchy and inconclusive. Thibaut and Coules (1952), for example, found that subjects who were allowed to communicate in writing with another person who had insulted them (and could therefore presumably express hostility) were later more friendly in their assessments of the insulter than other subjects who could not communicate. Such a finding might be indicative of aggression catharsis in the communicating subjects. However, in a second experiment subjects who were interrupted for 3 minutes before being allowed to communicate with the insulter were more hostile toward him than those allowed an immediate reply. As the researchers noted, the differences in friendliness between the communicating and noncommunicating subjects therefore might as likely be due to increased frustration in the latter (at not being able to reply) as to catharsis in the former.

Some evidence consistent with aggression catharsis is also found in an experiment by Rosenbaum and deCharms (1960). These investigators reported that subjects who either communicated hostility to a provocateur or watched as mother person berated the instigator later expressed less animosity toward their tormentor than other subjects who were allowed neither direct nor vicarious communication. This finding was true, however, only if the subjects were relatively low in self-esteem; those high in self-esteem revealed no such catharsis-like effect. Furthermore, Rosenbaum and deCharms commented that very little actual hostility was shown by any subjects and that the data were therefore probably not strictly relevant to a hypothesis of hostility catharsis.

In a study that grew out of the Rosenbaum–deCharms experiment, de-Charms and Wilkins (1963) found evidence for the opposite of catharsis. Some of the subjects were allowed to express hostility toward an insulter after having been attacked and again at the end of the experiment. It was shown that these subjects manifested an increase in hostility at the experiment's end (compared to how hostile they had felt before provocation) and that the increase in hostility was a positive function of the number of hostile comments made during the verbal retaliation. Moreover, subjects who observed a vicar express hostility against the provocateur but who did not engage in aggressive verbalizations themselves showed a similar increase in hostility. Thus, both direct and vicarious expression of hostility appeared to produce not catharsis but a heightened aggressiveness. A similar finding has also been reported by Wheeler and Caggiula (1966) and Wheeler and Smith (1967).

Several additional studies involving the verbalization of hostility not only fail to support the catharsis notion but indicate an opposite effect. Goldman, Keck, and O'Leary (1969) allowed some of the students in a class to express animosity toward a teacher who had frustrated them and later observed that these students actually manifested more residual hostility toward the teacher than did students who had not expressed their feelings. The classroom performance of the expressive subjects likewise suffered in proportion to the amount of hostility expressed. In an experiment by Nelsen (1969), subjects in one condition were encouraged to express hostility against a frustrator by an experimenter who gave verbal reinforcement for each such utterance. Compared to subjects who were either not frustrated or frustrated and encouraged to suppress hostility, the expressive subjects later rated themselves as more hostile. Unfortunately, the experiment lacked an additional control condition in which frustrated subjects expressed hostility but were not reinforced for doing so. As it stands, Nelsen's study confounds possible catharsis effects with the effects of social reinforcement. In a study mentioned in the previous section, Kahn (1966), after allowing some of his subjects to express angry feelings toward an insulting experimental assistant, gave all subjects a chance to indicate how much they liked the insulter. Subjects who had verbalized their anger reported liking the latter *less* than did other provoked subjects who had not, in the interim, expressed verbal hostility.

Finally, the results of a natural experiment carried out by Ebbesen, Duncan, and Konecni (1975) substantiates the laboratory finding that expression of verbal hostility facilitates further such expression. These investigators reported that technicians who had been allowed to verbalize hostility against either their former employers or their recent supervisor following a layoff were subsequently more punitive in their descriptions of these targets than were other discharged workers who had not previously given voice to their feelings. Expression of aggression against either company or supervisor facilitated later expression of hostility only toward the same target; it did not lead to a general tendency to be more verbally aggressive.

To summarize, experiments in which subjects aggress verbally against a provocateur offer scant support for the catharsis hypothesis and indicate that the opposite of catharsis is likely to occur. The expression of hostility appears to facilitate further expression of hostility, not to diminish it. One possible reason for this finding is that commission of a hostile act reduces socialized restraints against aggression, provided that nothing in the situation serves to augment those restraints (Buss, 1966a, 1966b; Wheeler, 1966). Another is that a person's acts of aggression may produce stimuli that in turn elicit still more aggression, much as would violent stimuli emanating from the environment (e.g., Berkowitz, 1962). In this case he stimulates himself to further aggression. Both of these matters will be discussed in greater detail later in the chapter.

B. AGGRESSIVE PLAY AND PHYSICAL ACTIVITY

The idea that participation in vigorous physical activity, such as contact sports, can supply a means of draining off aggressive motives has received considerable support among a number of psychologists. The principle has been expressed by Menninger (1948): "Competitive games provide an unusually satisfactory social outlet for the instinctive aggressive drive" (p. 343). Although the notion of indirect catharsis through substitute activity recently has been popularized by a number of contemporary writers (e.g., Lorenz, 1966), the data from controlled experiments and field studies fail to support it.

Ryan (1970) allowed three "cathartic" activities to subjects who had been angered by an experimental accomplice. Some subjects were allowed to pound on a box with a rubber hammer. Others likewise pounded on the box but in competition with the person who had angered them. Half of these subjects defeated their antagonist by out-pounding him; the other half were defeated. A group of control subjects merely sat and waited following the provocation. All subjects then shocked the confederate as part of a bogus learning task. Ryan found no evidence for catharsis. Subjects who pounded on the box alone or in the company of an enemy were as aggressive in shocking that enemy as subjects who had not participated in the physical activity, and subjects in all conditions were more punitive toward the instigator than toward another accomplice who had done nothing to arouse them. The failure of a pounding activity to reduce aggression has also been shown by Hornberger (1959), who found that insulted subjects who hammered nails for 10 minutes were later *more* verbally aggressive than control subjects. Evidence suggesting that expression of physical aggression in play increases aggressive arousal has also been reported by Kenny (1953) and Freeman (1962).

Zillmann (1971) has formulated a hypothesis (which he terms transfer of excitation) that helps to explain why vigorous physical activity in the general context of aggressive cues may lead to more, rather than less, aggression. Following S. Schachter and Singer (1962), Zillmann reasoned that arousal from any source is given the label of an emotion on the basis of salient cues in the environment. If the cues include attack or frustration, the aroused person will be quite likely to experience the emotion of anger, which, among other things, guides his behavior in the direction of expressing hostility toward the enemy. Furthermore, any residue of the arousal intensifies and energizes the behavior brought into play following the emotional labeling.

An experiment by Zillmann, Katcher, and Milavsky (1972) supported this line of reasoning. Subjects first interacted with an experimental accomplice who angered them or treated them in a more neutral manner. Some of the subjects then engaged in the strenuous activity of pedaling a bicycle, whereas others performed a more sedentary activity. Later when all subjects were allowed to deliver electric shocks to the accomplice, angered subjects who had performed the vigorous activity were more punitive than angered subjects who had carried out the other task. The difference in aggression between the two exercise groups was minimal among nonangered subjects. In this case, then, strenuous physical activity led to an increase in aggression among provoked subjects rather than to the decrease predicted by the catharsis hypothesis. Perhaps engaging in a strenuous aggressive activity provides both the arousal and the cues necessary for players to label themselves hostile and aggressive, with heightened aggression being the outcome.

The hypothesis that participation in an aggressive contact sport leads to the opposite of catharsis was supported in a field study by Patterson (1974). High school football players and physical education students were both given hostility rating scales 1 week before the football season began and again 1 week after the season's end. Whereas physical education students showed a nonsignificant decline in hostility across the two testing sessions, football players manifested a significant increase. Whether playing football caused this rise in hostility we cannot say within the context of such a natural experiment. It appears, however, that the experience of playing the rough game did nothing to decrease hostility.

Similar conclusions may be drawn on the basis of studies of the less vigorous, but perhaps more violent, behavior of shooting a gun. Mallick and McCandless (1966) used such an activity as the mode for aggressive play in an experiment with children. After having been frustrated by another child, the subject engaged in either target shooting or conversation with the experimenter. Half of those who talked to the experimenter simply chatted with him, whereas the other half were reassured that the frustration inflicted on them earlier had not been deliberate. Later every subject was able to hurt the frustrator by blocking his path to a desirable goal. The most important finding for our present purpose was that children who had engaged in aggressive play were as punitive towards the other child as were the subjects who had merely talked with the experimenter and more aggressive than those to whom the other's behavior had been rationalized. Aggressive play activity had not reduced the probability of subsequent aggression—a conclusion corroborated by the authors' further observation that children who had expressed hostility toward the frustrator immediately after being frustrated later expressed more dislike for him than did others who had not previously verbalized their feelings.

C. PHYSICAL AGGRESSION AGAINST AN ANTAGONIST

As observed earlier, experiments in which subjects express verbal hostility against a frustrator and are subsequently given an opportunity to aggress again generally fail to show evidence of a cathartic lowering of the instigation to aggression. As we noted, one reason for such findings may be that aggression facilitates continuing aggression by lowering socialized restraints against such behavior. Such a conclusion appears warranted by experiments in which provoked subjects, when allowed to aggress over a long series of trials, tend to increase the intensity of their attacks continuously across the series (e.g., Buss, 1966b; Geen, 1968). Thus, physical aggression may liberate the aggressor from feelings of inhibition and make possible increasing levels of violence over time.

Lowering of restraints through physical violence may also explain the findings of studies in which verbal hostility is enhanced by physical aggression. Berkowitz, Green, and Macaulay (1962) arranged to have some of their subjects angered by being given several electric shocks by a confederate, whereas others were subjected to only a few shocks. Half of the subjects in each condition were then allowed to give shocks to the confederate, whereas the other half were not. At the conclusion of the period each subject filled out a questionnaire on which he indicated how much he liked the confederate. The group whose rating was most critical for the catharsis hypothesis was that which had been attacked and allowed to retaliate, and this group reported the *least* friendliness of all the treatment conditions. Comparable findings have been reported by Berkowitz and Geen (1966, 1967) and by Geen (1968). In every case the experimental conditions that led to the greatest degree of physical aggression also produced the highest level of subsequent verbal rejection of the antagonist.

A major problem in the experimental investigation of aggression catharsis is showing that any observed decrease in aggression following acts of violence is due to decreased motivation and not to some active inhibitory process. Catharsis is a construct that is inferred from observations of behavior, but unless alternative explanations for such behavior can be ruled out, the inference is problematical. Furthermore, that aggression can elicit strong restraints against further violence when inhibitory cues are present in the situation has been demonstrated many times (Baron, 1971; Buss, 1966a, 1966b; Geen, 1970; Milgram, 1963). In view of the poverty of evidence supporting the catharsis hypothesis, it could be argued on grounds of parsimony that inhibition may be an even better explanation for any observed decreases in aggression hitherto explained as manifestations of catharsis. Any experimenter who wished to adduce evidence for catharsis certainly should be extremely careful to eliminate from his studies any conditions that might actually promote inhibitions against aggression. Furthermore, because the catharsis hypothesis is based on a model of motivation that emphasizes tension reduction, and in view of the evidence reviewed in the preceding section on autonomic recovery following aggression, catharsis experiments should probably also include both physiological and behavioral measures.

Two recent experiments that point to reduced aggressiveness following aggression may be interpreted as demonstrations of induced restraints against aggression. In one (Doob & Wood, 1972), subjects were verbally insulted by an experimenter's accomplice, after which a third of the subjects shocked the accomplice for making errors on a task, another third observed as the experimenter gave the shocks, and a final third merely waited as the confederate went unshocked. All subjects were then allowed to evaluate the confederate's performance on another task by giving shocks. Annoyed subjects who had previously shocked the confederate delivered fewer shocks than did those who had not been given an earlier opportunity to aggress. Subjects who had been provoked and who had observed the experimenter shock were slightly less aggressive than controls, but not significantly so. Although these data are consistent with the notion of catharsis, an inspection of the experimental procedures suggests that strong inhibitions against aggression may have operated to limit the amount of aggression shown by angry subjects. For one thing, subjects were both males and females, while the confederate was always a female. Other investigators have shown that both male and female subjects (especially females) are less likely to attack a woman than a man (e.g., Buss, 1966b). Furthermore, subjects who shocked the confederate may have felt that such behavior was more than enough to retaliate for a verbal insult and felt constrained not to engage in "overkill" by shocking her any more. While continuing to feel angry, the subjects may also have diminished the intensity of their attacks out of fear of social disapproval. A subsequent experiment by Konecni and Doob (1972), in which evidence was reported suggesting displaced aggression, used a similar methodology and can be reinterpreted in much the same way.

An experiment by Geen et al. (1975), while similar to the Doob and Wood experiment, avoided the possible situational restraints implicit in the latter by using only male subjects and a male confederate. Aggression against a fellow male has been shown not to arouse strong inhibitions against aggressing in male subjects (Buss, 1966a). Furthermore, Geen et al. included two additional measures: a self-rating of restraint against aggression made by the subject, and systolic and diastolic blood pressure taken at four points during the experiment. Briefly, the procedure called for an experimental confederate to attack some of the subjects with electric shocks, after which the subject either retaliated with shocks, observed as the experimenter shocked the confederate, or waited a short period of time during which the confederate was not attacked. Other subjects were controls who were not attacked but otherwise went through the same procedures as the ones who were. Finally, all subjects were given an opportunity to shock the confederate in connection with another task. The principal dependent measure was the intensity of shocks given by the subject on this latter occasion. The means, with 1.00 representing minimal intensity and 10.00 maximal, are shown in Table I. Subjects who had previously aggressed against a confederate who had attacked them were significantly more punitive than both control subjects who had not previously aggressed and others who had seen someone else attack their antagonist. Clearly, these results are in direct contradiction to the aggression catharsis hypothesis. A suggestion of what led to such findings may be seen in the reports made by subjects after the experiment of how restrained they had felt while shocking the confederate on the final task. Subjects in the Attack–Subject Shocks condition described themselves as less restrained than those in both the Attack–Experimenter Shocks (70.13 vs. 29.20[6]; $t = 4.93$, $df = 18$, $p < .01$) and the Attack–No Shocks (70.13 vs. 48.21; $t = 3.22$, $df = 18$, $p < .01$) conditions. Thus, subjects who had aggressed against the confederate once before were not only less restrained about attacking a second time than those who had not previously aggressed but also attacked with greater intensity.

Analysis of the blood pressure measurements showed that only DBP showed any variance across experimental conditions. Blood pressure was measured at four points: at the beginning of the session; just after the subject had been attacked (or not attacked) by the confederate; just after the Subject Shocks, Experimenter Shocks, or No Shocks treatment had been introduced; and, finally, just after the subject shocked on the last task. Diastolic changes from the first to the second, second to third, and third to fourth measurements are shown, respectively, as d_{12}, d_{23}, and d_{34} in Table II. It will be noted that the d_{12} scores show that the Attack–No Attack treatment was successful, with subjects attacked by the confederate becoming more aroused than those not attacked ($F = 29.12$, $df = 1/84$, $p < .01$).[7] Analysis of the d_{23} scores revealed that subjects in the Attack–Subject Shocks condition experienced a decrease in DBP to slightly below baseline level, whereas those in the Attack–Experimenter Shocks condition manifested a slight increase and those in the Attack–No

---

[6] Scores represent points checked by the subject along a 100-mm continuous scale from "Very" restrained to "Not at all" restrained.

[7] The six groups did not differ in baseline blood pressure.

TABLE I

MEAN INTENSITIES OF SHOCKS GIVEN BY SUBJECTS ON
CODE-LEARNING TASK[a]

Treatment of confederate on code-learning task	Treatment of subject by confederate	
	Attack	No attack
Subject Shocks	6.65_a	3.92_{bc}
Experimenter Shocks	4.13_{bc}	3.62_c
No Shocks	5.20_b	3.20_c

Note: Cells having common subscripts are not significantly different at the .05 level by a Duncan Multiple Range Test.

[a]From Geen, Stonner, and Shope (1975). Copyright 1975 by The American Psychological Association. Reprinted by permission.

Shocks condition revealed a slight decrease. Subjects in the No Attack condition showed a moderate decrease in blood pressure. These data produced a significant interaction between the two variables ($F = 6.82$, $df = 2/84$, $p < .01$). Analysis of the d_{34} scores showed main effects for both the Attack ($F = 10.33$, $df = 1/84$, $p < .01$) and Treatment of Confederate ($F = 3.15$, $df = 2/84$, $p < .05$) variables. Both effects are primarily due to the fact that subjects in the Attack–

TABLE II

MEAN DIASTOLIC BLOOD PRESSURE CHANGES ACROSS FOUR
MEASUREMENTS[a]

Treatment condition	Mean diastolic pressure change		
	d_{12}	d_{23}	d_{34}
Attack–Subject Shocks	$+6.66_a$	-8.80_a	-1.20_b
Attack–Experimenter Shocks	$+5.53_a$	$+1.83_c$	-10.67_a
Attack–No Shocks	$+5.56_a$	-1.30_{bc}	-6.57_{ab}
No Attack–Subject Shocks	-3.27_b	-1.87_{bc}	-1.07_b
No Attack–Experimenter Shocks	-1.83_b	-1.80_{bc}	-3.53_b
No Attack–No Shocks	$+0.10_b$	-6.60_{ab}	-0.07_b

Note: Cells having common subscripts within time periods are not significantly different at the .05 level by a Duncan Multiple Range Test.

[a]From Geen, Stonner, and Shope (1975). Copyright 1975 by The American Psychological Association. Reprinted by permission.

Experimenter Shocks condition experienced a greater drop in DBP than did subjects in any other condition.

The findings of the experiment reported here provide no support for the hypothesis of aggression catharsis and suggest instead that when an experimental situation is arranged to minimize restraints against aggression the opposite of catharsis occurs. The study also shows that aggressive behavior was followed by a reduction in blood pressure for all three groups of previously attacked subjects: Men in the Subject Shocks condition experienced decreased blood pressure after the maze task in which they aggressed, whereas men in the Experimenter Shocks and No Shocks conditions experienced decreased pressure following the learning task, in which they aggressed for the first time.

The finding that reduced physiological arousal in the subjects of the Attack–Subject Shocks condition was in turn followed by a high level of aggression rather than a low level casts doubt on the simple cause–effect assumption of the catharsis hypothesis. Aggression does lead to autonomic recovery, as previous reports have shown, but this cardiovascular change is in turn often followed by a relatively high level of aggressiveness. The results reported here are consistent with those of Kahn (1966), who showed that verbal aggression was followed by both reduced arterial pressure and a high degree of verbal hostility. Our findings, like Kahn's, suggest that future studies of aggression catharsis should include measures of both behavioral aggression and physiological arousal. We cannot assume simply that decreased arousal brings about a lowered instigation to aggress.

A study by Downey (1973) also has some relevance to the matters under discussion. Subjects in this experiment were drawn from a population of high school males that cut across social and economic class lines. The experimental sample therefore contained a number of subjects who might not be expected to manifest typical middle-class socialized behavior in the laboratory. By using all male subjects and male confederates, Downey minimized the presence of cues that might elicit inhibitions against aggression. Results of the study (described in greater detail in Section III,E,2) showed that subjects who had previously aggressed against an annoying confederate showed no subsequent evidence of catharsis and, in fact, were the most aggressive of any group in the study.

D. PREVIOUS SUFFERING BY THE VICTIM

The importance of controlling for possible disinhibition of aggression in catharsis experiments has been explicitly acknowledged by Bramel, Taub, and Blum (1968). These authors proposed that aggression against an antagonist may, by lowering of restraints against further aggression, mask an aggression catharsis that would otherwise occur. They therefore conducted an experiment in which an angered subject learned that his provocateur had suffered, but at some earlier time and not as a result of the subject's behavior. Each subject was insulted by an experimenter in the first part of the study, after which that individual left and was replaced by another person. In the second phase of the experiment, the new experimenter played for the subject a tape recording ostensibly made by the first experimenter to describe the latter's experiences after taking drugs several months earlier. These tapes made the insulting person appear to have either suffered, experienced euphoria, or felt indifferent as a result of taking the drugs. After hearing the tape the subject made ratings of his liking for the first experimenter as well as other feelings he experienced while listening to the recording. The results indicated that, relative to noninsulted subjects who had heard the same tapes, the insulted people expressed greater liking for the first experimenter after hearing him describe his suffering than after hearing him speak about his neutral experience with the drugs. Presumably, the subject experienced catharsis of hostility on learning that his former enemy had suffered, which was unconfounded by any disinhibitions he may have felt had he been the agent of that suffering.

The results of an experiment by Doob (1970) parallel those obtained by Bramel *et al.* As they filled out a questionnaire at the outset of the experimental session, some of the subjects were the targets of insulting remarks made by a confederate. Afterwards, this person attempted to learn a list of items. In half the conditions it was arranged that errors in learning would be punished by loss of money owed to the confederate for his participation in the study; in the other half, no mention was made of monetary incentives or loss. The confederate then proceeded to commit a series of errors, losing all of his money in the condition in which this was possible. The subject's only role was to observe and to record the number of errors made. In the final part of the experiment the subject gave electric shocks to the confederate. Those people who had been annoyed and had then watched the confederate lose money gave shocks of shorter duration than did those who had likewise been annoyed but had merely observed the confederate make errors without punishment. No such difference was observed among subjects who had not been annoyed. Thus, in this study as in the one previously described the subject observed his insulter suffer but was not responsible for the suffering; in the aggression that followed, aggression catharsis appeared to take place.

The most obvious alternative explanation of both the experiments of Bramel *et al.* and of Doob is that insulted subjects refrained from aggressing against the antagonist out of sympathy with him for having already suffered enough. In both cases the investigators were aware of this possibility and argued that if insulted subjects were inhibited about aggressing out of pity, noninsulted subjects should have shown similar restraints. In neither study were such restraints found, however, and Doob even observed that noninsulted subjects tended to give slightly *longer* shocks to a confederate who had lost money than to one who had not.

In response to this argument it may be suggested that aggression could have been inhibited in the insulted subjects not out of pity for the hapless victim but out of guilt over their anger toward him. They might have thought that it was wrong to feel anger toward a person who had already suffered, and consequently restrained themselves. Noninsulted subjects would not, of course, have felt especially guilty but might, in effect, simply have shrugged at the confederate's outcome and said "tough luck." Thus, it is quite possible that both the experiments of Bramel *et al.* and of Doob demonstrated some circumstances under which subjects feel restrained against aggressing and are not a set of conditions for catharsis.

E. FACILITATION OF AGGRESSION BY AGGRESSION

Overall, the data from experiments in which aggressive behavior is the major dependent variable do not offer much support for the catharsis hypothesis. Those studies which purport to lend credibility to the hypothesis are open to alternative explanation, and other studies that are designed to rule out such explanations by minimizing inhibition indicate that the opposite of catharsis often occurs. Furthermore, when both measures of autonomic activation and aggression are taken in the same experiment the results show that aggressive responses to the provocateur are followed by reduced blood pressure but increased aggressiveness. Such findings suggest that the linear cause–effect model for catharsis outlined earlier in this review is inadequate to explain behavior in the aftermath of aggression. We are left, then, with the question of why aggressive behavior seems to facilitate the expression of still more aggression while at the same time promoting reduction in arousal. Some of the possible answers are discussed next.

1. Disinhibition

The argument that aggression facilitates more aggression by helping to reduce socialized restraints has been offered repeatedly throughout this review. Altogether, it appears that aggression produces a reduction in blood pressure and also leads to further aggression under the same general conditions: when the aggressive act is regarded as appropriate to the situation, fear of retaliation is minimal, and internalized feelings of guilt or anxiety are unlikely to occur. The reduced arousal itself might possibly enhance the subject's willingness to aggress more. Having aggressed once and perceiving that he feels relatively good, the aggressor may be emboldened to do more of the same. The process is exemplified in the case of a Missouri man accused of murdering four people, as quoted by one of the arresting officers: "He said . . . he had a funny feeling in his stomach but after the first (killing) . . . it was easy" (*Kansas City Times,* September 19, 1973, p. 4).

The findings of a recent study by Konecni (1975) may be interpreted as support for the disinhibition hypothesis offered here. Subjects who had been verbally annoyed or not annoyed by an experimental confederate spent an interval of either 7 or 13 minutes engaged in solving mathematics problems, in shocking the confederate on a regular schedule, or in simply doing nothing. Overall, it was shown that annoyed subjects showed less aggression toward the confederate afterwards if they had spent the preceding interval either giving shocks or solving problems than if they simply waited. The significance of this finding will be discussed shortly.

In addition, Konecni found that annoyed subjects who gave shocks for 7 minutes were later less aggressive than either waiting subjects or problem solvers. However, those who shocked for 13 minutes were somewhat *more* aggressive subsequently than those in the 13-minute waiting and problem-solving conditions. Inhibitions against aggression might have been developing over the first 7 minutes, whereas over 6 additional minutes these inhibitions dissipated. Konecni suggested that the relatively high level of aggression shown in the 13-minute shock condition resulted from "adaptation" of subjects in this condition to the giving of shock, and the consequent adoption of a "many-shocks standard in the execution of the task . . ." (Konecni, 1975, p. 88), i.e., evaluating the confederate's bogus "performance." Konecni's notions of adaptation and adoption of higher shock levels as a standard are similar to our contention that by aggressing over a period of time a subject becomes accustomed to aggressing and more likely to use aggression in situations that permit it. In a follow-up experiment, Konecni (1975) showed that the 13-minute Aggress condition was not associated with relatively high levels of subsequent violence when the mode of aggressing (shock or noise) used in the first attack was different from that used in the second. This finding suggests that disinhibition effects are relatively specific to the mode of attack used.

2. Aggression as a Source of Cues

As has already been noted, some investigators (e.g., Berkowitz, 1962; Geen et al., 1975) have suggested that as people aggress they observe their own behavior, so that one's aggression may provide cues for subsequent acts of violence. Thus, an angered and aggressive subject will later behave as would an angered subject who has observed *other people* aggressing: he will be more violent than someone who has not previously observed aggression (cf. Berkowitz & Geen, 1966). In an experiment mentioned earlier in this chapter, Downey (1973) proposed the optimal condition for aggression catharsis is one in which the subject is given some distracting task after he has been provoked. Such a task should elicit responses that not only take the place of overt aggression but also, more importantly, interfere with the subject's thinking about his antagonist and thereby supply aggressive cues to himself.

Downey accordingly carried out an experiment in which male subjects were punished with harsh and aversive noise by a confederate. One-fourth of the subjects (Control condition) received minimal stimulation, whereas the remainder were exposed to several prolonged bursts of the noise. Thereafter, subjects who had been given the severe noise treatment either sat alone and awaited the next portion of the experiment (Wait condition), engaged in story-writing (Interference condition), or retaliated against the confederate by shocking him (Aggress condition). Finally, half of the subjects in all four conditions gave bursts of noise to the confederate, presumably for errors committed by the latter on another task. The other half shocked another person who had not previously been associated with them in any way. The mean number and intensity of noise bursts given in all eight groups are shown in Table III. Aggression toward the confederate was only slightly more intense than that visited upon an innocent bystander, so the data are collapsed across the two targets. Subjects who aggressed against the confederate just after being attacked were later more punitive in both number and intensity of responses than others who took part in interfering activity from the time they were provoked until they had an opportunity to aggress. Taking only number of attack responses into account, subjects in the Interference condition were also less aggressive than those who merely waited. The catharsis-like effects observed in this study therefore occurred not as a result of aggression but as the consequence of response interference.

Downey's findings give some support to Bandura's (1973) contention that the imposition of any activity following provocation leads to less subsequent

TABLE III
MEAN NUMBER AND INTENSITY OF BUZZES ACROSS
TARGETS[a]

Treatment	Number	Intensity
Aggress	6.80_a	6.72_a
Wait	6.60_a	5.96_{ab}
Interference	5.30_b	4.99_{bc}
Control	3.45_c	3.90_c

Note: Within each measure, means with subscripts having no letters in common are significantly different from each other at the .05 level of confidence by a Duncan Multiple Range Test; $N = 20$ in each cell.
[a]Data from Downey (1973).

aggression than does merely allowing the subject to wait and do nothing. Bandura proposed that subjects who do nothing following provocation constitute an improper control condition for those who retaliate because the latter, by simply engaging in a response, are distracted by response-produced stimuli from ruminating about the provocation. This notion has been supported by Konecni (1975), who showed that angered subjects were less aggressive toward the annoyer after either aggressing previously or after solving problems than after spending an interval of time doing nothing. Downey, it should be recalled, found a "catharsis-like" reduction in hostility after problem-solving activity, but slightly *greater* aggression in subjects who had attacked once before than in those who simply waited. This elevated aggression following previous aggression may have been due, as Downey proposed, to aggressive cues emanating from the aggressor's own behavior.

3. Reinforcement

Up to this point we have been dealing with behavior that occurs relatively soon after an initial act of aggression, during which interval short-term effects of disinhibition and self-stimulation may be maximal. Aggressive behavior may have implications for subsequent aggression over longer intervals of time as well. Berkowitz (1970) has argued that even when aggression produces short-run decreases in further violence, such behavior may in the long run make the person more likely to aggress. Attacking one's enemy may very well produce feelings of relief from tension (the physiological recovery that often accompanies aggression probably reflects this), but the relief in tension may reinforce the response that had lead to the relief. That aggression may be strengthened through such reinforcers as verbal praise has been demonstrated by several investigators (e.g., Geen & Stonner, 1971; Parke, Ewall, & Slaby, 1972). Autonomic recovery may serve as a reinforcer in much the same way. In addition, it may be rewarding merely to see one's enemy suffer. Feshbach, Stiles, and Bitter (1966) found that the sight of a person undergoing painful electric shock reinforced nonaggressive task responses made by subjects who had previously been attacked by that person. Swart and Berkowitz (cited in Berkowitz, 1974) have shown that a previously neutral stimulus acquires secondary reinforcement properties through association with suffering exhibited by the subject's enemy, suggesting that the observation of such suffering is rewarding.

4. Consistency

Another possible reason why aggression breeds further aggression is that the aggressor feels compelled to appear consistent in his behavior across the two situations. Doob and Wood (1972) have suggested that implicit demands for consistency can possibly be counteracted by using two different modes of aggressing for the two situations. A need for consistency presumably would be more likely to manifest itself in cases where the same mode of aggressing is used both times. As we have seen, however, in published studies using shock followed by verbal ratings of the victim, results tend to show that subjects who shock are subsequently *more* likely to express dislike than those who do not shock. Another question that might be raised is why a hypothesized need to seem consistent should be a more powerful motive than the need to appear just and equitable. If we are concerned with the subject's judgments of the behavior that is expected of him, it seems reasonable to argue that once he has attacked his enemy he should feel compelled to act as if equity has been restored and not to aggress further. Continued aggression would certainly not be expected under these conditions.

5. Termination of Aggressive Behavior

We are left with one question that must be answered. If aggression does not remove the instigating conditions for further aggression but instead tends to facilitate more violent behavior, when does aggression stop? Berkowitz (1962) has proposed that frustration or some other provocation to aggression creates a state of tension that motivates the person toward a distinct goal—the infliction of injury upon the provocateur. A "completion tendency" is therefore set in motion, and "inflicting injury on the anger instigator is the goal response completing the aggressive response sequence" (Berkowitz, 1962, p. 221). Thus, only when aggressive behavior is carried out to the extent that the aggressor perceives sufficient injury has been done to his victim will he cease his aggression. Closely related to this process is the aggressor's perceiving that justice has been done. The aggressor may regard his behavior as a means of restoring equity to his relationship with the victim, an equity that has been upset by the latter's previous attack. Thus, according to this reasoning, aggression will end when the aggressor perceives that his victim has suffered enough. Further aggression under these conditions would make the aggressor feel guilty or anxious by again upsetting the equity of the relationship. As we have noted above, studies involving verbal provocation of the subject followed by physical retaliation may create such conditions. Subjects may restrain themselves from shocking too much a confederate who has only irritated them verbally, because to do otherwise would be unjust.

IV. Summary

Theorizing on aggression catharsis that follows psychoanalytic or ethological reasoning, as well as that formulated in the frustration–aggression hypothesis, assumes a basic linear cause–effect model. According to this model, provocation to aggression creates a state of arousal that motivates aggression, which in turn lowers arousal and diminishes the probability of further violence.

Evidence from psychophysiological research indicates that under some conditions aggression does produce decreased arousal when the latter is quantified in terms of cardiovascular activity. Data regarding the effects of aggression on other indices of autonomic recovery are ambiguous. The conditions under which aggression does not promote cardiovascular recovery are those in which (1) the target possesses a higher social status than the attacker; (2) aggression is a manifestly inappropriate response in the given situation; and (3) the individual is predisposed to react to aggression with feelings of guilt. It is proposed that all three qualifications can be subsumed under one conclusion: aggression against a provocateur does not facilitate arousal reduction when it is likely to make the attacker experience anxiety.

Studies of the behavioral effects of aggression permit a similar conclusion to be drawn. In general, those experiments which report the strongest evidence for catharsis are susceptible to reinterpretation in terms of inhibitions against aggression because of the procedures used. Studies in which such procedural problems have been obviated tend to report results contradictory of the catharsis hypothesis. At present, therefore, we must conclude that the notion of catharsis has not been confirmed, that reductions in aggression following aggression, insofar as they have been demonstrated, might be more parsimoniously explained in terms of active inhibition, and that in the absence of such inhibitions the expression of aggression increases the likelihood of further such behavior.

REFERENCES

Alexander, F. *Psychosomatic medicine.* New York: Norton, 1950.

Ax, A. F. The physiological differentiation between fear and anger in humans. *Psychosomatic Medicine,* 1953, **15**, 433–442.

Baker, J. W., & Schaie, K. W. Effects of aggressing "alone" or "with another" on physiological and psychological arousal. *Journal of Personality and Social Psychology,* 1969, **12**, 80–86.

Bandura, A. *Aggression: A social learning analysis.* Englewood Cliffs, N.J.: Prentice-Hall, 1973.

Baron, R. A. Magnitude of victim's pain cues and level of prior anger arousal as determinants of adult aggressive behavior. *Journal of Personality and Social Psychology,* 1971, **17**, 236–243.

Berkowitz, L. *Aggression: A social psychological analysis.* New York: McGraw-Hill, 1962.

Berkowitz, L. The concept of aggressive drive: Some additional considerations. In L. Berkowitz (Ed.), *Advances in experimental social psychology.* Vol. 2. New York: Academic Press, 1965, 301–329.

Berkowitz, L. Experimental investigations of hostility catharsis. *Journal of Consulting and Clinical Psychology*, 1970, **35**, 1–7.

Berkowitz, L. Some determinants of impulsive aggression: Role of mediated associations with reinforcement for aggression. *Psychological Review*, 1974, **81**, 165–176.

Berkowitz, L., & Geen, R. G. Film violence and the cue properties of available targets. *Journal of Personality and Social Psychology*, 1966, **3**, 525–530.

Berkowitz, L., & Geen, R. G. Stimulus qualities of the target of aggression: A further study. *Journal of Personality and Social Psychology*, 1967, **5**, 364–368.

Berkowitz, L., Green, J. A., & Macaulay, J. R. Hostility catharsis as the reduction of emotional tension. *Psychiatry*, 1962, **25**, 23–31.

Bramel, D., Taub, B., & Blum, B. An observer's reaction to the suffering of his enemy. *Journal of Personality and Social Psychology*, 1968, **8**, 384–392.

Breuer, J., & Freud, S. *Studies in hysteria.* Boston: Beacon Press, 1961.

Buss, A. H. The effect of harm on subsequent aggression. *Journal of Experimental Research in Personality*, 1966, **1**, 249–255. (a)

Buss, A. H. Instrumentality of aggression, feedback, and frustration as determinants of physical aggression. *Journal of Personality and Social Psychology*, 1966, **3**, 153–162. (b)

deCharms, R., & Wilkins, E. J. Some effects of verbal expression of hostility. *Journal of Abnormal and Social Psychology*, 1963, **66**, 462–470.

Dollard, J., Doob, L., Miller, N. E., Mowrer, O. H., & Sears, R. R. *Frustration and aggression.* New Haven: Yale University Press, 1939.

Donnenwerth, G. V., & Foa, U. G. Effect of resource class on retaliation to injustice in interpersonal exchange. *Journal of Personality and Social Psychology*, 1974, **29**, 785–793.

Doob, A. N. Catharsis and aggression: The effect of hurting one's enemy. *Journal of Experimental Research in Personality*, 1970, **4**, 291–296.

Doob, A. N., & Climie, R. J. Delay of measurement and the effects of film violence. *Journal of Experimental Social Psychology*, 1972, **8**, 136–142.

Doob, A. N., & Wood, L. E. Catharsis and aggression: Effects of annoyance and retaliation on aggressive behavior. *Journal of Personality and Social Psychology*, 1972, **22**, 156–162.

Downey, J. An interference theory of the catharsis of aggression. Unpublished doctoral dissertation, University of Missouri, 1973.

Easterbrook, J. A. The effect of emotion on cue utilization and the organization of behavior. *Psychological Review*, 1959, **66**, 183–201.

Ebbesen, E. G., Duncan, B., & Konecni, V. J. Effects of content of verbal aggression on future verbal aggression: A field experiment. *Journal of Experimental Social Psychology*, 1975, **11**, 192–204.

Eibl-Eibesfeldt, I. *Ethology.* New York: Holt, 1970.

Feshbach, S. The drive-reducing function of fantasy behavior. *Journal of Abnormal and Social Psychology*, 1955, **50**, 3–11.

Feshbach, S., Stiles, W. B., & Bitter, E. The reinforcing effect of witnessing aggression. *Journal of Experimental Research in Personality*, 1967, **2**, 133–139.

Foa, E. B., Turner, J. L., & Foa, U. G. Response generalization in aggression. *Human Relations*, 1972, **25**, 337–350.

Freeman, E. Effects of aggressive expression after frustration on performance: A test of the catharsis hypothesis. Unpublished doctoral dissertation, Stanford University, 1962.

Freud, S. *Beyond the pleasure principle.* New York: Bantam Books, 1959.

Freud, S. Why war? In P. Reiff (Ed.), *Freud: Character and culture.* New York: Collier, 1963.

Funkenstein, D. G., King, S. H., & Drolette, M. E. *Mastery of stress.* Cambridge, Mass.: Harvard University Press, 1957.

Gambaro, S., & Rabin, A. Diastolic blood pressure responses following direct and displaced aggression after anger arousal in high- and low-guilt subjects. *Journal of Personality and Social Psychology,* 1969, **12,** 87–94.

Geen, R. G. Effects of frustration, attack, and prior training in aggressiveness upon aggressive behavior. *Journal of Personality and Social Psychology,* 1968, **9,** 316–321.

Geen, R. G. Perceived suffering of the victim as an inhibitor of attack-induced aggression. *Journal of Social Psychology,* 1970, **81,** 209–215.

Geen, R. G. Some effects of observing violence upon the behavior of the observer. In B. Maher (Ed.), *Progress in experimental personality research.* Vol. 8. New York: Academic Press, in press.

Geen, R. G., & Stonner, D. The effects of aggressiveness habit strength upon behavior in the presence of aggression-related stimuli. *Journal of Personality and Social Psychology,* 1971, **17,** 149–153.

Geen, R. G., Stonner, D., & Shope, G. L. The facilitation of aggression by aggression: A study in response inhibition and disinhibition. *Journal of Personality and Social Psychology,* 1975, **31,** 721–726.

Goldman, M., Keck, J. W., & O'Leary, C. J. Hostility reduction and performance. *Psychological Reports,* 1969, **25,** 503–512.

Hokanson, J. E. The effects of frustration and anxiety on overt aggression. *Journal of Abnormal and Social Psychology,* 1961, **62,** 346–351.

Hokanson, J. E., & Burgess, M. M. The effects of status, type of frustration and aggression on vascular processes. *Journal of Abnormal and Social Psychology,* 1962, **65,** 232–237. (a)

Hokanson, J. E., & Burgess, M. The effects of three types of aggression on vascular processes. *Journal of Abnormal and Social Psychology,* 1962, **64,** 446–449. (b)

Hokanson, J. E., Burgess, M., & Cohen, M. F. Effects of displaced aggression on systolic blood pressure. *Journal of Abnormal and Social Psychology,* 1963, **67,** 214–218.

Hokanson, J. E., & Edelman, R. Effects of three social responses on vascular processes. *Journal of Personality and Social Psychology,* 1966, **3,** 442–447.

Hokanson, J. E., & Shetler, S. The effect of overt aggression on physiological arousal. *Journal of Abnormal and Social Psychology,* 1961, **63,** 446–448.

Hokanson, J. E., Willers, K. R., & Koropsak, E. The modification of autonomic responses during aggressive interchanges. *Journal of Personality,* 1968, **36,** 386–404.

Holmes, D. Effects of overt aggression on level of physiological arousal. *Journal of Personality and Social Psychology,* 1966, **4,** 189–194.

Holt, R. R. A review of some of Freud's biological assumptions and their influence on his theories. In N. S. Greenfield & W. C. Lewis (Eds.), *Psychoanalysis and current biological thought.* Madison: University of Wisconsin Press, 1965.

Holt, R. R. On the interpersonal and intrapersonal consequences of expressing or not expressing anger. *Journal of Consulting and Clinical Psychology,* 1970, **35,** 8–12.

Hornberger, R. H. The differential reduction of aggressive responses as a function of interpolated activities. *American Psychologist,* 1959, **14,** 354.

Janov, A. *The primal scream.* New York: Dell Publ., 1970.

Kahn, M. The physiology of catharsis. *Journal of Personality and Social Psychology,* 1966, **3,** 278–286.

Kenny, D. T. An experimental test of the catharsis theory of aggression. Unpublished doctoral dissertation, University of Washington, 1953.

Konecni, V. J. Annoyance, type, and duration of postannoyance activity and aggression: The "cathartic" effect. *Journal of Experimental Psychology: General,* 1975, **104,** 76–102.

Konecni, V. J., & Doob, A. N. Catharsis through displacement of aggression. *Journal of Personality and Social Psychology,* 1972, **23,** 378–387.

Lacey, J. I. Somatic response patterning and stress: Some revision of activation theory. In M. H. Appley & R. Turnbull (Eds.), *Psychological stress: Issues in research.* Appleton, 1967. Pp. 14–37.

Lorenz, K. *On aggression.* New York: Harcourt, 1966.

Mallick, S. K., & McCandless, B. R. A study of catharsis of aggression. *Journal of Personality and Social Psychology,* 1966, **4,** 591–596.

McGinn, N. F., Harburg, E., Julius, S., & McLeod, J. M. Psychological correlates of blood pressure. *Psychological Bulletin,* 1964, **61,** 209–219.

Menninger, W. C. Recreation and mental health. *Recreation,* 1948, **42,** 340–346.

Meyer, R. G. The relationship of blood pressure levels to the chronic inhibition of aggression. Unpublished doctoral dissertation, Michigan State University, 1966.

Milgram, S. Behavioral study of obedience. *Journal of Abnormal and Social Psychology,* 1963, **67,** 371–378.

Mosher, D. Measurement of guilt in females by self-report inventories. *Journal of Consulting and Clinical Psychology,* 1968, **32,** 690–695.

Nelsen, E. A. Social reinforcement for expression vs. suppression of aggression. *Merill-Palmer Quarterly,* 1969, **15,** 259–278.

Parke, R. D., Ewall, W., & Slaby, R. G. Hostile and helpful verbalizations as regulators of nonverbal aggression. *Journal of Personality and Social Psychology,* 1972, **23,** 243–248.

Patterson, A. H. Hostility catharsis: A naturalistic quasi-experiment. Paper presented at the annual convention of the American Psychological Association, New Orleans, September 1974.

Rosenbaum, M. E., & deCharms, R. Direct and vicarious reduction of hostility. *Journal of Abnormal and Social Psychology,* 1960, **60,** 105–111.

Ryan, E. D. The cathartic effect of vigorous motor activity on aggressive behavior. *Research Quarterly,* 1970, **41,** 542–551.

Schachter, J. Pain, fear, and anger in hypertensives and normotensives: A psychophysiologic study. *Psychosomatic Medicine,* 1957, **19,** 17–29.

Schachter, S., & Singer, J. E. Cognitive, social, and physiological determinants of emotional state. *Psychological Review,* 1962, **69,** 379–399.

Schill, T. R. Aggression and blood pressure responses of high- and low-guilt subjects following frustration. *Journal of Consulting and Clinical Psychology,* 1972, **38,** 461.

Sosa, J. N. Vascular effects of aggression and passivity in a prison population. Unpublished master's thesis, Florida State University, 1968.

Spence, K. W. A theory of emotionally based drive (D) and its relation to performance in simple learning situations. *American Psychologist,* 1958, **13,** 131–141.

Stone, L. J., & Hokanson, J. E. Arousal reduction via self-punitive behavior. *Journal of Personality and Social Psychology,* 1969, **12,** 72–79.

Thibaut, J. W., & Coules, J. The role of communication in the reduction of interpersonal hostility. *Journal of Abnormal and Social Psychology,* 1952, **47,** 770–777.

Wheeler, L. Toward a theory of behavioral contagion. *Psychological Review,* 1966, **73,** 179–192.

Wheeler, L., & Caggiula, A. R. The contagion of aggression. *Journal of Experimental Social Psychology,* 1966, **2,** 1–10.

Wheeler, L., & Smith, S. Censure of the model in the contagion of aggression. *Journal of Personality and Social Psychology,* 1967, **6,** 93–98.

Worchel, P. Catharsis and the relief of hostility. *Journal of Abnormal and Social Psychology,* 1957, **55,** 238–243.

Zillmann, D. Excitation transfer in communication-mediated aggressive behavior. *Journal of Experimental Social Psychology,* 1971, **7,** 419–434.

Zillmann, D., Katcher, A. H., & Milavsky, B. Excitation transfer from physical exercise to subsequent aggressive behavior. *Journal of Experimental Social Psychology,* 1972, **8,** 247–259.

MERE EXPOSURE[1]

Albert A. Harrison

UNIVERSITY OF CALIFORNIA
DAVIS, CALIFORNIA

[1] The author would like to thank D. E. Berlyne, J. E. Crandall, R. Crandall, M. Matlin, J. T. Milord, R. Moreland, D. W. Rajecki, D. Stang, W. Underhill, W. R. Wilson, and R. B. Zajonc for critical comments on an earlier version of this review.

I. Introduction

One of the world's best-known and seemingly best-loved structures, the Eiffel Tower has come to symbolize Paris and, to some extent, all of France (Coutaud & Duclair, 1956). This Art Nouveau delight has been referred to as the "subject of lyrical raptures" (Cohen-Portheim, 1937, p. 13), as a sight which would "cause Louis XIV to die of envy" (Cohen-Portheim, 1937, p. 13), and as a friendly giant which invites picnicking and sunbathing at its feet (Simon, 1967). But the Eiffel Tower has not always been the subject of lyrical raptures, and Parisians have not always happily frolicked at its feet. Announcing the tower's completion in 1889, the journal *de Natuur* noted that its construction took place despite a storm of protest from Frenchmen who considered it an unforgivable profanation of the arts and a slap in the face for a nation which had previously upheld the banner of civilization and refinement (DeVries, 1972). This early condemnation bordered on the universal and, in the early 1900s, almost led to the tower's demolition (Coutaud & Duclair, 1956).

What might account for the seemingly massive shift in attitudes from condemnation and rejection to acceptance and liking? Some attitudes may have changed as engineering feats gained in vogue; some as the result of new contrasts provided by a changing Paris skyline; and some following disconfirmation of the prediction of a major financial disaster. There is, however, a factor that may have affected the attitudes of technophiles, aestheticians, and financiers alike. Because of its tremendous height, the tower was ubiquitous and inescapable and hence was likely to be seen day after day. According to one long-standing hypothesis, familiarity leads to liking, and perhaps attitudes towards the tower changed simply because it became a familiar part of the landscape. The purpose of the present paper is to examine the familiarity-leads-to-liking hypothesis, with specific reference to developments since it was formalized and revitalized by Zajonc (1965, 1968, 1969, 1970a, 1970b).

According to Zajonc's mere exposure hypothesis, the repeated exposure of an individual to a stimulus is a sufficient condition for the enhancement of his attitude toward that stimulus. Zajonc suggested that the function best describing the relationship between exposure and liking takes the form of a positive, decelerating curve, with attitude enhancement a function of the logarithm of the exposure frequency. "Mere" exposure refers to conditions which make the stimulus accessible to the organism's perception. The hypothesis does not preclude other bases for liking; it specifically allows that under some conditions liking can develop without repetition, and that under some conditions liking accruing from increased exposure can be partially offset by other factors. It also neither insists upon nor precludes other effects of varying stimulus familiarity.

In support of his hypothesis, Zajonc assembled an impressive array of prior findings and introduced a number of his own results. Many of the studies appearing or reappearing since Zajonc's monograph have yielded confirming exposure effects (that is, findings that organisms like or prefer repeatedly encountered or familiar stimuli), and few presently doubt that exposure sometimes leads to liking. What is disputed is the generality of this principle. For example, liking does not increase indefinitely with each successive exposure. In general, Zajonc and his associates have argued that although each successive exposure leads to successively smaller increments in liking, there is no such thing as "overexposure" and that results implying that incessant repetition eventually causes a stimulus to lose appeal reflect variables other than exposure itself (e.g., Zajonc, Crandall, Kail, & Swap, 1974a). Other investigators, however, have suggested that the "exposure effect" represents a myopic view of a more complex familiarity–liking relationship. Most commonly proposed is an inverted-U relationship between exposure and liking, such that stimuli of intermediate familiarity are the best liked (e.g., Berlyne, 1967, 1971, 1973, 1974c).

Our review will begin with a consideration of studies which have related assessed or varied familiarity to affective reactions. Then we shall focus directly on the conditions suspected of limiting the exposure effect or causing contrasting effects. After thus identifying the conditions under which different results prevail, we shall be in a position to consider major interpretations.

II. Attitudinal Effects of Mere Exposure

In his monograph, Zajonc (1968) discussed three types of studies bearing on the mere exposure hypothesis. These studies related (1) word frequency to the evaluation of that word or its referent; (2) interpersonal contact to interpersonal attraction; and (3) the familiarity of musical selections and other aesthetic stimuli to the liking expressed for them. Most of the studies appearing in the last decade may be classified into one of these three categories or into a fourth category involving message repetition and attitude change.

A. WORD FREQUENCY AND WORD EVALUATION

Both correlational and experimental studies have established a strong link between word familiarity and affective connotation. Correlational studies have related word frequency [as obtained from the Thorndike–Lorge (1944) count] to the evaluations given that word or its referent. Experimental studies have, of course, involved varying the number of times words are shown and then assessing the subject's attitudinal reactions.

1. Correlation Studies

Early frequency—meaning studies were an outgrowth of the perceptual defense controversy. In accordance with the hypothesis that people may defensively fail to perceive negatively toned stimuli such as "dirty words," McGinnies (1949) reported that dirty words had higher recognition thresholds than did neutral words. Howes and Solomon (1950, 1951) showed that infrequent words had higher recognition thresholds than did frequent words and explained McGinnies' findings in terms of the relative infrequency with which dirty words appeared in print. However, R. C. Johnson, Thomson, and Frincke (1960) raised the possibility that frequency and meaning are themselves interrelated. They found that (1) using three samples of words, strong positive correlations were obtained between word frequency and favorability of connotation; (2) in 26 of 30 pairs of words the high-frequency member was chosen as more positively toned than the low-frequency member of the pair; and (3) nonsense words which contained a number of letter combinations common in the English language received more favorable ratings than nonsense words which did not contain such familiar elements. Although L. R. Wilson and Becknell (1961) suggested that words which are easy to pronounce will be used frequently and liked, this interpretation cannot account for the Frincke and Johnson (1960) finding of a preference for the high-frequency member of homophonic pairs (e.g., team—teem).

Zajonc (1968) had students indicate which member of 154 antonym pairs had the most favorable meaning and found that in over 80% of the pairs the high-frequency member was designated. He also reported that (1) the most favorable adjectives in Gough's (1955) adjective checklist had a higher frequency count than the least favorable adjectives; and (2) the frequencies of Anderson's (1968) 555 personality-descriptive adjectives correlated +.83 with rated favorability. These findings have been conceptually replicated by Harrison (1968a). In addition, Zajonc (1970b) has noted that letter combinations and numbers with a high probability of occurrence (for example, low numbers) are rated more favorably than letter combinations and numbers with a low probability of occurrence (for example, high numbers). R. C. Smith and Dixon (1971) reported a correlation of .49 between log frequency and rated goodness of verbs; although the frequencies of "good" and "neutral" verbs did not appreciably differ, "bad" verbs were relatively infrequent. Matlin (1970) found that (presumably novel) nonsense words were less favorably rated than (presumably familiar) real words and that among the real words those with higher frequencies received better ratings. Such relationships are not culture bound; they have been noted in several languages (Zajonc, 1968), including Russian and Urdu (Matlin & Stang, 1976).

Other studies have focused on rated liking rather than on rated goodness of meaning. In one such study, Zajonc (1968) found that the log frequency of the names of ten countries and ten cities correlated better than .80 with ranked preference "as a place to live." In other studies, he had subjects rate fruits, flowers, vegetables, and trees, and for each class of stimulus the frequency–liking correlation exceeded .80. For example, the most-liked members of each class were pine, apple, corn, and rose (with frequency counts of 172, 220, 227, and 801, respectively) and the least-liked members of each class were acacia, mango, parsnip, and cowslip (with frequency counts of 4, 2, 8, and 2, respectively). Using this type of stimulus, Zajonc, Swap, Harrison, and Roberts (1971) obtained a significant correlation when ratings of stimuli of different frequencies were obtained from different subjects.

Although suggestive, such studies can provide only circumstantial support for the mere exposure hypothesis because alternative hypotheses are not overruled. One possibility is that exposure led to liking, but another is that liking for a stimulus increases the probability that it will appear or be discussed. Perhaps there are more roses than cowslips in this world because we like roses better and are more willing to exert effort to grow them; perhaps a positively toned word is used more frequently than a negatively toned word because use of the former brings us greater pleasure. Indeed, according to the "Pollyanna hypothesis," there is a universal tendency to structure conceptual worlds in a positive way by referring to pleasant rather than unpleasant things or events (Boucher & Osgood, 1969; Matlin & Stang, 1976; Osgood, 1964). To assess such alternatives we need data based on the experimental method with its distinguishing features of manipulation and control.

2. Manipulated Exposure–Word Evaluation

Most of the experimental tests of the relationship between word frequency and word meaning that have been generated by the mere exposure hypothesis have involved nonsense words. There are three reasons for this choice of stimulus. First, given a positive, decelerating exposure–liking curve, repetition of an already familiar stimulus should be expected to have a negligible effect on attitude. Second, past experiences with meaningful words can result in the formation of associations which could influence ratings independent of an exposure manipulation. Third, since nonsense words are unlikely to be encountered outside of the laboratory, they allow better control over overall familiarity. Studies which have manipulated the exposure of already-familiar stimuli may have implications for understanding mere exposure, but these studies will be taken up later in this discussion.

Using a pretest–posttest design, R. C. Johnson et al. (1960) had subjects rate 20 nonsense words which were presented five each in the frequencies of 1, 2, 5, and 10. Although these authors found a significant exposure effect, any given word appeared with a particular frequency for all subjects, and hence there was a confounding of familiarity and other stimulus properties. In a consumer preference study, Becknell, Wilson, and Baird (1963) presented nonsense words in differing frequencies and then had subjects choose among boxes which bore the nonsense words as "brand names." These investigators also found an exposure effect, but their use of forced-choice and preference ranking techniques to assess attitude admitted alteration of the exposure frequencies during the stimulus rating phase.

To circumvent these and other problems, Zajonc (1968) introduced a design which has served as a model for many subsequent studies. First, it is posttest only and thus minimizes the likelihood that anticipation of the rating task will lead to expectancies or sets which may influence postexposure ratings. Second, it involves counterbalancing to insure that across subjects each stimulus appears in each frequency category an equal number of times, and thus prevents a confounding of familiarity and other stimulus variables. Third, it involves assessing attitudes by rating scales and thus prevents alteration of the exposure frequencies in the course of attitude assessment. Using this design and the exposure frequencies of 0, 1, 2, 5, 10, and 25, Zajonc obtained strong mere exposure effects for both paralogs (nonsense words) and Chinese ideographs.

Exposure effects have been demonstrated in a number of subsequent studies which have used paralogs (Harrison & Hines, 1970; Harrison, Tufts, & Strayer, 1974; Janisse, 1970; Matlin, 1970, 1971, 1974a; Rajecki & Wolfson, 1973; Zajonc et al., 1974a; Zajonc & Rajecki, 1969) and ideographs (Brickman, Redfield, Harrison, & Crandall, 1972; R. Crandall, Harrison, & Zajonc, 1976; Harrison & Crandall, 1972; Harrison & Zajonc, 1970; M. A. Johnson, 1973; Saegert & Jellison, 1970; Zajonc et al., 1971). Although, as we shall see, some of these studies have reported other effects as well, for the most part they suggest that mere exposure effects are likely under a wide range of conditions, including when the exposure durations are reduced to a fraction of a second (Harrison & Hines, 1970), when the maximum frequency of exposure was raised to 241 (Zajonc et al., 1974a), and when favorability has been assessed by a stimulus's reward potential rather than by attitudinal ratings (Harrison et al., 1974). Field studies which have assessed word meaning after the manipulation of the number of times nonsense words were inserted in newspaper advertisements (Zajonc & Rajecki, 1969), written on a blackboard (R. Crandall, 1972) or placed in subjects' mailboxes (Rajecki & Wolfson, 1973) have shown that the effects of varying word frequency are by no means limited to the laboratory.

Against this array of results stand a number of findings which appear to conflict with the results just noted. Saegert and Jellison (1970) found that increased exposure of isolated brush strokes or components of the ideographs led first to increased and then to decreased liking. These authors believed that stimulus complexity was the responsible factor. J. E. Crandall and his associates have repeatedly found that low- or intermediate-frequency nonsense words receive the most favorable ratings (J. E. Crandall, 1967, 1968, 1970a, 1970b; J. E. Crandall, Montgomery, & Rees, 1973). These studies are difficult to interpret, for they departed considerably from a mere exposure manipulation: during the exposure, subjects engaged in such tasks as copying the stimulus each time that it was presented. There are additional differences in the Crandall and Zajonc procedures (cf. J. E. Crandall *et al.*, 1973). Crandall and his associates have typically used only three to five stimuli, but Zajonc and his associates have generally used ten to twelve stimuli. Thus, there is less variability in Crandall's presentation sequences than in Zajonc's. Furthermore, in the Crandall studies exposures and ratings were interspersed, but in the Zajonc studies all exposures were completed before ratings were obtained.

The effects of increasing or decreasing intraserial variability during the exposure phase and of joining or separating exposure and rating phases have been explored by Harrison and Crandall (1972), among others. Using ideographs and the frequencies of 0, 1, 3, 9, and 27, these investigators found the following: (1) mere exposure effects when the exposure phase involved a heterogeneous exposure sequence (presenting different stimuli in random or quasi-random order) and attitude measurement took place during a separate rating phase; (2) a severe attenuation of the mere exposure effect when the exposure phase involved a homogeneous exposure sequence (uninterrupted repetitions of a stimulus until the required number has been attained) and a separate rating phase; and (3) increased followed by decreased favorability ratings when the exposure sequence was homogeneous and exposures and ratings were interspersed. Confirmation of the finding of a reduced likelihood of exposure effects under homogeneous exposure sequences and an interspersal of exposures and ratings has come from nonsense word and other experiments by Stang and O'Connell (1974) and from Stang's (1974c) cross-study analysis. Thus, although manipulating the exposure of meaningless words has often yielded mere exposure effects, such studies also suggest that this effect is less likely when (1) the stimuli are simple; (2) the stimuli are presented in homogeneous sequences; and (3) the exposure and rating phases overlap.

B. INTERPERSONAL CONTACT AND INTERPERSONAL ATTRACTION

Two lines of research instigated prior to the mere exposure monograph suggested a link between exposure and interpersonal attraction. First, studies of propinquity and friendship suggest that people who are physically close to each other and hence are apt to come into repeated contact often become friends (Festinger, Schachter, & Back, 1950; Priest & Sawyer, 1967; Segal, 1974).

Second, studies in the area of race relations suggest that interracial contact can lead to a reduction of prejudice, although factors such as status inequality, competition, and prevailing custom limit this effect (Allport, 1954; Amir, 1969; Deutsch & Collins, 1951; Pettigrew, 1971). Although complex processes of interpersonal accommodation are traditionally invoked as mediators between interpersonal contact and interpersonal attraction, the mere exposure hypothesis raised the possibility that familiarity itself is a determining factor.

1. Familiarity—Attraction Correlations

Familiarity has been correlated with liking for individuals and for groups. Harrison (1969) found that liking ratings of a group of 200 public figures (politicians, actors, murderers, and so forth) and of 40 bogus individuals correlated with familiarity ratings made by a separate set of judges and with an exposure index based on the number of citations in the printed media. Stang (1975a) reported that ratings of presidents of the United States correlated .85 with an exposure index based on four archival sources. Zajonc (1968) obtained correlations between the frequency of usage of ethnic labels and occupational prestige. Similar results were reported by Harrison (1969), who found frequency—liking correlations ranging from +.20 to +.56 using as stimuli samples of religious, political, and ethnic groups. Still other studies have established a strong relationship between familiarity and ratings accorded people's first names (Harrison, 1969; McDavid & Harari, 1966).

2. Manipulated Exposure—Stimulus Persons

Many experimental tests of the effects of exposure on attraction have involved symbolically represented stimulus persons. Some of these studies have demonstrated exposure effects for names (Harrison, Tutone, & McFadgen, 1971; Maslow, 1937). In a recent field experiment, Stang (1974a) erected 0, 20, or 200 posters urging students to elect a fictitious person to the editorship of a student publication. Students who had seen the circulars were more likely to vote for the best publicized candidates.

Other experiments have used photographs. L. R. Wilson and Nakajo (1966) found that increasing the number of times a person's photograph was shown led to increasingly favorable ratings of personality, social appeal, and emotional stability. Zajonc (1968), using procedures which closely paralleled those of his word frequency—word meaning experiments, presented men's graduation portraits two each in the frequencies of 0, 1, 2, 5, 10, and 25. Ratings of liking for each man "as a person" closely followed the good/bad ratings obtained following exposure of the nonsense words and ideographs in the same frequencies. Also employing photographs, Hamm, Baum, and Nikels (1975) extended Zajonc's procedures and obtained mere exposure effects for stimulus persons of widely differing initial (or preexposure) likeability, for women, and for minorities.

Saegert, Swap, and Zajonc (1973) found exposure effects using live stimulus persons; this and related studies will be considered when we turn to the effects of the situation or context in which exposure occurs (Section III,B,1).

C. FAMILIARITY AND AESTHETIC PREFERENCES

Many of the studies bearing on the mere exposure hypothesis have dealt with people's reactions to musical selections, art works, and other aesthetic stimuli. Compared with the investigations thus far reviewed, these studies have often suggested that low-frequency or intermediate-frequency stimuli are the best liked.

1. Manipulated Exposure—Musical Selections

Predominant among the early studies of familiarity and liking were those which attempted to understand (and often to improve) people's musical tastes. Meyer (1903) played a novel composition "12 to 15 times"; introspective reports revealed that changes in the direction of increased liking outnumbered those in the opposite direction four to one. Gilliland and Moore (1924) played selections five times a session for five sessions; change scores indicated increased liking for three of the four selections, and in absolute terms the "negative change" of a tenth of a point was the smallest obtained. Downey and Knapp (1927) presented a program of musical selections during five weekly sessions and found a continuous increase in liking for all selections but one, and Washburn, Child, and Abel (1927) found that five repetitions in a homogeneous sequence more often led to exposure effects than to contrasting effects. Krugman (1943) selected three initially neutral selections and played them once a week for 8 weeks. Although there was some evidence of a decrease in liking following maximum exposure, this decrease was not reliable, and the .91 exposure–liking correlation suggested a rather strong linear component. Both Farnsworth (1926) and Mull (1957) have reported mere exposure effects for components of melodies: in the former case, endings; in the latter case, passages within a selection.

More recently, Lieberman and Walters (1968) found that evaluative ratings (but not nonevaluative ratings) improved for nine of ten selections following ten exposures of each selection, and Bradley (1971) noted that 84 exposures in the course of 28 sessions led to highly significant increases in liking for four classes of music. In a study which placed unusually strict controls on initial familiarity by using highly obscure selections, Heingartner and Hall (1974) increased both children's and adult's liking for Pakistani music. Finally, using attentional measures of liking (see Section III,C,2), Cross, Halcomb, and Matter (1967) were able to increase rats' preferences for selections by Mozart.

On the other hand, using sales as an indicator of liking, Jakobovits (1966) reported that as popular selections were aired, there was increased followed by decreased liking for the music. However, sales could have dwindled for other reasons, such as all affluent listeners having purchased copies of the song. Bush and Pease (1968) found that playing a song 30 times in succession led to increased polarization of ratings; since more individual ratings shifted towards the negative pole than towards the positive pole, there was, overall, increased liking for the low-frequency or novel selections. Skaife (1966) observed that exposure could lead to increased *or* decreased liking, depending on the specific selections employed. Curvilinear exposure—liking relationships have been reported by Verveer, Barry, and Bousfield (1933), who found that peak liking occurred after only a few repetitions, and by Alpert (1953), who showed that exposure led to successive reactions of displeasure, pleasure, and indifference.

The same variables which appear to reconcile the seemingly discrepant word frequency—word meaning results (that is, stimulus complexity, order of presentation, and time of rating) might also reconcile the apparently conflicting results with musical tastes. First, the Alpert and Skaife studies suggest that decreasing stimulus complexity lessens the chances of an exposure effect. Skaife found that whereas repetition of a simple tune decreased liking, repetition of a complex tune increased liking, and although cross-study comparisons are hazardous, Alpert's rhythms seem less complex than the stimuli used in all of the confirming studies except Farnsworth's. Second, whereas with the exception of Washburn *et al.* (1927), the confirming studies involved heterogeneous exposure sequences, both Alpert and Bush and Pease used homogeneous sequences. Third, again with the exception of Washburn *et al.*, although none of the confirming studies obtained ratings following each repetition or block of repetitions, Verveer *et al.* (1933), Alpert (1953), and Skaife (1966) did intersperse exposure and ratings. The study of Washburn *et al.* may not be a notable exception to this pattern because their maximum exposure frequency of 5 may have been insufficient for an eventual rating decline.

2. Manipulated Exposure—Visual Patterns and Designs

Studies of liking for visual stimuli have involved nonrepresentational patterns or designs, grains or checkerboards, cartoons, and art works. Some have found exposure effects. Pepper (1919) heightened liking for uncommon color combinations and Maslow (1937) increased liking for art slides by presenting them four times in the course of what was ostensibly a continuing study of work performance. Schick, McGlynn, and Woolam (1972) exposed *Peanuts* cartoons, as drawn by the original artist and as prepared by an unknown artist. The finding that the highly familiar original cartoons were better liked than the redrawn versions might only reflect the artistic merits of the two cartoonists, but increased ratings over exposures for the redrawn versions is an exposure effect. However, most such studies have used simple stimuli, homogeneous exposure sequences, or interspersed exposures and ratings and have yielded contrasting results.

Using paired-comparison rating procedures, G. N. Cantor (1968) and G. N. Cantor and Kubose (1969) found that children presented with previously exposed and unexposed Welsh figures were especially apt to respond to the familiar stimulus with the statement "I don't like it" and tended to designate the novel stimulus when indicating which member of a pair they liked best. Similarly, Siebold (1972) had children rate Welsh figures by pointing to pictures of faces arranged on a smiling–frowning continuum and found children liked the novel or low-frequency stimuli best. This occurred for stimuli of two levels of complexity, both when ratings immediately followed the exposure sequence and when they were obtained following 2-day and 1-week intervals. Although these experiments involved heterogeneous exposure sequences and separate exposure and rating phases, the relative simplicity of even the more "complex" Welsh figures may account for these results (Siebold, 1972).

Related studies which have systematically manipulated stimulus complexity have fairly consistently shown that complexity interacts with familiarity to influence ratings. Using nonrepresentational patterns and representational art works of varying degrees of complexity, Berlyne (1970) observed that, on the whole, increased exposure led to decreased ratings of pleasingness. However, he also found that, whereas the simple stimuli were less favorably rated as familiarity increased, pleasingness ratings of complex stimuli declined less or became more favorable as familiarity was increased. More recently, Fryrear and Cottrell (1976) used Vitz and Todd's (1971) model to generate stimuli of differing complexity. In one experiment, complexity was a within-subjects variable; in another (intended to eliminate contrast effects), a between-subjects variable. In both experiments, exposure led to more favorable ratings of complex stimuli but to less favorable ratings of simple stimuli. G. F. Smith and Dorfman (1975) used stimuli of three levels of complexity: in ascending order these comprised 2 X 2, 4 X 4, and 6 X 6 matrices. Exposures of simple stimuli led to less favorable ratings, exposure of complex stimuli led to more favorable ratings, and exposure of intermediate complexity stimuli yielded an inverted-U exposure–liking relationship.

Additional results in this area reflect upon the presentation sequence and the timing of the attitudinal measure. Berlyne (1970) presented representational and nonrepresentational art works of two levels of complexity in heterogeneous or in homogeneous exposure sequences. In the case of the nonrepresentational complex stimulus, exposure in a heterogeneous sequence led to greater reported pleasingness, whereas exposure in a homogeneous sequence led to lower levels of pleasingness. For the most part, exposure of the other stimuli led to a decline in rated pleasingness, but this decline was sharper in the homogeneous than in the heterogeneous conditions. Using random walks and other stimuli, Stang and O'Connell (1974) found attenuated exposure effects when homogeneous sequences were used and when no temporal interval separated the exposure and rating phase. Finally, we may refer again to the results of Stang's (1974c) interstudy comparison.

Thus, a sizable proportion of the studies which have assessed people's reactions to aesthetic stimuli have yielded results which appear to conflict with the mere exposure hypothesis. However, when complexity, presentation sequence, and time of rating are taken into account, they do not conflict with a previously noted overall pattern.

D. MESSAGE REPETITION AND ATTITUDE CHANGE

Finally, a few studies have related message repetition to attitude change. Weiss (1971) found that subjects who heard an argument three times agreed more quickly with its conclusions than did subjects who were given the argument only once, but in this study the dependent measure may have been one of information processing speed rather than one of evaluative reactions. L. R. Wilson and Miller (1968) presented arguments either once or thrice, and found that while the exposure manipulation had no immediate effects on attitudes, repetition increased the chances of agreement when attitudes were measured some time later. Roughly comparable are H. H. Johnson and Watkin's (1971) findings that while one or five repetitions of a message led to an equal amount of immediate acceptance, 4 weeks later the five-repetition subjects adhered the most closely to the advocated position. Finally we might note the finding of McCullough and Ostrom (1974) that when the same basic arguments were used (but there were variations in phrasing and the ordering of points) message repetition led to an immediate shift of attitudes. Thus, message repetition has yielded an exposure effect when ratings are delayed and when variability is introduced into the presentation sequence.

E. CONCLUSIONS

Since the appearance of Zajonc's (1968) monograph, the old hypothesis that familiarity leads to liking has been infused with new life. Many investigations conducted since Zajonc presented his impressive array of evidence have shown that exposure does increase favorability ratings under a wide range of conditions. Almost entirely consistent with the mere exposure hypothesis are the results of research which correlated word frequency with word meaning and of a preponderance of those studies which have manipulated the exposure of nonsense words or ideographs. Highly consistent are studies which have related mere exposure to interpersonal attraction. Partially consistent are the few studies of message repetition and attitude change. On the other hand, a number of investigations (especially those involving designs and works of art) have suggested qualifications and exceptions to the familiarity-leads-to-liking rule. In the next section, we shall focus directly upon the variables thought to pose difficulties for the mere exposure hypothesis.

III. Exposure and Other Variables

Some studies have yielded mere exposure effects, but others have not. Exposure frequency itself cannot account for this pattern of findings, for inconsistencies exist among studies which have manipulated frequency within identical ranges. Stimulus variables, presentation variables, and measurement variables interact with exposure to determine liking.

A. STIMULUS VARIABLES

Whether or not an exposure effect is obtained may depend in part on the properties of the stimuli selected. Hypothesized stimulus variables include: (1) initial or preexposure familiarity; (2) initial or preexposure meaning; (3) discriminability; (4) recognizability; and (5) complexity.

1. Initial Familiarity

Manipulating the exposure of an already familiar stimulus is unlikely to enhance attitudes. In the Washburn *et al.* (1927) study mere exposure effects became diminished or eliminated when the selections were initially familiar rather than novel. Similarly, although Maslow (1937) obtained exposure effects for initially novel paintings and names, he was not able to influence attitudes by varying the exposure of already familiar objects. Because the mere exposure hypothesis posits a positively-sloped, decelerating frequency–affect curve, it accommodates findings that repetition of an already familiar stimulus has a negligible effect on attitude.

2. Initial Meaning

Two conflicting hypotheses suggest that the mere exposure effect is dependent in part on the stimulus's meaning or valence prior to exposure. These hypotheses assume that the exposure effect reflects general changes in meaning of which a change in evaluative meaning is only one part (Grush, 1976; Jakobovits, 1968; Stang, 1976a). As we shall see later (Section IV,E,1), the semantic satiation interpretation suggests that stimulus repetition leads to a loss of meaning, with the result that initially negatively toned stimuli become less negative over exposures (an apparent exposure effect) whereas initially positively toned stimuli become less pleasing during repetition. The alternative, semantic generation interpretation suggests that exposure leads to increases in meaning, such that initially positively toned stimuli become more positive over exposures (an apparent exposure effect) whereas initially disliked stimuli become more negatively toned over exposures.

Accordingly, several studies have reported results suggesting that exposure will interact with initial meaning or valence to determine the consequences. Lambert and Jakobovits (1960) had subjects rate words before and after the word was presented for a 15-second interval (during which the subject repeated that word as quickly as possible) and found depolarization or satiation effects. Using the same stimuli and similar procedures as those of Lambert and Jakobovits (1960), Yelen and Schulz (1963) obtained a strong trend towards polarization or generation rather than towards satiation; other findings were trends towards satiation on some scales and trends towards generation on other scales. Amster and Glassman (1966) found "consistent generation" when meaningless materials were used; that is, there was a significant linear increase in the rated goodness of meaningless materials. Repetition of meaningful words yielded neither satiation nor generation. In a 1969 review, Esposito and Pelton (1969) concluded that the results of these and many other studies suggest that the repetition of initially meaningful words does not produce reliable changes in connotative meaning. One possibility, raised by Yelen and Schulz (1963), is that satiation and generation effects are statistical artifacts. If we assume some variability in successive ratings (Kaplan, 1972), initially polarized stimuli should show regression toward the mean whereas initially neutral stimuli should show increased polarity.

It is possible that regression towards the mean accounts for the results in a recent study of musical tastes by Bartlett (1973). He found that although selections which initially were only moderately liked became more liked over exposures, stimuli which were initially highly liked lost in favorability. In this investigation repeated measures were used, and the pretest ratings of the highly liked selections approached 8 on a 9-point scale. Conflicting with Bartlett's findings are the results of two aesthetic preference studies by Brickman et al. (1972). In one of these, subjects gave general reactions to 1950s-style rock and roll music; repetition led to decreased liking. In another study, which also utilized a pretest–posttest design, repetition led to increasingly favorable ratings of initially liked and initially neutral art works but to increasingly less favorable ratings of initially disliked artworks.

Satiation/generation research often involves a pretest–posttest design. This leads subjects to expect that the experimenter anticipates changes in ratings, and when stimuli are neutral or highly polarized certain types of changes are precluded (Esposito & Pelton, 1969; Yelen & Schulz, 1963). Using a posttest-only design would eliminate this problem. A recent experiment by Grush (1976) which employed a posttest-only design and words which were only moderately polarized (thereby precluding the problem of ceiling and floor effects) found that whereas repetition of the initially positive stimuli did not lead to significant changes, repetition of the initially negative stimuli led to lower favorability ratings.

Many of the studies which have not run the risk of ceiling or floor effects, activated associative processes, or departed from conditions of mere exposure are consistent with the proposition that exposure effects do not depend upon preexposure valence. Zajonc (1968) compared the ratings of stimuli following few and many exposures: although there was considerable variability following few exposures, in only 3 of 36 comparisons was there even a hint that many exposures led to decreased liking. Zajonc, Markus, and Wilson (1974b) reported that both socially desirable and socially undesirable individuals became better liked over exposures. Hamm et al. (1975) introduced preexposure valence as a major independent variable and found that exposure effects were not contingent upon preselected stimuli. In Zajonc's (1968) and many following studies (e.g., Harrison et al., 1971; Harrison & Zajonc, 1970), stimuli were rated below the midpoint of the scale following few exposures but above the midpoint following many exposures; neither satiation nor generation hypotheses accommodate such crossovers. A firm conclusion may not be warranted, because scalar neutrality is difficult to determine (Kaplan, 1972). It is conceivable that although mere exposure effects have been obtained using stimuli of differing initial valences, these stimuli have all nonetheless fallen within either the "disliked" or "liked" zone, and that interzone transitions are only illusory. Nonetheless, it has not been satisfactorily shown that the exposure effect requires selecting stimuli which fall within a narrow range on the affective or evaluative dimension.

3. Discriminability

Although Zajonc, Shaver, Tavris, and VanKreveld (1972) noted that paintings shown once prior to ratings were liked better than novel paintings, they also found that ratings decreased as exposure further increased. They suggested that these paintings were more discriminable (dissimilar) from one another than the stimuli used in studies yielding exposure effects. A second experiment revealed that although exposure led to increased and then decreased liking for both similar and dissimilar stimuli, maximum liking for the less-discriminable stimuli required a greater number of exposures. More recently, Bartlett (1973) hypothesized and found that exposure led to increased liking for music only as long as it led to new discriminations. Not many studies have thus far explored the effects of stimulus discriminability, and we cannot draw a definite conclusion.

4. Recognizability

Titchener spoke of a warm glow which accompanies recognition (see W. R. Wilson, 1975), and, as we shall see, a number of more recent discussions of stimulus repetition have held that stimulus recognition is a precondition for the exposure effect (see Section IV). But several strands of evidence suggest that attitude enhancement can occur over exposures even in the absence of stimulus recognition.

After presenting stimuli a certain number of times, Moreland (1975; Moreland & Zajonc, 1975) had some subjects rate the stimuli on Old–New scales (which provided several measures of recognition and subjective familiarity), while other subjects rated the same stimuli on the usual Like–Dislike scales. Repetition led to increased accuracy in recognition, greater confidence in recognition judgments, greater subjective familiarity, and greater liking. Multiple regression analyses, though, revealed that objective frequency of exposure was the best single predictor of liking, whereas subjective familiarity and recognition confidence added very little explanatory power. A second experiment, which involved somewhat similar procedures, demonstrated that whereas exposure frequency predicted evaluative responses, recognition confidence and recognition accuracy were not significant predictors of affect.

Compelling results have been presented in a recent dissertation by W. R. Wilson (1975). In two of his experiments, a distractor message was presented to one ear and the exposure stimuli to the "unattending" ear. In the first experiment, subjects proofread a written version of the distractor; in the second experiment, subjects shadowed (verbally repeated) one distracting message while proofreading another. In the first experiment, recognition of the critical stimuli was lessened, and there was a relationship between exposure and affect, independent of subjective familiarity. In the second experiment, postexposure recognition was eliminated entirely, but there was again an increase in positive affect with repeated exposures. These studies do not show that recognition variables play no role in evaluative reactions, but they do indicate that recognition and subjective familiarity are not preconditions for the mere exposure effect to occur.

5. Complexity

Reducing stimulus complexity lowers the likelihood of an exposure effect or causes the inflection point in an inverted-U curve to occur after relatively few exposures. As already noted, Skaife (1966) found that, whereas the repetition of a simple tune led to less favorable reactions, the repetition of a complex tune yielded exposure effects. Berlyne (1970) obtained greater declines over exposure when the stimuli were simple rather than complex. Saegert and Jellison (1970) found exposure led to liking for relatively complex ideographs but to increased followed by decreased liking for isolated components from the ideographs. Fryrear and Cottrell (1976) and G. F. Smith and Dorfman (1975) were able to produce increased liking, decreased liking, and increased followed by decreased liking through systematic variation of stimulus complexity. A satisfactory explanation of the exposure effect should take stimulus complexity into account.

B. PRESENTATION VARIABLES

The way in which the stimuli are presented may also influence the effects of exposure. Relevant here are (1) the situation or context in which exposure occurs and (2) order of presentation.

1. Context

The mere exposure hypothesis states that exposure to a given stimulus is a sufficient condition for its increased attractiveness and does not preclude other bases for evaluative reactions. However, exposure does not occur in a vacuum, and it has been suggested that the affective reactions elicited by the situation or context in which the exposure occurs will become increasingly associated with the exposure stimuli as exposure progresses. Thus, if a stimulus is presented in a context that elicits unpleasant emotional reactions, exposure should lead to decreased liking for that stimulus (Burgess & Sales, 1971; Perlman & Oskamp, 1971). Tests of this hypothesis have operationalized "context" in very different ways (Saegert et al., 1973). In some studies, "context" refers to a background or surround, and the transfer of affect would depend upon incidental learning. In other studies, which have been highly influenced by the Staats and Staats (1958) work on the classical conditioning of attitudes, "context" refers to an emotionally loaded word or other stimulus which becomes associated with the exposure stimulus by means of paired associate learning or other direct procedures.

Burgess and Sales (1971) considered the mere exposure effect a form of incidental learning during which favorable attitudes towards science and experimentation were transferred to the exposure stimuli. Although this interpretation requires showing indirect or incidental learning, the Burgess and Sales experiment involved a direct learning task which will be described shortly. Studies which have dealt with indirect learning, that is, manipulated the affective tone of the background or setting, have found that exposure, even in a negative context, leads to increasingly favorable reactions. M. A. Johnson (1973) treated subjects abrasively, perched them on hard stools in a formaldehyde-permeated room where the temperature was $90°F$, doubled the maximum exposure frequency, and still found an exposure effect comparable to one obtained in a condition where none of these unpleasantries were imposed. In another investigation, Saegert et al. (1973) had women participate in an experiment which ostensibly dealt with taste perception. In the course of this experiment the subjects moved from cubicle to cubicle and encountered each other varying numbers of times. Exposure led to increased interpersonal attraction both in conditions where subjects tasted pleasant solutions and in conditions where they sampled bitter concoctions of vinegar, quinine, and citric acid. This occurred whether or not nonverbal communication was possible, and whether or not the parties in the encounter experienced similar or dissimilar fates.

Under conditions of direct learning, stimulus ratings are of course influenced by the affective tone of contiguous associates. Burgess and Sales (1971) had subjects engage in a learning task in which nonsense words of varying frequency were paired with meaningful words of differing affective values. These authors found that exposure led to increasingly favorable ratings for stimuli paired with positively toned associates but to decreasingly favorable ratings of words paired with negatively toned associates. Similarly, when social stimuli are presented in such a way that the perceiver is encouraged to make attributions, impressions will be influenced. Perlman and Oskamp (1971) reported exposure effects for stimulus persons presented in desirable or neutral roles, but not for stimulus persons presented in undesirable roles. More recently, Swap (1976) had subjects incur rewards or losses at a maximizing-difference game (McClintock, 1972) and also varied exposure to the partner and the extent to which outcomes could be attributed to the partner. In most conditions, an exposure effect prevailed, and the finding that exposure did not lead to disliking in the Losses Incurred—Partner Not Responsible condition casts further doubt on the incidental learning hypothesis. However, even strong associative learning manipulations have not eradicated all evidence of an exposure effect. Burgess and Sales (1971) and Perlman and Oskamp (1971) found the favorability-increasing effects of exposure under positive conditions were more pronounced than the favorability-decreasing effects of exposure under negative conditions, even though negative information is usually assigned great weight (Kanouse & Hanson, 1972).

"Context" studies have gone beyond the conditions of mere exposure; stimulus repetition and the affective tone of an associate are not the same thing. Zajonc et al. (1974b) have shown that these two variables have independent effects. In one experiment, portraits of Chinese men were shown varying numbers of times. In some cases, stimulus persons were presented as "scholars and scientists who have made important contributions"; in other cases, they were presented as "criminals." To allow for associative learning, under one condition portraits were paired each exposure either with a lofty field of endeavor or with a crime. The results were, first, that although at any given frequency the "contributers" received more favorable ratings than the "criminals," in the absence of opportunity for associate learning greater exposure led to increasingly favorable ratings for both classes of stimulus persons. That is, presenting negatively valenced rather than positively valenced stimulus persons thus affected the *intercept*, not the slope, of the exposure—affect curve. Second, when a specific crime was indicated each time a "criminal" was presented, exposure did not lead to increased liking at as great a rate as when no associate appeared. The pairing of associates thus affected the *slope* of the exposure—affect curve.

Overall, the "context" studies demonstrate that mere exposure effects and associative learning effects are independent and additive. Attitudes following exposure "in a negative context" represent an algebraic sum of enhancement due to exposure and decrement due to conditioned negativity. When "contexts" are forcefully paired associates, exposure in a "negative context" may lead to disliking, but the mere exposure effect serves to inhibit this decline.

2. Presentation Sequence

For the most part, exposing a stimulus within a "heterogeneous" sequence in which other stimuli are interspersed is more likely to result in an exposure effect than is presenting a stimulus within an "homogeneous" or uninterrupted sequence in which the stimulus is repetitively presented. Washburn *et al.* (1927) were among the first to note the possible importance of this variable, and Berlyne (1970) was one of the first to provide experimental evidence by showing that high-frequency stimuli declined in judged pleasantness more rapidly when presented in homogeneous sequences. The already reviewed experiments by Harrison and Crandall (1972) and Stang and O'Connell (1974) and some of the semantic satiation studies (Amster, 1964) are consistent with this phenomenon, and also consistent are the results of Stang's (1974c) cross-study comparison. In many cases, however, repeated measures were used (Berlyne, 1970; Harrison & Crandall, 1972; Stang & O'Connell, 1974; Washburn *et al.*, 1927). If repeated measurement is a significant variable, as suggested earlier (Section III,A,2), some of these results may be open to an alternative interpretation. Spatial as compared to temporal massing does not seem to impair the mere exposure effect. Matlin (1974a) presented all stimuli simultaneously on a single sheet of paper and found exposure effects both when the different words were interspersed and when words of a given frequency were printed in an uninterrupted block.

C. MEASUREMENT VARIABLES

Finally, the effects of mere exposure will reflect in part the specific measures employed. Here we will consider the choice of scales, the use of attentional measures, the time of rating, and the use of repeated measures.

1. Scales

Although it seems trite to point out that assessed attitudes will depend on the specific questions asked, as Berlyne (1974b, 1974c, 1974d) notes, different scales which appear to be quite similar may not yield similar results. For example, both "interestingness" and "pleasingness" would seem to imply liking, yet Berlyne and his associates have repeatedly found that these items behave differently. Both types of ratings respond to variations in familiarity (among other variables), but the curves which express the two relationships are different. Similarly, it is important to separate scales which basically describe the stimulus or refer to its technical attributes from those which reflect evaluative or affective reactions (Berlyne, 1974c).

Word frequency—word meaning studies, which have generally supported the mere exposure hypothesis, have tended to use Good—Bad scales, whereas the aesthetic preference studies which have not so consistently supported the hypothesis have tended to use Like—Dislike scales. Both Saegert and Jellison (1970) and Zajonc *et al.* (1974a) found that the same manipulations which yielded exposure effects on Good—Bad scales produced other effects on Like—Dislike scales. Although both "good" and "like" imply favorable attitudes, there may be some important differences in the meanings of these two terms. Zajonc *et al.* (1974a) have suggested that whereas "good" scales measure a feeling of acceptance and affinity, "like" scales tap curiosity as well.

As we shall see in the next subsection, measures of curiosity are not good indicators of pleasant feelings. In consequence, studies using scales which straddle the two variables are particularly difficult to interpret. For example, it has been found that while children's willingness to associate with black stimulus persons increased as a function of portrait exposure, willingness to associate with white stimulus persons was either unaffected by exposures (G. N. Cantor, 1972) or decreased with exposures (Ball & Cantor, 1974). Although some of these results conflict with the mere exposure hypothesis, the dependent measures— "willingness to spend some time with this person and his family"—may assess curiosity and hence make these results open to alternative interpretations.

All this suggests that commonly obtained ratings may not be as easily interpretable as a cursory glance would suggest. A task for the future is to set aside assumed or face validity and seek other forms of validation for the affective rating scales.

2. Attentional Measures

Almost all studies which have used attentional measures have shown that people will attend to low-frequency or novel stimuli (Berlyne, 1950, 1958, 1960, 1966b, 1971; J. H. Cantor & Cantor, 1964a, 1964b, 1966; Endsley & Kessel, 1969; Harrison & Hines, 1970; Saegert & Jellison, 1970). If one equates curiosity with approach behavior and approach behavior with liking, then all of these studies appear to conflict with the mere exposure hypothesis. But such studies do not provide adequate tests of this notion. Attentional behavior has many causes and correlates (Berlyne, 1974d) and is therefore an unreliable indicator of liking.

In some cases we may attend to a stimulus because it is a welcome source of pleasure; in other instances, however, we may do so because it is threatening, uncertain, and worrisome. Berlyne (1960, 1966b), for example, has offered a distinction between two types of exploratory behavior. One, diversive exploratory behavior, is instigated by a lack of stimulation or by prolonged, unchanging stimulation. Its posited consequence is a boost in arousal which the organism finds pleasurable. Under these conditions, we would expect attention and liking to be positively correlated. The other type, specific exploratory behavior, is an orientational reaction provoked by unusual, uncertain, ambiguous, and potentially threatening circumstances (such as when a large, unidentified insect marches across the ceiling). In this latter case we would expect attention and liking to be inversely related.

Several studies have reported an inverse relationship between attentional behavior and verbally expressed liking. Harrison (1968b) found substantial negative correlations between viewing time and the favorability ratings accorded Zajonc's (1968) stimuli, and then later (Harrison, 1969) also obtained a negative correlation between ratings of curiosity and ratings of liking. Both Harrison and Hines (1970) and Saegert and Jellison (1970) found that the same operations which led to increased liking produced decreased exploratory behavior. Since such findings have been obtained on both within-subjects and between-subjects bases, they cannot be attributed to individual differences (Maddi, 1968) or to attribution of attitude given knowledge of attentional behavior (Kleinke, Gitlin, & Segal, 1973). The very least that can be said is that attentional responses and verbally expressed preferences are not identical functions of exposure, and that attentional behavior cannot be equated with liking.

Recently, Zajonc, Markus, and Wilson (1974c) have suggested that attentional behavior stemming from curiosity about a given stimulus decreases over time and that when attention to a given stimulus is prolonged this attentional behavior can be taken as an indicator of liking or affinity. Validation of this distinction is to be found in Brickman and D'Amato's (1975) results. Subjects were allowed to play a juke box and later rated the selections. Early in the experiment, subjects sampled different stimuli; this behavior decreased over time and was interpreted as curiosity. Later in the experiment, subjects played certain selections more and more frequently. Ratings revealed these to be the best-liked tunes, so this latter attentional behavior can be taken as signifying liking. Towards the end of the experiment, there was also alternation among the subset of frequently played stimuli, suggesting avoidance of homogeneous exposure sequences.

3. Immediate and Delayed Ratings

As already noted, mere exposure effects seem more likely and more pronounced when the exposure and rating phases are separated in time. The relevant studies may be classified into two groups according to the interval of delay.

Evidence suggesting that delays measured in minutes increase the likelihood of an exposure effect comes primarily from cross-study comparisons. For example, in Harrison and Crandall's (1972) first study, all stimuli were presented before ratings were obtained, and it was found that the homogeneous exposure sequence attenuated the attitude-enhancing effects of exposure. In their second experiment, exposure and rating phases were combined; each stimulus was rated after its last presentation and before the next stimulus was exposed. With these procedures, stimulus ratings dramatically declined (following three exposures). Stang's (1974c) cross-study comparison showed that although in most of the studies where "delay of ratings" occurred there was evidence of an exposure effect, in only a small proportion of the studies in which there was "no delay of ratings" was an exposure effect obtained.

Evidence indicating that lengthy delays measured in days increase the likelihood of an exposure effect is a bit more compelling. Both L. R. Wilson and Miller (1968) and M. A. Johnson and Watkins (1971) found that message repetition had more pronounced effects on attitudes under conditions of delayed assessment. Both Stang and O'Connell (1974) and Stang (1976b) have reported delay-of-rating effects. In the latter study, subjects tasted and rated spices and then returned a week later for additional tastings and ratings. Pleasantness ratings decreased over exposures within each session, but the initial ratings obtained during the second session were more favorable than the terminal ratings obtained during the first session. R. Crandall et al. (1976) found a greater exposure effect when ratings were obtained a week or more after the exposure manipulation than when ratings were required immediately following exposure. One of their findings was that whereas homogeneous exposure sequences were not associated with mere exposure effects when the ratings were made immediately, homogeneous exposure sequences did yield mere exposure effects when the ratings were obtained at a later point in time. This suggested that the homogeneous sequence only temporarily depressed the ratings of the maximum frequency stimuli.

Many of the studies involving immediate ratings have also involved another factor (Berlyne, 1970; Fryrear & Cottrell, 1976; Harrison & Crandall, 1972; Stang, 1976b; Stang & O'Connell, 1974). Subjects were either told in advance that they would rate the stimuli or exposures and ratings were interspersed so that subjects might have been led to anticipate subsequent ratings after the initial ratings had been made. As already noted (Section III,A,2), the effects of anticipating the ultimate rating task may itself influence ratings. Nonetheless, the studies reviewed here are suggestive of a temporal dynamic: how the subject feels about a stimulus depends, in part, on when it was last encountered.

D. CONCLUSIONS

Several analyses have suggested limitations and qualifications which would undermine the generality of the mere exposure hypothesis, but our review has shown that some of these alternative notions do not conflict with the mere exposure hypothesis and that others have not been consistently supported by the data. First, presentation of an already familiar stimulus does not reliably yield an exposure effect, but this does not conflict with the mere exposure hypothesis. Second, studies that have varied initial stimulus valence have not established that the exposure effect is dependent on having stimuli from a limited range of initial affective values. Third, stimulus recognition is not a precondition for the mere exposure effect to occur. Fourth, exposure, even "in a negative context" often produces greater liking. Finally, because verbal or behavioral measures of curiosity or attention are not good indicators of liking, experiments showing that repeated exposure leads to decreased exploratory behavior do not conflict with the mere exposure hypothesis.

Studies of the effects of initial meaningfulness are difficult to assess because they are highly contradictory and in some cases plagued with methodological flaws. Investigations in which stimulus discriminability is varied have been too few to allow a conclusion to be drawn. But, as we have repeatedly seen, three variables do seem to limit or reverse the exposure effect. We may conclude that mere exposure effects become less likely when stimulus complexity is decreased and when the heterogeneity or variability of the exposure sequence is reduced. It also appears that exposure effects become less likely when little or no temporal interval separates the exposure and rating phases. Any explanation of the attitudinal effects of exposure would do well to take these variables into account.

IV. Interpretations

Many explanations have been advanced to account for the mere exposure effect. Here we will consider five major explanations that have already entered the literature. These are the artifact, response competition, expectancy arousal, two-factor, satiation/generation, and arousal interpretations.

A. THE MERE EXPOSURE EFFECT AS AN EXPERIMENTAL ARTIFACT

To explain the exposure effect several investigators have invoked demand characteristics, subject expectancies, and other artifacts of experimentation. Burgess and Sales (1971), in their previously discussed study (see Section III,B,1) involving associative learning, argued that the effect resulted from differential association of the exposure stimuli with science, experimentation, and related concepts which are highly valued in our culture. However, as mentioned earlier, while their interpretation required a demonstration of incidental learning, their study dealt with paired associate learning. Suedfeld, Epstein, Buchanan, and Landon (1971) showed that it was possible to create expectancies or sets that made the exposure effect unlikely. One implication of their findings is that the mere exposure effect might require an alternative instructional set, perhaps resulting from intentional or unintentional manipulations by an overzealous experimenter. Hamid (1973), however, was unable to replicate the findings of Suedfeld *et al.*, and Rajecki and Wolfson (1973) obtained exposure effects even among a group of subjects who had been told that previous research had established a negative relationship between word frequency and goodness of meaning.

More recently, Stang (1974b) suggested that subjects intuit the mere exposure hypothesis and then perform in accordance with it. In two role playing studies subjects imagined participating in Zajonc's original exposure studies; their evaluative ratings did not differ appreciably from those given by Zajonc's active participants. In two other experiments, after rating stimuli of different frequencies, subjects were presented with a number of hypotheses and asked to indicate the one they thought of interest to the experimenter. Subjects tended to choose the hypothesis that best described their performance. The first two studies suggest that subjects have hypotheses about exposure and affect, and the latter investigations suggest that subjects perform in accordance with their intuitive hypotheses.

But these results do not prove that other familiarity–liking findings can be attributed to experimental artifacts. First, the hazards of role playing are many, and not the least of these is equating the amount of information available to role players and participants. Stang's role players were given minimal information, and certain critical aspects of the situation (such as cover stories) were omitted. Moreland and Zajonc (1976) found that when the situation, stimuli, and procedures were specified in detail (and hence the information available to role players and to participants were comparable) role players could not produce an exposure effect. In another sense, Stang's role players may have been given more information than is available to active participants. Each role player had an accurate exposure count for each stimulus. Real participants may not be good judges of the number of times a stimulus has been exposed (Gerard, Green, Hoyt, & Connolley, 1973), or they may preserve order relationships but seriously underestimate the number of exposures of the maximum frequency stimulus (Matlin & Stang, 1975; Matlin & Stone, 1975). Real participants may not even be able to tally frequencies, as was the case in the W. R. Wilson (1975) experiment where the stimuli were not recognizable. If real participants cannot correctly estimate the number of times they have seen a stimulus, it is unlikely that they could perform in accordance with an intuitive hypothesis which requires attitudes to improve as a function of the logarithm of the actual exposure frequency. Furthermore, we must consider the Moreland (1975) and Moreland and Zajonc (1975) findings which demonstrate that exposure leads to liking independent of subjective impressions of familiarity.

Second, as Stang (1974b) himself carefully observes, a correspondence between intuitive hypotheses and stimulus ratings does not show that the former caused the latter. Instead, the subjects' guesses may have been influenced by their behavior. As the verbal conditioning literature amply demonstrates, we cannot argue that awareness led to the particular outcome unless we can show that awareness precedes the effect and also rule out alternative explanations which accommodate both awareness and the effect (Kanfer, 1969). Neither of these conditions was satisfied in Stang's correlational studies. On the other hand, Moreland and Zajonc (1976) have eliminated awareness as a necessary condition for the exposure effect. In their research, which manipulated exposure as a between-subjects variable, an exposure effect was found even though each subject saw stimuli of only one frequency. Since individual subjects either could not tell that frequency was a variable or could not guess the number of times other subjects had seen a stimulus, it seems unlikely that they could divine or fulfill a familiarity–liking hypothesis. Artifact interpretations cannot account for the mere exposure data.

B. RESPONSE COMPETITION

Originated in an early theory of curiosity advanced by Berlyne (1954) and developed by Harrison (1968b), Matlin (1970), and others, the response competition interpretation sought to identify the psychological processes which mediate among exposure, liking, and curiosity. According to this conception, unless the organism is very young or primitive it will discover that even the most novel stimulus is composed of elements that it has encountered many times before in other stimuli. Associated with these other, previously encountered stimuli are different cognitive or behavioral responses. Consequently, a novel stimulus will tenuously elicit several responses, some of which will be incompatible or antagonistic. "Response competition" refers to the coexistence of conflicting or incompatible response tendencies. According to Berlyne (1954), the strength of the conflict will depend upon: (1) the number of competing responses; (2) the absolute and relative strength of these responses; and (3) their compatibility.

In accordance with traditional theorizing about the nature of response conflict (e.g., Brown & Farber, 1951), response competition is seen as an aversive, drive-like state which is associated with negative affect. This will be reflected in the low ratings given the associated (typically novel) stimulus. Subsequent exposure to the stimulus results in some response tendencies being strengthened while others are weakened or suppressed. These changes in response strength may result from an "implicit trial-and-error" or an "insightful restructuring" (Berlyne, 1954), or from subtler processes less contingent on recognition. As one response tendency achieves dominance, response competition is reduced. Concomitant with this is a reduction of tension and negative affect. This is manifested as the mere exposure effect. Response competition might also motivate exploratory behavior, which will in turn reduce response competition. In the course of exploration, then, liking should increase, but the motivation for exploration should decrease. Novel stimuli are thus expected to be associated with response competition, exploratory behavior, and disliking, and familiar stimuli are presumably associated with little response competition, little motivation to explore, and liking.

One test of this interpretation has involved intercorrelating response competition, liking, and exploratory behavior. Measures of response competition have included such things as: (1) response latencies in a free-association task, on the assumption that the greater the competition among a number of responses, the longer it will take for one of them to be omitted; (2) recall errors in a free-association task, on the assumption that the greater the number of responses attached to a stimulus, the less likely any one will be repeated; and (3) response communality in a free-association task, on the assumption that the more responses associated with a stimulus, the less likely one subject's initial associate will be matched by the initial associate of another subject. In keeping with response competition predictions, significant negative correlations have been found between response latency and liking (Harrison, 1968b; Matlin, 1970) and significant positive correlations between exploratory behavior and liking (see Section III,C,2).

In a second test of this interpretation, exposure was manipulated and the effects on response competition were assessed. In agreement with predictions, it has been found that increased exposure results in decreased response competition as assessed by response latencies (Harrison, 1968b; Harrison & Zajonc, 1970; Matlin, 1970) and recall errors (Matlin, 1970).

A third test has involved varying the number or strength of the responses associated with a stimulus, the expectation being that the greater the number of responses or the stronger the conflict among them, the less the associated stimulus will be liked. In one experiment, Matlin (1970) had subjects learn one, two, three, or six responses to initially novel stimuli and found that stimuli associated with fewer response alternatives were better liked. In another experiment, she had subjects pronounce nonsense words. Some nonsense words were pronounced the same way over trials, and others were pronounced different ways over trials. Again there was an inverse relationship between the number of responses and favorability ratings. Using more passive manipulations, Harrison *et al.* (1971) and Zajonc *et al.* (1974b) noted that pairing the test stimulus with consistent and redundant contiguous associates during the exposure phase enhanced the exposure effect, whereas pairing the test stimuli with inconsistent and changing stimuli caused an attenuation.

As advanced by Harrison (1968b), the response competition formulation did not explain why exposure might sometimes lead to decreased liking or to increased followed by decreased liking. Subsequently, two elaborations have been proposed. First, Saegert and Jellison (1970) raised the possibility that only up to a point does the reduction of response competition increase liking; further reduction is unpleasurable. This line of argument aligns the response competition model with several theories which we will encounter later. Second, Zajonc *et al.* (1972) offered an interpretation which not only accounts for the problem of "overexposure" but incorporates stimulus complexity and presentation sequence as well. These authors noted that in the typical exposure–liking experiment, subjects are confronted with an array of stimuli, and response competition is associated with each one. Repeated presentation of a given stimulus from the array will lessen the response competition associated with that stimulus, but the process is not infinite and after some number of exposures additional repetitions will have negligible effects on both response competition and attitude. The number of presentations required to reach this point should be relatively few when the stimuli are simple, that is, contain few elements to elicit associative responses. The number of repetitions should also be few when the presentation sequence is homogeneous and when ratings are promptly obtained, for under these conditions intraserial associations should make minimal contribution to response competition. Following the point at which the response competition associated with a given stimulus is already low, further repetition prevents the subject from reducing the response competition associated with the other stimuli in the array. Consequently disliking the maximum frequency stimulus might reflect frustration (or, indirectly, the response competition associated with other stimuli in the array).

Four major difficulties are associated with the response competition interpretation. First, there is a possibility that response latency measures do not reflect response competition but something else, such as variations in drive or arousal (Berlyne, 1966a) or meaningfulness (Stang, 1976a). Second, although this conception has been extended to account for variations in stimulus complexity, exposure sequence, and delay-of-ratings effects, such extensions have not yet received much in the way of direct experimental support. Third, this formulation predicts only a reduction in negative affect with exposure and does not predict the growth of positive feelings. Although, as we have already noted, scalar neutrality is difficult to determine, imprinting research (Rajecki, 1973; Zajonc, Reimer, & Hausser, 1973; Zajonc *et al.,* 1974c) suggests that exposure often leads to a development of positive affect. Not only have Parisians lost their distaste for the Eiffel Tower, they have learned to love it.

C. EXPECTANCY AROUSAL

Another possibility is that expectancies mediate between familiarity and liking, and that people will like best those stimuli which are neither totally unanticipated nor perfectly predictable. The expectancy arousal interpretation of J. E. Crandall (1967, 1968, 1970a, 1970b; also J. E. Crandall, Montgomery, & Rees, 1973) suggests that fragmentary cues which are first encountered in the course of stimulus inspection give rise to expectancies which will be confirmed or denied as stimulus inspection continues. As familiarity increases, increasingly stronger expectancies are aroused. Stimuli associated with moderately strong expectancies will be better liked than stimuli associated with very weak or very strong expectancies, and consequently an inverted U will best describe the relationship between familiarity and liking. Since stimuli associated with very weak expectancies are hypothesized to elicit exploratory behavior aimed at strengthening expectancies, an inverse relationship between curiosity and liking can be accommodated.

A distinction is made between expectancy arousal and expectancy confirmation. Cues encountered early in a temporal sequence (for example, the first syllable in a nonsense word) will gain expectancy arousal or predictive value; stimulus components encountered later (for example, the second syllable of a nonsense word) will gain expectancy confirmation value. Changes in either predictive or confirmation value could be responsible for evaluative reactions. In one experiment (J. E. Crandall, 1967) subjects rated two-syllable paralogs on a number of scales. Following this exposure manipulation, ratings were obtained for the first (or predictive) syllable, the second (or confirmation) syllable, and the two-syllable word. Ratings of the predictive syllable correlated more highly with the ratings of the paralog than did the ratings of the confirmation syllable, a finding repeatedly confirmed (J. E. Crandall, 1967, 1968, 1970a, 1970b). This suggests that expectancy arousal, rather than expectancy confirmation, mediated between exposure and liking.

A difficulty for both expectancy arousal and response competition formulations is that manipulations of expectancy arousal and of response competition are sometimes indistinct. For example, in one experiment, J. E. Crandall (1967) allowed some first syllables to accrue predictive value by pairing them with the same second syllable on each trial and prevented some syllables from accruing predictive value by pairing them with different second syllables on each presentation. Syllables which accrued predictive value were the most favorably rated. An alternative to the interpretation that the first syllables of the variable-ending paralogs did not acquire predictive value is that the variable-ending manipulation impaired the reduction of response competition.

Nonetheless, there are some important differences between the response competition and expectancy arousal approaches. First, although both formulations require some elaboration to account for complexity, presentation sequence, and delay-of-rating phenomena, the expectancy arousal formulation more easily accommodates results suggesting that low- or intermediate-frequency

stimuli are better liked than high-frequency stimuli. Second, the response competition researchers have generally used heterogeneous exposure sequences and
then obtained single ratings during a separate testing phase. The expectancy
arousal researchers, on the other hand, have generally used homogeneous exposure sequences and obtained multiple ratings in the course of stimulus repetition.
Third, although researchers in each tradition have manipulated the variables
posited to mediate between familiarity and liking, response competition has
been assessed independently of the liking measure whereas expectancy arousal
has not. Specification and exploration of the differences between response
competition and expectancy arousal formulation has only begun recently (J. E.
Crandall *et al.*, 1973).

D. TWO-FACTOR THEORIES

Two-factor theories hold that there is an inverted-U relationship between familiarity and liking, and they explain this relationship by invoking two separate
processes or factors. These separate factors have opposing effects but vary in
terms of relative strength over an exposure sequence in such a way that the
effects of first one factor and then the other will predominate. The two factors
proposed by Berlyne (1970) are (*a*) positive habituation (a reduction of uncertainty or conflict) and (*b*) tedium. Early in the course of exposures, positive
habituation will predominate and exposure will lead to increased liking. Later in
the course of exposures, tedium will predominate and exposure will decrease
liking. Variables such as complexity and presentation sequence will also affect
the relative strength of the two factors; habituation will be completed and
tedium will predominate after relatively few exposures when the stimuli are
simple or presented in homogeneous sequences. Each of the two factors, as we
shall see, can be related to changes in arousal (Section IV,F). Here, let us note
that because it provides an easy way of reconciling diverse results, Berlyne's
two-factor theory has gained considerable acceptance.

Stang (1973, 1974a, 1974b, 1975a, 1975b, 1976b) has used Berlyne's two-
factor formulation as a point of departure for developing his own analysis.
Stang's two factors are best described as learning and satiation. In the course of
exposure the subject learns about the stimulus, which in turn increases stimulus
favorability. Once learning has occurred, further repetition leads to satiation,
which causes a depression of ratings. In the initial formulation learning was
described in terms of perceptual recognition and recall. Accordingly, it has been
shown that exposure, learning, and affect are highly interrelated. For example,
using some measures, recall is a better predictor of linking than is frequency
(Stang, 1974a, 1975a), and stimuli whose serial position makes them easy to learn
are better liked than stimuli whose serial position makes them difficult to learn

(Matlin, 1974b, 1975; Stang, 1974a, 1975b). An alternative explanation of the relationship between recall and liking is that the more pleasant a stimulus is, the easier it is to remember (MacKinnon & Dukes, 1962).

Most recently, Stang (1976a) has described learning in terms of the attachment of new associative responses in the course of exposures. Thus, Stang's interpretation shares with the semantic generation interpretation (Section IV,E,2) the prediction that stimuli gain in meaningfulness in the course of exposures. However, unlike a generation interpretation, Stang's analysis can explain why exposure effects have been obtained using stimuli of differing initial valences. He suggests, in keeping with the Pollyanna principle (Section II,A,1), that the associations learned by subjects are more likely to be positively than negatively toned, because people tend to stress the good, the favorable, and the positive when organizing their phenomenological world. According to Stang, conditions which favor learning but minimize satiation (heterogeneous exposure, complex stimuli, delayed ratings) will promote exposure effects, whereas conditions favoring first learning and then satiation (massed exposures, complex stimuli, delayed ratings) will result in the inverted U.

At present, there would appear to be two major difficulties confronting Stang's two-factor formulation. First, as we have already seen, exposure in a "negative context" can lead to liking, even when the "context" is a forcefully paired, negatively toned associate. In the Zajonc et al. (1974b) experiment, for example, there was evidence of attitude enhancement even when subjects were not given the luxury of choosing their own cheerful associates. Second, W. R. Wilson (1975) suggests that while it is not a foregone conclusion that recognition is a prerequisite for the reduction of response competition, both Berlyne's and Stang's two-factor formulations suggest that "positive effects resulting from stimulus exposure are directly mediated by processes of subjective familiarity and stimulus recognition" (p. 76). But as the W. R. Wilson (1975) and Moreland (1975); also Moreland & Zajonc, 1975) research shows, neither subjective familiarity nor recognition is a prerequisite for liking high-frequency stimuli. Of course, as W. R. Wilson (1975) also points out, the mere exposure hypothesis does not eliminate subjective familiarity and recall as correlates of the exposure manipulation.

E. SEMANTIC SATIATION AND SEMANTIC GENERATION

Semantic satiation and semantic generation interpretations explain the mere exposure effect in terms of generalized changes in meaning (Grush, 1976; Jakobovits, 1968). The semantic satiation hypothesis suggests that repetition leads to decreases in meaningfulness with the consequence that initially negatively toned stimuli become less positive. The semantic generation hypothesis, on the other hand, proposes that repetition leads to increased rather than decreased polarization of ratings.

Because much of the evidence which supports one of these interpretations will disconfirm the other, we will have to consider each interpretation in turn. But there is some evidence which bears on both notions. First, both predict that changes in meaningfulness should appear on nonevaluative as well as evaluative scales. Some studies have found evidence of this (Amster & Glassman, 1966; Grush, 1976; Stang, 1976a), but others have not. Lieberman and Walters (1968) reported that although evaluative ratings gained in favorability following the repetition of musical selections, nonevaluative ratings were unaffected. Zajonc *et al.* (1974b) found that whereas repetition of portraits of Chinese lead to increased ratings of liking and goodness, ratings of honesty and complexity were not so affected. M. A. Johnson (1973) observed that although Good–Bad ratings improved over exposures in both pleasant and unpleasant contexts, ratings of activity and potency were not affected. Most bothersome of all are findings that the same manipulation which yields increased or decreased "meaning" on one scale leads to the opposite effect on another scale (Zajonc *et al.*, 1974a). Why, though, should some studies find changes on nonevaluative scales? One possibility is that even "nonevaluative" ratings have evaluative components (M. A. Johnson, 1973; Nunnally, 1967; Zajonc *et al.*, 1974a). Another possibility is that certain procedures do lead to generalized changes in meaning but are not a prerequisite for the mere exposure effect to occur.

There are three other difficulties shared by semantic satiation and semantic generation interpretations. First, both maintain that the effects of exposure will depend on the initial stimulus valence. This contention, as we have already seen, has not been satisfactorily verified (Section III,A,2). Second, neither hypothesis does a good job of explaining shifts from the "disliked" to the "liked" zones of the affective scales. Finally, both interpretations are hard pressed to account for an inverted-U exposure–favorability relationship, unless one cares to make assumptions about initial stimulus valence and view satiation and generation as sequential events (Amster, 1964).

1. Semantic Satiation

Semantic satiation would explain mere exposure and contrasting effects if we were to assume that in the former case experimenters have begun with initially disliked stimuli but that in the latter case they have begun with initially liked stimuli. The validity of this assumption has not been established, and much of the evidence is in direct opposition to it (Section III,A,2). Furthermore, a satiation interpretation would predict that concomitant with changes in connotative meaning as revealed on rating scales there would be changes in associative meaning as revealed by increased response latency and decreased response communality (Esposito & Pelton, 1969). The response competition studies have yielded the opposite result that increased exposure leads to decreased response latencies and to increased communality (Section IV,B). Finally, semantic satiation is usually considered to be a short-lived phenomena and dependent upon obtaining ratings as soon as possible after the last stimulus repetition. However, the exposure effect occurs even when the repetitions and ratings are quite distant in time (Section III,C,3).

2. Semantic Generation

Generation would explain mere exposure and contrasting effects if we were to assume that experimenters have begun with liked stimuli in the former case and with disliked stimuli in the latter. However, the validity of this assumption is also in doubt (Section III,A,2). Unlike a satiation interpretation, a generation conception may accommodate the response competition findings that increased exposure leads to decreased response latencies and increased reponse communality (Section IV,B). However, if generation is a result of attaching new responses to the stimulus in the course of exposures, it is not clear why the response competition and expectancy arousal studies have found that increasing the number and variety of attached responses and hence "meaningfulness" will result in disliking. Finally, we cannot say how this interpretation would explain exposure effects in a negative context (Section III,B,1). Neither semantic satiation nor semantic generation provide very satisfactory explanations of the exposure effect at present.

F. AROUSAL FORMULATIONS

Although their terms differ, a number of theorists hold that varying familiarity affects a stimulus's excitatory potential and that some form of activation or arousal mediates between stimulus exposure and affective reactions. Hebb (1946) and Bronson (1968) thought that early visual experience results in the encoding of perceptual patterns; following this, novel stimuli presumably disrupt these patterns and produce a state of negative emotion (fear). Later, the same stimuli will be incorporated into the pattern and will lose their disruptive ability. Thus, novel stimuli elicit negative reactions which diminish as the stimulus gains familiarity. McClelland, Atkinson, Clark, and Lowell (1953), Haber (1958), and others argued that the stimulation the organism has received in the past or is in the process of receiving produces a momentary level of adaptation. Stimuli with excitatory potential at the adaptation level are regarded with indifference. Stimuli with greater or lesser excitatory potential will induce a discrepancy from the momentary adaptation level. Small discrepancies are associated with positive affect, and large discrepancies with negative affect. Thus, a "butterfly curve" (with the juncture of the wings representing the adaptation level) would best describe the relationship between discrepancy from adaptation level and affective response. Consistent with this line of reasoning are Maddi's (1961) findings of a preference for a sequence of events that is neither highly predictable nor unpredictable; in other words, a sequence which departs somewhat but not too much from what would be expected. In a similar vein is Kagan's (1971) suggestion that the major sources of attraction (inspection time, smiling, change in heart rate, body movement) for babies between 3 and 12 months of age are objects that are moderately discrepant from schemas or internalized representations of the object. The difficulty with theories based on adaptation levels, as Zajonc *et al.* (1974a) note, is that mere exposure results suggest that stimuli which fall at the adaptation level are better liked than stimuli which depart from it.

Perhaps the most prominent of the arousal theorists is D. E. Berlyne. Although on the basis of his early writings (e.g., Berlyne, 1960) he is often described as an "optimal level of arousal" theorist, in the last decade or so he has expounded the view that there is an optimal degree of *change* in arousal which gives rise to feelings of pleasure (Berlyne, 1967, 1970, 1971, 1973, 1974c). Emphasis is thus on the effects of arousal increments and decrements.

According to Berlyne, a certain amount of arousal potential (capacity to increase arousal) will be associated with any given stimulus. Arousal potential is determined by the stimulus's psychophysical properties (brightness, loudness, etc.), ecological properties (association with other stimuli), and collative properties (such as novelty, surprisingness, incongruity, ambiguity, and complexity). The effects of these different sets of properties and of specific properties within a set are additive, and, to some extent, increases in one can compensate for decreases in the other. Most of Berlyne's research has focused on the collative properties, which are thus named because "in order to decide how novel, surprising, complex and so on a pattern is, one must compute or collate information from two or more sources" (Berlyne, 1971, p. 69).

Stimuli associated with moderate capacity to boost arousal are expected to elicit more favorable reactions than are stimuli with high or low arousal potential. Thus, as arousal potential is decreased from a high level, the consequence should be increased followed by decreased liking. One way of decreasing a stimulus's arousal potential is through repeated contact with it. Specifically, repetition of an initially novel stimulus should reduce that stimulus's arousal potential. However, the affective consequences of a given number of exposures will depend on all the psychophysical, ecological, and collative properties which contribute to overall arousal potential. The greater this overall arousal potential, the more exposures are required before reaching the inflection point in an inverted-U exposure–liking curve. Thus, while maximum liking for a simple stimulus (low arousal potential) should require few or no repetitions, maximum liking for a complex stimulus (high arousal potential) should require many exposures. Exposure sequence could be viewed as either an ecological or colla-

tive variable; in either case, in comparison to homogeneous sequences, heterogeneous sequences should be associated with higher arousal potential and
maximum liking should require relatively many exposures. Combining rather
than separating exposure and rating phases would also have ecological or collative effects; thus, short-term "delay of rating" phenomena become interpretable
within Berlyne's conceptual framework.

Although a property of the stimulus, arousal potential affects the organism's
arousal, which in turn activates various hedonic systems in the brain. Drawing on
studies of electrical stimulation of the brain (Olds, 1962; Olds & Olds, 1965),
Berlyne (1967, 1971, 1973, 1974c) posits three such systems. First, there is the
primary reward system, which is activated when arousal is raised. Second, there
is the aversion system, which requires a greater arousal increment for activation
than does the primary reward system. The aversion system will inhibit the
primary reward system. Thus, stimuli which provide a moderate boost in arousal
will be more pleasurable than stimuli with low or high arousal potential, for they
will be sufficiently arousing to activate the primary reward system but not so
arousing as to activate the aversion system. Finally, there is the secondary
reward system, which is activated by dearousal. The secondary reward system
serves to inhibit the aversion system; consequently, a dearousing stimulus is
"pleasurable" only in a roundabout way. Thus, as a stimulus with initially high
arousal potential gains in familiarity, declining arousal potential will inhibit the
aversion system and will seem relatively pleasurable, but if familiarization and a
loss of arousal potential continues, the stimulus will lose the capacity to activate
the primary reward system, with the result that an "overfamiliar" stimulus
becomes unpleasant.

Exploratory behavior can cause fluctuation in arousal. First, if the organism
is in a high state of arousal, exploration of novel stimuli serves to reduce the
surprisingness, incongruity, ambiguity, complexity, and so forth, with the result
that the novel stimulus will lose arousal potential and the aversion system will be
inhibited. Second, inspection of stimuli which are novel, complex, unpredictable, or have other collative properties serve to boost arousal and activate the
primary reward system. In the first instance we have specific exploratory
behavior, whereas in the second case we have diversive exploratory behavior
(Section III,C,2).

This carefully constructed formulation is highly attractive. First, it has a high
degree of coherence and internal consistency; although it involves two processes
and three systems, it all boils down to variations in arousal. Second, it would
seem to have generated a very large number of empirical tests—not only by those
associated with Berlyne's Laboratory for Aplopathematic and Thelematoscopic
Pneumatology (see Berlyne, 1973), but by many others as well (e.g., Fryrear &
Cottrell, 1976; Harrison & Crandall, 1972; G. F. Smith & Dorfman, 1975).
Third, it is a very general theory which can account not only for the effects of

familiarity but for the effects of many other stimulus properties, on both affective reactions and attentional behavior. Fourth, it is consistent with a hefty proportion of the data presented in this review. It can account for exposure leading to increased liking, decreased liking, or increased followed by decreased liking, and for complexity, presentation sequence, and possibly even time-of-ratings effects as well. Manipulated response competition and expectancy arousal results may also be consistent, if one assumes that these manipulations may have affected the associated stimulus's arousal potential. For example, attaching many conflicting response tendencies to a stimulus may drive arousal potential into the unpleasant range, and moderately strong expectancies may be associated with an optimal arousal increment.

However, there remain important gaps and inconsistencies in the intricate web of empirical evidence, and the physiological theorizing especially is best taken as provisional (Berlyne, 1971; Walker, 1973). Certain variables have received more attention than others, and the theory seems to do a better job of accommodating the effects of complexity than of accommodating the effects of novelty and familiarity (Zajonc et al., 1974a). Finally, as W. R. Wilson (1975) has pointed out, the positive habituation process (which causes a drop in arousal and should account for the exposure effect) rests upon the assumption that exposure provides a means by which elements of the stimulus are "discriminated, classified, recognized and grouped together" (Berlyne, 1970, p. 285). Wilson's findings that recognition is not necessary for the mere exposure effect to occur conflict with this view.

V. Ten Years of Exposure to Mere Exposure: Some Tentative Conclusions

For over a century psychologists have suspected an inverted-U relationship between familiarity and liking. Have we really learned anything since the preliminary version of the mere exposure monograph (Zajonc, 1965) appeared over a decade ago? A strong case can be made for an affirmative answer.

A good deal of research in the last 10 years has demonstrated that repeated exposure to some stimulus leads to liking for it under a wide range of conditions. The effect has been found when exposures have been reduced to a fraction of a second (Harrison & Hines, 1970), rendered unrecognizable (W. R. Wilson, 1975), or increased to ten times the number used in Zajonc's initial experiments (Zajonc et al., 1974a). The effect has been extended into the realm of interpersonal attraction, and considerable new data has been accrued concerning the relationship between familiarity and aesthetic preference.

Many hypotheses suggesting qualifications and exceptions to the mere exposure effect have been found to be invalid. The effect does not require choosing stimuli from a narrow range of preexposure valences; it does not require that the stimulus be recognized; and it certainly does not require that the exposure take place "in a positive context." Other studies suggesting that exposure does not enhance attitudes towards already familiar stimuli and suggesting that people attend to novel stimuli do not conflict with the mere exposure hypothesis.

On the other hand, three variables have raised complications for mere exposure advocates. Variations in stimulus complexity, presentation sequence, and time of rating affect the likelihood that an exposure or contrasting effect will appear. It may be, as Zajonc *et al.* (1974a) suggest, that such things as presentation sequence and time of rating are factors which surround the exposure manipulation and are not a natural result of stimulus repetition per se. Results showing that the homogeneous presentation sequence only temporarily depresses ratings are certainly consistent with this line of argument. However, it is not clear that complexity, usually considered to be a property of the stimulus, is quite so easy to dismiss.

The last decade has also seen many revelations about the cognitive and other processes which mediate among exposure, liking, exploratory behavior, and other variables. Some interpretations, such as the response competition interpretation, were built primarily on the exposure effect. Others, such as semantic satiation, semantic generation, and arousal interpretations, have viewed the effect as only one small part of a larger phenomenon.

Of the theories reviewed here, two have not fared well. First, the mere exposure effect is not an experimental artifact. It is not a result of associating strong positive attitudes towards psychology and experimentation; it occurs even in a "negative context." It is not a result of subjects' expectancies; it occurs when subjects are led to form conflicting hypotheses and when there is no possible way for the subjects to intuit the experimenter's anticipations. Second, the mere exposure effect is not easily explained away in terms of semantic satiation or generation. The critical predictions that the effect depends on selecting stimuli from a narrow range of preexposure valences and that the effects depend on generalized changes of meaning have not been borne out. Generalized changes in meaning may occur, but the mere exposure effect is not contingent upon these.

Of the remaining explanations, most can account for the overall patterns of results one way or another, and each offers some supportive studies which alternative formulations must take into account. Each has developed some strengths but retains some weaknesses. The response competition interpretation has done well in a number of tests, but its extension to account for complexity, presentation, and temporal effects is highly speculative. The expectancy arousal theory rests on a very limited number of experiments. Two-factor theories can account for any pattern of results (by drawing differentially on each factor). However, Stang's formulation has been challenged on the grounds that the processes identified by Stang are not necessary for the exposure effect to occur and on the grounds that it does not account for exposure in a "negative context." Berlyne's theory, based on changes in arousal, has a number of strong points. Yet the neuropsychological underpinnings may not be sound, and there remain some troublesome aspects of the data.

Is the ultimate key to be found in one of these theories? Most of them seem to be based on elaborate cognitive processes. Two findings thus pose a serious challenge. First, exposure effects appear among precocial birds, grasshoppers, and other organisms which seem to lack the neural prerequisites (Harrison & Fisicaro, 1974; Rajecki, 1973; Zajonc et al., 1973, 1974c). Second, as repeatedly noted, the exposure effect does not seem to depend on stimulus recognition, and recognition would seem to be a prerequisite for these elaborate processes to occur (W. R. Wilson, 1975).

To speculate a bit, there is a recent theory which might account for the exposure effect without involving complicated cognitive processes. This is the opponent process theory of motivation (Solomon & Corbit, 1974), thus far applied to cigarette addiction (Solomon & Corbit, 1973) and to imprinting (Hoffman & Solomon, 1974). The theory suggests that if the presentation of a stimulus triggers an affective reaction, the withdrawal of that stimulus will trigger an "opponent process" which in turn eventuates in feelings or moods with hedonic signs opposite to those associated with the initial reaction. This opponent process is a "slave" process which cannot under normal circumstances be triggered directly, and it decays over time so that feelings or moods will return to neutrality.

Suppose a novel stimulus is threatening (negative affect). In this case, withdrawal of that stimulus might trigger an opponent process which we might interpret as a flood of relief (positive affect). According to Solomon and Corbit, repetition of such a sequence would leave the initial process unaffected but strengthen the (in this case positive) opponent process, as indicated by measures of latency, asymptote, and decay. Through conditioning, the originally threatening stimulus will begin to trigger the opponent process, and stimulus withdrawal would no longer be required. Thus, repetition of a stimulus would strengthen the affective contribution of the opponent process, with the result that the stimulus becomes better liked.

Two other features are of note. First, just as repetition of the opponent process has a strengthening effect, disuse has a weakening effect. Thus, if stimuli were presented in uninterrupted sequences with little or no intertrial intervals, the opponent process would be weakened or extinguished through disuse; the initial process would contribute more and more heavily to the net affective reaction; and liking should decline. Second, the primary and opponent processes have different temporal-intensity gradients which vary as a function of both repetition and of stimulus properties such as complexity. Because of these gradients, such variables as the timing of the dependent measure should be very important. For example, if the viewer is observing a stimulus while rating, the rating should be relatively low because it will reflect both the primary process (−) and the opponent process (+). If the stimulus is withdrawn prior to rating, the rating should be relatively high because only the opponent process (+) remains activated. Finally, if the rating is obtained some time after the stimulus is withdrawn, it should be relatively low because the opponent process will have decayed over time.

Of course this is conjecture; although successfully applied in other areas, opponent process theory has not received direct testing in the "mere exposure" area. Furthermore, although it may overcome some of the problems associated with elaborate cognitive theories, other problems may arise to take their place. But all this remains to be seen. It is hoped that the next decade will see further inroads toward understanding the attitudinal effects of mere exposure.

REFERENCES

Allport, G. W. *The nature of prejudice*. Reading, Mass.: Addison-Wesley, 1954.
Alpert, R. Perceptual determinants of affect. Unpublished master's thesis, Wesleyan University, 1953. Discussed in D. E. Berlyne, *Aesthetics and psychobiology*. New York: Appleton, 1971. P. 191.
Amir, Y. Contact hypothesis in ethnic relations. *Psychological Bulletin*, 1969, 71, 319–342.
Amster, H. Semantic satiation and generation: Learning? Adaptation? *Psychological Bulletin*, 1964, 62, 273–286.
Amster, H., & Glassman, L. D. Verbal repetition and connotative change. *Journal of Experimental Psychology*, 1966, 71, 389–395.
Anderson, N. H. Likableness ratings of 555 personality-trait words. *Journal of Personality and Social Psychology*, 1968, 9, 272–279.
Ball, P. M., & Cantor, G. N. White boys' ratings of pictures of whites and blacks as related to amount of familiarization. *Perceptual and Motor Skills*, 1974, 39, 883–890.
Bartlett, D. L. Effect of repeated listenings on structural discrimination and affective response. *Journal of Research in Music Education*, 1973, 21, 302–317.
Becknell, J. C., Jr., Wilson, W. R., & Baird, J. C. The effect of frequency of presentation on the choice of nonsense syllables. *Journal of Psychology*, 1963, 56, 165–170.
Berlyne, D. E. Novelty and curiosity as determinants of exploratory behavior. *British Journal of Psychology*, 1950, 41, 68–80.
Berlyne, D. E. A theory of human curiosity. *British Journal of Psychology*, 1954, 45, 180–191.
Berlyne, D. E. The influence of complexity and novelty in visual figures on orienting responses. *Journal of Experimental Psychology*, 1958, 55, 289–296.
Berlyne, D. E. *Conflict, arousal, and curiosity*. New York: McGraw-Hill, 1960.
Berlyne, D. E. Conflict and reaction time: Reply to Kiesler. *Psychological Reports*, 1966, 19, 413–414. (a)
Berlyne, D. E. Curiosity and exploration. *Science*, 1966, 153, 23–33. (b)
Berlyne, D. E. Arousal and reinforcement. In D. Levine (Ed.), *Nebraska symposium on motivation*. Lincoln: University of Nebraska Press, 1967. Pp. 1–110.

Berlyne, D. E. Novelty, complexity, and hedonic value. *Perception and Psychophysics*, 1970, 8, 279–286.

Berlyne, D. E. *Aesthetics and psychobiology*. New York: Appleton, 1971.

Berlyne, D. E. The vicissitudes of aplopathematic and thelematoscopic pneumatology *or* The hydrography of hedonism. In D. E. Berlyne (Ed.), *Pleasure, reward, preference*. New York: Academic Press, 1973. Pp. 1–33.

Berlyne, D. E. The new experimental aesthetics. In D. E. Berlyne (Ed.), *Studies in the new experimental aesthetics: Toward an objective psychology of aesthetic appreciation*. Washington, D.C.: Hemisphere, 1974. Pp. 1–26. (a)

Berlyne, D. E. Novelty, complexity, and interestingness. In D. E. Berlyne (Ed.), *Studies in the new experimental aesthetics: Toward an objective psychology of aesthetic appreciation*. Washington, D.C.: Hemisphere, 1974. Pp. 175–181. (b)

Berlyne, D. E. (Ed.) *Studies in the new experimental aesthetics: Toward an objective psychology of aesthetic appreciation*. Washington, D.C.: Hemisphere, 1974. (c)

Berlyne, D. E. Attention. In E. C. Carterette & P. Friedman (Eds.), *Handbook of perception*. Vol. 1. *Historical and philosophical roots of perception*. New York: Academic Press, 1974. Pp. 123–147. (d)

Boucher, J., & Osgood, C. E. The Pollyanna hypothesis. *Journal of Verbal Learning and Verbal Behavior*, 1969, 8, 1–8.

Bradley, I. L. Repetition as a factor in the development of musical preferences. *Journal of Research in Music Education*, 1971, 19, 295–298.

Brickman, P., & D'Amato, B. Exposure effects in a free choice situation. *Journal of Personality and Social Psychology*, 1975, 32, 415–420.

Brickman, P., Redfield, J., Harrison, A. A., & Crandall, R. Drive and predisposition as factors in the attitudinal effects of mere exposure. *Journal of Experimental Social Psychology*, 1972, 8, 31–44.

Bronson, G. W. The fear of novelty. *Psychological Bulletin*, 1968, 69, 350–358.

Brown, J. S., & Farber, I. E. Emotions conceptualized as intervening variables—with suggestions toward a theory of frustration. *Psychological Bulletin*, 1951, 48, 465–495.

Burgess, T. D. G., & Sales, S. M. Attitudinal effects of mere exposure: A re-evaluation. *Journal of Experimental Social Psychology*, 1971, 7, 461–472.

Bush, P. A., & Pease, K. G. Pop records and connotative satiation: Test of Jakobovits Theory. *Psychological Reports*, 1968, 23, 871–875.

Cantor, G. N. Children's "like–dislike" ratings of familiarized and nonfamiliar visual stimuli. *Journal of Experimental Child Psychology*, 1968, 6, 651–657.

Cantor, G. N. Effects of familiarization on children's ratings of whites and blacks. *Child Development*, 1972, 43, 1219–1229.

Cantor, G. N., & Kubose, S. K. Preschool children's ratings of familiarized and nonfamiliarized visual stimuli. *Journal of Experimental Child Psychology*, 1969, 8, 74–81.

Cantor, J. H., & Cantor, G. N. Children's observing behavior as related to amount and recency of stimulus familiarization. *Journal of Experimental Child Psychology*, 1964, 1, 241–247. (a)

Cantor, J. H., & Cantor, G. N. Observing behavior in children as a function of stimulus novelty. *Child Development*, 1964, 35, 119–128. (b)

Cantor, J. H., & Cantor, G. N. Functions relating children's observing behavior to amount and recency of stimulus familiarization. *Journal of Experimental Psychology*, 1966, 72, 859–863.

Cohen-Portheim, P. *The spirit of Paris*. Philadelphia: Lippincott, 1937.

Coutaud, R., & Duclair, J. H. *Paris dans votre poche*. Paris: Edition Touristiques Francaises, 1956.

Crandall, J. E. Familiarity, preference, and expectancy arousal. *Journal of Experimental Psychology*, 1967, 73, 374–381.

Crandall, J. E. Effects of need for approval and intolerance of ambiguity upon stimulus preference. *Journal of Personality*, 1968, 36, 67–83.

Crandall, J. E. Predictive value and confirmability of traits as determinants of judged trait importance. *Journal of Personality*, 1970, 38, 77–90. (a)

Crandall, J. E. Preference and expectancy arousal: Further evidence. *Journal of General Psychology*, 1970, 83, 267–268. (b)

Crandall, J. E., Montgomery, V. E., & Rees, W. W. "Mere" exposure versus familiarity, with implications for response competition and expectancy arousal hypotheses. *Journal of General Psychology*, 1973, 88, 105–120.

Crandall, R. Field extension of the frequency-affect findings. *Psychological Reports*, 1972, 31, 371–374.

Crandall, R., Harrison, A. A., & Zajonc, R. B. The permanence of the positive and negative effects of stimulus exposure: A "sleeper effect"? Under editorial review, 1976.

Cross, H. A., Halcomb, C. G., & Matter, W. W. Imprinting or exposure learning in rats given early auditory stimulation. *Psychonomic Science*, 1967, 10, 223–234.

Deutsch, M., & Collins, M. E. *Interracial housing: A psychological evaluation of a social experiment*. Minneapolis: University of Minnesota Press, 1951.

DeVries, L. *Victorian inventions*. New York: American Heritage Press, 1972.

Downey, J. E., & Knapp, G. E. The effect on a musical program of familiarity and of sequence of selections. In M. Schoen (Ed.), *The effects of music*. New York: Harcourt, 1927.

Endsley, R. C., & Kessel, L. D. Effects of differential prior exposure on kindergarten children's subsequent observing and choice of novel stimuli. *Developmental Psychology*, 1969, 1, 193–199.

Esposito, N. J., & Pelton, L. H. Review of the measurement of semantic satiation. *Psychological Bulletin*, 1969, 75, 330–347.

Farnsworth, P. R. The effects of repetition on ending preferences in melodies. *American Journal of Psychology*, 1926, 37, 116–122.

Festinger, L., Schachter, S., & Back, K. *Social pressures in informal groups: A study of human factors in housing*. New York: Harper, 1950.

Frincke, G., & Johnson, R. C. Word value and word frequency in homophone pairs. *Psychological Reports*, 1960, 7, 470.

Fryrear, R. L., & Cottrell, N. B. Effects of stimulus complexity and repeated exposures on affective ratings. Under editorial review, 1976.

Gerard, H. B., Green, D., Hoyt, M., & Conolley, E. S. Influence of affect on exposure–frequency estimates. *Journal of Personality and Social Psychology*, 1973, 28, 151–154.

Gilliland, A. R., & Moore, H. T. The immediate and long-time effects of classical and popular phonograph selections. *Journal of Applied Psychology*, 1924, 8, 309–323.

Gough, H. G. Reference handbook for the Gough Adjective Checklist. University of California Institute of Personality Assessment and Research, Berkeley, 1955. (Mimeo.)

Grush, J. E. Attitude formation and mere exposure phenomena: A non-artifactual explanation of empirical findings. *Journal of Personality and Social Psychology*, 1976, 33, 281–290.

Haber, R. N. Discrepancy from adaptation level as a source of affect. *Journal of Experimental Psychology*, 1958, 56, 370–375.

Hamid, P. N. Exposure frequency and stimulus preference. *British Journal of Psychology,* 1973, **64,** 569–577.

Hamm, N., Baum, M. R., & Nikels, K. W. Effects of race and exposure on judgments of interpersonal favorability. *Journal of Experimental Social Psychology,* 1975, **11,** 14–24.

Harrison, A. A. Exposure, favorability, and item endorsement. *Psychological Reports,* 1968, **23,** 1970. (a)

Harrison, A. A. Response competition, frequency, exploratory behavior and liking. *Journal of Personality and Social Psychology,* 1968, 9, 363–368. (b)

Harrison, A. A. Exposure and popularity. *Journal of Personality,* 1969, **37,** 359–377.

Harrison, A. A., & Crandall, R. Heterogeneity–homogeneity of exposure sequence and the attitudinal effects of exposure. *Journal of Personality and Social Psychology,* 1972, **21,** 234–238.

Harrison, A. A., & Fisicaro, S. A. Stimulus familiarity and alley illumination as determinants of approach response latencies of house crickets. *Perceptual and Motor Skills,* 1974, **39,** 147–152.

Harrison, A. A., & Hines, P. Effects of frequency of exposure at three short exposure times on affective ratings and exploratory behavior. *Proceedings, 78th Annual Convention, American Psychological Association,* 1970, **5,** 391–392.

Harrison, A. A., Tufts, J. W., & Strayer, J. B. Task difficulty and the reinforcement effects of high and low frequency stimuli. *Journal of Personality and Social Psychology,* 1974, **29,** 628–636.

Harrison, A. A., Tutone, R., & McFadgen, G. The effects of frequency of exposure of changing and unchanging stimulus pairs on affective ratings. *Journal of Personality and Social Psychology,* 1971, **20,** 102–111.

Harrison, A. A., & Zajonc, R. B. The effects of frequency and duration of exposure on response competition and affective ratings. *Journal of Psychology,* 1970, **75,** 163–169.

Hebb, D. O. On the nature of fear. *Psychological Review,* 1946, **33,** 259–276.

Heingartner, A., & Hall, J. V. Affective consequences in adults and children of repeated exposure to auditory stimuli. *Journal of Personality and Social Psychology,* 1974, **29,** 719–723.

Hoffman, H. S., & Solomon, R. L. An opponent–process theory of motivation: III. Some affective dynamics in imprinting. *Learning and Motivation,* 1974, **5,** 149–164.

Howes, D., & Solomon, R. L. A note on McGinnies' "Emotionality and perceptual defense." *Psychological Review,* 1950, **57,** 229–234.

Howes, D., & Solomon, R. L. Visual duration thresholds as a function of word probability. *Journal of Experimental Psychology,* 1951, **41,** 401–410.

Jakobovits, L. A. Studies of fads: I. The "Hit Parade." *Psychological Reports,* 1966, **18,** 443–450.

Jakobovits, L. A. Effects of mere exposure: A comment. *Journal of Personality and Social Psychology,* 1968, 9 (Monogr. Suppl. 2), Part 2, 30–32.

Janisse, M. P. Attitudinal effects of mere exposure: A replication and extension. *Psychonomic Science,* 1970, **19,** 77–78.

Johnson, H. H., & Watkins, T. A. The effects of message repetition on immediate and delayed attitude change. *Psychonomic Science,* 1971, **22,** 101–103.

Johnson, M. A. The attitudinal effects of mere exposure and the experimental environment. Paper presented at the meeting of the Western Psychological Association, Anaheim, California, April 1973.

Johnson, R. C., Thomson, C. W., & Frincke, G. Word values, word frequencies and visual duration thresholds. *Psychological Review,* 1960, **67,** 332–342.

Kagan, J. *Change and continuity in infancy*. New York: Wiley, 1971.

Kanfer, F. H. Verbal conditioning: A review of its current status. In T. R. Dixon & D. L. Horton (Eds.), *Verbal behavior and general behavior theory*. Englewood Cliffs, N.J.: Prentice-Hall, 1969. Pp. 245–290.

Kanouse, D. E., & Hanson, L. R. Negativity in evaluations. In E. E. Jones, D. E. Kanouse, H. H. Kelley, R. E. Nesbit, S. Valins, & B. Weiner (Eds.), *Attribution: Perceiving the causes of behavior*. Morristown, N.J.: General Learning Press, 1972.

Kaplan, K. J. On the ambivalence–indifference problem in attitude theory and measurement: A suggested modification of the semantic differential technique. *Psychological Bulletin*, 1972, 77, 361–372.

Kleinke, C. L., Gitlin, K. S., & Segal, H. A. Effect of perceived looking time on evaluation of paintings. *Perceptual and Motor Skills*, 1973, 37, 421–422.

Krugman, H. E. Affective response to music as a function of familiarity. *Journal of Abnormal and Social Psychology*, 1943, 38, 388–392.

Lambert, W. E., & Jakobovits, L. A. Verbal satiation and changes in intensity of meaning. *Journal of Experimental Psychology*, 1960, 60, 376–383.

Lieberman, L. R., & Walters, W. M. Effects of repeated listening on connotative meaning of serious music. *Perceptual and Motor Skills*, 1968, 26, 891–895.

MacKinnon, D. W., & Dukes, W. F. Repression. In L. Postman (Ed.), *Psychology in the making*. New York: Knopf, 1962.

Maddi, S. R. Affective tone during environmental regularity and change. *Journal of Abnormal and Social Psychology*, 1961, 62, 338–345.

Maddi, S. R. Meaning, novelty and affect: Comment on Zajonc's paper. *Journal of Personality and Social Psychology*, 1968, 9 (Monogr. Suppl. 2), Part 2, 28–29.

Maslow, A. H. The influence of familiarization on preference. *Journal of Experimental Psychology*, 1937, 21, 162–180.

Matlin, M. W. Response competition as a mediating factor in the frequency–affect relationship. *Journal of Personality and Social Psychology*, 1970, 16, 536–552.

Matlin, M. W. Response competition, recognition, and affect. *Journal of Personality and Social Psychology*, 1971, 19, 295–300.

Matlin, M. W. Frequency–affect relationship in a simultaneous spatial presentation. *Psychological Reports*, 1974, 35, 379–383. (a)

Matlin, M. W. Serial position, perceived serial position, and affect. *Journal of General Psychology*, 1974, 91, 245–258. (b)

Matlin, M. W. Serial position and affect. *Bulletin of the Psychonomic Society*, 1975, 5, 489–491.

Matlin, M. W., & Stang, D. J. Some determinants of word-frequency estimates. *Perceptual and Motor Skills*, 1975, 40, 923–929.

Matlin, M. W., & Stang, D. J. *The Pollyanna principle: Affect and evaluation in language, memory and cognition*, 1976, in preparation.

Matlin, M. W., & Stone, M. R. The effects of evaluation, activity, and potency on frequency estimates. *Bulletin of the Psychonomic Society*, 1975, 5, 391–392.

McClelland, D. C., Atkinson, J. W., Clark, R. A., & Lowell, E. L. *The achievement motive*. New York: Appleton, 1953.

McClintock, C. G. Game behavior and social motivation in interpersonal settings. In C. G. McClintock (Ed.), *Experimental social psychology*. New York: Holt, 1972.

McCullogh, J. L., & Ostrom, T. M. Repetition of highly similar messages and attitude change. *Journal of Applied Psychology*, 1974, 59, 395–397.

McDavid, J. W., & Harari, H. Stereotyping of names and popularity of grade school children. *Child Development*, 1966, 37, 453–459.

McGinnies, E. Emotionality and perceptual defense. *Psychological Review*, 1949, **56**, 244–251.

Meyer, M. Experimental studies in the psychology of music. *American Journal of Psychology*, 1903, **14**, 155–163.

Moreland, R. L. Exposure, recognition, and affect. Paper presented at the meeting of the Midwestern Psychological Association, Chicago, May 1975.

Moreland, R. L., & Zajonc, R. B. A strong test of exposure effects. *Journal of Experimental Social Psychology*, 1976, **12**, 170–179.

Moreland, R. L., & Zajonc, R. B. Is stimulus recognition a necessary condition for exposure effects? Unpublished manuscript, University of Michigan, 1975.

Mull, H. K. The effect of repetition upon enjoyment of modern music. *Journal of Psychology*, 1957, **43**, 155–162.

Nunnally, J. C. *Psychometric theory*. New York: Wiley, 1967.

Olds, J. Hypothalamic substrates of reward. *Physiological Review*, 1962, **42**, 554–604.

Olds, J., & Olds, M. E. Drives, rewards and the brain. In F. Barron, W. C. Dement, W. Edwards, H. Lindman, L. D. Phillips, J. Olds, & M. Olds (Eds.), *New directions in psychology*. Vol. 2. New York: Holt, 1965.

Osgood, C. E. Semantic differential technique in the comparative study of cultures. *American Anthropologist*. 1964, **66**, 171–200.

Pepper, S. C. Changes of appreciation for color combinations. *Psychological Reports*, 1919, **26**, 389–396.

Perlman, D., & Oskamp, S. The effects of picture content and exposure frequency on evaluations of negroes and whites. *Journal of Experimental Social Psychology*, 1971, **7**, 503–514.

Pettigrew, T. F. *Racially separate or together?* New York: McGraw-Hill, 1971.

Priest, R. F., & Sawyer, J. Proximity and peership: Bases of balance in interpersonal attraction. *American Journal of Sociology*, 1967, **72**, 633–649.

Rajecki, D. W. Imprinting in precocial birds: Interpretation, evidence, and evaluation. *Psychological Bulletin*, 1973, **79**, 48–58.

Rajecki, D. W., & Wolfson, C. The rating of materials found in the mailbox: Effects of frequency of receipt. *Public Opinion Quarterly*, 1973, **37**, 110–114.

Saegert, S. C., & Jellison, J. M. Effects of initial level of response competition and frequency of exposure on liking and exploratory behavior. *Journal of Personality and Social Psychology*, 1970, **16**, 553–558.

Saegert, S. C., Swap, W. C., & Zajonc, R. B. Exposure, context, and interpersonal attraction. *Journal of Personality and Social Psychology*, 1973, **25**, 234–242.

Schick, C., McGlynn, R. P., & Woolam, D. Perception of cartoon humor as a function of familiarity and anxiety level. *Journal of Personality and Social Psychology*, 1972, **24**, 22–25.

Segal, M. W. Alphabet and attraction: An unobtrusive measure of the effect of propinquity in a field setting. *Journal of Personality and Social Psychology*, 1974, **30**, 654–657.

Siebold, J. R. Children's rating responses as related to amount and recency of stimulus familiarization and stimulus complexity. *Journal of Experimental Child Psychology*, 1972, **14**, 257–264.

Simon, K. *Kate Simon's Paris*. New York: Putnam, 1967.

Skaife, A. M. The role of complexity and deviation in changing tastes. Unpublished doctoral dissertation, University of Oregon, 1966. Discussed in D. E. Berlyne, *Aesthetics and psychobiology*. New York: Appleton, 1971. Pp. 191–194.

Smith, G. F., & Dorfman, D. D. The effect of stimulus uncertainty on the relationship between frequency of exposure and liking. *Journal of Personality and Social Psychology*, 1975, **31**, 150–155.

Smith, R. C., & Dixon, T. R. Effects of exposure: Does frequency determine the evaluative connotations of words? *Journal of Experimental Research in Personality*, 1971, **5**, 124–126.

Solomon, R. L., & Corbit, J. D. An opponent–process theory of motivation: II. Cigarette addiction. *Journal of Abnormal Psychology*, 1973, **81**, 158–171.

Solomon, R. L., & Corbit, J. D. Opponent–process theory of motivation. *Psychological Review*, 1974, **81**, 119–145.

Staats, A. W., & Staats, C. K. Attitudes established by classical conditioning. *Journal of Abnormal and Social Psychology*, 1958, **57**, 37–40.

Stang, D. J. Six theories of repeated exposure and affect. *Catalog of Selected Documents in Psychology*, 1973, **3**, 126.

Stang, D. J. An analysis of the effects of political campaigning. Paper presented at the 66th annual meeting of the Southern Society for Philosophy and Psychology, Tampa, 1974. (a)

Stang, D. J. Intuition as artifact in mere exposure studies. *Journal of Personality and Social Psychology*, 1974, **30**, 647–653. (b)

Stang, D. J. Methodological factors in mere exposure research. *Psychological Bulletin*, 1974, **81**, 1014–1025. (c)

Stang, D. J. Is learning necessary for the attitudinal effects of mere exposure? Paper presented at the annual meeting of the American Psychological Association, August 1975. (a)

Stang, D. J. The effects of mere exposure on learning and affect. *Journal of Personality and Social Psychology*, 1975, **31**, 7–13. (b)

Stang, D. J. Response competition and meaningfulness as predictors of the attitudinal effects of mere exposure. Under editorial review, 1976. (a)

Stang, D. J. When familiarity breeds contempt, absence makes the heart grow fonder. *Bulletin of the Psychonomic Society*, 1976, in press. (b)

Stang, D. J., & O'Connell, E. J. The computer as experimenter in social psychological research. *Behavior Research Methods and Instrumentation*, 1974, **6**, 223–232.

Suedfeld, P., Epstein, Y. M., Buchanan, E., & Landon, P. B. Effects of set on the "effects of mere exposure." *Journal of Personality and Social Psychology*, 1971, **17**, 121–123.

Swap, W. C. The effects of repeated exposure of meaningful stimuli on attitude formation and change. *Proceedings, 81st Annual Convention, American Psychological Association*, 1973, **8**, 107–108.

Swap, W. C. Interpersonal attraction and repeated exposure to rewarders and punishers. Under editorial review, 1976.

Thorndike, E. L., & Lorge, I. *The teacher's word book of 30,000 words*. New York: Columbia Teachers College Press, 1944.

Verveer, E. M., Barry, H., Jr., & Bousfield, W. A. Change in affectivity with repetition. *American Journal of Psychology*, 1933, **45**, 130–134.

Vitz, P. C., & Todd, T. C. A model of the perception of simple geometric figures. *Psychological Review*, 1971, **78**, 207–228.

Walker, E. L. Arousal potential and Beethoven's Fifth Symphony. *Contemporary Psychology*, 1973, **18**, 363–364.

Washburn, M. F., Child, M. S., & Abel, T. M. The effects of immediate repetition on the pleasantness or unpleasantness of music. In M. Schoen (Ed.), *The effects of music*. New York: Harcourt, 1927.

Weiss, R. F. Role playing and repetition effects on opinion strength. *Journal of Social Psychology*, 1971, **85**, 29–35.

Wilson, L. R., & Becknell, J. C. The relation between the association value, pronounciability and affectivity of nonsense syllables. *Journal of Psychology*, 1961, **52**, 47–49.

Wilson, L. R., & Miller, H. Repetition, order of presentation, and timing of arguments and measures as determinants of opinion change. *Journal of Personality and Social Psychology*, 1968, 9, 184–188.

Wilson, L. R., & Nakajo, H. Preference for photographs as a function of frequency of presentation. *Psychonomic Science*, 1966, 3, 577–578.

Wilson, W. R. The unobtrusive induction of positive attitudes. Unpublished doctoral dissertation, University of Michigan, 1975.

Yelen, D. R., & Schulz, R. W. Verbal satiation? *Journal of Verbal Learning and Verbal Behavior*, 1963, 1, 372–377.

Zajonc, R. B. The attitudinal effects of mere exposure. Technical Report No. 34, Institute for Social Research, Ann Arbor, Michigan, 1965.

Zajonc, R. B. The attitudinal effects of mere exposure. *Journal of Personality and Social Psychology*, 1968, 9 (Monogr. Suppl. 2), Part 2, 1–27.

Zajonc, R. B. Attraction, affiliation, and attachment. In J. F. Eisenberg, W. S. Dillon, & S. D. Ripley (Eds.), *Men and beast: Comparative social behavior*. Washington: Smithsonian Institution Press, 1969.

Zajonc, R. B. Brain wash: Familiarity breeds comfort. *Psychology Today*, 1970, 3, 32–62. (a)

Zajonc, R. B. Some empirical and theoretical continuities in the social behavior of animals and men. In Chauvin, R. (Ed.), *Colloques Internationaux du C.N.R.S.* No. 198. *Modeles animaux du comportment humain*. Paris: CNRS, 1970. Pp. 303–342. (b)

Zajonc, R. B., Crandall, R., Kail, R. B., & Swap, W. Effect of extreme exposure frequencies on different affective ratings of stimuli. *Perceptual and Motor Skills*, 1974, 38, 667–678. (a)

Zajonc, R. B., Markus, H., & Wilson, W. R. Exposure effects and associative learning. *Journal of Experimental Social Psychology*, 1974, 10, 248–263. (b)

Zajonc, R. B., Markus, H., & Wilson, W. R. Exposure, object preference, and distress in the domestic chick. *Journal of Comparative and Physiological Psychology*, 1974, 86, 581–585. (c)

Zajonc, R. B., & Rajecki, D. W. Exposure and affect: A field experiment. *Psychonomic Science*, 1969, 17, 216–217.

Zajonc, R. B., Reimer, D. J., & Hausser, D. Imprinting and the development of object preference in chicks by mere repeated exposure. *Journal of Comparative and Physiological Psychology*, 1973, 83, 434–440.

Zajonc, R. B., Shaver, P., Tavris, C., & VanKreveld, D. Exposure, satiation, and stimulus discriminability. *Journal of Personality and Social Psychology*, 1972, 21, 270–280.

Zajonc, R. B., Swap, W. C., Harrison, A. A., & Roberts, P. Limiting conditions of the exposure effect: Satiation and relativity. *Journal of Personality and Social Psychology*, 1971, 18, 384–391.

MORAL INTERNALIZATION: CURRENT THEORY AND RESEARCH

Martin L. Hoffman
UNIVERSITY OF MICHIGAN
ANN ARBOR, MICHIGAN

Psychologists have long been intrigued with moral internalization, probably because it epitomizes the age-old problem of how individuals come to manage the inevitable conflict between personal needs and social obligations. The legacy of both Sigmund Freud and Emile Durkheim is the agreement among social scientists that most people do not go through life viewing society's moral norms as external, coercively imposed pressures to which they must submit. Though the norms are initially external to the individual and often in conflict with his desires, the norms eventually become part of his internal motive system and guide his behavior even in the absence of external authority. Control by others is thus replaced by self-control. Examples of internalization concepts are Freud's "superego" and Durkheim's "collective conscience."

Perhaps the most succinct statement of the assumed societal value of internalization to society was made long ago by Simmel (1902, p. 19): "The tendency of society to satisfy itself as cheaply as possible results in appeals to 'good conscience,' through which the individual pays to himself the wages for his righteousness, which otherwise would probably have to be assured to him in some way through law or custom." Internalization processes may thus serve the social control function of making conformity to moral norms rewarding in its own right, which is especially important when rewards for correct behavior and punishments for deviation are not consistently forthcoming from society. We shall return to the societal function of internalization later.

Among psychologists, theoretical disagreement revolves around which socialization experiences are most likely to foster the internalization process. The purpose of this article is to review the rather large body of pertinent research and evaluate it in relation to the guiding theoretical notions. The paper is organized around three broad categories that encompass most of the research: parental discipline, identification and modeling, and cognitive disequilibrium A fourth topic, consistency of moral behavior and the influence of the situation, which does not deal directly with internalization but has a definite bearing on it, will also be included.

I. Parental Discipline

The general rationale for assuming that parental discipline is important is as follows. Moral internalization implies the motivation to weigh one's desires against the moral requirements of the situation without regard to external sanctions. The central conflict in the moral encounter, then, is between the person's egoistic needs and the moral standards applicable in a given situation. It seems reasonable to assume that the key socialization experiences must therefore include the child's early encounters with an analogous conflict, that between his desires and the prevailing moral standards, which are at first, of course, external to him. These standards are embedded in many of the physical and verbal messages from the parent regarding how the child should and should not act, that is, in the parent's discipline techniques. The discipline encounter, then, has much in common with many later moral encounters. In each, there is conflict and the individual is compelled to work out a balance between behaving in accord with his desires, on the one hand, and subordinating his desires and acting in line with moral standards, on the other. The moral requirements are external in the discipline encounter and, with proper socialization, they eventually become internalized in the moral encounter. The child's experiences in the discipline encounter—the type of discipline to which he is repeatedly exposed and which determines the options available to him—must therefore weigh heavily in determining the extent to which he acquires internal resources for controlling egoistic impulses and behaving morally. Some discipline techniques, for example, may help perpetuate the child's initial sense of opposition between his desires and external demands, whereas others may provide him with the inner re-sources—both cognitive and motivational—for changing his views about these demands and adopting them as internal guides to his own behavior.

When does the discipline encounter become important? During the first year or so it is not significant, because the parent is primarily a caretaker. The anger the parent may feel when the infant fusses, wets, and cries is tempered by the knowledge that these misdeeds are often distress responses largely out of the infant's control. There is also evidence that adults may be biologically pro-grammed to cuddle and nurture infants (Hess, 1967; Lorenz, 1965) and to be especially responsive when the babies are around 5 or 6 months of age and begin to show selective attachment to the parent (Bowlby, 1969). Whether biologically based or not, the parent's primary aim appears to be to maximize the infant's comfort, which is entirely consistent with the infant's desires.

The pattern changes in the second year. Owing to a rapid increase in neuromuscular development and gross motor activity, the baby's behavior is often at odds with the parent's wishes. Something distinctly new then begins to characterize many more parent–child interactions than previously: The parent frequently attempts to change the child's behavior against his will, and the child attempts to have his way even though he may know what the parent wants. The stage is thus set for sustained conflicts of will, and the parent's role shifts dramatically from primarily that of caretaker to that of socialization agent. His actions change from being facilitative and nurturant to disciplinary.

Research findings attest to this shift. Home observations by Moss (1967) indicate that mothers spend most of their time with their 1- and 3-month-old infants in caretaking and affectionate interaction. Even at 10 months, Tulkin and Kagan (1972) found that over 90% of the mother's behaviors consisted of affection, caretaking, or play; only 5% involved any attempt to prohibit the child from an ongoing act. By 2 years, however, the picture changes dramati-cally. Minton, Kagan, and Levine (1971) found that, in 65% of the interactions between 2-year-old children and their mothers, the mother attempted to change the child's behavior against his will. More importantly, the children were ob-served to obey, or were compelled by the mothers to obey, in 60% of these instances. In my unpublished research on 3½-year-old children, the frequency of discipline encounters and the percentage of compliance by the children were slightly higher.[1]

The available evidence suggests, then, that in the 2- to 4-year-old range children experience pressures from mothers to change their behavior on the

---

[1] The children in these studies were all first-born and mostly middle class.

average of every 6 to 8 minutes throughout their waking hours, and in the main they end up complying.[2] Comparable data on discipline frequency are unavailable for older children. It is with older children, however, that the relationship between different types of discipline and moral internalization has been investigated. This research will now be summarized, followed by an attempt at theoretical interpretation.

A. CORRELATIONAL RESEARCH

Most of the correlational research on discipline and moral internalization was done in the late 1950s and early 1960s. I reviewed this research several years ago (Hoffman, 1970b) and organized the findings into three broad types of discipline: *(a) Power assertion*—which includes physical force, deprivation of material objects and privileges, or the threat of these; the term is used to highlight the fact that in using these techniques the parent seeks to control the child by capitalizing on his physical power or control over the child's material resources. *(b) Love withdrawal*—which includes techniques whereby the parent simply gives direct but nonphysical expression to his anger or disapproval of the child for engaging in some undesirable behavior (e.g., ignores the child, turns his back on him, refuses to speak or listen to him, explicitly states a dislike for the child, isolates or threatens to leave him). Love withdrawal, like power assertion, has a highly punitive quality. It poses no immediate physical threat to the child, however, but rather the ultimate threat of abandonment or separation. Whereas power assertion ordinarily consists of discrete aversive acts that are quickly over and done with, love withdrawal is typically more prolonged—lasting many minutes, hours, or even days—and its duration may be variable and unpredictable. *(c) Induction*—which includes techniques in which the parent gives explanations or reasons for requiring the child to change his behavior, or directly appeals to conformity-inducing agents that may already exist within the child. Examples are appealing to the child's pride, mastery strivings, or concern for others; and pointing out the implications of the child's behavior for others (e.g., "You hurt his finger"; "Don't yell at him, he was only trying to help"; "He was proud of his tower and you knocked it down"). These techniques rely less on fear and more on the child's connecting their cognitive content with his own resources for comprehending the requirements of the situation and controlling his behavior accordingly.

The moral internalization indices used in the research represent different levels of behavior (overt, affective, cognitive). Included are the extent to which *(a)* the child resists temptation without external constraint, usually in a labo-

---

[2] The discipline attempts are by no means spaced evenly throughout the day. On the basis of Lytton and Zwirner's (1975) observations, for example, it appears that they may occur at the rate of one per minute in the period before bedtime.

ratory situation in which the child is tempted to violate a rule in order to obtain a prize (e.g., he is left alone, observed through a one-way mirror, and assigned scores based on whether or not and how much he cheats and how long he holds out before cheating); *(b)* the child makes cognitive judgments about the transgressions of others that are based on moral principles (e.g., "It was wrong to do that because the man trusted him") rather than external considerations (e.g., "He'll go to jail if he's caught"); *(c)* the child confesses and accepts responsibility for a misdeed even though no one apparently witnessed it—usually based on parents' or teacher's reports; *(d)* the child experiences guilt (as opposed to fear of punishment) following a transgression—usually measured in terms of responses to deviation story–completion items. This last technique presents the subject with a story that begins by focusing on someone who has committed a transgression under conditions that minimize the likelihood of detection. The subject is instructed to complete the story, telling what the protagonist thinks and feels and what happens afterwards. The subject is assumed to identify with the protagonist and thus reveal his own internal (although not necessarily overt) reactions in his completion. To maximize the likelihood of this rather than a more detached, morally evaluative response, the protagonist is portrayed as a basically well-meaning person of the same age and sex as the subject, someone who commits the transgression under pressure. Completions are usually scored on the extent to which the protagonist exhibits an aversive, self-critical reaction.

It should be noted that the attempt in all these measures is to obtain an index of the child's behavior in the absence of external surveillance. This is done in order to assess the extent to which the individual's moral orientation has an internalized component that may operate in real life regardless of the presence or absence of surveillance.

The findings support the following empirical generalizations:

(a) A moral orientation characterized by independence of external sanctions and high guilt is associated with the mother's frequent use of inductive discipline—especially "other-oriented" inductions, in which the implications of the child's behavior for other people are pointed out—and with her relatively frequent expression of affection in nondiscipline situations.

(b) A moral orientation based on fear of external detection and punishment is associated with the mother's use of discipline techniques which have high power-assertive components.

(c) There appears to be no consistent relationship between moral orientation and love withdrawal, although there is some evidence that love withdrawal, especially its more subtle forms, may contribute to inhibition of anger (Hoffman, 1963b; Hoffman & Saltzstein, 1967; Sears, 1963).

These generalizations do not appear to be the spurious result of social class, IQ, or sex—each of which relates to discipline and to some moral indices—since sex was usually controlled, and in one study all three variables were controlled with no detrimental effect on the relation (Hoffman & Saltzstein, 1967). Furthermore, the generalizations gain strength from the fact that they reflect a convergence of results from studies using a variety of measures (Campbell & Fiske, 1959).

There is also evidence for two types of internal moral orientation: a "flexible-humanistic" type in which antimoral impulses are tolerated and guilt tends to be experienced due to awareness of the harmful effects of one's behavior on others; and a "rigid-conventional" type which appears to be based to a greater extent on the need to control hostility, and guilt is often the result of one's hostile feelings rather than awareness of the harm done to others (Hoffman, 1970a). The mothers of both types express affection and use inductive discipline frequently, in keeping with the foregoing generalization. Those whose children are flexible-humanistic, however, use more varied discipline techniques, ranging from a totally permissive response to the occasional use of power assertion when the child is openly and unreasonably defiant; they cushion their handling of aggression by focusing on the precipitating issues and suggesting reparative action where possible. In contrast, the mothers of the rigid-conventional subjects rarely use power assertion, and their techniques often have a pronounced love-withdrawing component, especially in situations in which the child expresses anger. A recent study by DePalma (1974) indicates that flexible-humanistic children may be somewhat less dependent on the environment as a source of evaluation of their actions and thus more internalized than rigid-conventional children.

Despite the consistency of the findings, these studies have methodological shortcomings. The discipline data, for example, are usually obtained by interviewing the parents, which makes them subject to memory lapses and possible "social desirability" effects. These problems may be lessened somewhat in the studies employing child reports of the parent's discipline, but the child's feelings and attitudes toward the parent may color his response, and there is the further problem of a lack of independence in the data sources for discipline and moral orientation. The virtues and defects of the moral internalization indices have been discussed elsewhere (Hoffman, 1970b). Guilt and moral judgment, for example, may clearly differentiate internal and external responses, but they are far removed from overt moral action. Confession is usually measured in terms of overt behavior, but it may often be an attempt to seek approval rather than a moral act, since confession is often rewarded. The resistance-to-temptation measures have the special virtue of tapping overt moral behavior in highly standardized situations, but here too the motivation may be external (e.g., a pervasive fear of detection despite being left alone) rather than internal (e.g., wishing not to betray the experimenter's trust). There is evidence that this may be more of a problem in males than in females (Hoffman, 1975d). In addition, motivation for the prize, hence degree of temptation, has not been controlled. Despite the flaws, general support for the utility of these measures comes from the consistency of the results obtained regardless of the particular measures used.

A more fundamental limitation is that this research is correlational, which raises the problem of inferring causal direction. This limitation has been highlighted recently by several investigators who cite, as evidence against the assumption of parental influence, the burgeoning research showing that children often affect their parent's behavior (see especially Bell, 1968, 1971). I cannot disagree with the general argument here but do think that although causal direction cannot automatically be assumed, there may be a greater scientific risk associated with being overly cautious and assuming nothing about causality than in making a tentative causal inference when there are reasonable grounds for doing so. And I have argued elsewhere that there are grounds for inferring that parental discipline is more likely to be an antecedent than a consequence of the child's moral internalization (Hoffman, 1975c). Two of the main points will be summarized here.

1. Evidence was given in the preceding section showing that from an early age children are often compelled by the parent to change their behavior against their will. There is also evidence that parental discipline exerts more constraint on the child than the child exerts on the parent (Schoggen, 1963; Simmons & Schoggen, 1963). The child is thus often in the position of complying in response to parental discipline. It follows that personality characteristics that derive at least in part from the behaviors and inner states associated with compliance to a discipline pattern are likely to be consequences rather than antecedents of that pattern. Moral internalization appears to be such a characteristic, since the responses elicited in the moral encounter by internalized and noninternalized persons (guilt, fear) are remarkably similar to those often associated with compliance in the discipline encounter (e.g., self-blame when the parent points out the harmful effects of one's actions on others; complying out of fear). Furthermore, early discipline encounters obviously predate the development of an internal moral orientation. It follows that parental discipline is more likely to be an antecedent than a consequence of moral internalization.

2. Certain dispositions deriving from congenital factors and from the child's previous interactions with the parent (e.g., aggressiveness, "person orientation," rate of cognitive development) may affect the parents' choice of discipline techniques, as has been suggested (Bell, 1968). This does not, however, negate the immediate impact of the discipline techniques on the child's inner states; hence it does not negate the contribution of discipline to moral internalization. Rather, all of the antecedent contributing factors may be thought of as summing up to produce the behavioral response tendency that the parent brings to the discipline encounter, and the discipline techniques themselves may be viewed as

the environmental events that directly affect the child's experience in ways pertinent to moral internalization.

A final resolution of the causality issue awaits the application of sophisticated longitudinal designs such as those employing cross-lagged correlations (e.g., Eron, Huesmann, Lefkowitz, & Walder, 1972). In view of the foregoing arguments, however, it seems reasonable tentatively to interpret the findings as reflecting the contribution of inductive discipline to the development of an internal moral orientation in children.

B. THEORETICAL INTERPRETATION

An analysis of the effects of discipline on the child, presented in parts elsewhere (Hoffman, 1960, 1963b, 1970a; Hoffman & Saltzstein, 1967), is summarized below.

1. Power Assertion

Any discipline encounter is apt to generate some anger in the child because it interrupts an ongoing motivated act. Power assertion is especially likely to arouse anger, particularly when applied without explanation, because it dramatically underscores the extent to which his action is circumscribed by the superior power and resources of the adult world. The parent's disciplinary act also serves as a model, for example, of direct discharge or control of anger. Power assertion may thus both elicit anger and simultaneously provide a model for expressing it outwardly although, because of the fear also aroused, it may not be expressed toward the parent. This may explain why preschool and adolescent children of power-assertive parents are aggressive toward peers but not parents (Bandura & Walters, 1959; Hoffman, 1960).

In a discipline encounter the child's attention is directed toward certain aspects of the situation. Power assertion directs his attention to the consequences of his behavior for himself, that is, to the anticipated punitive reaction of the parent. It should therefore accentuate his perception of the source of moral standards as external. And the frequent experience of subordinating his impulses and complying out of external pressure should help perpetuate the sense of opposition between his desires and the standards. Power assertion should therefore contribute to behavior controls based on external threat, which is what the research suggests.

2. Love Withdrawal

All discipline encounters communicate parental disappointment and may thus be expected to arouse the child's needs for approval in varying degrees. At one extreme, techniques with highly pronounced love-withdrawal components direct the child's attention to the emotionally punitive consequences of the child's behavior for himself and may at times arouse intense anxiety over loss of love. He may then comply merely to restore harmony. Such compliance is obviously not based on internal considerations; nor does it highlight the will conflict between parent and child as sharply as does power assertion. This may be why love withdrawal shows no relation to moral internalization, although it does relate to inhibition of anger (Hoffman, 1963b; Hoffman & Saltzstein, 1967). Techniques in which love withdrawal is minimal and induction predominates may arouse some need for approval but not intense anxiety because the reasons given indicate that the parent is responding to the child's act rather than rejecting him.

3. Induction

Inductions are unique in that they direct the child's attention to the consequences of his actions for others, that is, they point up the other's distress and indicate that it resulted from the child's behavior. Inductions should therefore contribute to an awareness of the social consequences of the child's actions; they should also enlist an important motivational resource that exists within the child and is especially applicable in situations involving the child's harming another person, namely, empathy, defined as the vicarious affective response to another person (Hoffman, 1975b). There is evidence that preschool as well as older children respond empathically to others (Hoffman, in press). The capacity for empathy that the child brings to the discipline encounter is significant because it adds to his need for approval the discomfort that he may vicariously experience when inductions are employed. He may thus feel badly due to the other person's distress rather than because of anticipated punishment to himself. Furthermore, the empathy aroused may interact with the awareness of harming another, in a process of cognitive—affective synthesis much like that postulated by Schachter and Singer (1962) in which any stirred up emotional state is labeled, interpreted, and identified in terms of the characteristics of the situation and the individual's cognitive appraisal of these characteristics. Becoming aware that one is the agent of another's disgress may thus transform the empathic affect into a subjective feeling having all the attributes of guilt: affectively unpleasant and cognitively self-blaming.

4. Optimal Arousal and Information Processing

The hypothesized effects just discussed assume that the child processes the information contained in inductions. Why does he do this? The answer requires making explicit something thus far implicit: Most discipline techniques are not unidimensional but contain elements of power assertion and love withdrawal, and sometimes induction. The power-assertive and love-withdrawal aspects, alone or in combination, put varying degrees of pressure on the child and may be called the motive-arousal component of the technique, which may be necessary to get the child to stop what he is doing, attend to the parent, and process the information contained in the inductive component. If there is too little arousal, the child may ignore the parent. Too much arousal and the resulting hostility, fear, or anxiety may prevent effective processing of the information. Techniques having pronounced inductive components may be expected to attain the optimal arousal level often. They are thus more likely than other techniques to contribute to the child's knowledge about the social consequences of his actions, to allow him to use the knowledge as a basis for controlling his own behavior, and thereby to help diminish the feeling of opposition between his desires and the moral standards communicated by the parent.

This optimal-arousal model is consistent with the general experimental research indicating that moderate arousal enhances perceptual and cognitive functioning, whereas intense arousal is disorganizing and interferes with attention to relevant cues (Easterbrook, 1959; Kausler & Trapp, 1960). It is also supported somewhat more directly by experimental work to be cited later.

5. Memory, Self-Attribution, and Internalization

To fully account for internalization requires explaining how the guilt and knowledge about the social consequences of the child's actions, acquired through exposure to inductions, become dissociated from the discipline encounters in which they originated, and are experienced by the child as his own. How does he come to feel guilty even if no one points out the harm he has done? Casting the problem in terms of differential memory offers a possible solution. If the informational component of a discipline technique is salient, as is true for inductions, then its message content should persist in memory longer than its other attributes. The child may thus remember the message long after having forgotten its origin in a parentally administered discipline technique. Consequently, on subsequent occasions when the content of the message enters the child's mind it may be perceived as his own idea, which would certainly add an internal, autonomous quality to his moral orientation. Parents often report this type of phenomenon, as do clinicians. It is also similar to the so-called sleeper effect found in attitude-change research in which the persuasive arguments are recalled but not the source.

More importantly, this conception of a differential memory for the content and source of inductions finds support in recent memory research, notably Tulving's (1972) distinction between two types of memory, episodic and semantic (see also Brown, 1975). Briefly, episodic memory refers to the receiving and storing of information about temporally dated episodes and events, and the temporospatial relations among these events. The events are often stored in terms of their perceptual attributes and may have no special meaning or reference to anything outside the particular episode. Examples are memory for whether a word occurred in an experimental list, its position in the list, or its exact spelling. Semantic memory is concerned with the storage and utilization of knowledge about an event independently of its actual occurrence in a particular situation or its temporal cooccurrence with other events. Semantic memory registers not the perceptual or physical properties of inputs but rather their cognitive referents, which are then stored and integrated with the organized knowledge a person has, for example, about words and their meanings, about concepts and relationships among concepts, and about rules and when they can be generalized and applied. The two types of memory are quite independent of each other. And what is especially important here is that semantic memory for an event is apt to be far more enduring than episodic memory. There are several reasons for this: mainly, the material in semantic memory, but not episodic memory, is embedded in the person's organized knowledge, hence protected from interference by other inputs.

Tulving illustrates the distinction as follows: In listening to a story the information regarding the episode, including the perceptual properties of the storyteller and the precise words used, is entered in episodic memory and relatively soon forgotten. The story contents (e.g., concepts and meanings) are registered in semantic memory, largely stripped of their connection to the circumstances surrounding the storytelling, and become part of the individual's relatively enduring categories of knowledge. There are obvious parallels between listening to a story and responding to an induction, (e.g., storyteller and parent, story content and informational content of induction). There are also differences: mainly, whereas inductions occur in the context of parent–child conflict, storytelling usually does not. Since conflict is minimized with induction, however, we may assume a basic similarity between the two events as regards factors pertinent to memory: the child attends to a verbal communication from another person. It thus seems reasonable to expect that the idea content of inductions will ordinarily be put into semantic memory and become part of the child's store of knowledge about the effects of his behaviors on others and the needs and intentions of others that should be considered before acting. And the empathy and guilt generated by this information should add to his repertoire of responses to the awareness of harming others. Other aspects of inductions which contribute little to their meaning, such as the exact words and sentence structure employed, the fact that they originated with the parent, and the physical setting in which they occurred, will be put mainly into episodic memory where they are relatively soon forgotten. Subsequently, when the child is reminded of the ideas communicated in the inductions and perhaps feels empathy or guilt (for example, when he acts or contemplates acting in ways similar to his past socially harmful actions), he may not remember that he originally had these thoughts and feelings in response to parental discipline.

Who then will he perceive as the source? Recent work on self-attribution may provide an answer: If the external sources of one's actions and thoughts are salient, unambiguous, and sufficient to explain them, the person attributes them to these external agencies. But if these external sources are not perceived, or if they are unclear or invisible, the research, much of it done with 4- and 5-year old children, suggests that he will experience these actions and thoughts as his own (e.g., Bem, 1972; Lepper & Greene, 1973). Similarly, without an external agent to whom to attribute the idea content of inductions, the child will presumably experience it as deriving from his own dispositions. In this way, moral norms that originate externally in the form of inductive communications from the parent in the discipline encounter may become internalized, autonomous components of the child's moral orientation.

Though this interpretation is consistent not only with discipline research but also with developmental research in such diverse areas as empathy, memory, and self-attribution, further study is needed in which new hypotheses derived specifically from this approach are tested.

C. ROLE OF THE FATHER

Data on the father's discipline were obtained in less than a fourth of the studies. In contrast to that of mothers, very few statistically significant relationships were found, and there was no apparent pattern among them There is evidence that fathers may have an indirect effect, however. Thus, their behavior toward the mother is often one of the factors affecting the mother's discipline pattern, which in turn affects the child (Hoffman, 1963c). And, in a study of the effects of father absence, seventh-grade boys without fathers (for at least 6 months prior to the study) obtained significantly lower scores on three out of four moral internalization indices (guilt, internal moral judgment, confession) than a group of boys—controlled for sex, IQ, and social class—who had fathers (Hoffman, 1971b). No differences were obtained for girls.

D. SEX DIFFERENCES

In Freud's view, owing to anatomical differences, girls are not compelled to resolve the Oedipus complex quickly and dramatically and thus do not identify with the parent as fully as boys do. Consequently, girls have less internalized moral structures. Freud's followers differed in details but drew the same conclusion. In a recent study of sex differences at three age levels (fifth graders, seventh graders, and adults—all middle class) females gave strong evidence of having a more internalized moral orientation than males (Hoffman, 1975d). The results in all child and adult samples, for example, indicate that moral transgressions are more likely to be associated with guilt in females and fear in males. On a measure of personal values, females revealed a consistently more positive orientation toward humanistic concerns (e.g., going out of one's way to help others). Males placed a far greater value on achievement, and there was evidence that the males' achievement values may reflect an egoistic rather than a moral orientation.

The sex difference in children may be due in part to childrearing differences: more induction and affection for girls, and power assertion for boys (Hoffman, 1975d; Zussman, 1975). The results for adults, which are actually more pronounced than those for children, might best be explained by the increasing pressures on males, especially in adolescence and adulthood, to achieve and succeed, which may often conflict with the moral concerns acquired earlier.[3] This interpretation raises questions for research that might have societal as well as theoretical importance: When does achievement socialization in males begin to conflict with moral socialization? What might parents and other socialization agents be doing that often tips the balance in favor of achievement? Is this a deliberate attempt to help assure the future success of male children, and are the adults aware of the potentially negative consequences for moral socialization? An unpublished experimental study by Burton (1972) brings into bold relief the dilemma that may confront many parents in their efforts to socialize their children in terms of both morality and achievement. It also demonstrates that under certain conditions parents may communicate to their children that when success and honesty are in conflict it is more important to succeed than to be honest.

E. EXPERIMENTAL RESEARCH

The experimental research began in the mid-1960s and has now virtually replaced the correlational approach to the study of discipline and moral internalization. Although experimental work in general has been criticized because of the frequent influence of "demand characteristics" and lack of "ecological validity," this particular body of research has not been critically examined. To fill this gap, the following discussion will be more concerned with methodological than conceptual issues.

In the most frequently used experimental paradigm the child is first trained or "socialized" by presenting him with several toys of varying degrees of attractiveness. When he handles a particular toy (e.g., the most attractive one) he is "punished" by an unpleasant noise, the timing and intensity of which may be varied. The child is then left alone with the toys and observed through a one-way mirror. Resistance-to-temptation scores are based on whether or not, how soon after the experimenter left, and for how long the child plays with the prohibited toy. In the early version of this paradigm the child was usually given no verbal instructions about what to do (e.g., Aronfreed, 1966; Aronfreed & Reber, 1965;

---

[3] Females also appear to be more empathic, which may contribute to their internal moral orientation (Hoffman, in press).

R. G. Walters & Dembow, 1963; R. H. Walters, Parke, & Cane, 1965). The noise thus served not only as the punishment but also as the indicator or what was expected of the child.

Recently, a verbal component has been added to the training session (e.g., Cheyne, Goyeche, & Walters, 1969; Cheyne & Walters, 1969; LaVoie, 1973, 1974a, 1974b). This may be a simple instruction, say, "Don't touch the green toy" (Cheyne *et al.*, 1969), or a complex reason resembling induction, such as the following:

> Now, some of these toys you should not touch or play with because I don't have any others like them, and if they were to get broken or worn out from boys playing with them, I wouldn't be able to use them anymore, so for that reason I don't want you to touch or play with some of these toys. And if you touch one of the toys you're not supposed to touch or play with, I'll tell you and you will hear a sound like this. . . . [Cheyne & Walters, 1969, p. 234].

In general, these studies have found that: *(a)* without a verbal component, variations in timing and intensity of punishment have effects similar to those observed with lower animals—the child is less likely to perform a deviant act when the training consists of intense punishment or punishment that was applied at the onset of that act rather than after it has begun; *(b)* these effects of timing and intensity are reduced when a verbal component is added; *(c)* the verbal component is more effective with mild than with severe punishment, and with older than with younger children.

A second, less frequently used paradigm deals not with inhibition of an overt act but with creating a self-critical verbal response following a deviant act. The usual procedure is to give the subject a task to perform such as guessing which direction a doll is facing, or knocking toy soldiers down so as to move a toy nurse to safety. The subject has no control over the task, nor can he see the actual results of his actions. There are a number of training trials, on some of which, according to a predetermined schedule, the subject receives punishment (e.g., the experimenter takes candy from a supply that was given the subject earlier, or frowns and expresses disappointment). The experimenter verbalizes the word designated as the critical label (e.g., careless, rough, bumper, blue) when the punishment is administered. In the test trial the child is not punished but a cue is provided indicating that he has transgressed (e.g., the toy nurse is made to appear to break; or a buzzer sounds). The subject's self-criticism score depends on whether or not he then applies the self-critical label to his act. The relevance of the earlier studies to moral internalization is questionable because an adult was present throughout the experiment (e.g., Aronfreed, 1966). The most recent study (Grusec & Ezrin, 1972), in which this and other deficiencies were corrected, will be described here in detail.

The subject's task was to drive a toy bulldozer through a "forest" by pushing on a metal rod, without bumping into "trees." The experimenter explained that the subject could not see the trees because it was foggy, encouraged the subject to do his best anyway, and added, "If you bump into too many trees you will hear a buzzer . . . which means that you are a 'bumper' and that's the worst thing you can be in this game."

There were 16 training trials. Punishment was administered on eight. On the first punishment trial, the experimenter sounded a concealed buzzer and said, "You're a bumper. Remember, in this game, that's the worst thing you can be." On the remaining punishment trials, there were four experimental conditions involving combinations of two types of discipline and the presence or absence of reinforcement: *(a) Withdrawal of love induction*—The experimenter says, "You're a bumper. Because you're a bumper, I'm not happy with the way you're playing" and lowers her head, glancing occasionally at the subject with a distressed look on her face. *(b) Withdrawal of material reward*—Like *a* except instead of expressing disapproval and unhappiness, the experimenter says, "You will have to lose three chips" and takes the chips from the subject's container. *(c) Reinforcement of self-criticism*—If the subject calls himself a bumper the experimenter expresses her approval and happiness with his behavior (in *a*), or returns chips to the subject's container (in *b*). Probe questions were asked where necessary, e.g., "What happened?"; "Can you tell me why I'm unhappy with you?"; "Was it because of the way you drove the bulldozer?"; "What did I say you were?" The reinforcement was greater when fewer probe questions were required. *(d) No reinforcement*—The subject was instructed to proceed to the next trial whether or not he gave the self-critical response.

After the 16 training trials, the experimenter left the room and instructed the child to finish eight more trials by himself and to keep a record of his performance. The experimenter then observed the child through a one-way mirror and sounded the buzzer on the first three trials in which the child played alone. The score for internalizing the self-critical label depended on whether the child used the word "bumper" when the buzzer sounded on these trials. The findings were that the internalization score was not affected by the two types of discipline, but the score was increased by direct reinforcement of the label.

The assumptions made in both paradigms are that the experimental treatments are valid simulations of different types of parental behaviors, and the child's response represents the degree of moral internalization resulting from the treatments. These assumptions may be criticized on several grounds.

1. The problem that first comes to mind in examining this research is that, with one exception (LaVoie, 1973), the quality and intensity of the parent–child relation, which may be assumed to influence the child's response to discipline, is lost by having the child interact with a stranger. Furthermore, the

simulated discipline techniques themselves, though fitting certain theoretical categories of the investigator, often bear little resemblance to what parents actually do. It is difficult to imagine a parent, for example, using anything like the technique designated as "withdrawal of love induction" in the self-criticism study just described, or the associated probe questions. Other questionable examples are the statements, "It is wrong for you to want to play with that toy or to think about playing with that toy" and "I wasn't told that you could handle that object" (LaVoie, 1973, 1974a); and the use of a loud noise as a method of punishment.

Another unrealistic feature of these studies is that the act designated as deviant is not a spontaneous transgression by the child but is actually induced by the adult's instructions, arbitrarily defined as deviant, and punished. The subject is instructed to choose one of several toys, for example, and is then punished for choosing a particular one. Or he is given a task and punished for doing something over which he has no control, as in the self-criticism studies.

2. The behavior designated as moral often amounts to nothing more than compliance with an adult's arbitrary prohibition. This may be a valid index of compliance in real life, but is it a valid index of morality? When we consider the well-known finding by Milgram (1963) that many people will violate their moral values in the service of compliance to an experimenter's instructions, we must be skeptical about the use of compliance as a moral index.

The self-criticism index has another problem which has a bearing on its validity and also points up the difficulty of operationally defining in simple behavioral terms concepts involving inner states. The child who verbalizes the self-critical label is probably not actually being self-critical, that is, judging himself as good or bad and experiencing a sense of wrongdoing. More likely, what happens is that the experimenter applies the label to a particular behavior, and a few moments later the subject merely repeats the label since it is the only description of the act given him, hence the only sensible response available at the time. The rote, parrotlike quality of the self-criticism score is also enhanced by the usual scoring procedure in which the subject's response is scored as self-criticism only if it includes the precise label used by the experimenter. Similar but nonidentical responses, which might provide a truer index of self-criticism, are not counted. It is interesting to note in this connection that Grusec and Ezrin (1972) report that children who used the self-critical label showed very little emotional disturbance when they "deviated" (i.e., when the experimenter sounded the buzzer), which supports the idea that the use of the labels in these experiments does not reflect moral internalization.

3. A more subtle problem is that the moral socialization process is so drastically telescoped in these experiments that it loses some of its essential features, notably the distinction between a moral act and the child's immediate response to discipline techniques. This is most apparent in the forbidden-toy

paradigm in which the child is exposed to a type of "discipline," left alone, and observed. The observed behavior, that is, the child's initial response to a discipline technique that was administered moments earlier, is the moral index. Thus the studies obviously lack a moral index that is independent of the response to discipline. In one study, resistance-to-temptation scores were obtained both immediately after the discipline manipulations and 15 days later (Leizer & Rogers, 1974). This is an important improvement, though perhaps limited because the delayed test was identical to the immediate test and may thus reflect the child's learning of a specific response inhibition rather than a new moral orientation.

It follows from these limitations that there are two directions that might be considered for future experimental work in this area. One is to make drastic changes in design so that the experiments become truer paradigms of real-life socialization. This requires devising more realistic adult interventions and valid moral internalization indices that are independent of the child's response to the interventions. Employing the child's actual parent as the experimenter might also be considered, although—except for the finding of Landauer, Carlsmith, and Lepper (1970) that 4-year-old children are less likely to obey their mothers than strangers—we know little about the child's response to a parent acting as experimenter.

A second direction is to design experiments to do what they may well be best qualified to do, that is, to investigate the processes involved in the child's immediate reactions to various types of discipline. The resistance-to-temptation experiments, for example, despite their limitations, may tell us something useful about the effectiveness of different parental behaviors in gaining the child's compliance: the effects of timing and intensity of punishment, the reduction in these effects when reasons are given, and the effectiveness of reasons accompanied by moderate punishment. Experimental research may also be the only way to study the inner states associated with compliance and noncompliance. Consider the experiments done by Cheyne *et al.* (1969) and by Cheyne and Walters (1969). This research suffers from the defects enumerated above but incorporates an important innovation: telemetered heart-rate data were obtained throughout. By noting the changes in the amount and type of heart rate that occurred at different points in the experiment, the investigators were able to make tentative inferences about such inner states as the subject's anxiety and attentional level that accompanied his overt response. The forbidden-toy design was used, in which children were exposed to these conditions: severe punishment *(a)* with and *(b)* without a verbal rule; mild punishment *(c)* with and *(d)* without a rule. The major result, for present purposes, was that only condition *c* resulted in the apparently ideal combination of both resistance to temptation and heart-rate deceleration, which is generally associated with attention and cognitive processing. Condition *d* produced little resistance to temptation and heart-rate change. And, although some subjects in condition *b* resisted temptation, this was generally accompanied by heart-rate acceleration, which has been found to be associated with emotional stress. These findings suggest that compliance to severe punishment alone may function primarily to alleviate fear and anxiety. When reasons are employed and the punishment is mild, attentional processes rather than anxiety seem to be involved.

These findings fit the model of optimal arousal in the discipline encounter, as discussed earlier. The parallel is limited because the rule used was too simple to qualify as an induction, but with certain modifications this type of experiment may be uniquely well suited for investigating the processes in the child's immediate reactions to discipline, knowledge about which may be necessary for full understanding of the role of discipline in moral internalization. This example also illustrates the potential value of coordinating the experimental and correlational research on this topic. Whereas correlational research is a convenient way of spotting real-life associations between parent and child characteristics, to fully understand the cognitive and affective processes underlying these associations may require zeroing in on the child's immediate reactions in the discipline encounter, which may best be done experimentally.

II. Identification and Imitation

It has been commonly held, since Freud, that parent identification is a major process in conscience development. The details of Freudian theory have by no means been accepted, but many human developmentalists still assume that by adopting the parent's evaluative orientation with respect to his own behavior, the child eventually stops striving only for impulse gratification. Furthermore, since the parent's orientation derives largely from his cultural group, identifying with the parent is a means of internalizing the standards of the culture.

The intriguing theoretical question for most writers, though neglected by researchers, is: What impels the child to emulate the parent? Psychoanalytic writers stress two motives: First, the child's anxiety over losing the parent's love, to overcome which he strives desperately to be like the parent in every way. This "anaclitic identification" leads the child to adopt the parent's behavioral mannerisms, thoughts, feelings, and even the capacity to punish himself and experience guilt when he violates a moral standard. It contributes to lasting developmental changes in the child such as the acquisition of a sex-role identity and an internalized conscience. Some reformulations—termed "developmental," "emotional," or "true" identification—stress the child's love for the parent rather than the threat of loss of love. The second motive, derived from Freud's notion of castration anxiety, is fear of physical attack. The resulting "identification with the aggressor" or "defensive identification" is currently viewed as a transitory defense mechanism, or possibly as contributing to aggressive behavior but not to moral internalization.

Social learning theorists view the child as emulating the parent to acquire the parent's power, mastery, and other resources. A self-reinforcing process is sometimes postulated in which the child fantasizes himself as the model who controls or consumes the valued resources; he then acts like the model, and the resulting similarity is reinforcing because it signifies that he may be able to attain the model's desired goal states.

A. CORRELATIONAL RESEARCH

The research relating parent identification to moral internalization is meager. Two basic approaches have been used. One predicts that if the moral attributes are acquired through identification there should be consistency among them. The other predicts that if moral internalization is the product of identification it should be related to parental discipline techniques in ways predictable from anaclitic identification theory, that is, it should relate positively to love withdrawal. The research is nonsupportive in both cases. As we have seen, moral internalization does not relate to love withdrawal; and as will be noted later, the intercorrelations among the moral indices are generally low. This casts doubt on the notion of identification as an encompassing, unitary process. To see if identification plays any role in moral development requires independent assessment of the child's tendency to identify and also his moral orientation. This was done in one study (Hoffman, 1971c). The identification scores of the subjects, all seventh-grade children, were based on the extent to which they consciously admired and strived to emulate their parents. Few significant relationships were obtained: father identification related positively to conformity to rules, internal moral judgments, and salience of moral values in boys; and to conformity to rules in girls. Mother identification related to conformity to rules in boys. Neither mother nor father identification related significantly to the major moral internalization indices: guilt, confession, and acceptance of blame.

These findings may reflect the fact that parents do not often express guilty, self-critical feelings openly and thus do not provide the child with an effective model for these internal moral states. In addition, young children may lack the cognitive, especially role-taking skills needed to infer another person's inner states from overt behavior. Finally, the child's motive to identify may not be strong enough to overcome the natural aversion to the pain associated with a self-critical perspective. In other words, it appears that identification may contribute to the adoption of certain moral attributes that are visible and do not require complex cognitive functions or self-denial [see also Hoffman (1975a) for evidence that parents who place a high value on helping others often have children who help others]. These attributes may be internalized in the sense that the child uses them rather than external sanctions as the criteria for right and wrong, as in making moral judgments about others. The data do not suggest, however, that identification contributes to the use of moral standards as an evaluative perspective with which to examine one's own behavior. As indicated earlier, this internalized perspective may be fostered under certain conditions in the discipline encounter—in being criticized by another rather than in emulating another's self-criticism. The relative effectiveness of the discipline encounter may be due in part to the fact that it requires far simpler cognitive operations for the child to learn to view his own actions critically on the basis of his parent's criticisms of these actions than on the basis of the parent's self-criticism. That is, the child's attention in the discipline encounter need only be directed toward his own act and its effects; he need not attend to the inner states and take the role of the parent.

B. EXPERIMENTAL RESEARCH

Bandura (1969) and others have argued that identification and imitation refer essentially to the same behavioral phenomenon and are therefore inter-changeable concepts. Imitation lends itself readily to experimental investigation, and in the past decade numerous laboratory studies have attempted to show the influence of imitative modeling on many types of behavior. Those investigating the effects of adult models are especially pertinent here because of their possible bearing on the parent's role as model in the child's moral development.

1. Resistance to Temptation

In a study by Stein (1967), fourth-grade boys were assigned to do a boring job (watch for a light and push a button when it goes on) while an attractive movie was being shown just outside their line of vision. The prohibition against looking at the movie was stated as follows: "The lights probably won't come on very often so you may do whatever you like as long as you stay in your chair. You must stay in your chair, though, so you'll be ready when the lights do come on." Then followed one of three conditions: exposure to an adult model doing the same task who said aloud, "I sure wish I could see the movie" and then yielded to the temptation to do so; an adult model who said the same thing but resisted temptation; and no model. After that the child was left alone and observed through a one-way mirror. The findings were that observing a model who yielded to temptation resulted in more yielding than the other two conditions. The subjects who observed a model who resisted temptation, how-ever, showed no more resistance than the control group. This suggests that observing deviant models may serve to legitimize deviancy and undermine the subject's prior socialization against it. Observing models who resist the tempta-tion to deviate, however, is likely to be ineffective as an agent of inhibition.

Other interpretations are possible. One, that the high level of resistance shown by the no-model control group produced a "ceiling effect," is not supported by the data, as noted by Stein, since the resistance scores of the controls were actually slightly higher than those who observed the resisting model. It remains possible, however, that the control group's deviation scores were spuriously low because the deviant response had little salience for them. In any case, the study provides no evidence that observing a resisting model contributes to resistance to temptation.

Recent research raises the possibility that Stein's results may reflect the predominantly middle-class background of her subjects. Rosenkoetter (1973) used a similar design with lower-class, mostly white, third-grade students in a Lutheran parochial school, half of whom were from broken homes. He found, as did Stein, that the effects of observing a model who yielded to temptation far exceeded the effects of observing a model who resisted temptation; the resisting model in this case, however, did have a statistically borderline effect. Fry (1975) studied 8- and 9-year-old Indian children and American middle-class children living in India, using the forbidden-toy paradigm. For the Americans, the yielding model was effective but not the resisting model, which fits Stein's findings. With Indian children, however, the resisting and yielding models were both effective, though marginally. Fry suggests that adult models who resist temptation may be effective in cultures which stress the importance of obedience. This explanation may also apply to Rosenkoetter's findings, since lower class parents typically place great stress on obedience (e.g., Kohn, 1959), although it is not known whether this was true in Rosenkoetter's sample.

These studies, it might be noted, are subject to some of the criticisms made earlier of the discipline experiments. The ecological validity of the experimental manipulations does not seem to be much of a problem here, but the moral indices used are similar to those used in the discipline research and therefore may be questioned on similar grounds. Also, as in the discipline experiments, the socialization process is telescoped and a moral index independent of the child's immediate response to the model is lacking. What these studies may provide, then, is an index of the subject's susceptibility to immediate influence by a model.

2. Self-Denial in Relation to Performance Standards

A series of experiments, beginning with Bandura and Kupers (1964), deal with the child's adoption of a model's performance standards. The typical procedure is one in which the subject participates in a bowling game with a model. The range of scores obtained is controlled by the experimenter. At the outset, the subject and model are given access to a plentiful supply of candy or chips (exchangeable for toys later) from which they can help themselves in accord with instructions. In one experimental condition, the model sets a high standard of self-reward (e.g., on trials in which he obtains or exceeds a score of 20, he rewards himself with one or two candies and says something like "I deserve an M & M for that high score"). On trials in which the model fails to meet the standard, he takes no reward and makes some comment like "No M & M's for that" or "That does not deserve an M & M treat." After exposure to their respective models, the subjects play the bowling game a number of times, and the performance level for which they reward themselves is recorded.

Most of these experiments have limited relevance to moral internalization because an adult (usually not the model) is present at all times. In the two studies in which the children are left to play the game alone, however, the findings were essentially the same as in the others: the children's pattern of self-reward and self-denial resembled that of the model to which they were exposed (Grusec, 1971; Liebert & Ora, 1968). That is, the children who observed a model apply a low standard rewarded themselves generously even for minimal performance. Children who observed a model apply a high, self-denying standard helped themselves to rewards sparingly and only when they achieved relatively high levels of performance.

It is difficult to interpret these findings because only two studies included control groups not exposed to any model. And whereas in both of these studies the observation of models with low standards resulted in the use of low standards by the children, such consistency was not obtained with high standards. In one study the subjects who observed models with high, self-denying standards demonstrated more self-denial than did the control group (Liebert & Ora, 1968); in the other study, they did not (Bandura & Whelan, 1966). It is difficult to know which finding to weigh more heavily. Of the two, only Liebert and Ora employed an "alone" condition on which to base the children's self-denial scores. On the other hand, the Bandura and Whelan study included six different independent tests, each with its own control group, and in all six the subjects who observed models with high, self-denying standards actually rewarded themselves *more* often than did the control groups (significantly so in two cases)—a pattern much like that found in the resistance-to-temptation research discussed previously. It is possible that the self-denying behavior of the control groups, which may partly account for these findings, is due to the presence of an adult; but this adult was also present for the subjects who observed self-denying models. Furthermore, in a study by Bandura and Perloff (1967), children who were instructed to set their own performance standard and reward themselves only when they attained it, tended to set high standards to which they then adhered even when left alone. The Bandura and Whelan findings thus cannot be ignored.

Even if we conclude from these experiments that self-denial may be fostered in children by having them observe self-denying models, there is evidence that the resulting self-denial is short-lived. Bandura, Grusec, and Menlove (1967) reported that high, self-denying standards were readily abandoned in favor or more lenient standards used by a peer model. This finding takes on added significance in light of the evidence that children will ordinarily emulate an adult rather than a peer who uses the same standard (Bandura & Kupers, 1964). All in all, the evidence is not compelling that observing models who set high standards and deny themselves rewards when they fail to attain them results in self-denying behavior by the child. Models exhibiting lenient standards, however, do appear to be quite effective in producing self-rewarding behavior.

3. Effects of Punishing a Deviant Model

Many experiments have been done on the effects of having children observe models—mostly peers—who are punished for behaving in a manner forbidden by the experimenter. This research has little bearing on parental practices (except insofar as the punishment administered to one child may affect his onlooking sibling). It may be directly pertinent to the impact of the mass media on moral internalization, however, and so warrants brief mention here. The studies were done in the 1960s, and I reviewed them several years ago (Hoffman, 1970b). The most clear-cut generalization to emerge is that direct observation of a model who behaves aggressively or yields to temptation and acts in the experimentally prohibited manner without being punished has a disinhibiting effect on the observer. The effects of observing a deviant model who is punished, however, are unclear. That is, children who observe a deviant model who is punished display less aggression and more resistance to temptation than do children who observe a deviant nonpunished model, but they behave no differently than do control subjects who observe no model (see also Collins, 1973).

It should be noted that this research used power-assertive punishment. Consequently, even if punishment to the model were found to produce inhibition and self-denial in the subject, this would have little or no bearing on moral internalization, since the subject's most likely motive would be to avoid punishment. Future investigators might take their cue from the parent discipline research discussed earlier and try "punishing" the model with induction rather than power assertion. The effect might still not be due to imitation of the model, however, but to the message from the experimenter. As in all these studies, the model may simply serve as the medium for what is essentially a discipline technique administered to the subject by the experimenter.

The most reasonable conclusion to draw from the modeling research to date is that exposure to deviant, unpunished models has a disinhibiting effect that may reflect a temporary undermining of the observer's prior socialization in impulse control and self-denial; exposure to models who resist temptation, or who deviate and are punished, on the other hand, appears to be a questionable way of promoting impulse control and self-denial. The research also suggests that the failure to imitate a model's self-denying behaviors is not due to deficiencies in cognitive capacity, since the children were able to imitate the models, sometimes in remarkable detail, when self-denial was not involved. And prior nurturant interactions with the model, which have been found to increase the imitation of neutral acts (e.g., Bandura & Huston, 1961; Sgan, 1976) appear to be ineffective when it comes to self-denying behaviors (e.g., Bandura *et al.*, 1967). Perhaps the observation of models is not enough to arouse sufficiently powerful identificatory motives to overcome the child's natural tendency towards self-gratification. This may be due to the artificiality of the typical laboratory experiment and the use of models who are strangers to the child. As noted earlier, however, even the motive to emulate the parent may have this same limitation.

We expressed concern earlier about the adequacy of the conceptions of morality underlying the experimental research and mentioned the need to investigate more significant moral behaviors. A suggestive example is provided in a study of college students reported by Rosenhan (1969). He used a Milgram-type paradigm and found that the observation of a model who *(a)* discontinued administering the shock, *(b)* delegitimized the experimenter by questioning his credentials and good sense, and *(c)* expressed sympathy for the victim resulted in a substantial reduction in the subject's compliance, hence in the amount of shock he administered to the victim. It is interesting to note that despite the obvious difference between the model's behavior in this study and in the research discussed previously, the effects on the observer have certain things in common. Thus the "deviant" model in the Rosenhan study served to diminish the effectiveness of the experimenter's instructions, just as the deviant models did in the previous research. And, as in the previous research, the model functioned to enable the subject to do what he wanted to do in the first place—only in this case what he wanted was to perform a moral act. The important difference between this and the previous research is that it suggests models may at times provide the support needed to resist pressures to deviate from one's existing moral standards. Whether identification with parents serves a similar purpose is a problem worth investigating.

III. Cognitive Disequilibrium

The cognitive-developmental theorists—notably J. Piaget and L. Kohlberg—view moral internalization as occurring in a series of fixed, qualitatively distinct stages whose end product is a universal sense of justice or concern for reciprocity among individuals. Each stage is a homogeneous type of moral reasoning strategy or conceptual framework designed to answer moral questions and evaluate issues; moral reasoning within a stage is thus consistent across different moral problems and situations. Each stage builds upon, reorganizes, and encompasses the preceding one and is therefore more comprehensive, providing new perspectives and criteria for making moral evaluations. The content of moral values does not play an important role in defining a stage.

All individuals regardless of culture are viewed as going through the stages in the same order, varying only in how quickly and how far they move through the stage sequence. The stages are held to be constructed by the individual as he tries to make sense out of his own experience, rather than implanted by culture through socialization. The dialectical quality of this model of stage progression should be noted in contrast to other conceptions, for example, Gesell's (1929), in which stages form an invariant sequence through the maturational unfolding of a series of innate biological patterns, that is, each stage is simply a direct reflection of the individual's maturational level at the time.

A. PIAGET'S MODEL

Piaget's two stages were derived from the attitudes expressed by different-aged children toward the origin, legitimacy, and alterability of rules in the game of marbles, and the responses to stories such as the well-known one in which children are asked to judge who is naughtier, a boy who accidentally breaks fifteen cups as he opens a door or a boy who breaks one cup while trying to sneak jam out of the cupboard (Piaget, 1932). In Piaget's first stage—referred to as moral realism, morality of constraint, or heteronomous morality—the child feels an obligation to comply with rules because they are sacred and unalterable. He tends to view behaviors as totally right or wrong and thinks everyone views them in the same way. He judges the rightness or wrongness of an act on the basis of the magnitude of its consequences, the extent to which it conforms to established rules, and whether it is punished. He believes in "immanent justice"— that violations of social norms are followed by physical accidents or misfortunes willed by God or by some inanimate object.

The child in the more advanced stage—called autonomous morality, morality of cooperation, or reciprocity—views rules as established and maintained through reciprocal social agreement and thus subject to modification in response to human needs. He recognizes a possible diversity in views. His judgments of right and wrong place stress on intentions as well as consequences. He thinks that punishment should be reciprocally related to the misdeed (e.g., through restitution) rather than painful, arbitrary, and administered by authority. Also, duty and obligation are no longer defined in terms of obedience to authority, but more in terms of conforming to peer expectations, considering their welfare, expressing gratitude for past favors, and, above all, putting oneself in the place of others.

Piaget believes that both cognitive development (hence, maturation) and social experience play a role in the transformation from one stage to the next.

Although he is not clear about how the two interact, here is my impression of the threads of his argument. The young child's moral immaturity is based on *(a)* two cognitive limitations, namely, egocentrism (assuming that others view events the same as he does) and "realism" (confusing subjective with objective experience, e.g., perceiving dreams as external events); and *(b)* his heteronomous respect for adults—a syndrome of feelings including inferiority, dependency, affection, admiration, and fear, which produces feelings of obligation to comply with their commands and to view their rules as sacred and unchangeable. Moral growth requires that the child give up egocentrism and realism and develop a concept of self as distinct from others who have their own independent perspectives about events. This shift occurs in interactions with peers, in two ways.

1. By growing older the child attains relative equality with adults and older children, which lessens his unilateral respect for them and gives him confidence to participate with peers in decisions about applying and changing rules on the basis of reciprocity. This new mode of interaction makes the child's initial conception of the rules no longer tenable. They are no longer seen as having an infinite past and a divine or adult origin but increasingly as products of cooperation and agreement based on the human goals they serve, and amenable to change by mutual consent.

2. Interacting with peers often requires taking alternate and reciprocal roles with them, which facilitates awareness that one is coordinate with others—that he reacts to similar situations in similar ways, that the consequences of his acts for them and theirs for him are similar, and yet events seem different when viewed from different vantage points. The child thus becomes sensitized to the inner states that underlie the acts of others, which contributes, among other things, to the tendency to take their intentions into account.

Social experience, then, serves to stimulate and challenge the individual because it contradicts his expectations. The resulting cognitive disequilibrium then motivates him to utilize his newly attained cognitive capabilities to resolve the contradiction; and it is through this effort that preexisting patterns of moral thought are reorganized.

Although Piaget's theory appeared in the late 1920s, most of the published research based on it was done in the 1950s and 1960s. The earlier findings, critically reviewed by Hoffman (1970b), provide considerable support for Piaget's postulated age-developmental sequence in Western countries (England, United States, Switzerland), although adults may sometimes use earlier forms of moral reasoning in certain situations. There is no support, however, for the assumption that this sequence occurs in other types of societies, or that peer interaction fosters moral growth. The assumption of consistency across stage attributes (subjects with high scores on one attribute such as "consequences" are also high on other attributes such as "immanent justice") is generally not upheld, but the research appears to lack some of the controls needed for a critical test. More recently, level of moral judgment has been found to relate positively to the cognitive level displayed in solving mathematics and physics problems by 4- to 8-year olds and to the role-taking ability of children at various ages (Ambron & Irwin, 1975; Damon, 1975; Moir, 1974; Selman, 1971).

An interesting series of experiments beginning with the investigation of Bandura and McDonald (1963) and continuing into the present have been conducted to test Piaget's assumption that the child's progression from one stage to the next requires cognitive disequilibrium The attempt in these studies was to see if the individual's level of moral reasoning could be changed by simply exposing him to models who verbalize moral judgments at higher or lower levels than his own. The social learning theorists who did most of this work expected that such exposure would produce changes, whereas cognitive-developmentalists would not ordinarily expect social influences to operate in such a direct manner. In general, these experiments did show that the subjects' moral judgments were affected by the model's verbalizations. The earlier experiments were criticized as perhaps demonstrating nothing more than momentary, specific response shifts rather than actual changes in level of moral reasoning (Turiel, 1966). The more recent research, however, does indicate that children not only shift their verbal responses toward the model but also increase their understanding of the principle that intentions should be taken into account when making moral evaluations of behavior. Furthermore, the effects appear to last up to a year, although not beyond that (Cowan, Langer, Heavenrich, & Nathanson, 1969; Crowley, 1968; Dorr & Fay, 1974; Glassco, Milgram & Youniss, 1970; Sternlieb & Youniss, 1975).

That mere exposure to models can produce such shifts has been interpreted as evidence against cognitive developmental theory (e.g., Kurtines & Greif, 1974). Another interpretation (Hoffman, 1971a) is that the children did not merely imitate the model. Rather, they knew that acts may or may not be intentional but gave intentions less weight than consequences, perhaps because the stories used, like Piaget's, portrayed more harmful consequences for accidental than for intended acts. This fits the recent evidence (Imamoglu, 1975; Rule, Nesdale, & McAra, 1974) that children as young as 5 years of age use intentions when the consequences of accidental and intended acts are equal (the modeling studies in question used older children). Repeated exposure to an adult model who consistently assigns greater weight to intentions despite the disparity in consequences might then have produced cognitive disequilibrium, which the subjects reduced by reexamining and changing their views. This interpretation is consonant with cognitive developmental theory, but it does not make the cognitive developmental assumption that movement is always progressive, since a model who espouses "consequences," the less mature response, should also produce cognitive disequilibrium. Further research, in which the subjects' reports of their thoughts and feelings on hearing the model's expressed views were obtained, would be illuminating.

B. KOHLBERG'S STAGE SCHEME

In developing his stage scheme Kohlberg attempted to retain the best of Piaget's analysis and to fit it into a more refined, comprehensive, and logically consistent framework. Kohlberg's six stages are based on extensive case analyses of boys ranging from 10 to 16 years of age (Kohlberg, 1958). The data were obtained from 2-hour interviews focused on nine hypothetical moral dilemmas in which acts of obedience to laws, rules, or commands of authority conflict with the needs or welfare of other persons. The subject was asked to choose whether one should perform the obedience-serving act or the need-serving act and to answer a series of questions probing the thinking underlying his choice. Kohlberg's interest was not in the action alternatives selected by the subjects, which presumably reflect the content of their moral values, but in the quality of their judgments as indicated in the reasons given for their choices and their ways of defining the conflict situations.

Each stage was defined in terms of its position on 30 different moral issues which the subjects brought into their thinking. The six stages were ordered into three levels of moral orientation, the basic themes and major attributes of which may be summarized as follows.

Premoral. Control of conduct is external in two senses: standards consist of outer commands or pressures; the motive is to avoid external punishment, obtain rewards, have favors returned, etc.

Stage 1—Obedience and punishment orientation. Definition of good and bad is based on obedience to rules and authority. Deference to superior power or prestige exists but is not heteronomous in Piaget's sense, that is, punishment is feared like any other aversive stimulus.

Stage 2—Naive hedonistic and instrumental orientation. Acts are defined as right which satisfy the self and occasionally others. Values are relative to each actor's needs and perspectives.

Morality of conventional role-conformity. Morality is defined as maintaining the social order and conforming to expectations of others. Control of conduct is external in that standards consist of rules and expectations held by those who are significant others by virtue of personal attachment or delegated authority. Motivation is largely internal—though based on anticipation of praise or censure by significant others, the child now takes their role and respects their judgment. Thus the personal reactions of authority now serve as cues to the rightness or wrongness of an act and the moral virtue of the actor.

Stage 3—Good-boy morality of maintaining good relations. Orientation is to gain approval and to please and help others. The morally good person is one who possesses moral virtues. In judging others, intentions are considered.

Stage 4—Authority and social-order maintaining morality. Orientation is to "doing one's duty," showing respect for authority, and maintaining social order for its own sake. Takes the perspective of others who have legitimate rights and expectations in situation. Believes that virtue must be rewarded.

Morality of self-accepted moral principles. Morality is defined as conformity to shared or sharable standards, rights, duties. Possibility of conflict between two socially accepted standards is acknowledged and attempts at rational decision between them are made. Control of conduct is internal in two senses: the standards have an inner source, and the decision to act is based on an inner process of thought and judgment concerning right and wrong.

Stage 5—Morality of contract, individual rights, and democratically accepted law. Norms of right and wrong are defined in terms of laws or institutionalized rules, which are seen to have a rational base; for example, they express the will of the majority, maximize social utility or welfare, or are necessary for institutional functioning. Although recognized as arbitrary, sometimes unjust, and one of many alternatives, the law is generally the ultimate criterion of the right. Duty and obligation are defined in terms of contract, not the needs of individuals. When conflict exists between the individual and the law or contract, though there may be sympathy for the former the latter prevails because of its greater functional rationality for society.

Stage 6—Morality of individual principles of conscience. Orientation is not only to existing rules and standards but also to conscience as a directing agent, mutual respect and trust, and principles of moral choice involving appeal to logical universality and consistency. Conduct is controlled by an internalized ideal that exerts pressure toward action that seems right regardless of reactions of others present. If the individual acts otherwise, self-condemnation and guilt result. Though aware of the importance of law and contract, moral conflict is generally resolved in terms of broader moral principles such as the Golden Rule, the greatest good for the greatest number, or the categorical imperative.

Kohlberg's stage descriptions are more fully developed than his conception of the processes involved in the individual's progress through the stages. His recent writings stress two processes: cognitive disequilibrium and role taking. The first is an extension of the concepts of cognitive disequilibrium and equilibration in Piaget's theory of intellectual (rather than moral) development The hypothesis, as formulated by Turiel (1966), is that moral growth results from exposure to levels of moral reasoning that are moderately higher than one's current level ("structural match"). The resulting cognitive conflict or disequilibrium is tension producing, which results in the person's becoming motivated to make sense out of the contradiction. This notion of a strain toward equilibrium obviously has much in common with motivational concepts that stress the importance of curiosity or exploratory drives, activity and sensory needs, effectance and mastery strivings, and the need to reduce dissonance (e.g., Berlyne, 1960; Festinger, 1957; Maslow, 1954; R. W. White, 1959).

The moral stages, according to Kohlberg, also reflect a sequence of successive changes in role taking ability. The ability to take another person's perspective is seen as having special significance in the transition from premoral to conventional morality (from stage 2 to 3). Indeed, Kohlberg at times seems to imply that role taking is the defining characteristic of conventional morality. At other times, however, role taking is seen as functioning primarily in the service of cognitive conflict, that is, role-taking experiences provide the individual with different perspectives and thus instigate cognitive conflict and its resolution through modification of the existing moral structure.

Kohlberg has devised a Moral Judgment Scale to determine an individual's stage of moral development. The only complete description of the scale is given in his dissertation (Kohlberg, 1958). The instrument consists of the same nine hypothetical dilemmas used initially to derive the stages. An interviewer presents the subject with one dilemma at a time, and the person must make a judgment about the situation and justify his choice. The subject is encouraged to respond freely and asked probe questions to elicit additional responses, all of which are recorded. The scoring is based not on a subject's specific judgment to each moral dilemma, but rather on the reasoning which he gives in support of his judgment. The scale is complex and difficult to score. Precise scoring instructions are available only from Kohlberg personally, and extensive training is necessary in order to score protocols correctly. There are two scoring methods: a global intuitive one in which the rater assigns the subject both a stage score for each dilemma (resulting in a profile) and an overall score consisting of his dominant stage; and a highly detailed system of coding the responses in terms of a classification scheme based on the 30 moral issues, each defined by a 6-point scale corresponding to the six stages.

The detailed scoring system, obviously the one most potentially useful for other researchers because of its greater objectivity, recently underwent a drastic revision (Colby, Speicher, & Kohlberg, 1973; Kohlberg, 1976). The new procedure puts emphasis on fewer moral issues and more weight on the highest stage attained by the subject on each issue. An earlier, minor change in the scoring was prompted by the finding in the Kohlberg and Kramer (1969) longitudinal study that a number of subjects attained higher scores (usually stage 4) in high school than in their early college years (often stage 2). This finding initially appeared to be a challenge to the theory, which postulates forward but not backward movement. It was also for a time viewed as possibly reflecting a kind of disorganization that may characterize movement from conventional to autonomous morality. Careful examination of the protocols, however, showed that the stage 2 responses of the retrogressors did not show the unconcerned, self-centered, hedonistic reasoning characteristic of the "natural" stage 2 responses of younger subjects. Rather, these subjects appeared to view morality in conventional stage 4 terms, to have thought about it and questioned its validity. In the revised scoring system these responses were assigned stage scores of 4.5. It should be noted that by age 25 all of these subjects are reported by Kohlberg as having developed strong, principled reasoning (stages 5 or 6).

1. Application to Moral Education

Kohlberg's work has aroused considerable interest among educators—perhaps due in part to the post-Watergate surge of interest in morality, but also more fundamentally because it appears to provide an answer to a long-felt need. Kohlberg (1973) has noted that educators see the need for moral education in the classroom but they are equally concerned that it may be an elitist, authoritarian imposition of their own moral values on their students. He has also criticized the relativistic and the so-called "bag of virtues" approaches, which suffer from lack of agreement on what the virtues should be. He offers as a solution to this dilemma his own theoretical model as a scientifically based "non-relativistic strategy for defining educational aims." Since later stages of moral development reflect a more adequate, mature approach to moral issues, Kohlberg concludes that what *is* at later stages is what *ought* to be (Kohlberg, 1973).

In other words, Kohlberg claims that his is a schema of objectively desirable moral objectives and the various developmental steps in their attainment. To stimulate moral growth, the teacher need only provide a congenial environment, the nature of which follows also from the theory, that is, an environment that provides the students with exposure to higher levels of moral reasoning. The technique suggested is to encourage group discussion of moral dilemmas (either Kohlberg's own dilemmas or others that may be more pertinent to the students' experiences) about certain essential moral issues. The cognitive conflict required for moral growth is assured by the inevitable differences in moral stages among the participants, together with provoking but not value-specific questions from the teacher when necessary. The teacher is thus a catalyst for the student's construction of his own increasingly more adequate moral orientation.

2. Research Review and Critique

Kohlberg's model has stimulated a great deal of research, especially in the past 10 years. Most of it uses Kohlberg's measures but is peripheral to the theory and will not be treated here—studies relating moral reasoning to IQ (e.g., Selman, 1971), to Piaget's cognitive developmental levels (e.g., Tomlinson-Keasy & Keasy, 1972), to other ego factors (Grim, Kohlberg, & White, 1968), to political ideology (Fishkin, Keniston, & MacKinnon, 1973), and to political activism (e.g., Haan, Smith, & Block, 1968). What follows is a critical review of the research bearing on the central tenets of the theory: the postulated stage sequence is invariant; moral growth is fostered by cognitive conflict and role taking opportunities; the stages are homogeneous or consistent.

   a. *Invariance of stage sequence.* In Kohlberg's initial study, age trends were found to be consistent with the view of the stages as developmental. Furthermore, two aspects of these trends—earlier stages decrease with age whereas later ones increase, and the further apart two stages are in the postulated developmental sequence the lower the correlation between them—were cited by Kohlberg as evidence that later stages replace rather than merely add to earlier stages. These conclusions are premature, however, since they are based on findings obtained in the very same study in which Kohlberg initially constructed his stage schema, and the subjects' ages were a known and important factor in this construction. From an unpublished study of age trends in moral reasoning in several cultures, Kohlberg (1969) has also reported data that appear to provide some support for the first three stages. These data cannot be evaluated properly because the sample size and the details of administering and scoring the tests are not given.

   Kohlberg and Kramer (1969) have reported the results of a follow-up of Kohlberg's original sample. Moral reasoning scores for lower and middle class males at 16, 20, and 24 years of age were available. Moral judgment profiles for the two classes at the three ages were presented which appeared to demonstrate the developmental invariance of the six stages. As noted by Kurtines and Greif (1974), however, there were actually few significant changes in the moral judgment profiles over time. Stage 4 was predominant at all ages in both samples; few people reached stages 5 and 6; and there was no evidence to show that the subjects passed through the stages in a fixed order, or even that people who reached stage 4 had gone through any of the previous stages. Furthermore, as mentioned earlier, college students often had lower stage scores than high-school students. Although, as already pointed out, this finding was reinterpreted as a measurement problem which does not exist in the revised scoring system, the fact remains that the longitudinal results do not support the postulated developmental sequence. A 3-year longitudinal study by Holstein (1976) also provides evidence against the expected stepwise progression, since stages were skipped and some backsliding occurred.

   The study most often cited as basic support for the invariant sequence of the stages was done by Turiel (1966). Forty-seven seventh-grade boys were assigned stage scores based on their responses to six Kohlberg dilemmas. In the experimental condition, three different dilemmas were administered. In each, the subjects were instructed to take the role of the central figure and "seek advice" from the experimenter. To produce cognitive conflict without suggesting what action the central figure should take, the experimenter's advice consisted of arguments on both sides of the issue, each cast in terms of moral concepts at a level which diverged from the subject's own stage position by certain specified amounts—either one or two stages above (+1 or +2) or one stage below (−1). The subjects were retested a week later on all nine dilemmas.

The results confirmed one hypothesis: a person's existing stage of thought limits how far he can go, and therefore he will be more likely to assimilate moral reasoning one stage above rather than two stages above his current level. The more crucial hypothesis was based on the assumption that *(a)* higher stages are reorganizations and displacements of preceding stages rather than mere additions to them, and *(b)* there is a tendency toward forward movement through the stage sequence, that is, irreversibility. The group exposed to the +1 treatment was therefore expected to shift in the +1 direction to a greater degree that the −1 group would shift in the −1 direction. The findings were just the opposite from those expected, and furthermore the experimental groups did not shift to a significantly greater degree than the control group which had experienced no treatment. The control group, however, for some unknown reason showed considerably more shift in the −1 direction than in the +1 direction. As a result, the net shift (experimental minus control) was greater for the +1 than the −1 group. This difference is in the hypothesized direction and of borderline significance. In other words, it is only if the action of the control group, which is inexplicably more dramatic than either experimental group, is taken into account that the findings may be interpreted as providing the slightest evidence in favor of the hypothesis. This problem together with others mentioned by Kurtines and Greif (1974), casts doubt on the support this study provides for Kohlberg's theory.

In a recent study using an improved version of Turiel's design (Tracy & Cross, 1973) seventh-grade children who initially scored at Kohlberg's lowest two moral stages (but not the higher-stage subjects) were influenced in the expected manner, that is, they shifted more in the direction of higher than of lower levels of moral judgment. These same lower-stage subjects, however, also obtained high scores on a social desirability measure; furthermore, within this group, social desirability was found to relate positively to the amount of shift. Since these subjects had an external moral orientation to begin with (the lowest two stages are external), these findings suggest that direct social influence processes may account for their shift in judgment rather than the disequilibrium and "structural match" postulated in cognitive-developmental theory.

The studies of comprehension and preference for higher moral levels, which also follow Turiel's format (e.g., Rest, 1973), appear to have other problems. The findings were that comprehension was high, up to the subject's own predominant stage, and then fell off rapidly; and the highest stage comprehended was the most preferred of those comprehended. Stage 6 statements, however, were the most preferred of all, which means that the subject's predominant stage did not predict his preference. This casts doubt on the implications of the entire study. It also raises a possible question about the design of all these studies. The investigators themselves apparently constructed the statements of "advice," and despite their attempts to balance each pro—con pair for stage, attitude, and issue, it is possible that high-stage statements were inadvertently phrased more attractively than low-stage statements. This would introduce a spurious element in the subjects' choices. Perhaps a better procedure in studies like these would be to have independent persons construct the statements.

   b. *Moral growth through cognitive conflict and role taking.* The studies just discussed also bear on the importance of cognitive disequilibrium, but in view of their limitations they cannot be seen as providing support for the idea that cognitive disequilibrium promotes moral growth.

   As for role taking, studies by Moir (1974) and Selman (1971) found, with IQ controlled, a positive relationship between Kohlberg's moral stages and nonmoral role-taking ability (visual perspective taking, and ability to predict another's feelings and motives in interpersonal situations). And Holstein (1972) reports that children whose parents permitted them to participate in an experimental family decision-making situation obtained high moral reasoning scores as compared to children whose parents made most of the decisions. These correlational studies tell us nothing about whether role taking is an antecedent or a consequence of moral reasoning development or whether moral reasoning is a form of role taking, with development in moral and nonmoral role taking occurring simultaneously or through mutual influence. In a 1-year follow-up of 10 subjects who had initially scored low on both role taking and moral reasoning, Selman (1971) found that more children advanced in role taking than in moral reasoning, and the two who did advance in moral reasoning were among those who advanced in role taking. He interprets this as suggesting that development of role-taking skills may be a necessary but not sufficient condition for development of moral thought. This interpretation, however, overlooks the fact that 1 year earlier a third of the children with high moral-reasoning scores in Selman's initial, larger sample had *low* role-taking scores.

   Thus, although it seems reasonable that cognitive conflict and role taking would help foster growth in moral thinking, clear empirical evidence is still lacking.

   c. *Stage consistency.* Kohlberg assumes that each stage is homogeneous and there is a high degree of uniformity in a person's moral reasoning level in different situations. The assumption of homogeneity cannot be tested in most of the published research because total moral maturity scores or dominant stage scores are given, with no indication of the individual moral dilemma scores. The few studies reporting such data do not support the assumption. Thus not one subject in a sample of 75 college students obtained the same stage score in five

Kohlberg dilemmas (Fishkin *et al., 1973*). The scores obtained by adolescent boys, and also by their mothers, showed considerable "scatter" (Hudgins & Prentice, 1973). And two-thirds of a large college sample used different stages in Kohlberg's dilemmas than in evaluating a social protest movement (Haan, 1975). A small amount of situational variation might be expected due to random errors of measurement and might justify the use of Piaget's concept of "décalage." The high degree of variation obtained in these studies, however, argues against décalage and therefore perhaps against the assumption that the stages are homogeneous.

  d. Moral reasoning and behavior. Kohlberg's theory does not predict a direct relationship between moral reasoning and behavior. Individuals may exhibit the same behavior for different reasons, or different behaviors for the same reason. There should be some relationship between moral reasoning and behavior, however, and Langer (1969) has suggested a possible mechanism: A discrepancy between one's level of moral reasoning and overt behavior creates a state of disequilibrium, to reduce which the individual is compelled to lessen the discrepancy by bringing behavior and reasoning closer together. Whatever the mechanism, there is some evidence of a relationship between moral reasoning and behavior. Kohlberg has reported informally that moral stages in his initial study related positively to teacher ratings of fairness to peers and adherence to rules in the absence of authority; and that male college students at stages 5 and 6 resisted the experimenter's request to administer severe electric shocks in a Milgram-type study to a greater extent than students at stages 3 and 4. A positive relation between moral reasoning scores and resistance to temptation has been found in sixth-grade children (R. L. Krebs, 1968) and in college students (Schwartz, Feldman, Brown, & Heingartner, 1969). No relation was found between these two variables in seventh graders, however (Nelson, Grinder, & Challas, 1968). And, finally, Fodor (1972) found delinquent adolescents to have moral reasoning scores lower than a matched nondelinquent group, although the mean score for both groups was at stage 3.

  Some interesting anomalies in these findings have been pointed up by Kurtines and Greif (1974). Examples are the fact that stage 3 could characterize both the delinquents in the Fodor study and the conformers in a study by Saltzstein, Diamond, and Belenky (1972); and that Haan *et al.* (1968) found many stage 2s among college students, whereas Schwartz *et al.* (1969) found none. Variations in administering and scoring the Kohlberg measures may account for these strange patterns.

  All things considered, there appears to be a generally positive relationship between moral-reasoning scores and moral behavior. There is no clear evidence as yet, however, that any distinctive pattern of behavior is associated with any particular stage—or that knowing how a person reasons morally indicates anything about how he will behave.

It seems evident that the research as yet provides no clear support for Kohlberg's claim that the stages are homogeneous, that their postulated sequence is universal and invariant, and that moral growth results from role-taking opportunities and exposure to moderately higher levels of moral reasoning. Whether the problem lies in the inadequacies of method, as Kohlberg (1975) has suggested, or in the theory itself remains to be seen.

Aside from the issue of empirical verification, Kohlberg's theory has been taken to task by Simpson (1974) for being a culturally biased approach which claims universality but is actually based on the style of thinking and social organization peculiar to Western culture. Stage 5, for example, makes sense only in a constitutional democracy; and stage 6 requires a level of abstract thought that may disqualify most people in the world. The theory has also been criticized from various philosophical perspectives by Alston (1971), Baier (1974), and Peters (1971). Peters has also suggested that it is important to understand the development of the motivation to be concerned for others, which is ignored in Kohlberg's theory, because this motive is presumably needed to provide direction for translating Kohlberg's abstract moral concepts of justice into actual behavior.

In my view, Kohlberg's major contribution has been to sensitize researchers to the highly complex nature of moral development and the cognitive dimensions that may be necessary for a mature moral orientation. Both he and Piaget have also called attention to the possible importance for moral growth of the person's own direct social experience and his active efforts to draw meaning from its contradictions. And, despite the lack of empirical support to date, certain of the concepts in the theory continue to have appeal. Cognitive disequilibrium and structural match, for example, may help account for the developmental progression from a rudimentary moral sense that perhaps originates in the discipline encounter to the complex moral concepts often held by adults. Finally, Kohlberg's theory has already spawned a great deal of research as well as conceptual and philosophical discussion. For these reasons, further tests of the theory may be worth making.

IV. Generality vs. Specificity

The major theoretical positions differ as to whether moral development is a unitary process. The cognitive-developmental and the Freudian approaches, though vastly different, both view morality as unitary and assume that the individual is consistent across situations. Learning theorists have traditionally held the "specificity" view. Mischel and Mischel (1976), for example, suggest it is the individual's ability to discriminate between situations and anticipate different outcomes, rather than a general moral tendency, that determines whether he will act morally or not.

The best known and most elaborate research relevant to this issue was done by Hartshorne and May in the 1920s (Hartshorne & May, 1928–1930). Over a 5-year period tests designed to disclose cheating and other forms of dishonesty, along with tests of moral knowledge and other variables, were administered to several thousand children between the ages of 8 and 16. The major findings, low intercorrelations among tests, led to Hartshorne and May's "doctrine of specificity": honesty and dishonesty are not unified traits but specific functions of life situations; furthermore, consistency across situations is due to stimulus elements which they may have in common.

Burton (1963) factor analyzed that portion of Hartshorne and May's behavioral honesty data that was based on their six most reliable cheating tests and found some support for a "generality" dimension. He also found an increase in generality with age. Similar support for generality, as well as specificity, was obtained by Sears, Rau, and Alpert (1965) and Nelson, Grinder, and Mutterer (1969), who tested preschool children under more controlled conditions. Sears et al. found correlations ranging from 0 to .45 (mostly statistically significant) among six different resistance-to-temptation measures all given in a play situation. Nelson et al. also studied six different resistance-to-temptation tests and, depending on the statistical procedure employed, anywhere from about 15 to 50% of the variance in the test scores appear to be due to "persons."

With regard to story-completion guilt, Allinsmith (1960) reports no relation between guilt scores on different stories. I have obtained the same results using Allinsmith's scoring procedure. In this procedure, responses expressing concern about punishment and detection are interpreted as guilt responses. It may therefore provide a better index of total deviation anxiety rather than guilt. When guilt was defined more strictly as an affective but also internally self-critical response, significant positive relations were obtained between responses to two very different stories (see Hoffman, 1970a) administered a week apart and scored by independent "blind" raters.

In summarizing the Kohlberg research the finding of inconsistency in type of moral reasoning used by individuals across different situations was pointed up. It should be noted, however, that although there was inconsistency with regard to particular stages there was nevertheless a general tendency for high scores on one dilemma to be associated with high scores on another. Thus, while the findings may provide evidence against Kohlberg's claim that each stage is a "structured whole," they do suggest that there may be some degree of generality across situations.

It seems clear that one can find both generality and specificity in moral, as in any other behavior. Individuals may be more or less disposed to honest or dishonest behavior, for example, but their actions are also affected by the situation—as common sense would dictate.

As for the relation between different aspects of moral behavior, the findings are just as equivocal. We have already mentioned the inconclusive findings regarding the relation between moral reasoning and other indices of moral behavior. In a recent study, Hoffman (1975d) found no relation between guilt and moral reasoning. And the studies relating guilt to resistance-to-temptation are just as inconclusive: whereas MacKinnon (1938) and Grinder (1960) reported low positive relations between the two, Allinsmith (1960) and Maccoby (1959) reported no relation, and Burton, Allinsmith, and Maccoby (1966) found a negative one. A possible explanation for these mixed results is that consistency between levels, or "dynamic consistency" (Hoffman, 1963a), can only be expected when the same value is used, that is, the particular moral standard must be controlled. This view fits both the MacKinnon study, which obtained a positive relation between resistance to temptation in a cheating situation and amount of guilt following cheating, and Hoffman's (1970a) finding of a positive relationship between use of humanistic moral reasoning and amount of guilt following transgressions involving harm to others. It is also in keeping with the finding by Henschel (1971) that the correlation between placing a positive value on honesty and overt honesty in an anonymous resistance-to-temptation test, though very low in fourth-grade children, increased dramatically by the fifth grade, and reached the rather high level of .78 in the seventh grade.

Further research with appropriate controls is needed before the issues of behavioral generality and dynamic consistency can be resolved. Generality across different cheating tests might increase considerably, for example, if motivation and expectations of success or failure in the particular test were controlled, as they have thus far not been. Similarly, there are many reasons why a person who would feel guilty if he violated a standard might nevertheless not predictably resist temptation, even with respect to the same standard: (a) though committed to the standard he might become so involved in striving for highly desired objectives that he fails to discriminate relevant cues and anticipate consequences of his actions; (b) he might lack the necessary behavioral controls; or (c) he might be willing to tolerate guilt in order to attain highly desired immediate objectives. It follows that a strong relationship between guilt and resistance to temptation may occur only when relevant motivational, cognitive and behavior-control variables are controlled. With increasing age we can expect the minimal cognitive and ego-control requisites of moral action to be acquired by more individuals. Hence, behavioral generality and dynamic consistency should both increase with age. Both Henschel's findings and Burton's reanalysis of the Hartshorne and May data indicate that this is the case.

As a possible guide to further research on generality, I would suggest the following formulation. In the very young child generalization takes place on the basis of common stimulus elements, as suggested by Hartshorne and May. After 4 or 5 years of age, when cognitive mediation becomes possible, generalization begins to occur on the basis of conceptual similarity, as suggested by Burton. At some later point in development, after certain moral principles have been internalized—perhaps in the discipline encounter as suggested earlier—the individual may also begin to experience strains towards consistency between these principles and his conduct. Whether these strains toward consistency result in consistent behavior will be determined in part by other aspects of the personality in interaction with situational factors.

V. Concluding Remarks

The major focus of research thus far has been on abstract conceptions of justice, cognitive aspects of moral thought, and prohibitions against one or another type of egoistic need gratification. Research has burgeoned on altruism [reviewed by Bryan (1975) and by Schwartz, in this volume] and on equity and other forms of distributional justice (e.g., Lerner, 1975), but little of it pertains to antecedent social influences, and adequate provision has not been made to rule out egoistic motives that may underlie the subject's prosocial behavior. This is true of both the experimental and the correlational child-rearing research (e.g., Hoffman, 1963b, 1975a; Mussen, Harris, Rutherford, & Keasey, 1970; Rosenhan & White, 1967; Staub, 1974).

Though limited in focus, the variety of research designs, measuring instruments, and theoretical concepts attest to the complex, multifaceted nature of moral internalization. Furthermore, each approach appears to capture a part of reality and each hypothesis can claim some empirical support, though none has yet been subject to the crucial test.

A. TYPES OF INTERNALIZATION

As an attempt to integrate the findings and most promising hypotheses to date, I would suggest, pending further research, that there may be at least three types of internalization processes, each with its own experiential base:

1. The first refers to the general expectation that people often have, without necessarily being aware of it, that their actions are constantly under surveillance. In extreme, this may reflect an irrational fear of ubiquitous authority figures, or retribution by gods or ghosts. The result in any case is that the individual often behaves in the morally prescribed way even when alone, in order to avoid punishment. The socialization experiences contributing to this orientation very likely include a long period in which significant others have punished deviant acts, with the result that painful anxiety states become associated with them. Due to repeated punishment, for example, the kinesthetic and other cues produced by the deviant act may arouse anxiety, which may subsequently be

avoided only by inhibiting the act. This is basically the view advanced by Mowrer (1960) that led to the early experiments on timing and intensity of punishment. From the standpoint of the observer, the individual is behaving in an internalized manner because external surveillance is not necessary. Applying a subjective criterion, however, moral action based on fear of external sanctions, whether realistic or not, cannot be considered an instance of internalization. When the anxiety over deviation is unaccompanied by conscious fears of detection, however, as sometimes happens, this may be viewed as a primitive form of internalization.

2. The second type pertains to the integration of the human capacity for empathy, and the cognitive awareness of other people's inner states and how they are affected by one's behavior. As a contributing socialization experience, I have suggested exposure to inductive discipline, which fosters the simultaneous experiencing of empathy with awareness of harming another person. Reciprocal role taking with peers, in Piaget's sense, that is, in which the person alternately affects others and is affected by them in similar ways, may also help heighten the individual's sensitivity to the inner states aroused in others by his own behavior. Having been in the other person's place helps one to know how the latter feels in response to one's behavior.

3. The third type pertains to the individual's active efforts to cognitively process morally relevant information which is at variance with his preexisting conceptions, and the proclivity to adopt perspectives more comprehensive than his own. It seems likely that the person will feel a special commitment to—and in this sense internalize—moral concepts that he has been actively involved in constructing. The cognitive-developmental theorists may thus be correct in stressing cognitive disequilibrium although, as discussed earlier, there is no evidence that the newly adopted perspectives follow a preordained hierarchical order. I am suggesting in short that the cognitive-conflict and equilibration notions be separated from stage theory and investigated in their own right as possibly contributing to moral internalization.

These three processes are best not thought of as moral stages. The first may be the most pervasive and in one form or other may account for a good deal of moral behavior in many societies. The second may also be prevalent, especially in liberal, humanistically oriented groups. The third may be applicable to a relatively small number of individuals for whom intellectually attained values are of special importance. The three processes may thus develop independently. They may coexist and be mutually supportive, for example, an empathy-based concern for others may provide direction for one's cognitive efforts to resolve conflicting moral concepts. Or they may be nonsupportive, for example, early anxiety-based inhibitions may prevent behaviors from occurring later when their control might be acquired on the basis of awareness of their effects on others.

B. MORAL INTERNALIZATION AND SOCIETY

This article has focused on psychological processes in moral internalization. To round out the picture requires some discussion of the views of several writers who challenge the presumed importance of internalization for society (e.g., Reiss, 1966; Sanford, 1953; Wrong, 1961). Reiss in particular contends that the individual's moral standards are highly vulnerable to external pressures and must be firmed up by continuing social support. He states further that internalization is not necessary for society because of the web of external surveillance that inevitably exists. He also cites the extensive shifts in behavioral norms that often occur from one generation to the next as evidence that the parent–child relationship cannot be the major agency of cultural transmission. Rather, standards of conduct are disseminated by institutionally organized systems (e.g., religious, political, legal, educational) and regulated by collectively enforced sanctions. Innovation also originates at the social organization level, according to Riess, whereas changes emerging within the family are minor. Finally, parents are less important in determining the values that govern an individual's behavior in adult life than the larger social system which may counteract and replace parentally taught values. Internalization is therefore not a necessary requisite and should not enter into the definition of moral behavior.

The view that internalization has a powerful influence on behavior is also challenged by Milgram's (1963) demonstration that people will sometimes obey requests by respectable authority figures to behave in ways that contradict their professed and presumably internalized standards. The findings in two surveys are also suggestive. In one, a majority of executives agreed with the statement that "businessmen would violate a code of ethics whenever they thought they could avoid detection" (Baumhart, 1961). In the other, Harvard graduate students in political science, when presented with details of actual cases of official duplicity, gave responses which indicated an "apparently untroubled acceptance of widespread deceit and lying; an orientation toward seeing things not in ethical but in cost-benefit terms and whether one might get caught" (as reported by Otten, 1974). Finally, Ross and DiTecco (1975) cite several instances suggesting that morality may break down on a large scale when policing agencies are removed. For example, when the Montreal police went on strike for 16 hours in 1969, many people engaged in wholesale looting; and in 1945 when the Norwegian government required taxpayers to register bank accounts and securities, large amounts of money surfaced that had not previously been declared for tax purposes. These, together with the more recent Watergate and corporate bribery revelations, must make us less sanguine about the ubiquity of moral internalization.

These arguments and facts certainly help place internalization in proper perspective. In my view they do not negate its importance, however. Once we discard the simplistic notion that moral standards internalized from parents persist unchanged throughout life, and accept the vulnerability of internalized standards to extreme temptations and to situational pressures, the concept that remains—moral standards which were at first external to the individual may acquire internal motive force—is still viable. The potential long-range power of this motive can often be seen in the clinical realm, though less durability is ordinarily to be expected. How long an internalized standard will effectively guide behavior undoubtedly depends in part on the amount of counterpressures that the individual encounters.

Reiss's view that the family is rarely the source of normative innovation is compelling, although I would suggest that parents may take a more active role than he indicates. While it is true that the adult's internalized standards may influence his child-rearing behavior and thus serve as a conservative social force, the adult is also aware of social reality and is often capable of subordinating his standards to it. When faced with strong pressures against an internalized standard, he may, with some exertion of will and perhaps a twinge of conscience, suppress the tendency to behave in accord with the standard. In this way new circumstances may have a considerable impact on his behavior, including his child-rearing practices. Some of my unpublished findings may be relevant (Hoffman, 1957, 1960). When the parents were asked for the rationale behind the way they disciplined their preschool-aged children, many especially in the middle class mentioned long-range character goals and cited the views of experts. This is in keeping with findings reported by Kohn (1959), M. S. White (1957), and others. What may be of special interest here is that to achieve their aims the parents stated that they sometimes did not do what came naturally but deliberately altered their behavior. For example, they often held back and did not punish the child for something they had been punished for as children, because they could see no point to it now. Our earlier discussion of the possible impact of achievement pressures on moral internalization in males may also be relevant.

What the child internalizes, then, will often be different from the parent's own internalized standards, and closer to the new societal demands. Normative change may be facilitated by this process, in which the adult's internalized standards are filtered through his own cognitive and control systems before finding overt expression in his child-rearing behavior. The parent's own standards, though presumably still internalized, may thus give way to societal pressures, and the parent may actually contribute to the child's internalization of new norms.

The facts of social change may thus be entirely compatible with both the existence of moral internalization and the importance of the parent's role. What function then does internalization serve in society? I would suggest that though internalization is not impervious to external (e.g., economic, technological) pressures for change, the presence of internalization is likely to soften the impact of such pressures on society. That is, when many individuals have internalized the society's moral standards, this may act as a brake against the impact of external pressures for change. The situation is complicated because subgroups—age, socioeconomic, ethnic—undoubtedly vary in the extent to which they both internalize the moral standards and are exposed to pressures against these standards. As a result conflicts between subgroups, as well as between internalized standards and external pressures, may be expected. All of these conflicts constitute a major dynamic in social change. Moral internalization, then, though vulnerable to external pressures, may nevertheless serve a central, primarily stabilizing function in the social process. For this reason it commands the continued attention of social researchers.

REFERENCES

Allinsmith, W. Moral standards: II. The learning of moral standards. In D. R. Miller & G. E. Swanson (Eds.), *Inner conflict and defense.* New York: Holt, 1960. Pp. 141–176.

Alston, W. P. Comments on Kohlberg's "From Is to Ought." In T. Mischel (Ed.), *Cognitive development and epistemology.* New York: Academic Press, 1971. Pp. 269–284.

Ambron, S. R., & Irwin, D. M. Role-taking and moral judgment in five- and seven-year olds. *Developmental Psychology,* 1975, **11**, 102.

Aronfreed, J. The internalization of social control through punishment: Experimental studies of the role of conditioning and the second signal system in the development of conscience. *Proceedings, XVIIIth International Congress of Psychology, Moscow,* 1966, August.

Aronfreed, J., & Reber, A. Internalized behavioral suppression and the timing of social punishment. *Journal of Personality and Social Psychology,* 1965, **1**, 3–16.

Baier, K. Moral development. *Monist,* 1974, **58**, 601–615.

Bandura, A. Social-learning theory of identificatory processes. In D. A. Goslin & D. C. Glass (Eds.), *Handbook of socialization theory and research.* Chicago: Rand McNally, 1969.

Bandura, A., Grusec, J. E., & Menlove, F. L. Some determinants of self-monitoring reinforcement systems. *Journal of Personality and Social Psychology,* 1967, **5**, 449–455.

Bandura, A., & Huston, A. C. Identification as a process in incidental learning. *Journal of Abnormal and Social Psychology,* 1961, **63**, 311–318.

Bandura, A., & Kupers, C. J. Transmission of patterns of self-reinforcement through modeling. *Journal of Abnormal and Social Psychology,* 1964, **69**, 1–9.

Bandura, A., & MacDonald, F. J. Influence of social reinforcement and the behavior of models in shaping children's moral judgments. *Journal of Abnormal and Social Psychology,* 1963, **67**, 274–281.

Bandura, A., & Perloff, B. Relative efficacy of self-monitored and externally-imposed reinforcement systems. *Journal of Personality and Social Psychology,* 1967, **7**, 111–116.

Bandura, A., & Walters, R. H. *Adolescent aggression.* New York: Ronald Press, 1959.

Bandura, A., & Whalen, C. The influence of antecedent reinforcement and divergent modeling cues on patterns of self-reward. *Journal of Personality and Social Psychology,* 1966, **3**, 373–382.

Baumhart, R. C. How ethical are businessmen? *Harvard Business Review,* 1961, **39**, 6–19.

Bell, R. Q. A reinterpretation of the direction of effects in studies of socialization. *Psychological Review,* 1968, **75**, 81–95.

Bell, R. Q. Stimulus control of parent or caretaker behavior of offspring. *Developmental Psychology,* 1971, **4,** 63–72.

Bem, D. J. Self-perception theory. In L. Berkowitz (Ed.), *Advances in experimental social psychology.* Vol. 6. New York: Academic Press, 1972.

Berlyne, D. E. *Conflict, arousal, and curiosity.* New York: McGraw-Hill, 1960.

Bowlby, J. *Attachment and separation.* New York: Basic Books, 1969.

Brown, A. L. The development of memory: Knowing, knowing about knowing, and knowing how to know. In H. W. Reese (Ed.) *Advances in child development and behavior.* Vol. 10. New York: Academic Press, 1975. Pp. 103–152.

Byan, J. H. Children's cooperation and helping behaviors. In E. M. Hetherington (Ed.), *Review of child development research.* Volume 5. Chicago: University of Chicago Press, 1975. Pp. 127–181.

Burton, R. V. The generality of honesty reconsidered. *Psychological Review,* 1963, **70,** 481–499.

Burton, R. V. Cheating related to maternal pressures for achievement. Unpublished manuscript, Psychology Department, University of Buffalo, 1972.

Burton, R. V., Allinsmith, W., & Maccoby, E. E. Resistance to temptation in relation to sex of child, sex of experimenter, and withdrawal of attention. *Journal of Personality and Social Psychology,* 1966, **3,** 253–258.

Campbell, D. T., & Fiske, D. W. Convergent and discriminant validation by the multitrait-multimethod matrix. *Psychological Bulletin,* 1959, **56,** 81–105.

Cheyne, J. A., Goyeche, J. R. M., & Walters, R. H. Attention, anxiety, and rules in resistance-to-deviation in children. *Journal of Experimental Child Psychology,* 1969, **8,** 127–139.

Cheyne, J. A., & Walters, R. H. Intensity of punishment, timing of punishment, and cognitive structure as determinants of response inhibition. *Journal of Experimental Child Psychology,* 1969, **7,** 231–244.

Colby, A., Speicher, D., & Kohlberg, L. Standard form scoring. Paper presented at the Moral Development and Education Workshop, Harvard University, Cambridge, Mass., 1973.

Collins, W. A. Effect of temporal separation between motivation, aggression, and consequences. *Developmental Psychology,* 1973, **8,** 215–221.

Cowan, P. A., Langer, J., Heavenrich, J., & Nathanson, M. Social learning and Piaget's cognitive theory of moral development. *Journal of Personality and Social Psychology,* 1969, **11,** 261–274.

Crowley, P. M. Effect of training upon objectivity of moral judgment in grade school children. *Journal of Personality and Social Psychology,* 1968, **8,** 228–232.

Damon, W. Early conceptions of positive justice as related to the development of logical operations. *Child Development,* 1975, **46,** 301–312.

DePalma, D. J. Effects of social class, moral orientation, and severity of punishment on boys' moral responses to transgression and generosity. *Developmental Psychology,* 1974, **10,** 890–900.

Dorr, D., & Fay, S. Relative power of symbolic adult and peer models in the modification of children's moral choice behavior. *Journal of Personality and Social Psychology,* 1974, **29,** 335–341.

Easterbrook, J. A. The effect of emotion on cue utilization and the organization of behavior. *Psychological Review,* 1959, **66,** 183–201.

Eron, L. D., Huesmann, L. R., Lefkowitz, M. M., & Walder, L. O. Does television violence cause aggression? *American Psychologist,* 1972, **27,** 253–263.

Festinger, L. *A theory of cognitive dissonance.* Evanston, Ill.: Row, Peterson, 1957.

Fishkin, J., Keniston, K., & MacKinnon, C. Moral reasoning and political ideology. *Journal of Personality and Social Psychology,* 1973, **27**(1), 109–119.

Fodor, E. M. Delinquency and susceptibility to social influence among adolescents as a function of moral development. *Journal of Social Psychology,* 1972, **86**, 257–260.

Fry, P. S. The resistance of temptation: Inhibitory and disinhibitory effects of models in children from India and the United States. *Journal of Cross-Cultural Psychology,* 1975, **6**, 189–202.

Gesell, A. Maturation and infant behavior pattern. *Psychological Review,* 1929, **36**, 307–319.

Glassco, J., Milgram, N. A., & Youniss, J. The stability of training effects on intentionality of moral judgment in children. *Journal of Personality and Social Psychology,* 1970, **14**, 360–365.

Grim, P., Kohlberg, L., & White, S. Some relationships between conscience and attentional processes. *Journal of Personality and Social Psychology,* 1968, **8**, 239–252.

Grinder, R. E. Behavior in a temptation situation and its relation to certain aspects of socialization. Unpublished doctoral dissertation, Harvard University, 1960.

Grusec, J. E. Power and the internalization of self-denial. *Child Development,* 1971, **42**, 93–105.

Grusec, J. E., & Ezrin, S. A. Techniques of punishment and the development of self-criticism. *Child Development,* 1972, **43**, 1273–1288.

Haan, N. Hypothetical and actual moral reasoning in a situation of civil disobedience. *Journal of Personality and Social Psychology,* 1975, **32**, 255–270.

Haan, N., Smith, M. B., & Block, J. Moral reasoning of young adults: Political–social behavior, family background, and personality correlates. *Journal of Personality and Social Psychology,* 1968, **10**, 183–201.

Hartshorne, H., & May, M. S. *Studies in the nature of character.* Vol. I. *Studies in deceit.* Vol. II. *Studies in self-control.* Vol. III. *Studies in the organization of character.* New York: Macmillan, 1928–1930.

Henschel, A. M. The relationship between values and behavior: A developmental hypothesis. *Child Development,* 1971, **42**, 1997–2007.

Hess, E. H. Ethology. In A. M. Freedman & H. I. Kaplan (Eds.), *Comprehensive textbook of psychiatry.* Baltimore: Williams & Wilkins, 1967. Pp. 180–189.

Hoffman, M. L. An interview method for obtaining descriptions of parent-child interaction. *Merrill-Palmer Quarterly,* 1957, **4**, 76–83.

Hoffman, M. L. Power assertion by the parent and its impact on the child. *Child Development,* 1960, **31**, 129–143.

Hoffman, M. L. Childrearing practices and moral development: Generalizations from empirical research. *Child Development,* 1963, **34**, 295–318. (a)

Hoffman, M. L. Parent discipline and the child's consideration for others. *Child Development,* 1963, **34**, 573–588. (b)

Hoffman, M. L. Personality, family structure, and social class as antecedents of parental power assertion. *Child Development,* 1963, **34**, 869–884. (c)

Hoffman, M. L. Conscience, personality, and socialization techniques. *Human Development,* 1970, **13**, 90–126. (a)

Hoffman, M. L. Moral development. In P. H. Mussen (Ed.), *Carmichael's handbook of child psychology.* Vol. 2. New York: Wiley, 1970. (b)

Hoffman, M. L. Discussion of Symposium: Moral judgment and delinquency. Presented at the meeting of the American Psychological Association, Washington, D.C., September 1971. (a)

Hoffman, M. L. Father absence and conscience development. *Developmental Psychology,* 1971, 4, 400–406. (b)

Hoffman, M. L. Identification and conscience development. *Child Development,* 1971, 42, 1071–1082. (c)

Hoffman, M. L. Altruistic behavior and the parent–child relationship. *Journal of Personality and Social Psychology,* 1975, 31(5), 937–943. (a)

Hoffman, M. L. Developmental synthesis of affect and cognition and its implications for altruistic motivation. *Developmental Psychology,* 1975, 11, 607–622. (b)

Hoffman, M. L. Moral internalization, parental power, and the nature of parent-child interaction. *Developmental Psychology,* 1975, 11(2), 228–239. (c)

Hoffman, M. L. Sex differences in empathy and related behaviors. *Psychological Bulletin,* in press.

Hoffman, M. L. Empathy, its development and prosocial implications. In C. B. Keasey (Ed.), *Nebraska Symposium on Motivation,* in press.

Hoffman, M. L., & Saltzstein, H. D. Parental discipline and the child's moral development. *Journal of Personality and Social Psychology,* 1967, 5, 45–57.

Holstein, C. B. The relation of children's moral judgment level to that of their parents and to communications patterns in the family. In R. C. Smart & M. S. Smart (Eds.), *Reading in child development and relationships.* New York: Macmillan, 1972.

Holstein, C. B. Irreversible stepwise sequence in the development of moral judgment: A longitudinal study of males and females. *Child Development,* 1976, 47, 51–61.

Hudgins, W., & Prentice, N. Moral judgment in delinquent and nondelinquent adolescents and their mothers. *Journal of Abnormal Psychology,* 1973, 82, 145–152.

Imamoglu, E. O. Children's awareness and usage of intention cues. *Child Development,* 1975, 46, 39–45.

Kausler, D. H., & Trapp, E. P. Motivation and cue utilization in intentional and incidental learning. *Psychological Review,* 1960, 67, 373–379.

Kohlberg, L. The development of modes of moral thinking and choice in the years 10 to 16. Unpublished doctoral dissertation, University of Chicago, 1958.

Kohlberg, L. The contribution of developmental psychology to education—examples from moral education. *Educational Psychologist,* 1973, 10(1).

Kohlberg, L. The cognitive-developmental approach: New developments and a response to criticism. Paper presented at the meeting of the Society for Research in Child Development, Denver, March 1975.

Kohlberg, L. Moral stages and moralization: The cognitive-developmental approach. In T. Likona (Ed.), *Moral developmental and behavior.* New York: Holt, 1976.

Kohlberg, L., & Kramer, R. Continuities and discontinuities in childhood and adult moral development. *Human Development,* 1969, 12, 93–120.

Kohn, M. L. Social class and parental values. *American Journal of Sociology,* 1959, 64, 337–351.

Krebs, R. L. Some relationships between moral judgment, attention, and resistance to temptation. Unpublished doctoral dissertation, University of Chicago, 1968.

Kurtines, W., & Greif, E. B. The development of moral thought: Review and evaluation of Kohlberg's approach. *Psychological Bulletin,* 1974, 81, 453–470.

Landauer, T. K., Carlsmith, J. M., & Lepper, J. Experimental analyses of the factors determining obedience of four-year-old children to adult females. *Child Development,* 1970, 41, 601–611.

Langer, J. Disequilibrium as a source of development. In P. H. Mussen, J. Langer, & M. Covington (Eds.), *Trends and issues in developmental psychology.* New York: Holt, 1969.

LaVoie, J. C. Punishment and adolescent self-control. *Developmental Psychology,* 1973, **8**, 16–24.

LaVoie, J. C. Cognitive determinants of resistance to deviation in seven-, nine-, and eleven-year-old children of low and high maturity of moral judgment. *Developmental Psychology,* 1974, **10**, 393–403. (a)

LaVoie, J. C. Type of punishment as a determinant of resistance to deviation. *Developmental Psychology,* 1974, **10**, 181–189. (b)

Leizer, J. I., & Rogers, R. W. Effects of method of discipline, timing of punishment, and timing of test on resistance to temptation. *Child Development,* 1974, **45**, 790–793.

Lepper, M. R., & Greene, D. Turning work into play: Effects of adult surveillance and extrinsic rewards on children's intrinsic motivation. *Journal of Personality and Social Psychology,* 1973, **28**, 129–137.

Lerner, M. J. The justice motive in social behavior. *Journal of Social Issues,* 1975, **31**, 1–20.

Liebert, R. M., & Ora, J. P., Jr. Children's adoption of self-reward patterns: Incentive level and method of transmission. *Child Development,* 1968, **39**, 537–544.

Lorenz, K. Z. *Evolution and modification of behavior.* Chicago: University of Chicago Press, 1965.

Lytton, H., & Zwirner, W. Compliance and its controlling stimuli in a national setting. *Developmental Psychology,* 1975, **11**, 769–779.

Maccoby, E. E. The generality of moral behavior. *American Psychologist,* 1959, **14**, 358. (Abstract)

MacKinnon, D. W. Violation of prohibitions. In H. W. Murray (Ed.), *Exploration in personality.* New York: Oxford University Press, 1938. Pp. 491–501.

Maslow, A. H. *Motivation and personality.* New York: Harper, 1954.

Milgram, S. Behavioral study of obedience. *Journal of Personality and Social Psychology,* 1963, **67**, 371–378.

Minton, C., Kagan, J., & Levine, J. Maternal control and obedience in the two-year-old. *Child Development,* 1971, **42**, 1873–1894.

Mischel, W., & Mischel, H. N. A cognitive-social learning approach to morality and self-regulation. In T. Likona (Ed.), *Moral development and behavior.* New York: Holt, 1976.

Moir, D. J. Egocentrism and the emergence of conventional morality in preadolescent girls. *Child Development,* 1974, **45**, 299–304.

Moss, H. Sex, age, and state as determinants of mother-infant interaction. *Merrill-Palmer Quarterly,* 1967, **13**, 19–26.

Mowrer, O. H. *Learning theory and behavior.* New York: Wiley, 1960.

Mussen, P., Harris, S., Rutherford, E., & Keasey, C. B. Honesty and altruism among preadolescents. *Developmental Psychology,* 1970, **3**, 169–194.

Nelson, E. A., Grinder, R. E., & Challas, J. H. Resistance to temptation and moral judgment: Behavioral correlates of Kohlberg's measure of moral development. Mimeographed paper, University of Wisconsin, 1968.

Nelson, E. A., Grinder, R. E., & Mutterer, M. L. Sources of variance in behavioral measures on honesty in temptation situations: Methodological analyses. *Developmental Psychology,* 1969, **1**, 265–279.

Otten, A. L. Politics and people. *Wall Street Journal,* 1974, April 11.

Peters, R. S. Moral development: A plea for pluralism. In T. Mischel (Ed.), *Cognitive development and epistemology.* New York: Academic Press, 1971. Pp. 237–267.

Piaget, J. *The moral judgment of the child.* New York: Harcourt, 1932.

Reiss, A. Social organization and socialization: Variations on a theme about generations. Mimeographed paper, Department of Sociology, University of Michigan, 1966.

Rest, J. R. The hierarchical nature of moral judgment: A study of patterns of comprehension and preference of moral stages. *Journal of Personality*, 1973, **41**, 86–109.

Rosenhan, D. Some origins of concern for others. In P. H. Mussen, J. Langer, & M. Covington (Eds.), *Trends and issues in developmental psychology*. New York: Holt, 1969.

Rosenhan, D., & White, G. N. Observation and rehearsal as determinants of prosocial behavior. *Journal of Personality and Social Psychology*, 1967, **5**, 424–431.

Rosenkoetter, L. I. Resistance to temptation: Inhibitory and disinhibitory effects of models. *Developmental Psychology*, 1973, **8**, 80–84.

Ross, M., & DiTecco, D. An attributional analysis of moral judgments. *Journal of Social Issues*, 1975, **31**, 91–110.

Rule, B. G., Nesdale, A. R., & McAra, M. J. Children's reactions to information about the intentions underlying an aggressive act. *Child Development*, 1974, **45**, 794–798.

Saltzstein, H. D., Diamond, R. M., & Belenky, M. Moral judgment level and conformity behavior. *Developmental Psychology*, 1972, **7**, 327–336.

Sanford, R. N. Individual and social change in a community under pressure: The oath controversy. *Journal of Social Issues*, 1953, **9**, 25–42.

Schachter, S., & Singer, J. E. Cognitive, social and physiological determinants of emotional state. *Psychological Review*, 1962, **69**, 379–399.

Schoggen, P. Environmental forces in the everyday lives of children. In R. G. Barker (Ed.), *The stream of behavior: Explorations of its structure and content*. New York: Appleton, 1963.

Schwartz, S. H., Feldman, K. A., Brown, M. E., & Heingartner, A. Some personality correlates of conduct in two situations of moral conflict. *Journal of Personality*, 1969, **37**, 41–57.

Sears, R. R. Dependency motivation. In M. R. Jones (Ed.). *Nebraska symposium on motivation*. Lincoln: University of Nebraska Press, 1963. Pp. 25–36.

Sears, R. R., Rau, L., & Alpert, R. *Identification and child rearing*. Stanford: Stanford University Press, 1965.

Selman, R. The relation of role taking to the development of moral judgments in children. *Child Development*, 1971, **42**, 79–91.

Sgan, M. L. Social reinforcement, socioeconomic status, and susceptibility to experimenter influence. *Journal of Personality and Social Psychology*, 1967, **5**, 202–210.

Simmel, G. The number of members as determining the sociological form of the group. *American Journal of Sociology*, 1902, **8**, 1–46.

Simmons, H., & Schoggen, P. Mothers and fathers as sources of environmental pressures on children. In R. G. Barker (Ed.), *The stream of behavior: Explorations of its structure and content*. New York: Appleton-Century Crofts, 1963.

Simpson, E. L. Moral development research: A case study of scientific cultural bias. *Human Development*, 1974, **17**, 81–106.

Staub, E. Helping a distressed person: Social, personality, and stimulus determinants. In L. Berkowitz (Ed.), *Advances in experimental social psychology*. Vol. 7. New York: Academic Press, 1974.

Stein, A. H. Imitation of resistance to temptation. *Child Development*, 1967, **38**, 157–169.

Sternlieb, J. L., & Youniss, J. Moral judgments one year after intentional or consequence modeling. *Journal of Personality and Social Psychology*, 1975, **31**, 895–897.

Tomlinson-Keasey, C., & Keasey, C. Formal operations and moral development. Paper presented at the meeting of the American Psychological Association, Honolulu, September 1972.

Tracy, J. J., & Cross, H. J. Antecedents of shift in moral judgment. *Journal of Personality and Social Psychology*, 1973, **26**, 238–244.

Tulkin, S. R., & Kagan, J. Mother-infant interaction in the first year of life. *Child Development*, 1972, **43**, 31–42.

Tulving, E. Episodic and semantic memory. In E. Tulving & W. Donaldson (Eds.), *Organization of memory*. New York: Academic Press, 1972. Pp. 381–403.

Turiel, E. An experimental test of the sequentiality of developmental stages in the child's moral judgments. *Journal of Personality and Social Psychology*, 1966, **3**, 611–618.

Walters, R. G., & Dembow, L. Timing of punishment as a determinant of response inhibition. *Child Development*, 1963, **34**, 207–214.

Walters, R. H., Parke, R. D., & Cane, V. A. Timing of punishment and the observation of consequence to others as determinants of response inhibition. *Journal of Experimental Child Psychology*, 1965, **2**, 10–30.

White, M. S. Social class, child-rearing practices, and child behavior. *American Sociological Review*, 1957, **22**, 704–712.

White, R. W. Motivation reconsidered: The concept of competence. *Psychological Review*, 1959, **66**, 297–333.

Wrong, D. H. The oversocialized conception of man. *American Sociology Review*, 1961, **26**, 183–193.

Zussman, J. U. Demographic factors influencing parental discipline techniques. Paper presented at the meeting of the American Psychological Association, Chicago, September 1975.

SOME EFFECTS OF VIOLENT AND NONVIOLENT MOVIES ON THE BEHAVIOR OF JUVENILE DELINQUENTS[1]

Ross D. Parke,[2] Leonard Berkowitz,[3]
Jacques P. Leyens,[4] Stephen G. West,[5]
and Richard J. Sebastian[6]

[1] The research reported in this chapter was supported by National Institute of Mental Health Grant MH 17955 from the Center for the Study of Crime and Delinquency to Leonard Berkowitz and Ross D. Parke. Preparation of this report was assisted by National Science Foundation Soc 72-05-220A03 to Parke. A large number of individuals contributed to this project. We are grateful to Lloyd Mixdorf and Roland Hershman, Assistant Superintendant and Superintendant, respectively, of the Wisconsin School for Boys at Wales, for their fine cooperation in the conduct of the American phases of this research and to Thomas Bassett, James Cowden, and Asher Pacht for their general assistance throughout our research programs.

For assistance in the conduct of the Belgian phase of the program we wish to thank S. Vanderelst, Director, and A. Louvet, Psychologist, of the Foyer de Roucourt, for their cooperation, Leoncio Camino for his able assistance in the execution of this project, and Bernard Rime for his critical suggestions. And finally we thank the individuals who participated in this series of investigations. To these young men and women, we dedicate this chapter.

[2] University of Illinois, Urbana, Illinois.
[3] University of Wisconsin, Madison, Wisconsin.
[4] University of Louvain, Louvain, Belgium.
[5] Florida State University, Tallahassee.
[6] University of Notre Dame, Notre Dame, Indiana.

I. Introduction

Few recent topics in social psychology have generated as much controversy as the impact of exposure to film and television violence on the behavior of observers. Although a large number of laboratory investigations have demonstrated that viewing aggression can increase subsequent viewer aggression, skeptics have seriously questioned the generalizability of these laboratory-derived results to real-life situations (Howitt & Cumberbatch, 1975; Klapper, 1968).

The purpose of studies to be reviewed in this chapter was to provide a more adequate test of the effects of exposure to movie violence in a naturalistic setting. Three field experiments are described in which adolescent boys are exposed to several full-length unedited commercial films in their usual environment. Observations of interpersonal aggression formed the basis for the dependent indices. By this approach, it was hoped some of the usual problems of generalizability would be overcome. We first turn to a brief examination of these problems, as well as a review and critique of previous field experimental studies of movie violence.

II. Problems in Generalizing from Laboratory Studies

There are many factors that limit the generalization of laboratory results to naturalistic contexts. In considering the effects of movie violence, however, four problems merit special attention: the nature of the stimulus materials, the frequency of exposure to violent stimuli, the type of viewing context, and the choice of dependent measure.

A. STIMULUS MATERIALS

Two types of media stimuli have typically been employed in experimental laboratory investigations of the effects of film or TV violence on aggression.

First, investigators have experimentally produced films designed to test a particular theoretical issue (e.g., Bandura, Ross, & Ross, 1963; Hartmann, 1969); the extent to which these film sequences characterize ecologically valid film and TV materials has not been determined. The second type of stimulus materials which are commonly employed are edited versions of either commercial films (Berkowitz, 1965; Walters & Llewellyn-Thomas, 1963) or TV programs (e.g., Liebert & Baron, 1972). Typically, a limited and usually violent episode is excerpted from the full-length film or program, such as the boxing match from *The Champion* or the knife fight scene from *Rebel Without a Cause*. It is assumed that these film excerpts will have the same impact on observers as the full-length unedited version. However, this assumption is questionable since the effect of viewing an isolated violent film clip may be different from the consequences of watching an entire film. First, the context in which the sequence is embedded may alter the interpretation of the violence, which, in turn, may affect the subsequent behavior of the viewer. The type of plot, the events before and after the critical clip, and the mood shifts produced by the film may all affect the viewer reaction, as studies of justification of violence (Berkowitz, 1965) and response consequences (Bandura, 1965) have demonstrated. In short, it cannot be assumed that the edited film clips used in the laboratory and full-length films or programs viewed under naturalistic viewing conditions produce similar effects; consequently, results from laboratory studies may have only limited generalizability to the impact of film and TV violence in real-life settings.

B. FREQUENCY OF EXPOSURE

The second problem that arises in generalizing from laboratory investigations of the effects of film violence on aggression to naturalistic situations concerns the frequency of exposure to the stimulus materials. In the typical laboratory investigation, subjects are presented with a single exposure to film violence and then tested for aggression. The usual assumption underlying the generalization of conclusions from the laboratory studies to naturalistic viewing contexts is that the sight of a single display has the same kind of effect, although perhaps somewhat weakened, that repeated exposure to aggressive stimuli produces. This may be termed the cumulative impact hypothesis, which is derived from an additive model suggesting that the probability of aggression increases in a monotonic manner with repeated exposure to film violence. However, there is no compelling empirical basis for such a contention. In fact, the effects of frequent or long-term exposure may be quite different from the effect of a briefer exposure to filmed violence. One possible alternative result of repeated viewing is satiation or habituation to the film violence; rather than producing a heightened probability of aggressive consequences, such a satiation effect might well *lessen* the likelihood that observed aggression will elicit aggressive responses. There is a growing body of evidence in support of the satiation principle (cf.

Gewirtz, 1967), which predicts that continuous or repeated presentation of various stimuli reduces their capacity to evoke their associated responses. Based on this principle, one might hypothesize that frequent exposure to aggressive stimuli will lessen their ability to elicit aggressive behaviors.

Although the impact of repeated presentations of aggressive scenes has received little attention, some investigators have examined the effects of this type of exposure on emotionality of viewers. For example, Cline, Croft, and Courrier (1973) found that children who are frequent TV users showed less emotional reactivity to aggressive displays than children who see TV less often. Tannenbaum (1972) exposed subjects to aggressive stimuli on four occasions in the form of either brief violent excerpts and/or still photographs taken from an excerpt the subjects had previously viewed. Although not statistically significant, there was a habituation trend over trials. More conclusive evidence comes from a recent experiment by Averill, Malmstrom, Koriat, and Lazarus (1972), who showed college subjects 20 presentations of an isolated accident scene from a movie. Habituation, as indexed by skin conductance heart rate and self-reported distress, was found, not only for the isolated scene, but for the scene embedded in the complete film. Similar findings of decreased emotional responsivity as a result of repeated exposure have been found for erotic materials as well (Howard, Reifler, & Liptzin, 1971). Together, these studies suggest that repeated exposure to emotionally arousing material may lessen physiological reactions to stimuli of this class. However, other research (Lang, 1968) indicates that cognitive, emotional, and behavioral response systems should be treated independently; therefore, emotional habituation to a class of stimuli does not necessarily imply that behavioral and cognitive reactions will be similarly affected. In fact, Menzies (1972) recently found that repeated observation of violent movies increased acceptance and approval of aggressive tactics for solving social conflict. Anxiety reactions might conceivably decline more rapidly than aggressive ones with repeated exposure, so that for a while the likelihood of overt aggression actually increases. It is clear that further research on the behavioral effects of repeated exposure to filmed aggression is required.

C. THE GROUP VIEWING CONTEXT

Another feature that often differs between field and laboratory contexts is the nature of the viewing situation. In most laboratory studies individuals see the film alone, whereas in a typical field setting other people are watching the scene as well. Freidson (1953), for example, noted that television was usually viewed in a family situation, whereas movie watching involved the presence of peers. Maccoby (1951) also reported that television serves to bring family members physically closer together.

What are the effects of group observation? Hicks (1968) found that the presence of adults who either approved or disapproved of the televised model's aggression affected the subsequent behavior of child viewers. Specifically, adult approval led to an increased amount of viewer imitation, whereas adult disapproval of the TV model inhibited aggressive behavior.

More recently, Martin, Gelfand, and Hartmann (1971) exposed children to a play situation in the presence of an adult, or a peer, or when they were alone, after they observed an aggressive model. The data showed that the presence of an adult served as an inhibiting cue, but having a same-sexed peer nearby disinhibited aggression in comparison to the control group.

It is reasonable to think that the audience has reinforcing value for the subject; the others in the room may facilitate as well as inhibit aggressive reactions depending on the type of reinforcement that would be provided. In that sense "the effect of an observer's presence is apparently more a function of *who* is watching (i.e., observing) than simply whether or not *anyone* is watching" (Borden, 1975). It is clear that the impact of group viewing vs. individual viewing needs to be closely examined with particular attention to the *nature* of the co-viewing group.

D. DEPENDENT INDEX

A fourth feature of laboratory paradigms that might limit their generalizability has to do with the dependent measures of aggression they have employed. Criticisms have been leveled against the use of physical attack against an inanimate object, such as a Bobo doll, as a measure of aggression (Hartley, 1964; Klapper, 1968); it is typically argued that the measure is play activity which may bear little or no relationship to interpersonal aggression directed against another individual. There have been attempts to overcome these criticisms in recent years. First, a number of studies have demonstrated similar effects where the target of aggression is a human dressed as a clown (e.g., Hanratty, Liebert, Morris, & Fernandez, 1969; Hanratty, O'Neal, & Sulzer, 1972; Savitsky, Rogers, Izard, & Liebert, 1971). Perhaps more importantly, a number of studies have indicated that Bobo doll training does transfer to interpersonal situations (Walters & Brown, 1963) and that children with high hitting rates against a Bobo doll are judged as typically aggressive by their peers (Dubanoski & Kong, 1973). In short, as social learning theory maintains, aggressive responses may be acquired in "play contexts" but still be performed through transfer to interpersonal contexts (Bandura, 1969, 1973). By maintaining the acquisition—performance distinction, both the relevance and contribution of these Bobo doll studies might be more clearly recognized.

A second type of dependent index that has been extensively used in laboratory experiments is the Buss aggression machine (Buss, 1961), whereby an individual has an opportunity to deliver electric shocks to another person. Variations of this general procedure have been developed for studies with children in which a loud noise is substituted for the electric shock (Williams,

Meyerson, Eron, & Semler, 1967). In spite of the criticism that these situations are of questionable ecological validity, there have been a number of recent demonstrations of the validity of both the adult and child procedures. Both Berkowitz, Parke, Leyens, and West (1974) and Shemberg, Leventhal, and Allman (1968) found positive relationships between counselor ratings of adolescent boys and the intensity of electric shock delivered by the boys in the Buss situation. Similarly, Williams *et al.* (1967) reported that children who were rated aggressive by their peers were especially likely to deliver noxious noises to their peers in an experimental task. But in spite of these demonstrations researchers have increasingly sought to investigate the effects of exposure to media violence on interpersonal behavior in naturalistic contexts. We next turn to these field studies.

III. Previous Field Experimental Research

There have been a number of previous field experimental investigations of the effects of exposure to movie violence. However, they fail to yield a very consistent picture, and a close examination of these efforts is necessary before describing our own work in this area.

One of the earliest, most ambitious projects, and the study that is most closely related to our own investigations, is the Feshbach and Singer (1971) field experiment. The TV diets of 9- to 15-year-old boys attending seven residential schools and institutions were controlled for a 6-week period. During this time the boys were required to watch at least 6 hours of TV per week. Half of the boys were on an aggressive program diet (e.g., "Branded," "Gunsmoke," "Combat"), while the remaining boys watched nonaggressive programs (e.g., "Amateur Hour," "The Dick Van Dyke Show"). The major dependent measures of aggression were observer ratings in the form of behavior checklists made by the boys' supervisors. Contrary to the aggression activation hypothesis, Feshbach and Singer found no evidence that televised violence leads to increases in aggression. In fact, they found lowered aggression among highly aggressive working-class boys who had been exposed to violent TV programs. However, the study has been criticized on a number of methodological grounds (Bandura, 1973; Liebert, Sobol, & Davidson, 1972). In summarizing a number of the criticisms, Stein and Friedrich (1975, p. 203) note:

> The two groups differed in aggression from the beginning of the viewing period, and there was no way of knowing whether this difference existed before viewing. Little information was obtained on the amount of previous television viewing or program preferences, nor was the amount of viewing during the experiment carefully monitored. Complaints from boys with the nonviolent diet made it clear, however, that their assigned programs were less attractive than the violent

programs. Their increased aggression may have resulted from the resentment generated by deprivation of their television favorites and from boredom created by the unavailability of their usual television fare. When adolescent boys have nothing to do, they are likely to engage in fights, rough-house play, and complaints.

In addition, ratings, not behavioral observations, were used which could be easily biased by single aggressive incidents or by general attitudes toward the boys. Observer bias was a potential problem as well, since supervisors, not outside observers, made the ratings. In light of these criticisms and the marked inconsistency between these findings of Feshbach and Singer and earlier theory and data, this study afforded no resolution of the movie violence—behavior issue.

Wells (1973), in a replication of the Feshbach and Singer experiment, attempted to overcome some of these methodological shortcomings in an extensive study of ten residential schools. First, the experimental and control groups were matched for their initial levels of aggression. Second, the boys' behavior was assessed during a baseline period. Third, behavior ratings were made not only by the institution staff but also by nonparticipant trained observers. Wells found that there were few differences in aggression as a function of the type of TV fare. Contrary to the Feshbach—Singer results, there was no decrease in aggression but a slight increase in physical aggression. However, to cloud the issue further, in both of these field studies the TV diet manipulations involved depriving some of the boys of their usual TV fare, mostly aggressive programs. In other words, these studies, actually evaluated the dual impact of *both* exposure to neutral programs as well as the inability to view the customary aggressive programs.

A methodologically superior effort by Friedrich and Stein (1973) appeared soon after these investigations. Friedrich and Stein exposed nursery school children to aggressive, neutral, or prosocial programs over a 4-week period. Interpersonal behavior, including aggression, was measured by outside observers during a 3-week baseline period, the 4-week viewing period, and during a 2-week follow-up. Results indicated that those children who were above the group median for aggressive behavior during the baseline interval were affected by the aggressive films. Specifically, these children were more aggressive after exposure to violent movies than were children who saw neutral films. Subjects who were below the median in their aggressiveness during the baseline period did not differ as a function of exposure to aggressive films. Still, the results of this study must be interpreted cautiously due to the statistical problem of regression toward the mean. Moreover, a recent study by Sawin (1973), using lower-class nursery school children failed to verify these findings. In fact, Sawin found no difference between the violent and nonviolent movie groups.

To add to an already uncertain picture, Milgram and Shotland (1973) reported a series of field experimental studies of the effects of TV exposure on various forms of antisocial behavior, such as stealing, and found no differences in social behavior among viewers. On the basis of these inconclusive results, further field investigations are clearly necessary to clarify the effects of aggressive films on observers' behavior.

IV. The Present Investigations

In addition to providing a more adequate evaluation of the impact of movie violence on observer behavior in a naturalistic setting, the series of investigations considered here was designed to assess the impact of movie violence on a particular subject population: juvenile delinquents. There has been little research on the effects of movie violence on this population to date. Such investigation is important for two reasons: First, it will permit an assessment of the assumption that individuals with a prior history of violent offenses will be more strongly affected by film violence than are individuals with a less violent history. Second, an assessment of the susceptibility of juvenile delinquents, as a group, to observed aggression may yield some clues concerning the antecedents of aggressive-delinquent behavior. In addition to these theoretical justifications, however, there is also a methodological reason for this choice of subject population. The use of institutionalized participants enabled us to control the boys' viewing experiences and also gave us opportunities to observe the subjects in their daily environments. All of the studies involved repeated exposure to either aggressive or nonaggressive, commercially available, unedited films shown in a naturalistic situation; the dependent measures were the interpersonal behaviors of the boys as assessed by trained observers in the youngsters' normal daily environment.

Three field experimental studies were conducted—two in the United States and one in Belgium. All the studies used a similar type of design, as well as similar behavioral observation procedures.

A. FIRST AMERICAN STUDY

In our American field experiments, the research site was a minimum security penal institution for juvenile offenders. The boys, ranging in age from 14 to 18 years, were mainly white (68%), with a sizable black minority (26%). The basic living unit in the institution is the self-sufficient and self-contained cottage to which approximately 30 boys are randomly assigned by the institution. From a research viewpoint this provided a relatively ideal setting, since the observations and manipulations could be executed in these units.

1. Design

The design of the study involved four phases of observations and measures over a total time span of 7 weeks. During the first phase, a 3-week baseline period, pairs of trained observers recorded the behavior of the boys in each of two cottages for approximately 2 hours a day on 3 consecutive days a week.

The next phase was a 5-day experimental period. On each weekday boys in one cottage saw an aggressive movie on each evening, while boys in a second cottage watched a neutral nonaggressive film. Behavioral observations were made each evening before, during, and after the movies. In addition, the boys rated the movies on a series of 5-point scales in terms of aggressiveness (brutal, violent, aggressive, cruel) and interest (boring, interesting, funny, exciting, silly, stupid). Ratings were made after each movie and again at the end of the movie week. TV watching was eliminated during this phase.

On the day following the final film the boys from both cottages participated in a laboratory assessment of aggression (the amount of electric shock delivered to a confederate) under either angered or nonangered conditions.

The fourth and final phase was a 3-week follow-up period, which was included to assess the long-term effects of the movies on the boys' social behavior. As in the baseline period, behavioral observations were obtained on three consecutive evenings for each of the 3 weeks.

2. Observational Procedure

A brief description of the observational system and categories is necessary in order to fully understand this project. A nonhierarchical, minimally inferential, time-sampling observational procedure was employed. Each boy in each cottage was to be observed for three consecutive 30-second intervals at two separate times each evening, for an evening's total of 3 minutes. The order in which the boys were observed was randomly determined, with new random orders generated daily for each of the observers.

The observational record considered 14 behavioral categories, the descriptions of which are given in Table I. Since aggression was the main dependent variable of interest, 8 of the 14 categories pertained to different forms of aggression. All other social or nonsocial behaviors could be coded into one of the remaining 6 categories. An activity measure was included because it has been found to be related to aggression, at least for young children (Patterson, Littman, & Bricker, 1967).

In addition to these observations, the observers also recorded the behavior of the boys during the showing of the movies. The observers recorded the occurrence of ten different overt behaviors every 30 seconds. The behaviors recorded during the movies are (1) shouting; (2) laughter; (3) talking; (4) leaving the room; (5) clapping; (6) foot stamping; (7) shifting chairs; (8) pushing–shoving (9) poking; and (10) changing seats. Each behavior was recorded only once in each 30-second interval, and a *group* score was derived from these observations.

University of Wisconsin undergraduates served as observers. Training in use of the observational code began 1 week prior to the onset of the study; after the observers had learned the code, two practice sessions were held at the institution

TABLE I
OBSERVATIONAL CATEGORIES

1. *Social Request* (SR)—making a request from another person or counselor
   (e.g., "Give me some candy"; "Move over"; "What is the score?")
2. *Yell* (Y)—yelling loudly with or without communicative value
3. *Physical Threat* (PT)—attack without physical contact; fist waving, fist threatening
4. *Physical Attack* (PA)—physical contact of sufficient intensity to potentially inflict pain
   on the victim (e.g., hitting, slapping, choking, kicking)
5. *Verbal Aggression* (VA)—verbal interaction with hostile intent such as namecalling,
   teasing, taunting, and humiliating; or cursing if directed toward another person
6. *Noninterpersonal Physical Aggression* (NPA)—damaging or destroying an
   object or attempting to hit or kick it
7. *Noninterpersonal Verbal Aggression* (NVA)—an angry outburst or cursing
   but with no clear social target
8. *Self-Aggression Verbal* (SAV)—an aggressive statement directed to
   oneself (e.g., "Boy, am I crazy!")
9. *Self-Aggression Physical* (SAP)—hitting oneself on head or jumping
   around wildly when disappointed
10. *Alone-Active* (AA)—walking, running, or playing an active game
11. *Alone-Passive* (AP)—sitting, lying, sleeping, or waiting silently in line
12. *Social Interaction Active* (SIA)—playing ping-pong, pool, or basketball
13. *Social Interaction Passive* (SIP)—playing cards, monopoly, or talking
14. *Television* (TV)—watching TV

to insure that the observers were in agreement. Inter-rater reliabilities ranged from 80 to 100% in one cottage and from 95 to 100% in the other cottage. Prior to the first visit of the observers to the institution, the counselors were instructed to tell the boys the schedule of the observers and to assure the boys that the observers were merely interested in finding out what goes on daily in the cottage recreational rooms. The counselors were also instructed to inform the boys at this time that they were to be paid $5.00 for their participation.

Ten commercially available, unedited movies were selected for use in this first study. The following aggressive movies were shown: *The Chase, Death Rides a Horse, The Champion, Corruption,* and *Ride Beyond Vengeance.* The nonaggressive films were *Buenna Serra Mrs. Campbell, Ride the Wild Surf, Countdown, Beach Blanket Bingo,* and *A Countess from Hong Kong.* Content analyses of these movies indicated that the aggressive films contained significantly more interpersonal physical and noninterpersonal physical aggression. On the other hand, the nonaggressive movies depicted significantly more dancing and bathing suit incidents than their violent counterparts. This latter difference is largely attributable to the movies *Beach Blanket Bingo* and *Ride the Wild Surf.* Not only did the movies differ in their content, but the viewers perceived the movies differently as well. The boys rated the aggressive films as more brutal, violent, aggressive, and cruel than the neutral ones. Unfortunately, the nonaggressive movies were also rated as less exciting, less likeable, and more boring and silly. We were clearly only partially successful in our film selection and, as a result, movie content and audience interest were confounded in the first study.

These ratings are consistent with the boys' behavior during the film presentations. The aggressive movie viewers engaged in more yelling $[t(8) = 5.45; p < .01]$, talking $[t(8) = 3.16; p < .05]$, and seat changing $[t(8) = 6.18; p < .001]$ than did those who watched the nonaggressive movies. Moreover, there were trends $(p < .10)$ toward greater laughing and clapping, as well as more pushing, shoving, and poking, among the boys who saw the aggressive movies.

Correlational analyses indicated positive relationships between the interest ratings and the viewer behavior during the film showings. These findings yield a consistent picture: the aggressive movies were both more interesting and exciting than the neutral films.

3. Results

What were the effects of watching the aggressive and nonaggressive movies on the boys' subsequent social behavior?

The fourteen behavior categories which constituted the observational code were combined to form the following composite indices: (1) the *general aggression index* (GA), which was the sum of the rates for physical threat, physical attack, verbal aggression, noninterpersonal physical and verbal aggression, and physical and verbal self-aggression; (2) the *physical aggression index* (PA), which combined all measures of physical aggression including physical attack, noninterpersonal physical aggression, and physical self-aggresion; (3) the *interpersonal verbal and physical aggression index* (PVA) consisted of only interpersonal physical attack and verbal aggression.

An initial analysis of variance of the rates, with two levels of one "between" factor (aggressive or nonaggressive movies) and three levels of one "within" factor (premovie weeks, movie week, or postmovie weeks) yielded results which indicated baseline differences between the two cottages in aggression. The boys in the cottage receiving the aggressive movie treatment were initially more aggressive than the boys in the cottage shown the nonaggressive films. It was therefore necessary to carry out analyses which would statistically eliminate these initial baseline differences in order to assess the effects of the movies. An adjustment by subclassification procedure recommended by Cochran (1968) was adopted. In this procedure subject are placed in classes (high, low) on the basis of their baseline scores. This technique not only eliminates baseline differences but also permits comparisons between levels of behavior at subsequent time periods and the level during the baseline. This analysis by subclassification procedure was employed in all of the analyses of the observational data.

The boys who saw the aggressive movies were significantly more aggressive than were those who saw the nonaggressive ones, with a variety of measures including the general aggression index $[F(1,33) = 8.61; p < .05$; see Fig. 1], the physical and verbal aggression index $[F(1,33) = 4.13; p < 0.61$; see Fig. 2], or the physical aggression measure $[F(1,33) = 5.94; p < .05]$. In addition, there were no interactions between baseline levels of aggression and the subsequent impact of the films. Both high and low aggressive viewers were affected by the movie violence. In some cases (physical aggression index), we should also note, it was the low aggressive boys rather than the high aggressive individuals who were most affected immediately after viewing the movies. While the results generally support the hypothesis that exposure to film violence increases subsequent aggression, there was no clear evidence concerning the impact of predispositional factors, such as level of prior aggression, on viewer reactions. Moreover, there was no cumulative impact of seeing movies each night of the experimental period. Had there been a cumulative effect, we would have expected more aggression during the last part of the week than during the earlier days of exposure. Comparisons between the first 3 and last 2 days of this period revealed no differences.

Nor are the effects due simply to an increase in activity level among the boys who saw the aggressive movies. In fact, the adolescents who saw the *nonaggressive* movies participated in more active social interaction than did the boys who watched the aggressive films $[F(1,31) = 4.48; p < .05]$. The boys in the aggressive movie group engaged in more solitary activity (playing alone, reading, etc.) than did their counterparts in the other group $(F(1,31) = 5.96; p < .05]$.

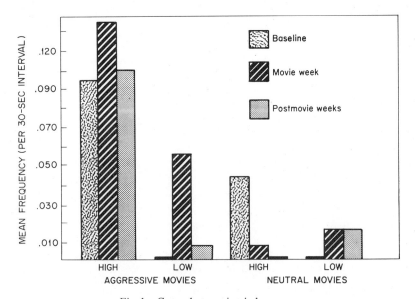

Fig. 1.   General aggression index.

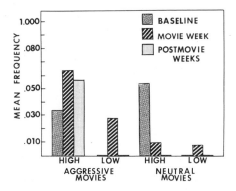

Fig. 2.   Interpersonal physical and verbal aggression index.

Finally, the effects of the films were reexamined after controlling for the amount of social interaction by use of the following ratio score:

$$\frac{PVA}{PVA + SIA + SIP}$$

Consistent with the earlier analyses, subjects who saw the aggressive movies displayed more interpersonal aggression than viewers of nonaggressive films $[F(1,33) = 4.21; p < .05]$.

In summary, the observational data provide some support for the hypothesis that exposure to movie violence increases subsequent aggressive behavior among viewers.

4. Laboratory Phase

On the Saturday following the movie week a laboratory measure of aggression was obtained. A modified Buss (1961) procedure was employed. One-half of the boys from each of the movie treatments was insulted by the confederate under the pretense of evaluating their performance on a test of "common sense," whereas the other half received a neutral evaluation (cf. Hartmann, 1969). Afterwards, all the subjects were given an opportunity to deliver shocks to the confederate whenever he made a mistake in his task. These shocks could vary in intensity from 1 to 10.

The yield from this phase was small. The initial data analysis revealed no overall significant effects for the intensity of shock index. However, evaluation of the confederate feedback tapes used for the insult–no-insult manipulation indicated that the insult manipulation was successful only in the case of one of the two confederates. The second confederate delivered his evaluation in a very mild, noninsulting tone. Consequently, a further analysis was executed, using only the data from the first (effective) confederate. This analysis yielded a borderline interaction between film condition and type of evaluation [$F(1,22) =$ 3.12; $p < .10$]. As can be seen in Fig. 3, the boys who viewed the aggressive movies were more aggressive following an insulting evaluation than the boys in the other three conditions. Although this result must be interpreted cautiously, the similarity between this interaction pattern and previous results from Berkowitz's laboratory is noteworthy. Across a wide range of experiments, it has been found that increases in aggression are most likely to occur when subjects are both insulted and exposed to an aggression-eliciting cue such as an aggressive film (Berkowitz, 1970, 1973).

In light of the problems and limitations of the first study, a second investigation was executed which attempted to overcome some of the shortcomings of the initial field experiment. Next we turn to an examination of this second study.

B. SECOND AMERICAN STUDY

A number of changes were introduced in the second investigation. First of all, more interesting neutral films were chosen so that the aggressive and nonaggressive film series would be more equivalent on this dimension. Second, the number of observation sessions was extended to include all 5 days of the week immediately preceding and immediately following the movie week. In the first study, there were only 3 observation days per week (Wednesday–Friday),

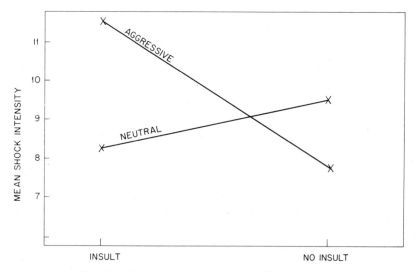

Fig. 3. Laboratory index of aggression (Saturday test).

and as a result there were no field observations after the movie viewing until the following Wednesday. Given the possibility that the experimental effect may dissipate over time, the field assessments in this later study commenced on the Monday of the postmovie period. To equate the frequency of observations during the pre- and postmovie periods, a full week of observations was included before the movie week as well.

A third change was introduced to clarify the effects of the repeated exposure to the films on the field measures of aggression. To permit a direct comparison of the repeated-exposure and single-exposure effects, two additional groups of boys were included in the study who saw only the final aggressive or neutral movie in the series. These youths were observed for a week before and a week after this single-exposure session. Finally, all subjects underwent a laboratory test for verbal aggression using a procedure developed by Mosher, Mortimer, and Grebel (1968).

1. Procedure

The same population and setting was available for the second study, and four cottages not previously used in the first run were chosen for this partial replication.

There were two sets of conditions: (a) those who participated in the 7-week replication study and who saw five films; and (b) those who participated in a 2-week assessment of the impact of a single movie. For the first group, the procedures were similar to those used in the initial study, with one exception: instead of only three observation days in the pre- and postmovie weeks, five observations a week were made for these two periods. For the groups who saw only a single film, another schedule was followed for 2 weeks on Monday through Thursday. They were observed in their cottages in the evening at the same times as the boys in the full-scale study. Then, on Friday evening, they were observed before and after watching either an aggressive film (*Ride Beyond Vengeance*) or a neutral film (*The Absent-Minded Professor*). Observations were made in the cottage during the following week, from Monday through Friday evenings. In essence, this was a shortened version of the full-scale study. Observer training, observational codes, and procedures were identical to the original full-scale study. Reliability estimates ranged between 92 and 100%.

Ten unedited commercial films were again selected. In order of presentation, the aggressive movies were *The Chase, Harper, Champion, The Wild One*, and *Ride Beyond Vengeance*. The five neutral movies were *The Harlem Globetrotters, Beach Blanket Bingo, Boy on a Dolphin, Ride the Wild Surf*, and *The Absent-Minded Professor*. Content analyses revealed that there was significantly more interpersonal physical aggression in the violent than in the nonaggressive films. The boys perceived the aggressive movies as more violent, brutal, cruel and aggressive than the neutral films. However, unlike the earlier study, the boys found both types of films equally interesting and exciting. The prior confounding of interest and content was thus avoided in this study.

Similar analyses were executed for the single exposure groups as well. Although the aggressive film and nonaggressive film did not significantly differ in amount of interpersonal physical aggression (x = 1.08 vs. .57), the boys clearly perceived the two films differently. The aggressive movie (*Ride Beyond Vengeance*) was viewed as more brutal, violent, and cruel and exciting, whereas the neutral film (*The Absent-Minded Professor*) received higher ratings on funniness, stupidity, and strangeness. In general, these analyses indicate that both the set of five films and the single film were perceived in the anticipated way.

The behavior of the boys during the five movies was generally similar to the pattern of the previous study. During the aggressive movies, the boys yelled and shouted [$t(8)$ = 3.76; p < .01], stamped their feet (t = 2.67; p < .05), shifted their chairs (t = 5.27; p < .01), and changed seats (t = 4.20; p < .01) more than during the neutral movies. In addition, the boys tended to do more poking (t = 1.98; p < .10) during the aggressive films.

2. Results

Now, let us examine the observational data. As in the first study, the main indices of aggression were (*a*) general aggression; (*b*) physical aggression; (and (*c*) interpersonal aggression. Unfortunately baseline differences were present in this study as well, and therefore, Cochran's subclassification procedure was used again. The main finding for the five movie groups was straightforward: boys who watched the five violent movies were more aggressive than those who saw the five nonviolent films as measured by the general aggression index [$F(1,47)$ = 6.79; p < .05], as can be seen in Fig. 4. A similar but nonsignificant pattern was present for the physical (F = 3.68; p < .10) and interpersonal aggression measures (F = 3.49; p < .10).

What about the impact of a single film on viewer behavior? While neither the general aggression nor the interpersonal aggression indices yielded any significant film effects, the boys' physical aggression level was affected by the movies. Specifically, there was a type of movie X baseline level interaction [$F(1,20)$ = 4.85; p < .05]; boys who were high in aggression during the baseline period displayed more physical aggression following exposure to the aggressive film than to the neutral film. Subjects who were low in physical aggression during baseline did not significantly differ as a function of the type of movie.

Do five movies have more impact than a single film? Analyses revealed that this was not the case. In fact, the boys who saw only the single aggressive film showed more aggression on both the general and physical aggression indices than did their peers who were exposed to the series of five films.

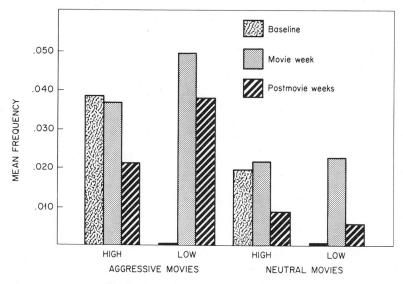

Fig. 4. General aggression index (Study 2).

Again, the amount of active social interaction was examined. In this investigation, unlike the first, boys who saw the five aggressive movies engaged in *more* interpersonal active behavior during the movie week than did viewers shown the series of neutral films, whereas the reverse pattern was present in the follow-up period [$F(1,45) = 9.64; p < .005$]. There were few significant effects for the single-exposure cottages on those activity variables: The amount of solitary active behavior increased from the movie week to the postmovie week [$F(1,20) = 4.36; p < .05$], whereas there was a decrease in social interaction passive behaviors (playing cards, talking, etc.) across these same time periods [$F(1,20) = 7.90; p < .05$].

Since the pattern of results is not exactly the same as that found in the initial study, it is important to examine the impact of the movies while controlling for the amount of social interaction. This examination showed that the movie effects are not dependent on the boys' level of social interaction. Analyses revealed that viewers of the violent films were more interpersonally aggressive than viewers of the nonaggressive films [$F(1,67) = 6.95; p < .025$], even with interaction level held constant. The observational results clearly suggest that exposure to movie violence increases aggressive behavior.

3. Laboratory Phase

As in the first study, a laboratory test was included as well as the observational measures. This time, instead of the shock measure, a verbal aggression

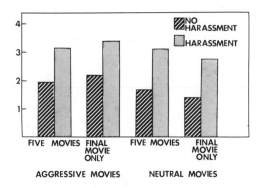

Fig. 5.   Verbal aggression index (Mosher laboratory procedure).

index derived from Mosher *et al.* (1968) was used. Briefly, the subject attempted to solve a puzzle while being verbally harassed by a confederate. Half of the boys received mild harassment; the confederate intermittently distracted the subject by asking questions or making comments about the puzzle (e.g., "What did you do last night?" or "This is a weird puzzle"). For the remaining boys, the confederate continually attacked the subject by negatively evaluating his work and by making stereotypic, derogatory remarks about him (e.g., "Come on—you can do better than that. You stupid idiot!"). Following his treatment, the subject was given an opportunity to verbally harass the confederate while the confederate worked on a puzzle task. Judges' ratings of the subjects' verbal aggression over a 2-minute period constituted the dependent index. As expected, the boys who were exposed to aggressive movies, regardless of the frequency of exposure (1 vs. 5 movies), exhibited more verbal aggression toward the confederate than did boys exposed to nonaggressive films $[F(1,66) = 3.72; p < .06]$. In addition, the subjects who were severely harassed by the confederate were more verbally hostile than were those subjects who experienced only mild harassment $[F(1,66) = 34.95; p < .01]$, as shown in Fig. 5. (See Sebastian, Parke, Berkowitz, & West, 1974, for more details.)

4. Summary

The same general conclusion seems reasonable for both studies: exposure to film violence increased aggressive behavior by the viewers. This conclusion is strengthened by the fact that the confounding of movie type and viewer interest was avoided in this second investigation. Unfortunately, no consistent picture emerged concerning the influence of the average level of aggression displayed in the premovie period on reactions to aggressive films. In the first study, there were no significant interactions between baseline levels of aggression and reactions to the violent films. In the second study, the high aggressive viewers were more affected by the aggressive movies; but this pattern held only in the case of the single-exposure subjects. It is obvious that no conclusion concerning the role of predispositional factors in determining aggressive reactions to violent films can be drawn from these two studies.

The laboratory data were consistent with the observational findings. However, in the first study only insulted subjects reacted differentially to the treatments, whereas in the second investigation subjects displayed more verbal aggression following the diet of violent films regardless of the level of harassment. This difference is probably due to the difference in the nature of the dependent indices: verbal vs. physical. It is likely that the threshold and/or eliciting cues for verbal and physical aggression differ, with verbal aggression having a lower threshold and requiring fewer situational eliciting cues than physical aggression.

C. BELGIAN STUDY

A question of continuing interest concerns the cross-cultural generality of the effects of exposure to movie violence on aggressive behavior. On the one hand, it has been argued that the peculiarly violent and aggressive attitudes prevalent in American society facilitate the eliciting effects of violent films. An alternative viewpoint suggests that the reactions to aggressive movies are universal, or at least not limited to Americans. As a partial test of these possibilities a similar study was conducted in Belgium, a country that does not suffer the heavy load of aggressive TV programs and films to which the United States is exposed. Although cross-cultural comparisons are often difficult to make because of differences in procedures and measures, comparability across the cultural groups was insured by the fact that Leyens, who was intimately involved in the design and execution of the original experiment, was also responsible for the Belgian study. A similar experimental design was used, as well as the same observational scoring system. With the limited availability of American films, and to insure the best selection for the Belgian audiences, a different set of films were selected. However, the same content analyses and viewer ratings that were used in the American studies permitted an assessment of the interstudy comparability of the movies. [See Leyens & Camino (1974), and Leyens, Camino, Parke, & Berkowitz (1975) for a more detailed presentation.]

A unique feature of the Belgian study involved the measurement of group dominance hierarchies in the cottages. A recent report by Sundstrom and Altman (1974) indicates that groups similar to those observed in this study possess dominance hierarchies. Moreover, data from primate and human studies of the relationship between dominance hierarchies and aggression (e.g., Bernstein, 1971; McGrew, 1972) suggest the usefulness of dominance hierarchy information for making predictions concerning the amount and targets of aggression.

1. Institution, Procedures, and Measures

In this case the setting was a minimum security institution for teen-age boys who were sent there because of delinquency, personality problems, or inadequate home care. The basic units were four cottages housing 16, 18, 19, and 31 boys, respectively. The principal difference between the Belgian and American institutions was "disciplinary," with strictness and discipline being less in the Belgian setting. In addition, the Belgian institution places more severe restrictions on TV viewing, permitting no violent or sexual programs to be viewed. The age range of the all-white sample was 12 to 19 years old, and each cottage received a small sum to purchase common play material for its participation in the study.

The design of the study was a shortened version of the original American investigations and was divided into three phases over a 3-week period. First, subjects were observed for a 1-week baseline period for 3 hours on each of 5 weekdays. One observation session of $1\frac{1}{2}$ hours was scheduled in the early afternoon, while a second 1.5-hour session took place in the evening. During the second phase, a 1-week experimental period, two cottages of boys saw aggressive movies, while boys in two other cottages saw nonaggressive films for 5 evenings. Observations were again made for $1\frac{1}{2}$ hours in the early afternoon and in the evening after the movie. After each one the boys rated the movie. No TV was permitted during the week. In the third and final phase, the boys were observed for a $1\frac{1}{2}$-hour period in the early afternoon for the 5 days of the postmovie week. No evening measures were possible, nor were laboratory measures secured in this study due to institutional restrictions. As in the earlier studies, a time-sampling observational procedure was employed whereby each boy was observed for three consecutive 30-second intervals on approximately two separate times in the afternoon and two times during the evening viewing period. To assess interobserver reliability, a fifth observer went from one cottage to another, always coding the boys in the same order as that followed by the regular observer. Inter-rater reliability ranged between 78 and 100% for all categories.

Unedited commercial films were again used. The aggressive movies were, in order, *Iwo-Jima*, *Bonnie and Clyde*, *The Dirty Dozen*, *Zorro*, and *The Left-Handed Gun*. The neutral movies were *Lily*, *Alexandre le Bienheureux*, *Daddy's Fiancee*, *Sebastien Parmi Les Hommes*, and *La Belle Americaine*.

Content analyses revealed more incidents of physical threat [$t(8) = 4.05; p < .01$] and physical attack [$t(8) = 10.56; p < .01$] in the aggressive movies than in the neutral films—a finding that parallels the results obtained with the movies used in the two previous investigation. In addition, the boys rated each film using the same adjectives used in the earlier studies. The youngsters rated the aggressive films as more brutal [$F(3,78) = 67.14; p < .01$], cruel ($F = 57.97; p < .01$), and aggressive ($F = 26.55; p < .01$) than the neutral movies. Neutral and aggressive films were regarded as equally interesting and exciting, and viewers indicated equal interest in seeing the films again. The neutral films were perceived as funnier, whereas the more intricate plots of the aggressive films led to higher "confusing" ratings for them than for the neutral movies.

To ensure comparability across the three studies, similar aggression indices were used, namely, GA, PA, and PVA. In addition, verbal aggression was included. To avoid the confounding between baseline levels of aggression and film groups, the aggression levels in the four cottages were carefully assessed before final film treatment decisions were made. As before, there were cottage differences in baseline level of aggression, with the boys in two of the cottages being more aggressive and more passive in their interaction patterns than were those in the other two cottages. Therefore, one cottage of each pair saw the neutral films while the other cottage of each pair watched aggressive movies.

2. Results

Since observations were made both in the evening after the films and on the next afternoon, it was possible to assess both the immediate and the intermediate effects of exposure to aggressive and neutral films. The evening measures are similar to the measures secured in the earlier studies, and so we will examine these results first. As Fig. 6 shows, boys in both cottages exposed to the

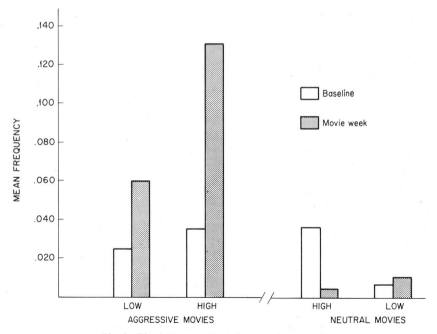

Fig. 6. Physical aggression index (evening period).

aggressive movies increased their physically aggressive behavior, whereas the teen-agers who watched the nonaggressive movies either decreased in their physical aggression or were unaffected by this exposure [$F(3,69) = 2.81$; $p <$ .05]. For the other measures (general aggression, verbal aggression), the boys who were initially high in aggression became more aggressive after viewing the aggressive films, whereas boys exposed to the neutral films showed a decrease in aggression [$F(3,69) = 14.14$ and 11.29 for general and verbal aggression indices; both $p < .001$; see Fig. 7].

Not surprisingly, the medium- and long-term effects were less marked. As Fig. 8 shows, the boys in the cottages that were initially high in aggression remained more verbally aggressive in both the afternoon and postmovie week periods, whereas the boys who saw the neutral movies were less verbally aggressive during these periods [$F(3,69) = 13.08$; $p < .001$].

Were activity and interaction levels affected? Both types of films influenced the rates in the behavioral categories related to the activity–passivity and interaction–solitude dimensions. First, both treatments increased the frequency of socially active interactions and decreased the occurrences in the alone-passive category. Second, the neutral films increased the amount of passive social

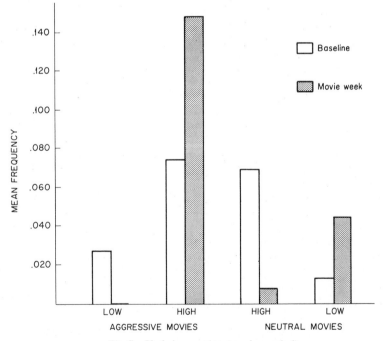

Fig. 7. Verbal aggression (evening period).

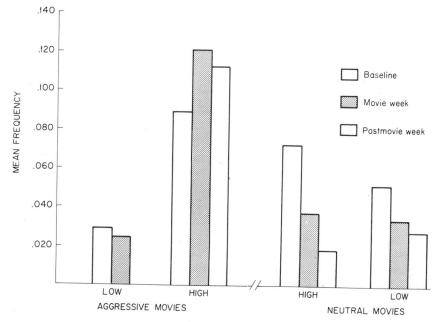

Fig. 8.   Verbal aggression (noon period).

interaction, whereas the amount of solitary active behavior increased after subjects watched the aggressive films. However, none of the correlations between activity and aggression were significant, which suggests that the increases in aggression were not necessarily due to elevated activity levels.

A final set of assessments, measures of group dominance, cohesion, and popularity was included in this study.

The hierarchy of dominance and the cohesion in each cottage were determined at the end of the third observational week. To measure dominance each boy was asked to categorize the other subjects in his group according to whether they were relatively dominant or submissive to him. On a list of all the members of the group, each boy had to mark a plus (+) in front of the more dominant members and a minus (−) in front of the less dominant ones.

Cohesion was measured in two different ways. First, the boys were asked to rate their willingness to remain as members of their group. Second, they had to rate their attraction toward each of their cottage mates on a 10-point scale. This also constituted a measure of popularity. At the end of the first and third weeks the boys were given questionnaires to determine how aggressive, active, and sociable they perceived themselves and their companions to be.

To assess the relationship between levels of group dominance and aggression subsequent to the movies, an analysis was executed using the two cottages which were initially higher in aggression. The levels of dominance were based on the received ranks, which were divided into three groups having approximately equal numbers of boys. As Table II indicates, dominance did not differentially affect the level of general aggression in the neutral movie cottage. In the aggressive movie group, however, the increase in general aggression was related to the levels of dominance: the most dominant teen-agers reacted most strongly to the violent movies. A more qualitative analysis indicated that the most dominant boys reacted immediately and powerfully, whereas the least dominant members delayed their reactions, which were notably weaker.

As with dominance, the popularity scores were also divided into three groups of approximately equal number, and the analysis was calculated only for the two cottages initially high in aggression. The general level of aggression was not affected in the neutral movie cottage. In the aggressive movie group, however, the medium popular subjects were least influenced by the aggressive films.

These effects for dominance and popularity are restricted to the evening period. No differences were found for the afternoon observational period. Moreover, the differences in dominance and cohesion among the four cottages cannot account for the differential impact of the treatment nor for the initial level of aggression spontaneously displayed by the four groups.

Other interesting findings concern the relationship between the effects of the films and the level of initial aggression: First, there is no correlation between the observed aggression and aggression estimated by the peers. This is consistent with the findings of the American studies when aggression was measured by

TABLE II

MEANS OF GENERAL AGGRESSION CHANGE SCORES AS A
FUNCTION OF LEVELS OF DOMINANCE AND PEER-RATED
AGGRESSION (EVENING PERIOD)

Category	Cottage	Levels[a]		
		High	Medium	Low
Dominance	High-aggressive aggressive treatment	$.281_a$	$.098_b$	102_b
	High-aggressive neutral treatment	$-.087_c$	$-.115_c$	$-.071_c$
Estimated aggression	High-aggressive aggressive treatment	$.244_a$	$.230_a$	$.017_b$
	High-aggressive neutral treatment	$-.129_b$	$-.106_b$	$-.068_b$

[a]Values having the same subscript are not significantly different at the .05 level by the Duncan Multiple Range Test.

objective indices (e.g., seriousness of offense) and by counselors and social workers. Second, the boys rated as least aggressive by their companions were least influenced by the films in their aggressive behavior. This was true only for the evenings, and the analysis was restricted to the two initially higher aggressive cottages. In the violent-films cottage the least aggressive subjects increased general aggression the least, whereas in the neutral-films cottage GA decreased the least $[F(2,37) = 2.48; p < .10]$; see Table II.

3. Summary

The results of the Belgian investigation are very similar to those of the earlier American studies. Exposure to movie violence again led to an increase in viewer aggression. Physical aggression was affected most clearly, which is precisely the type of aggressive behavior that significantly discriminated between the aggressive and nonaggressive films. There are two possible explanations. First, the movies may have an eliciting effect whereby the most predominant type of aggressive responses in the observers' habit hierarchies is displayed after viewing the films. This is plausible, since physical aggression is a common form of aggressive exchange among delinquent boys. Another possibility suggests that the viewers copied the physically aggressive actions displayed on the screen. Although there was no information available from this Belgian study concerning the boys' behavior during the movie viewing period, data from the earlier studies suggested that some of the youngsters imitated the physical aggression they saw on the screen during the films. Qualitative observations indicated this was especially true in the case of the boxing scenes from *The Champion*. However, the wide range of aggression measures that were affected in these studies, such as the index of verbal aggression in the Belgian investigation and the laboratory attacks on the accomplice (either with electric shocks or verbal harassment) in the American studies demonstrates that the boys did not merely copy the behaviors carried out by the movie aggressors. They displayed forms of aggression that they had not seen in the films.

Although physical aggression was altered immediately after the movie viewing, the films had greater long-term impact on verbal aggression. Unlike physical aggression, in the high aggression cottage exposed to the aggressive films the increase in verbal aggression persisted during both the afternoon periods of the movie week and the posttreatment week. The greater persistence of verbal aggression is probably due to the fact that it is much less likely to be punished by the counselors than are displays of physical aggression. In short, situational restraints probably interact with the films in determining both the form and stability of behavioral effects.

One of the innovations of the Belgian study involved an examination of the impact of group membership characteristics on the viewers' reaction to movie violence. The findings indicated that it was the most dominant, popular, and aggressive boys who were most clearly affected by the exposure to the violent films. In addition, the least popular boys were also influenced by this treatment. This pattern of findings is congruent with the high value placed on aggressive behavior by the boys in this type of institutional setting: Members of the group having the most prestige conceivably display aggressive behavior and possibly use aggressive tactics to maintain their position in the dominance hierarchy. The least popular boys, on the other hand, may often be involved in aggressive encounters—not as initiators but as victims in aggressive exchanges. Alternatively, unpopular boys may often exhibit inappropriate aggression, which is the source of their low group status (Olweus, 1974; Pope, 1953). Unfortunately, our measurement techniques did not permit an evaluation of these possibilities, since information concerning either the identification of the victims of aggressive attacks or the sequence of aggressive behaviors was not available.

V. Some Remaining Issues

Our results across the three field experimental studies just discussed support the proposition that exposure to movie violence increases aggressive behavior by the viewers. More importantly, these effects were obtained with unedited commercially available films, and the measures of aggression were based on observations of boys in a naturalistic setting. The findings are generally consistent with the earlier research of Friedrich and Stein (1973), who studied children of nursery school age.

However, unlike the findings of Friedrich and Stein, our data did not consistently suggest that predispositional variables such as baseline levels of aggression were important predictors of reactions to film violence. Only in the final study was there a clear indication that high aggressive individuals are more likely to be affected by violent movies than are low aggressive individuals. It is clear that more research on the issue of predispositional factors is necessary.

Our studies raise a variety of unresolved issues, and next we turn to a discussion of these problems.

A. HABITUATION TO FILM VIOLENCE

The question of whether there is a satiation or habituation to film violence remains unsettled by these studies. There was no evidence of any systematic decrease across film exposures over the 5-day viewing period in any of the three studies. While the greater eliciting effect produced by the single vs. the repeated exposure might be regarded as evidence of habituation, closer analyses argued against such a conclusion. There was an overall difference between the single-exposure groups and the repeated-exposure groups, even when the comparison is limited to the *first* exposure for the five-exposure subjects. This also may be due to the day of testing or to a sampling of the films; both explanations are more parsimonious than the habituation one.

We now come to another question: Is it possible to evaluate the effects of repeated exposure with a sample of teen-age boys who already have a significant history of watching aggressive TV and films? This is particularly problematic for a sample of individuals who prefer aggressive media diets. Our addition of five exposures is rather paltry after they have seen an average of thousands of movie gunfights, knifings, and beatings. The increment is probably less than a 1% additional exposure to this type of fare. In light of this, it is not surprising that there was no clear evidence of habituation in the boys' level of aggression.

This does not imply that it is not possible to demonstrate such an effect. We may have to give much closer attention to a variety of variables, in addition to frequency, that may control this type of habituation phenomenon. The simi-·larity of the aggressive content seems especially important. Although the films were all roughly classifiable as aggressive, there were great differences in the type of aggression, the plots, and the manner in which the conflict was resolved. There was some similarity of content, but only in the crudest sense, and greater attention to this dimension is clearly necessary.

In addition, there are a variety of other important parameters that may control habituation to movie violence, such as the time between exposures, the time between exposure and test, the novelty of the content, and the potency of the stimuli. Is it possible that the recent spate of blatantly violent films, such as *Clockwork Orange, Dirty Harry*, and *Straw Dogs*, has come about because, as a culture, we have become accustomed to tamer versions of violence? The escalation of violence in movies may, in fact, be necessary to maintain audience interest. On the other hand, this type of cultural shift may also consistently provide eliciting stimuli for aggressive action and prevent any true habituation from occurring.

B. NATURE OF THE VIEWING CONTEXT

One feature of the field studies which differs from the majority of laboratory studies is the group viewing context. Since all movies were seen in a group, it is possible that any one person's reactions to the movies may have been influenced by the behavior of the other members of the audience around him. This may be a particularly important factor in accounting for the effects of the aggressive movies; for the first two studies in the series, our observations indicated that the boys showed greater excitement and responsiveness during the viewing of the aggressive films. (Ratings were not available for the Belgian study.) Other evidence indicates that positive reactions from coobservers to an aggressive movie increased the amount of aggression displayed by a fellow observer (Hicks, 1968; Lefcourt, Barnes, Parke, & Schwartz, 1966). More research is needed to evaluate the impact of individual vs. group viewing contexts on the impact of films. Moreover, is the carry-over effect dependent on the similarity between the audience and the group that one interacts with later? In this case the viewers watched with the same cabin mates with whom they interacted in the postmovie period. Whether this same effect would occur with a group that did *not* share the same movie experience has to be determined.

C. NATURE OF THE MEASUREMENT CONTEXT

Another issue merits discussion, namely, the nature of the social context in which the observational assessments are made [see Parke (1974) for a fuller treatment of this issue]. Although individuals were treated in our studies as separate and distinctive reactors to a series of movie stimuli, it is questionable whether this type of analysis is sufficient.

Our assumption underlying the choice of analyses is that the results were due either to direct imitation of the actions of the movie characters by individual viewers or the direct eliciting or disinhibiting of nonimitative aggressive acts. Another possibility, however, involves *secondary exposure effects*. We can distinguish between two such effects. In one type, one member of the audience acts aggressively as a function of exposure to the film violence, and this person serves as an aggressive model or stimulus for other group members. In the other kind of secondary effect, movie-elicited attacks, provocations, or insults generate retaliatory aggressive behaviors in the victims. Both of these effects may interact with prior movie exposure. Possibly, the likelihood of imitating the aggressive actions of a peer, retaliating against a tormentor, or even attacking a nearby target is heightened by having watched an aggressive film—even though the movie itself was insufficient to elicit an aggressive response. It is clear that our typical scoring procedure, which treats all types of aggressive behavior as if they are direct responses to movie exposure, obscures the relative contribution of two interacting processes; (a) the elicitory effects of the films; and (b) the subsequent maintaining and transmitting effects of vicarious and direct peer instigation.

In addition, further research such as the Belgian study, which included measures of the existing group structure, is necessary. This Belgian investigation confirmed that dominance hierarchy arrangements are related to the level of aggression. More detailed analyses of both the direct and secondary effects of movie violence on viewer behavior clearly are necessary in order to determine how the effects are modified and transmitted through existing group structures. A two-track analysis is required in which sociometric assessments are made of shifting dominance hierarchies and molecular observational analyses are made of interpersonal exchanges of individual members of the group.

Much work obviously is necessary if we are to move beyond the simple assertion that exposure to movie violence increases aggression—and, in field settings, become able to specify the group processes that enhance or diminish this effect. It is not only the stimulus side that needs more attention. The contexts in which our behavioral measures are obtained need careful study as well if we are not only to predict but even to understand the effects of movie violence in naturalistic settings.

D. GENERALIZATION BETWEEN DELINQUENT AND NONDELINQUENT SAMPLES

An issue that is, in part, independent of the problem of field vs. laboratory analyses of movie aggression concerns the similarity between the reactions of delinquent and nondelinquent populations. Are the results of the present field experiments limited to male juvenile delinquents? In light of the parallel findings obtained by Friedrich and Stein (1973), who used normal children of nursery school age, it is unlikely that our results are restricted to only a delinquent population. However, in order to provide further evidence on this issue, a laboratory experiment was conducted to determine whether delinquent and nondelinquent boys exhibit similar reactions to film violence.

Our strategy involved carrying out an experiment with delinquents that had previously yielded clear, replicable results with a nondelinquent population. Previous experiments with middle-class university students have repeatedly found that the observer's response to filmed violence depends in part on his judgment of the propriety of the depicted aggression. If he is angry at the time the movie is presented and then has an opportunity to attack his tormentor at the end of the film he is likely to show the strongest aggression if he believes that the witnessed violence was justified (Berkowitz, 1965; Berkowitz & Geen, 1967; Hoyt, 1970; Meyer, 1972).

In this research the filmed violence was usually defined as justified or not by varying the information given the subjects about the defeated character. Most of the experiments used an excerpt from the movie *The Champion* in which the protagonist, a prize fighter, takes a bad beating during a title bout. A brief synopsis provided before the movie started (supposedly so that the subjects would better understand the scene) portrayed the champion in either a sympathetic or a less sympathetic manner. In the latter case he was described as a person who had frequently and shamelessly exploited other people in his rise to the championship. The college students therefore generally regarded the beating he receives in the fight as justified punishment for his past misdeeds. In the opposing condition, by contrast, the story summary depicted him more favorably and, as a consequence, the students viewed his defeat as less justified aggression.

Our question was whether juvenile delinquents would respond in the same way as did the university students employed in these earlier experiments. One could argue either way. Findings obtained by some investigators suggest that there would be differences. Whether or not there is a separate, delinquent subculture, various authorities contend that delinquents generally value being hard, tough, and able to outsmart others (Lerman, 1968). Consistent with this orientation, delinquent boys are especially likely to think of social relationships as hostile interactions (Shore, Massimo, & Moran, 1967) and are greatly concerned with their ability to exert power over their peers (Gold, 1969). They are also likely to be exploitative, believing that they have the right to take advantage of "suckers" (Hirschi, 1971). All in all, in the words of some of these researchers, the delinquent boy seems to be "sensitive to and aware of many ingenious techniques for manipulating others." Furthermore, "Rather than withdrawing from others, he appears more oriented toward aggressively taking, demanding, and doing" (Shore et al., 1967, p. 247). We might expect from all this that delinquents would not be unsympathetic to the tough, hard-hearted exploiter—as the fight loser, the champion, is described in the supposedly justified film aggression condition. They might even be attracted to him. As a consequence, the beating the champion receives in the movie would appear relatively unwarranted and the delinquents should therefore be less willing to act aggressively themselves immediately afterwards. Following this reasoning, then, the difference between the "justified" and "less justified" film aggression conditions found in the earlier studies with university students should be minimized or even reversed in the present delinquent population.

We should be careful not to exaggerate the uniqueness of the values held by juvenile delinquents, however. Several investigations have shown that these youngsters have many of the same beliefs and values as their middle-class, normal counterparts. Much like university students, they too could be affronted by the fight loser's callous exploitation of other people and would, therefore, also regard his beating as entirely proper and deserved. To the extent that this is the case, angry delinquent boys viewing the presumably justified film aggression should be more aggressive soon afterwards than other delinquents seeing the less warranted violence.

This study employed 44 boys (median age 16 years) from the same institution used in the field experiments. Subjects were randomly assigned to a 3 × 2 design involving insult vs. no insult and three film conditions: no film, justified film aggression, or less justified film aggression.

Subjects were first required to complete a "test of common sense," which we described earlier. Briefly, a partner evaluated the boys' answers to a series of simple questions by either belittling the boy's answer (insult condition) or by providing innocuous, nonevaluative feedback (noninsult condition). In the next phase, two-thirds of the subjects watched a $6\frac{1}{2}$-minute film of a prize fight from The Champion, a film in which the protagonist, Kirk Douglas, receives a severe beating. The scene was introduced by a synopsis summarizing the story up to the fight, supposedly so that the viewer would better understand what was happening. As indicated earlier, the "justified aggression" summary portrayed Kirk Douglas as a scoundrel who had frequently exploited the people in his life, whereas the "less justified aggression" synopsis depicted him in a rather sympathetic manner.

The remaining subjects saw no film. Next, the boys' aggression was measured by the use of the Buss machine. Subjects were permitted to choose among ten levels of electric shock whenever the partner, who had previously evaluated him, made an error on a questionnaire. Each subject had ten opportunities to shock his partner. Table III presents the results. The principal finding concerns the heightened aggression displayed by the subjects in the insult-justified aggression condition: as in the experiments with college student subjects, the provoked boys who had watched a "bad person" being beaten subsequently attacked their tormentor more severely than did any other group. These juvenile delinquents evidently regarded the witnessed aggression in this condition as being warranted or "proper," so that their own aggression also seemed justified for the time being. Like the university students, they apparently thought an unfeeling exploiter of others deserved a severe beating.

The present results extend the generality of the earlier findings obtained with university students. In this sample, as in the university groups, when angry people watch a "bad" person receive a beating, they are subsequently more inclined to attack the "bad" individual in their own lives who had previously insulted them. These comparable results also suggest that the delinquents in our sample had employed the same kind of moral standards as did the university students in evaluating the defeated movie character; in both cases this character was evidently viewed as getting his "just deserts" if he had been depicted as someone who had ruthlessly exploited other people.

TABLE III
MEAN INTENSITY OF SHOCKS GIVEN TO CONFEDERATE[a]

	Film conditions		
Treatment	No film	Less-justified film aggression	Justified film aggression
Neutral	5.58_{abc} (7)	6.40_{ab} (7)	5.66_{abc} (7)
Insult	4.28_c (7)	6.56_{ab} (7)	7.70_a (8)

[a]Cells having different subscripts are significantly different, at the .05 level, by Duncan Multiple Range Test. The numbers in parentheses are the number of cases in each cell.

Moreover, the similarity in the pattern of results across the delinquent and nondelinquent populations suggests that our field study findings are probably not restricted to delinquent populations. It obviously remains both desirable and necessary to replicate the field studies with nondelinquent groups in order to generalize more conclusively to these other populations.

E. MOVIE VIOLENCE AND FEMALE DELINQUENT VIEWERS

As a further evaluation of the generality of our findings, we also examined the effect of viewing movie violence on verbal aggression in juvenile delinquent girls (West, Berkowitz, Sebastian, & Parke, 1975). Little attention has been devoted to date to effects of film aggression on female viewers, and no research has considered the influence on female delinquents. In considering the reactions of female delinquents we will have further data concerning the generalizability of previous findings obtained with nondelinquent male populations.

In addition, we investigated another aspect of the generalization issue: whether watching physical aggression enhances verbal aggression. Specifically, we asked whether exposure to films which depict only physical aggression increases the level of verbal aggression in the viewer. Some previous research by (Berkowitz, Corwin, & Heironimus (1963) has demonstrated that male college students who view a film depicting a brutal beating give more negative ratings to a confederate who had previously angered them than do subjects who view a more neutral film. Others have found that reinforcement for physical aggression can increase verbal aggression (Geen & Pigg, 1970), and vice versa (Loew, 1967; Parke, Ewall & Slaby, 1972). It was therefore expected that subjects who viewed physical aggressive displays would increase their verbal aggressive behavior.

To investigate these issues, 63 adolescent girls at the Wisconsin School for Girls were assigned to one of the conditions of a 2 X 3 design. Subjects saw an aggressive scene from a movie of a roller derby match involving either male or female participants. The aggressive films began with one player hitting another and ended with fighting between the two teams. None of the films included a significant amount of verbal aggression. Subjects in the control condition watched a fast-paced but nonaggressive segment from the TV comedy series "Laugh-In." The Mosher Verbal Aggression procedure described earlier was used to measure aggression. In addition to various film presentations, half of the subjects were submitted to a mild verbal harassment, while the remaining subjects received a severe harassment from a trained female confederate. The amount of verbal aggression exhibited by the subjects during the Mosher procedure is presented in Table IV.

First, verbal aggression was greater in the high- than in the low-harassment condition $[F(1,42) = 13.38; p < .001]$. Second, subjects in the three film

TABLE IV
MEAN MOSHER SCALE RATINGS

| | Treatment | | |
| | Aggressive film | | |
	Male model	Female model	Control
Harassment			
Mild	2.17	2.34	1.20
Severe	3.03	3.61	2.79
Mean	2.60	2.98	2.00

conditions tended to differ in their level of verbal aggression $[F(2,42) = 2.85; p < .10]$; subsequent analyses revealed that the two aggressive film conditions combined produced a significantly higher level of aggression than did the control film condition $[F(1,42) = 4.18; p < .05]$.

A second measure of verbal aggression was provided by the subjects' ratings on a 7-point scale of "How well do you think (confederate's name) will do in technical training school?" The experimenter emphasized that the confederate wanted to attend such an institution and that their rating would be taken into consideration in deciding whether or not to admit her. While no effect of harassment was obtained, the film treatments produced different ratings of the confederate $[F(2,75) = 3.48; p < .05]$. Although the two aggressive conditions did not themselves differ, the subjects who saw the aggressive films rated the confederate more poorly than did subjects in the control condition $[F(1,57) = 5.31; p < .05]$.

These results indicate that female delinquents who are exposed to aggressive films show a higher level of verbal aggression on both the Mosher Scale and the questionnaire ratings of the confederate. These results, together with the present research by the authors, demonstrate that both male and female delinquents exhibit increases in aggression following exposure to film violence in a manner similar to that of college students in previous research.

Next, let us turn to an evaluation of the usefulness of the two main strategies represented by this research project: the field experiment and the laboratory experiment.

F. FIELD VS. LABORATORY STUDIES

Two strategies are represented in this chapter: field and laboratory studies. Although it has become increasingly fashionable to advocate field methodological approaches, to a large degree the advice has been too unqualified and undifferentiated to serve as a useful basis for deciding which research strategy to employ. Social psychology will not necessarily advance by merely becoming more naturalistic. Nor is there much evidence that this has happened. We might therefore ask whether it is necessary or even desirable to continue to execute the types of field experimental studies that are represented in this chapter. Probably not. It surely is unnecessary merely to accumulate further demonstrations in support of the relatively simple statement that exposure to media violence increases viewer aggression. There already is sufficient supporting evidence, and further effort on behalf of this relatively unqualified conclusion does not seem warranted. Unfortunately, the field experimental approach is not well suited for testing subtle theoretical issues. Rather, this approach more typically yields main effect outcomes or, at most, a simple interaction. Theoretical analyses of the operation of film violence, in short, have moved to a level of complexity that is difficult to test adequately in field contexts.

This does not imply that we should discontinue field studies. Instead, we should alter the nature of our question from "Do the mass media have an effect on the viewer?" to "How does this influence occur in naturalistic settings?" Concern for the ways in which the group context modifies the impact of media viewing is an example of this type of question.

We recognize, of course, that our field studies were not specifically designed to answer subtle theoretical issues. Rather, these investigations were in part a response to the shift in the nature of the questions that confronted social scientists in the late 1960s. Under increased pressure to provide information that could guide public policy decisions and, specifically, decisions about the nature of mass-media programming, the issue of the generalizability of laboratory-derived findings to real-life behavior in naturalistic situations came to the forefront. Field studies, then, were executed partly to define the limits of the laboratory findings, on the one hand, and to provide evidence for the scientist-cum-policy maker regarding the desirability of changes in mass-media programming, on the other. The field studies were to a large degree dictated by the policy-relevant nature of this research topic. In the future a combination of laboratory studies and periodic excursions into the field to evaluate the generalizability of laboratory findings would seem to be the most reasonable approach to understanding the impact of the mass media. Guidelines that aid in deciding among various strategies are necessary.

G. NEED FOR MULTICAUSAL MODELS

There is another issue which also warrants more attention in the future, namely, the relative influence of various social forces on the acquisition and modification of aggression. We too often proceed on the assumption that TV and movie viewing is a primary causal agent in the development and maintenance of aggressive behavior. However, there are a variety of influences in addition to mass-media violence that can affect aggressive behavior, including societal values and attitudes, parental values, family interaction patterns, and parental disciplinary practices. Although we often recognize these alternative sources of influence, seldom do we attempt to assess the relative impact of these different sources. Models that would permit a strategy for partitioning the various sources of influence are badly needed. More important than merely ranking the relative contribution of such sources are models that permit assessment of the interactions among these sources. As noted in this chapter, mass-media fare is not consumed in a vacuum. It is modified or intensified by the context in which both the viewing and testing take place. The investigation of the impact of the family, school, and peer contexts as significant modifiers of the impact of mass-media viewing would seem to be long overdue. Just as we have discovered that the stimulus is not fixed in mass-media presentations, neither are the viewing and testing contexts. Future research strategies should involve simultaneous assessment of a variety of influence sources in order to begin to articulate the relative impact of various socialization agents on the development and maintenance of aggressive behavior.

REFERENCES

Averill, J. R., Malmstrom, E. J., Koriat, A., & Lazarus, R. S. Habituation to complex emotional stimuli. *Journal of Abnormal Psychology*, 1972, **80**, 20–28.

Bandura, A. Influence of model's reinforcement contingencies on the acquisition of imitative responses. *Journal of Personality and Social Psychology*, 1965, **1**, 589–595.

Bandura, A. *Principles of behavior modification*. New York: Holt, 1969.

Bandura, A. *Aggression: A social learning analysis*. Englewood Cliffs, N.J.: Prentice-Hall, 1973.

Bandura, A., Ross, D., & Ross, S. A. Imitation of film-mediated aggressive models. *Journal of Abnormal and Social Psychology*, 1963, **66**, 3–11.

Berkowitz, L. Some aspects of observed aggression. *Journal of Personality and Social Psychology*, 1965, **2**, 359–369.

Berkowitz, L. The contagion of violence: An S-R mediational analysis of some effects of observed aggression. In W. J. Arnold & M. M. Page (Eds.), *Nebraska symposium on motivation*. Lincoln: University of Nebraska Press, 1970. Pp. 95–136.

Berkowitz, L. Words and symbols as stimuli to aggressive responses. In J. F. Knutson (Ed.), *The control of aggression*. Chicago: Aldine, 1973.

Berkowitz, L., Corwin, R., & Heironimus, M. Film violence and subsequent aggressive tendencies. *Public Opinion Quarterly*, 1963, **27**, 217–229.

Berkowitz, L., & Geen, R. B. Stimulus qualities of the target of aggression. *Journal of Personality and Social Psychology*, 1967, **5**, 364–368.

Berkowitz, L., Parke, R. D., Leyens, J., & West, S. The effects of justified and unjustified movie violence on aggression in juvenile delinquents. *Journal of Research in Crime and Delinquency*, 1974, **11**, 16–24.

Bernstein, I. S. Group behavior. In A. M. Schrier & F. Stollnitz (Eds.), *Behavior of nonhuman primates.* Vol. 3. New York: Academic Press, 1971.

Borden, R. J. Witnessed aggression: Influence of an observer's sex and values on aggressive responding. *Journal of Personality and Social Psychology,* 1975, **31**, 567–573.

Buss, A. *The psychology of aggression.* New York: Wiley, 1961.

Cline, V. B., Croft, R. G., & Courrier, S. Desensitization of children to television violence. *Journal of Personality and Social Psychology,* 1973, **27**, 360–365.

Cochran, W. G. Planning and analysis of non-experimental studies. Technical Report No. 19, April 26, 1968, Harvard University, Contract No. 1866 (37)-NR 042-097, Office of Naval Research.

Dubanoski, R. A., & Kong, C. The effects of pain cues on hitting behavior. Paper presented at the meeting of the Society for Research in Child Development, Philadelphia, March 1973.

Feshbach, S., & Singer, R. D. *Television and aggression.* San Francisco: Jossey-Bass, 1971.

Freidson, E. The relation of the social situation of contact to the media of mass communication. *Public Opinion Quarterly,* 1953, **17**, 230–238.

Friedrich, L. K., & Stein, A. H. Aggressive and prosocial television programs and the natural behavior of preschool children. *Monographs of the Society for Research in Child Development,* 1973, **38** (4, Whole No. 151).

Geen, R. G., & Pigg, R. Acquisition of an aggressive response and its generalization to verbal behavior. *Journal of Personality and Social Psychology,* 1970, **15**, 165–170.

Gewirtz, J. L. Deprivation and satiation of social stimuli as determinants of their reinforcing efficacy. In J. P. Hill (Ed.), *Minnesota symposia on child psychology.* Vol. 1. Minneapolis: University of Minnesota Press, 1967.

Gold, M. Juvenile delinquency as a symptom of alienation. *Journal of Social Issues,* 1969, **25**, 212–135.

Hanratty, M. A., Liebert, R., Morris, L., & Fernandez, L. Imitation of film mediated aggression against live and inanimate victims. *Proceedings of the 77th Annual Convention, American Psychological Association,* 1969, **4**, 457–458.

Hanratty, M. A., O'Neal, E. C., & Sulzer, J. L. Effect of frustration upon imitation of aggression. *Journal of Personality and Social Psychology,* 1972, **21**, 20–34.

Hartley, E. R. The impact of viewing aggression: Studies and problems of extrapolation. In *A review and evaluation of recent studies on the impact of violence.* Office of Social Research, C.B.S., Inc., 1964.

Hartmann, D. P. Influence of symbolically modeled instrumental aggression and pain cues on aggressive behavior. *Journal of Personality and Social Psychology,* 1969, **11**, 280–288.

Hicks, D. J. Effects of co-observer's sanctions and adult presence on imitative aggression. *Child Development,* 1968, **39**, 303–309.

Hirschi, T. *Causes of delinquency.* Berkeley: University of California Press, 1971.

Howard, J. L., Reifler, C. B., & Liptzin, M. B. Effects of exposure to pornography. *Technical report of the Commission on Obscenity and Pornography.* Vol. 8. Washington, D.C.: U.S. Government Printing Office, 1971.

Howitt, D., & Cumberbatch, G. *Mass media violence and society.* New York: Wiley, 1975.

Hoyt, J. L. Effect of media violence "justification" on aggression. *Journal of Broadcasting,* 1970, **14**, 455–464.

Klapper, J. T. The impact of viewing "aggression": Studies and problems of extrapolation. In O. N. Larsen (Ed.), *Violence and the mass media.* New York: Harper, 1968.

Lang, P. J. Fear reduction and fear behavior: Problems in treating a construct. In J. M. Shlien (Ed.), *Research in psychotherapy.* Vol. 3. Washington, D.C.: American Psychological Association, 1968. Pp. 90–102.

Lefcourt, H., Barnes, K., Parke, R. D., & Schwartz, F. Anticipated social censure and aggression conflict as mediators of response to aggression induction. *Journal of Social Psychology*, 1966, 70, 251–263.

Lerman, P. Individual values, peer values, and subcultural delinquency. *American Sociological Review*, 1968, 33, 219–235.

Leyens, J. P., & Camino, L. The effects of social structures and repeated exposure to film violence on aggression. In W. W. Hartup & J. DeWit (Eds.), *Determinants and origins of aggressive behavior*. The Hague: Mouton, 1974.

Leyens, J. P., Camino, L., Parke, R. D., & Berkowitz, L. The effects of movie violence on aggression in a field setting as a function of group dominance and cohesion. *Journal of Personality and Social Psychology*, 1975, 32, 346–360.

Liebert, R. M., & Baron, R. A. Short-term effects of televised aggression on children's aggressive behavior. In *Television and social behavior*. Rockville, Md.: U.S. Department of Health, Education and Welfare, 1972.

Liebert, R. M., Sobol, M. D. and Davidson, E. S. Catharsis of aggression among institutionalized boys: fact or artifact? In *Television and social behavior*. Rockville, Md.: U.S. Department of Health, Education and Welfare, 1972.

Loew, C. A. Acquisition of a hostile attitude and its relationship to aggressive behavior. *Journal of Personality and Social Psychology,* 1967, 5, 335–341.

Maccoby, E. E. Television: Its impact on school children. *Public Opinion Quarterly,* 1951, 15, 421–444.

Martin, M. F., Gelfand, D. M., & Hartmann, D. P. Effects of adult and peer observers on boys' and girls' responses to an aggressive model. *Child Development,* 1971, 42, 1271–1275.

McGrew, W. C. *An ethological study of children's behavior*. New York: Academic Press, 1972.

Menzies, E. S. The effects of repeated exposure to televised violence upon attitudes towards violence among youthful offenders. Unpublished manuscript, Florida State University, 1972.

Meyer, T. P. Effects of viewing justified and unjustified real film violence on aggressive behavior. *Journal of Personality and Social Psychology*, 1972, 23, 21–29.

Milgram, S., & Shotland, R. L. *Television and antisocial behavior*. New York: Academic Press, 1973.

Mosher, D. L., Mortimer, R. L., & Grebel, M. Verbal aggressive behavior in delinquent boys. *Journal of Abnormal Psychology*, 1968, 73, 454–460.

Olweus, D. Personality factors and aggression: With special reference to violence within the peer group. In J. DeWit & W. W. Hartup (Eds.), *Determinants and origins of aggressive behavior*. The Hague: Mouton, 1974.

Parke, R. D. A field experimental approach to children's aggression: Some methodological problems and some future trends. In W. W. Hartup & J. DeWit (Eds.), *Determinants and origins of aggressive behavior*. The Hague: Mouton, 1974.

Parke, R. D., Ewall, W., & Slaby, R. G. Hostile and helpful verbalizations as regulators of nonverbal aggression. *Journal of Personality and Social Psychology,* 1972, 23, 243–248.

Patterson, G. R., Littman, R. A., & Bricker, W. Assertive behavior in children: A step toward a theory of aggression. *Monographs of the Society for Research in Child Development*, 1967, 32 (5, Whole No. 113).

Pope, B. Socio-economic contrasts in children's peer culture prestige values. *Genetic Psychology Monographs*, 1953, 48, 157–220.

Savitsky, J. C., Rogers, R. W., Izard, C. E., & Liebert, R. M. The role of frustration and anger in the imitation of filmed aggression against a human victim. *Psychological Reports*, 1971, 29, 807–810.

Sawin, D. B. Aggressive behavior among children in small playgroup settings with violent television. Unpublished doctoral dissertation, University of Minnesota, 1973.

Sebastian, R. J., Parke, R. D., Berkowitz, L., & West, S. The effects of repeated and single exposures to naturalistic film violence on laboratory verbal aggression. Unpublished manuscript, University of Wisconsin, 1974.

Shemberg, K. M., Leventhal, D. B., & Allman, L. Aggression machine performance and rated aggression. *Journal of Experimental Research in Personality,* 1968, **3,** 117–119.

Shore, M. F., Massimo, J. L., & Moran, J. K. Some cognitive dimensions of interpersonal behavior in adolescent delinquent boys. *Journal of Research in Crime and Delinquency,* 1967, **4,** 243–247.

Stein, A. H., & Friedrich, L. K. Impact of television on children and youth. In E. M. Hetherington (Ed.), *Review of child development research.* Vol. 5. Chicago: University of Chicago Press, 1975.

Sundstrom, E., & Altman, I. Field study of dominance and territorial behavior. *Journal of Personality and Social Psychology,* 1974, **30,** 115–125.

Tannenbaum, P. H. Studies in film- and television-mediated arousal and aggression: A progress report. In *Television and social behavior.* Rockville, Md.: U.S. Department of Health, Education and Welfare, 1972.

Walters, R. H., & Brown, M. Studies of reinforcement of aggression III. Transfer of responses to an interpersonal situation. *Child Development,* 1963, **34,** 563–571.

Walters, R. H., & Llewellyn-Thomas, E. Enhancement of punitiveness by visual and audio-visual displays. *Canadian Journal of Psychology,* 1963, **16,** 244–255.

Wells, W. D. Television and aggression: Replication of an experimental field study. Unpublished manuscript, Graduate School of Business, University of Chicago Press, 1973.

West, S. G., Berkowitz, L., Sebastian, R. J., & Parke, R. D. The effect of viewing physical aggression on verbal aggression in delinquent girls. Unpublished manuscript, Florida State University, 1975.

William J. F., Meyerson, J. L., Eron, L. D., & Semler, I. J. Peer-rated aggression and aggression responses elicited in an experimental situation. *Child Development,* 1967, **38,** 181–189.

THE INTUITIVE PSYCHOLOGIST AND HIS SHORTCOMINGS: DISTORTIONS IN THE ATTRIBUTION PROCESS[1]

Lee Ross

STANFORD UNIVERSITY
STANFORD, CALIFORNIA

[1] The author gratefully acknowledges the assistance of Teresa Amabile, Daryl Bem, Phoebe Ellsworth, Baruch Fischhoff, David Greene, Larry Gross, Mark Lepper, Richard Nisbett, Julia Steinmetz, Amos Tversky, and Philip Zimbardo, all of whom have contributed useful comments and suggestions concerning both the manuscript and the research and conceptual analysis it reports. The preparation of this chapter and reported research were supported by National Institute of Mental Health Research Grant MH 24134.

I. Introduction to Attribution Theory and
Attribution Error

A. ATTRIBUTION THEORY AND INTUITIVE PSYCHOLOGY

Attribution theory, in its broadest sense, is concerned with the attempts of ordinary people to understand the causes and implications of the events they witness. It deals with the "naive psychology" of the "man in the street" as he interprets his own behaviors and the actions of others. The current ascendancy of attribution theory in social psychology culminates a long struggle to upgrade that discipline's conception of man. No longer the stimulus–response (S–R) automaton of radical behaviorism, promoted beyond the rank of information processor and cognitive consistency seeker, psychological man has at last been awarded a status equal to that of the scientist who investigates him. For man, in the perspective of attribution theory, is an intuitive psychologist who seeks to explain behavior and to draw inferences about actors and their environments.

To better understand the perceptions and actions of this intuitive scientist we must explore his methods. First, like the academic psychologist, he is guided by a number of implicit assumptions about human nature and human behavior, for example, that the pursuit of pleasure and the avoidance of pain are ubiquitous and powerful human motives, or that conformity to the wishes and expectations of one's peers is less exceptional and less demanding of further interpretation than is nonconformity. The amateur psychologist, like the professional one, also relies heavily upon data. Sometimes these data result from first-hand experience; more often, they are the product of informal social communication, mass media, or other indirect sources. Moreover, the representativeness or randomness of the available data is rarely guaranteed by formal sampling procedures. The intuitive psychologist must further adopt or develop techniques for coding, storing, and retrieving such data. Finally, he must resort to methods for summarizing, analyzing, and interpreting his data, that is, rules, formulas, or schemata that permit him to extract meaning and form inferences. The intuitive scientist's ability to master his social environment depends in large measure upon the accuracy and adequacy of his hypotheses, evidence, and methods of analysis and inference. Conversely, sources of oversight, error, or bias in his assumptions and procedures may have serious consequences, both for the lay psychologist himself and for the society that he builds and perpetuates. These shortcomings, explored from the vantage point of contemporary attribution theory, provide the focus of the present chapter.

While the label "attribution theory" and some of the jargon of its proponents may be relatively new and unfamiliar, its broad concerns—naive epistemology and the social inference process—have a long and honorable history in social psychology. The Gestalt tradition, defying the forces of radical behaviorism, has consistently emphasized the *subject's* assignment of meaning to the events that unfold in the psychological laboratory and in everyday experience (cf. Asch, 1952). Icheiser (1949) explicitly discussed some fundamental social perception biases and their origins almost 30 years ago. Long before attribution theory's current vogue, Kelly (1955, 1958) brought an attributional perspective to the study of psychopathology and, in fact, explicitly suggested the analogy between the tasks of the intuitive observer and those of the behavioral scientist. Schachter and Singer (1962) and Bem (1965, 1967, 1972) further anticipated current attributional approaches in their respective analyses of emotional labeling and self-perception phenomena.

The broad outlines of contemporary attribution theory, however, were first sketched by Heider (1944, 1958) and developed in greater detail by Jones and Davis (1965), Kelley (1967), and their associates (e.g., Jones, Kanouse, Kelley, Nisbett, Valins, & Weiner, 1972; Weiner, 1974). These theorists emphasized two closely related tasks confronting the social observer. The first task is causal judgment: the observer seeks to identify the cause, or set of causes, to which some particular effect (i.e., some action or outcome) may most reasonably be *attributed.* The second task is social inference: the observer of an episode forms inferences about the *attributes* of relevant entities, that is, either the dispositions of actors or the properties of situations to which those actors have responded.

Causal judgment and social inference tasks have both been the subject of intensive theoretical and empirical inquiry and, until recently, had constituted virtually the entire domain of attribution theory. Lately, however, a third task of the intuitive psychologist has begun to receive some attention; that task is the *prediction* of outcomes and behavior. Episodes characteristically lead the intuitive psychologist not only to seek explanations and to make social inferences but also to form expectations and make predictions about the future actions and outcomes. Thus, when a presidential candidate promises to "ease the burden of the average taxpayer," we do attempt to judge whether the promise might have resulted from and reflected the demands of political expediency rather than the candidate's true convictions. However, we are likely also to speculate about and try to anticipate this candidate's and other candidates' future political actions. The psychology of intuitive prediction, is thus a natural extention of attribution theory's domain.

The three attribution tasks are, of course, by no means independent. Explanations for and inferences from an event are obviously and intimately related, and together they form an important basis for speculation about unknown and future events. Each task, moreover, can reveal much about the assumptions, strategies, and failings of the intuitive psychologist. Each, however, provides some unique problems of interpretation and methodology that we should explore before proceeding.

In describing causal judgments, researchers from the time of Heider's early contributions to the present have relied heavily upon a simple internal–external or disposition–situation dichotomy. That is, they have tried to identify those configurations of possible causes and observed effects that lead the observer to attribute an event to "internal" dispositions of the actor (e.g., abilities, traits, or motives) or to aspects of the "external" situation (e.g., task difficulties, incentives, or peer pressures).[2] While this seemingly simple dichotomy has undeniable intuitive appeal, it creates a host of conceptual problems and methodological pitfalls (see also Kruglanski, 1975). For instance, attribution researchers (e.g., Nisbett, Caputo, Legant, & Maracek, 1973) frequently require subjects to explain why a particular actor has chosen a particular course of behavior. These attributions are then coded as "situational" or "dispositional" on the basis of the *form* of the subject's response. Thus the statement "Jack bought the house because it was so secluded" is coded as an external or situational attribution, whereas "Jill bought the house because she wanted privacy" is coded as an internal or dispositional attribution. The rationale for such coding seems straightforward: The former statement cites something about the object or situation to which the actor responded while the latter statement cites something about the actor. However, when one attends not to the *form* of the attributer's statement but to its *content,* the legitimacy of many such situation–disposition distinctions becomes more dubious. First, it is apparent that causal statements which explicitly cite situational causes implicitly convey something about the actor's dispositions; conversely, statements which cite dispositional causes invariably imply the existence and controlling influence of situational factors. For instance, in accounting for Jack's purchase of a house the "situational" explanation (i.e., "because *it* was so secluded") implies a disposition on the part of this particular actor to favor seclusion. Indeed, the explanation provided is no explanation at all unless one *does* assume that such a disposition controlled Jack's response. Conversely, the dispositional explanation for Jill's purchase (i.e., because *she* likes privacy) clearly implies something about the house (i.e., its capacity to provide such privacy) that, in turn, governed Jill's behavior. Thus the content of both sentences, notwithstanding their differences in form, communicates the information that a particular feature of the house exists and that the purchaser was disposed to respond positively to that feature. In fact, the form of the sentences could have been reversed without altering their content to read "Jack bought the house because he wanted seclusion" and "Jill bought the house because it provided privacy."

Is there a more meaningful basis for a distinction between situational and dispositional causes? One possibility merits consideration. One could ignore the form of subjects' causal statements and, by attending to content, distinguish

---

[2] Most contemporary researchers have been concerned with attributional rules or principles that apply commonly to all social perceivers. However, a few investigators [most notably Rotter (1966)] have used a similar dichotomy in discussing individual differences in such strategies (see also Collins, 1974; Collins, Martin, Ashmore, & Ross, 1973; Crandall, Katkovsky, & Crandall, 1965; Lefcourt, 1972).

between (1) explanations that do not state or imply any dispositions on the part of the actor beyond those typical of actors in general, and (2) explanations that do state or imply unique relatively atypical or distinguishing personal dispositions. Thus the causal statements "I was initially attracted to Sally because she is so beautiful" and "I was initially attracted to Sally because her astrological sign is Libra" should be coded differently in terms of the proposed distinction despite their similar form. Specifically, while the former explanation conveys that I, *like* most men, am particularly attracted to beautiful women, the latter implies that I, *unlike* most men, am particularly attracted to women of one specific astrological sign. In a sense, the former statement constitutes a situational explanation because it invokes a widely accepted and generally applicable S–R law; the latter explanation, by contrast, is dispositional because it resorts to an individual difference or distinguishing personality variable.[3]

The interpretation of causal statements in the manner just described is obviously a difficult undertaking and many investigators may favor the second attribution task, i.e., the formation of social inferences. This task, at first glance, seems to offer a far less forbidding but no less rewarding research target. For instance, the subject who learns that Joan has donated money to a particular charity may infer that the relevant act reflected [or, in Jones and Davis' (1965) terms, "corresponded" to] some personal disposition of Joan. Alternatively, the subject may infer that Joan's actions reflected not her personal characteristics but the influence of social pressures, incentives, or other environmental factors. The attribution researcher, accordingly, can measure the subject's willingness to assert something about Joan's traits, motives, abilities, beliefs, or other personal dispositions on the basis of the behavioral evidence provided. Specifically, the subject could be required to characterize Joan by checking a Likert-type scale anchored at "very generous" and "not at all generous" with a midpoint of "average in generosity." An alternative version of the scale might deal with the degree of confidence the rater is willing to express in his social inferences.

Such measures of social inference are, indeed, simple to contrive and simple to score. Nevertheless, nontrivial problems of interpretation do arise. Most obvious is the fact that the meaning of a given point on these scales differs for different subjects. More importantly, that meaning may depend upon subtle features of research context and instruction, features often beyond the experimenter's knowledge or control.

---

[3] The reader should recognize, however, that the form or structure of a causal statement may have a significance that cannot be predicted from a logical analysis of its contents and meaning. Thus, Mary's statement that she loves John because of his qualities rather than her own needs may be an important reflection of her feelings and an important determinant of their subsequent relationship, notwithstanding the dubious logical status of the implied distinction.

Even subtler problems of interpretation may arise. One common format, for instance, asks subjects to indicate whether the specified person is "generous" or "ungenerous," or that they "can't say, depends upon circumstances." Superficially, the first two options indicate willingness to infer the existence or influence of a personal disposition, whereas the third option suggests unwillingness to do so. But a more careful examination of the rater's perceptions may reveal that the third option reflects the rejection only of a *broad* or *general* dispositional label. Thus, further interrogation might reveal that the rater judged the relevant actor to be unexceptional with respect to the behavioral domain in question, that is, like most actors behaving generously or not as situational pressures and constraints dictate. In such a case it seems that no disposition has been inferred (and that the rater has made a situational rather than a dispositional attribution of relevant behavior). On the other hand, the rater's reluctance to choose either trait label may convey his judgment that the actor is relatively more generous than his fellows in some specific circumstances but less generous in others, i.e., that his generosity is inconsistent or idiosyncratic (cf. Bem & Allen, 1974). In the latter case a disposition *has* been inferred, albeit a relatively specific one, for example, a tendency to be unusually generous to one's employees but not to one's family, or vice versa. In fact, several important papers in the attribution area (e.g., Jones & Nisbett, 1971; Nisbett *et al.,* 1973), have failed to distinguish adequately between the absence of trait inferences and the rejection of broad trait labels in favor of narrow or situation-specified ones. Inevitably, confusion and unwarranted conclusions have been the product of this failure.

The third type of attribution task, prediction of behavior (e.g., Nisbett & Borgida, 1975), permits simple unambiguous questions and produces responses that can be scored objectively. Thus the witness to an ostensibly generous act by Joan might be required to predict Joan's behavior in a series of other episodes that seemingly test an actor's generosity or lack of it. Alternatively, the question put to the social observer might be: "What percentage of students (or of people, or of women, or of Joan's socioeconomic peers, etc.) would have behaved as generously as Joan did?" The logical relationship of the prediction task to the tasks of causal judgment and social inference is worth reemphasizing [although the relevant empirical correlations between attribution measures may prove surprisingly weak; cf. Bierbrauer (1973)]. To the extent that a given action or outcome is attributed to the actor rather than his situation and that some stable disposition is inferred, the attributer should prove willing to make confident and listinguishing predictions about the actor's subsequent behaviors or outcomes. Conversely, to the extent that an act is attributed to situational pressures that would dispose all actors to behave similarly, and to the extent that no inferences are made about the actor's dispositions, the observer should eschew such "distinguishing" predictions; instead, he should invoke the "null hypothesis" and rely upon his baseline information or estimates about how "people in general" respond in the specified situation.

Prediction measures of attribution processes have a crucial advantage (beyond their simplicity and seeming objectivity). Unlike causal judgments or social inferences, predictions can often be evaluated with respect to their *accuracy*. That is, whenever authentic information is available about the behavior of various actors in more than one situation, the success of the intuitive psychologist's attribution strategy can be measured and the direction of biases can be determined. To illustrate this advantage, research on "nonconservative" prediction biases will be discussed later in this chapter (Section III,C; cf. also Amabile, 1975; Ross, Amabile, Jennings, & Steinmetz, 1976a).

B. LOGICAL SCHEMATA AND NONLOGICAL BIASES

Contemporary attribution theory has pursued two distinct but complementary goals. One goal has been the demonstration that, by and large, social perceivers follow the dictates of logical or rational models in assessing causes, making inferences about actors and situations, and forming expectations and predictions. The other goal has been the illustration and explication of the sources of imperfection, bias, or error that distort these judgments. We shall consider briefly the so-called logical or rational schemata employed by the intuitive psychologist and then devote the remainder of the chapter to the sources of bias in his attempts at understanding, predicting, and controlling the events that unfold around him.

1. Two Logical Schemata

Individuals must, for the most part, share a common understanding of the social actions and outcomes that affect them, for without such consensus, social interaction would be chaotic, unpredictable, and beyond the control of the participants. Introspection on the part of attribution theorists, buttressed by some laboratory evidence, has led to the postulation of a set of "rules" that may generally be employed in the interpretation of behaviors and outcomes. These "commonsense" rules or schemata are analogous, in some respects, to the more formal rules and procedures that social scientists and statisticians follow in their analysis and interpretation of data.

H. Kelley, E. E. Jones, and their associates have distinguished two cases in which logical rules or schemata may be applied: In the *multiple* observation case the attributer has access to behavioral data which might be represented as rows or columns of an Actor × Object × Situation (or Instance) response matrix. Typically, summary statements are provided rather than actual responses. Thus the potential attributer learns that "Most theatergoers like the new Pinter play," or "Mary can't resist stray animals," or "The only television program that Ann watches is Masterpiece Theater." In the *single* observation case the attributer must deal with the behavior of a single actor on a single occasion. For instance, he may see Sam comply with an experimenter's request to deliver a painful shock to a peer, or he may learn that "Louie bet all his money on a long shot at Pimlico."

The logical rules or principles governing attributions in these two cases are rather different (Kelley, 1967, 1971, 1973). In the multiple observation case the attributer applies the Covariance Principle; that is, he assesses the degree to which observed behaviors or outcomes occur in the presence, but fail to occur in the absence, of each causal candidate under consideration. Accordingly, the attributer concludes that the new Pinter play is a good one (and attributes praise to the play rather than the playgoer) to the extent that it is liked by a wide variety of playgoers, that it is liked by individuals who praise few plays (e.g., "critics"), and that it is applauded as vigorously on the ninetieth day of its run as on the ninth.

In the single observation case the attributer's assessment strategy involves the application of the Discounting Principle, by which the social observer "discounts" the role of any causal candidate in explaining an event to the extent that other plausible causes or determinants can be identified. This attributional principle can be restated in terms of social inferences rather than causal attributions: To the extent that situational or external factors constitute a "sufficient" explanation for an event, that event is attributed to the situation and no inference logically can be made (and, presumably, no inference empirically *is* made) about the dispositions of the actor. Conversely, to the extent that an act or outcome seems to occur *in spite of* and *not because of* attendant situational forces, the relevant event is attributed to the actor and a "correspondent inference" (Jones & Davis, 1965) is made, i.e., the attributer infers the existence and influence of some trait, ability, intention, feeling, or other disposition that could account for the actor's action or outcome. Thus, we resist the conclusion that Louie's longshot plunge at Pimlico was reflective of his stable personal attributes to the extent that such factors as a "hot tip," a desperate financial crisis, or seven prewager martinis could be cited. On the other hand, we judge Louie to be an inveterate longshot player if we learn that his wager occurred in the face of his wife's threat to leave him if he ever loses his paycheck at the track again, his knowledge that he won't be able to pay the rent if he loses, and a track expert's overheard remark that the favorite in the race is "even better than the track odds suggest."

It is worth noting that the application of these two different principles places rather different demands upon the intuitive scientist. The Covariance Principle requires the attributer to apply rules that are essentially logical or statistical in nature and demands no further insight about the characteristics of the entities in question. Application of the Discounting Principle, by contrast, demands considerable insight about the nature of man and the impact of such situational forces as financial need, alcohol consumption, and a spouse's threat of abandonment. In a sense, the Covariance Principle can be applied by a mere "statistician," whereas the Discounting Principle requires a "psychologist" able to assess the role of various social pressures and situational forces and even to distinguish intended acts and outcomes from unintended ones (cf. Jones & Davis, 1965).

Evidence concerning the systematic use of commonsense attributional principles comes primarily from questionnaire studies in which subjects read and interpret brief anecdotes about the responses of one or more actors to specified objects or "entities" under specified circumstances (e.g., McArthur, 1972, 1976). Occasional studies of narrower scope have also exposed the attributer to seemingly authentic responses, encounters, and outcomes (e.g., Jones, Davis, & Gergen, 1961; Jones & DeCharms, 1957; Jones & Harris, 1967; Strickland, 1958; Thibaut & Riecken, 1955). Such research has demonstrated that attributers can, and generally do, make some use of the hypothesized principles or rules of thumb. That is, manipulations involving information about either the covariance of causes and effects or the number of potential causes for a given effect have produced statistically significant effects upon subjects' judgments. Some studies have even provided evidence about the *relative* impact of various competing attributional principles or criteria (cf. McArthur, 1972, 1976).

What the methodologies employed to date have not assessed (and, logically, could never assess) is the accuracy of the attributer's judgments and the sufficiency of his judgmental strategies. As we have noted earlier, such determinations become possible only when attributers are presented with authentic information and are required to make predictions or other judgments that can be verified.

2. Motivational and Nonmotivational Sources of Bias

The central concern of the present chapter, and an increasingly important goal of contemporary research and theory, is not the logical schemata which promote understanding, consensus, and effective social control; instead, it is the sources of systematic bias or distortion in judgment that lead the intuitive psychologist to misinterpret events and hence to behave in ways that are personally maladaptive, socially pernicious, and often puzzling to the social scientist who seeks to understand such behavior.

In speculating about possible distortions in an otherwise logical attribution system, theorists were quick to postulate "ego-defensive" biases through which attributers maintained or enhanced their general self-esteem or positive opinion of their specific dispositions and abilities (Heider, 1958; Jones & Davis, 1965; Kelley, 1967). Attempts to prove the existence of such a motivational bias have generally involved demonstrations of asymmetry in the attribution of positive and negative outcomes—specifically, a tendency for actors to attribute "successes" to their own efforts, abilities, or dispositions while attributing "failure" to luck, task difficulty, or other external factors. Achievement tasks (e.g., Davis & Davis, 1972; Feather, 1969; Fitch, 1970; Wolosin, Sherman, & Till, 1973) and teaching performances (e.g., Beckman, 1970; Freize & Weiner, 1971; Johnson, Feigenbaum, & Weiby, 1964) have provided most of the evidence for this asymmetry. It has also been shown that actors may give themselves more credit for success and less blame for failure than do observers evaluating the same outcomes (Beckman, 1970; Gross, 1966; Polefka, 1965).

Critics, skeptical of broad motivational biases, however, have experienced little difficulty in challenging such research. [See D. T. Miller and Ross (1975) for a detailed discussion.] First, it is obvious that subjects' private perceptions and interpretations may not correspond to (and may be either less or more "defensive" than) their overt judgments. Second, asymmetries in the attributions of success and failure or differences in the judgments of actors and observers need not reflect motivational influences. As several researchers have noted, success, at least in test situations, is likely to be anticipated and congruent with the actor's past experience, whereas failure may be unanticipated and unusual. Similarly, successful outcomes are intended and are the object of plans and actions by the actor, whereas failures are unintended events which occur in spite of the actor's plans and efforts. Observers, furthermore, rarely are fully aware of the past experiences or present expectations and intentions of the actors whose outcomes they witness.

Challenges to the existence of pervasive ego-defensive biases have been empirical as well as conceptual. Thus, in some studies subjects seem to show "counterdefensive" or esteem-attenuating biases. For example, Ross, Bierbrauer, and Polly (1974), using an unusually authentic instructor—learner paradigm, found that instructors rated their own performances and abilities as more important determinants of failure than of success. Conversely, the instructors rated their learner's efforts and abilities as less critical determinants of failure than success. In the same study these seemingly counterdefensive attributional tendencies proved to be even more pronounced among professional teachers than among inexperienced undergraduates, a result which contradicted the obvious derivation from ego-defensiveness theory that those most directly threatened by the failure experience would be most defensive.

Researchers who insist that self-serving motivational biases exist can, of course, provide alternative interpretations of studies that seem to show no motivational biases or counterdefensive biases. Indeed, in many respects the debate between proponents and skeptics has become reminiscent of earlier and broader debates in learning theory and basic perception in which the fruitlessness of the search for a "decisive" experiment on the issue of motivational influences (i.e., one that could not be interpreted by the "other side") became ever more apparent as data multiplied and conceptual analysis sharpened. One approach favored by many researchers has been an attempt to specify relevant moderator variables that might determine when ego defensiveness will distort the attribution process and when it will not do so. An alternate and perhaps more fruitful strategy, however, may be to temporarily abandon motivational constructs and to concentrate upon those informational, perceptual, and cognitive factors that mediate and potentially distort attributional judgments "in general." A fuller understanding of such factors, in turn, might well allow us, ultimately, to understand and anticipate the particular circumstances in which attributions of responsibility will unduly enhance or attenuate an attributer's self-esteem (cf. D. T. Miller & Ross, 1975).

Unfortunately the existing attribution literature provides relatively little conceptual analysis or evidence pertaining to nonmotivational biases. The first identified (Heider, 1958) and most frequently cited bias or error, one which we shall term the *fundamental* attribution error, is the tendency for attributers to underestimate the impact of situational factors and to overestimate the role of dispositional factors in controlling behavior. The evidence for this error and its broader implications for our understanding of social psychological phenomena receive detailed consideration in Section II,A.

Our consideration of other previously cited nonmotivational biases shall be brief. Perhaps the most provocative contribution concerning nonmotivational biases has been Jones and Nisbett's (1971) generalization regarding the "divergent" perceptions of actors and observers (cf. also Jones, 1976). Essentially, it was proposed that actors and observers differ in their susceptibility to the fundamental attribution error; that is, in situations where actors attribute their own behavioral choices to situational forces and constraints, observers are likely to attribute the same choices to the actors' stable abilities, attitudes, and personality traits. An interesting and unusual feature of the Jones and Nisbett paper is its careful consideration of underlying processes—informational, cognitive, and perceptual in nature—which might *account for* these divergent perceptions of actors and observers (cf. also Jones, 1976). Another interesting line of investigation (one, incidentally, which promises to subsume Jones and Nisbett's actor–observer generalization) involves "perceptual focusing" (Duncker, 1938; Wallach, 1959). It appears that whatever or whomever we "focus our attention on" becomes more apt to be cited as a causal agent (Arkin & Duval, 1975; Duval & Wicklund, 1972; Regan & Totten, 1975; Storms, 1973; Taylor & Fiske, 1975).

Other attributional biases that have been proposed in the literature have been less systematically investigated. Our list, although incomplete, is perhaps representative. Jones and Davis (1965), for instance, proposed that actions directed towards the attributer, or having consequences for him, are more likely to be attributed to dispositions of the actor than are acts which do not personally involve or affect the attributer. Walster (1966) reported a questionnaire study suggesting that actors are held more responsible (and "chance" or "luck" less responsible) for acts that have serious consequences than for acts with trivial consequences. Finally Kelley (1971), summarizing the results of several prior questionnaire studies, observed that the actor is also held more responsible for acts which lead to reward than for acts which prevent loss or punishment.

II. Attributional Biases: Instances, Causes, and Consequences

A. THE FUNDAMENTAL ATTRIBUTION ERROR

Our exploration of the intuitive psychologist's shortcomings must start with his general tendency to overestimate the importance of personal or dispositional factors relative to environmental influences. As a psychologist he seems too often to be a nativist, or proponent of individual differences, and too seldom an S–R behaviorist. He too readily infers broad personal dispositions and expects consistency in behavior or outcomes across widely disparate situations and contexts. He jumps to hasty conclusions upon witnessing the behavior of his peers, overlooking the impact of relevant environmental forces and constraints. Beyond anecdotes and appeals to experience, the evidence most frequently cited for this general bias (e.g., Jones & Nisbett, 1971; Kelley, 1971) involves the attributer's apparent willingness to draw "correspondent" personal inferences about actors who have responded to very obvious situational pressures. For instance, Jones and Harris (1967) found that listeners assumed some correspondence between communicators' pro-Castro remarks and their private opinions even when these listeners *knew* that the communicators were obeying the experimenter's explicit request under "no choice" conditions. A more direct type of evidence that observers may ignore or underestimate situational forces has been provided by Bierbrauer (1973), who studied subjects' impressions of the forces operating in the classic Milgram (1963) situation. In Bierbrauer's study, participants witnessed a faithful verbatim reenactment of one subject's "obedience" to the point of delivering the maximum shock to the supposed victim. Regardless of the type and amount of delay before judging (see Fig. 1), regardless of whether they actually played the role of a subject in the reenactment or merely observed, and regardless of their perceptual or cognitive "set," Bierbrauer's participants showed the fundamental attribution error; that is, they consistently and dramatically underestimated the degree to which subjects in general would yield to those situational forces which compelled obedience in Milgram's situation. In other words, they assumed that the particular subject's obedience reflected his distinguishing personal dispositions rather than the potency of situational pressures and constraints acting upon all subjects. The susceptibility of observers to the fundamental attribution error has been noted

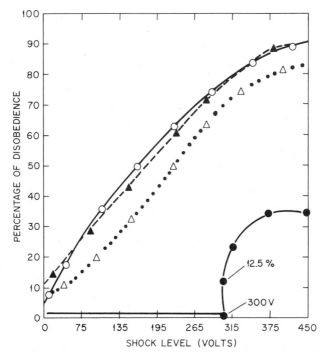

Fig. 1. Comparison of predicted and actual disobedience rates: *open circles,* no delay prediction; *black triangles,* distracted delay prediction; *open triangles,* undistracted delay prediction; *black circles,* rates obtained by Milgram (1963). From Bierbrauer (1973).

by many theorists (e.g., Heider, 1944, 1958; Icheiser, 1949) and disputed by few.[4] The relevance of this error to the phenomena and research strategies of contemporary social psychology, however, has been less widely recognized. To illustrate, we shall first discuss its critical role in mediating the effects of "forced compliance" or "role playing" upon attitude change; then we shall digress slightly to consider the *professional* psychologist's apparent susceptibility to this error.

1. Attribution Error and Forced Compliance Effects

Proponents of cognitive consistency and self-perception theories have regarded demonstrations of attitude change following forced compliance as impor-

---

[4] Insufficient attention, perhaps, has been given to the possibility that while many situational forces are typically underestimated, there may be others which generally are correctly estimated or even overestimated. Notably, an intriguing series of studies (Deci, 1971; Greene & Lepper, 1974; Lepper & Greene, 1975; Lepper, Greene, & Nisbett, 1973) suggest that actors, in certain circumstances, may inappropriately attribute intrinsically motivated behavior to the influence of salient extrinsic rewards and constraints.

tant evidence for their theoretical viewpoint. Upon closer examination, however, it becomes apparent that these theories "explain" the relevant phenomenon only to the extent that one additionally assumes the operation of the fundamental attribution error. Consider the classic Festinger and Carlsmith (1959) experiment in this regard. Why *does* the compliant actor in the "one dollar" condition experience dissonance? Or, in self-perception terms, why does he incorrectly infer that his compliant behavior reflects liking for the experimental task? Why don't the actors, or the observers in Bem's (1967) interpersonal "simulations," correctly identify the actual "external" causes of the actor's compliance and hence draw no inferences about the actor's attitudes from his counterattitudinal behavior?

The answer is clear: Actors and observers alike must systematically *underestimate* the sufficiency of the particular complex of situational factors in the Festinger and Carlsmith study to produce compliance and must *overestimate* the role played by personal dispositions in producing such behavior. "Correct" attributions, presumably, would produce little dissonance and certainly no erroneous "correspondent inferences" concerning the compliant actor's attitudes. (That is why the "twenty dollar" condition, which presumably facilitates "correct" attributions, produces no attitude change among actors and no tendency for observers to assume congruence between actors private attitudes and their public utterances.) In short, self-perception theory, attribution theory, and dissonance theory "explain" the Festinger and Carlsmith results only if one additionally recognizes the role of the fundamental attribution error.

2. Fundamental Attribution Error by Psychologists

The professional psychologist, like the intuitive psychologist, is susceptible to the fundamental attribution error. This susceptibility, in fact, is crucial to the strategy of designing so-called nonobvious research. Many of the best known and most provocative studies in our field depend, for their impact, upon the reader's erroneous expectation that individual differences and personal dispositions will overcome relatively mundane situational variables or "channel factors." Thus Darley and Batson's (1973) study of Good Samaritanism is noteworthy because it seems to contradict our intuition that an individual's ethical principles are more important determinants of bystander intervention than an experimental manipulation of the individual's earliness or lateness for an appointment. Similarly, Bavelas, Hastorf, Gross, and Kite (1965) earn our professional applause and recognition because they show that one can "overcome" those personal qualities which presumably propel the leader into his role through a banal manipulation of the amount of talking done by group members. Most notable of all, perhaps, are the now classic studies showing the vulnerability of actors to situational forces strongly challenging their judgments, preferences, or beliefs (cf. Asch, 1955; Milgram 1963). These studies were professional successes not because they showed that the relevant target behavior or perceptions could be influenced by a situational manipulation, but because they demonstrated control by a situational factor that the reader had previously assumed to be too weak to exert such control.

In this context it is instructive to consider the heated response of many professionals to Mischel's (1968) summary of evidence indicating that, for most behavior domains of interest to social psychologists, the degree of cross-situational consistency is very modest, making personality scales poor predictors of behavior. Adding insult to injury of the "trait theorists," Mischel and associates (Mischel, 1974; Mischel & Ebbesen, 1970; Mischel, Ebbesen, & Zeiss, 1972) have further demonstrated that in at least one paradigm of general interest—the "delay of gratification paradigm"—relatively subtle situational factors (i.e., the experimenter's suggestion concerning cognitive strategies) overwhelm any individual differences that might be anticipated. Why have Mischel's assertions and demonstrations proven so controversial and prompted such energetic rebuttal research? One reason may be that Mischel's work contradicted not only the formal theories of his critics but also the working assumptions that guide their everyday personal encounters.

The deep conviction that personal dispositions control and are reflected in everyday social behavior will no doubt continue to inspire research in personality theory and personality assessment. Similarly, successful social psychologists will continue to exploit the undue faith of their readers (and their subjects) in the impact of personal beliefs or standards relative to that of situational manipulations. In subsequent sections of this chapter we shall attempt to understand how erroneous trait inferences and trait theories survive or "persevere" in the face of logical challenges and empirical disconfirmations. We shall also explore further the relevance of attributional biases to the tactics and strategy of experimental social psychology.

B. THE "FALSE CONSENSUS" OR "EGOCENTRIC ATTRIBUTION" BIAS

The professional psychologist relies upon well-defined sampling techniques and statistical procedures for estimating the commonness of particular responses. Where such estimates are relevant to subsequent interpretations and inferences, he can proceed with confidence in his data. Intuitive psychologists, by contrast, are rarely blessed either with adequate "baseline" data or with the means of acquiring such data. To the extent that their systems for interpreting social responses depend upon estimates of commonness or oddity they must, accordingly, rely largely upon subjective impressions and intuitions.

The source of attributional bias that we shall consider next relates directly to the subjective probability estimates of intuitive psychologists. Specifically, we shall report research demonstrating that laymen tend to perceive a "false consensus," that is, to see their own behavioral choices and judgments as relatively common and appropriate to existing circumstances while viewing alternative responses as uncommon, deviant, and inappropriate. Evidence shall also be reported for an obvious corollary to the false consensus proposition: The intuitive psychologist judges those responses that differ from his own to be more revealing of the actor's stable dispositions than those responses which are similar to his own. Thus, we contend that the person who feeds squirrels, votes Republican, or drinks Drambuie for breakfast will see such behaviors or choices by an actor as relatively common and relatively devoid of information about his personal characteristics. By contrast, another person who ignores hungry squirrels, votes for Democrats, or abstains at breakfast will see the former actor's responses as relatively odd and rich in implications about the actor's personality.

The term *relative* is critical in this formulation of the false consensus bias and requires some clarification. Obviously, the man who would walk a tightrope between two skyscrapers, launch a revolution, or choose a life of clerical celibacy recognizes that his choices would be shared by few of his peers. It is contended, however, that he would see his personal choices as less deviant than would those of us who would *not* walk tightropes, launch revolutions, or become celibate clerics. Similarly, the present thesis concedes that for some response categories virtually all raters' estimates may be biased in the same direction. The incidence of infant abuse, for instance, might be underestimated by abusing and nonabusing parents alike. The relative terms of the false consensus hypothesis leads only to the prediction that abusing parents will estimate child abuse to be more common and less revealing of personal dispositions than will nonabusing parents.

References to "egocentric attribution" (Heider, 1958; Jones & Nisbett, 1971), to "attributive projection" (Holmes, 1968), and to specific findings and phenomena related to false consensus biases have appeared sporadically in the social perception and attribution literatures (cf. Katz & Allport, 1931; Kelley & Stahelski, 1970). Perhaps the most compelling evidence, however, is provided in a series of studies by Ross, Greene, and House (1977b) which we shall review in some detail.

1. Empirical Evidence and Implications

In the first study reported, subjects read descriptions of hypothetical conflict situations of the sort they might personally face. One of the four stories, for example, describes the following dilemma:

> As you are leaving your neighborhood supermarket a man in a business suit asks whether you like shopping in that store. You reply quite honestly that you do like shopping there and indicate that in addition to being close to your home the

supermarket seems to have very good meats and produce at reasonably low prices. The man then reveals that a videotape crew has filmed your comments and asks you to sign a release allowing them to use the unedited film for a TV commercial the supermarket chain is preparing.

The subjects then were asked to *(a)* estimate the commonness of the two response alternatives (e.g., signing or refusing to sign the commercial release in the supermarket story); *(b)* indicate the alternative they, personally, would follow; and *(c)* assess the traits of the "typical" individual who would follow each of the two specified alternatives.

The relevant estimates and ratings made by subjects strongly supported both the false consensus hypothesis and its corollary. For example, subjects reading the foregoing episode who claimed that they personally would sign the commercial release guessed that more than 75% of their peers would show the same response in the same circumstances; by contrast, subjects who reported that they personally would refuse to sign the release estimated that only 57% would sign. Furthermore, signers made more confident and extreme judgments about the distinguishing traits of the typical nonsigner, while nonsigners reported more confident and extreme impressions about the distinguishing dispositions of the signers.

A second questionnaire study by Ross *et al.* (1977b) dealing with a broad range of habits, preferences, fears, daily activities, expectations, and other personal characteristics greatly extended the apparent domain of the false consensus effect. That is, subjects' estimates of the commonness of the various responses and personal characteristics cited in the questionnaire were consistently biased in accord with their own responses and characteristics.

In a final demonstration by Ross, Greene, and House the hypothetical questionnaire methodology was abandoned and subjects were confronted with a real and consequential conflict situation: Subjects (in the context of a purported experiment on communication techniques) were asked to walk around campus for 30 minutes wearing a large sandwich-board sign bearing the message "EAT AT JOE'S." The experimenter made it clear to subjects that they could easily refuse to participate in the sandwich-board study but that he would prefer that they did participate and thereby "learn something interesting while helping the research project." Subjects were subsequently asked to make their own decision about taking part in the study, to estimate the probable decisions of others, and to make trait inferences about particular peers who agreed or refused to participate.

The results using this "real" conflict situation (Table I) confirmed the findings of earlier questionnaire studies dealing with hypothetical responses. Overall, subjects who agreed to wear the sandwich-board sign estimated that 62% of their peers would make the same choice. Subjects who refused to wear the

TABLE I
THE FALSE CONSENSUS EFFECT: RATERS' ESTIMATES OF COMMONNESS AND
TRAIT INFERENCES REGARDING TWO BEHAVIORAL ALTERNATIVES[a]

Raters	Estimated commonness of:		Strength of trait inferences[b] about subject who:	
	Agreement (%)	Refusal (%)	Agrees to wear sign	Refuses to wear sign
Subjects who agree to wear sign (n = 48)	62	38	120.1	125.3
Subjects who refuse to wear sign (n = 32)	33	67	139.7	106.8

[a]Summarized from Ross et al. (1977b).
[b]Sum of ratings for four traits: higher number indicates more confident and more extreme inferences by rater.

sign estimated that only 33% of their peers would comply with the experimenter's request. Furthermore, as predicted, "compliant" and "noncompliant" subjects disagreed sharply in the relative strength of inferences that they were willing to make about one peer who agreed and one who refused to wear the sandwich board. Compliant subjects made more confident and more extreme inferences about the personal characteristics of the noncompliant peer; noncompliant subjects made stronger inferences about the compliant peer.

Some broad implications of the Ross, Greene, and House demonstrations for our conception of the intuitive psychologist should be clear. His estimates of deviance and normalcy, and the host of social inferences and interpersonal responses that accompany such estimates, are systematically and egocentrically biased in accord with his own behavioral choices. More generally, it is apparent that attributional analyses may be distorted not only by errors in the intuitive psychologist's eventual analysis of social data, but also by earlier biases in sampling or estimating such data.

The present findings are interesting to consider in the light of Jones and Nisbett's (1971) contentions that (1) we see our peers' behavior as the product of broad consistent personal dispositions while attributing our own responses to situational forces and constraints, and (2) we are reluctant to agree that we ourselves possess the type of stable personality traits that we readily apply in characterizing our peers. To explain their results, Jones and Nisbett suggested important differences in the perceptual and informational "perspectives" enjoyed by actors and observers. The Ross et al. (1977b) results, however, lead one to speculate that attributional differences of the sort described by Jones and

Nisbett may arise, at least in some measure, simply from attributers' misconceptions about the degree of consensus enjoyed by their own responses and by the alternative responses of their peers.

The derivation is a simple one: To the extent that particular responses by one's peers differ from one's own responses in a given situation, such responses are likely to be seen as relatively odd or deviant—the product, therefore, not of situational forces (which, presumably, guide one's own *contrary* responses) but of distinguishing personality dispositions or traits. Moreover, since any peer responds differently from oneself in at least some situations, it is inevitable that one's peers be seen as the possessors of more numerous and more extreme distinguishing personal characteristics than oneself. The false consensus effect thus allows us to account for many of the phenomena and experimental results that have been mustered in support of Jones and Nisbett's thesis (cf. Jones & Nisbett, 1971; Nisbett *et al.*, 1973) without resorting to the "differing perspective" mechanisms they suggested.

2. Sources of the False Consensus Bias

Investigators who have discussed false consensus phenomena or egocentric attributional biases have typically emphasized their motivational status or function for the individual. Such biases, it is contended, both foster and justify the actor's feelings that his own behavioral choices are appropriate and rational responses to the demands of the environment, rather than reflections of his distinguishing personal dispositions. More dynamic interpretations (e.g., Bramel, 1962, 1963; Edlow & Kiesler, 1966; Lemann & Solomon, 1952; Smith, 1960) have stressed the ego-defensive or dissonance-reducing function of attributive projection, particularly as a response to failure or negative information about one's personal characteristics.

Several nonmotivational factors, more directly relevant to our present concern with the methods of the intuitive psychologist, may play some role in producing false consensus phenomena. Principal among these are (1) "selective exposure" and "availability" factors, and (2) factors pertaining to the resolution of situational ambiguity.

Selective exposure factors underlying false consensus are fairly straightforward. Obviously, we know and associate with people who share our background, experiences, interests, values, and outlook. Such people *do*, in disproportionate numbers, respond as we would in a wide variety of circumstances. Indeed, our close association is determined, in part, by feelings of general consensus, and we may be inclined to avoid those whom we believe unlikely to share our judgments and responses. This exposure to a biased sample of people and behavior does not demand that we err in our estimates concerning the relevant populations, but it does make such errors likely. More subtle, and more cognitive in character, are the factors which increase our ability to recall, visualize, or imagine paradigmatic instances of behavior. In a given situation the specific behaviors that we have chosen, or would choose, are likely to be more readily retrievable from memory and more easily imagined than opposite behaviors. In Kahneman and Tversky's (1973) terms, the behavioral choices we favor may be more cognitively "available," and we are apt to be misled by this ease or difficulty of access in estimating the likelihood of relevant behavioral options.

A second nonmotivational source of the false consensus effect arises from the intuitive psychologist's response to ambiguity—both about the nature and magnitude of situational forces and about the meaning and implications of various response alternatives. Attempts to resolve such ambiguity involve interpretation, estimation, and guesswork, all of which can exert a parallel effect on the attributer's own behavior choices and upon his predictions and inferences about the choices of others.

The biasing effect of ambiguity resolution perhaps is most obvious when the attributer's knowledge of a response or situation is secondhand and lacking in important specific details. Consider, for example, the subject who must decide on the precise meaning of such modifiers as *often* or *typically* or of any other potentially ambiguous descriptors encountered in the context of questionnaire items. It is obvious that both the response category to which that subject assigns himself and his categorizations of his peers will be similarly influenced by these decisions about the precise meaning of terms.

Similarly, the subject who reads about a dilemma regarding the signing of a release form for an impromptu television commercial [in Study 1 of Ross *et al.* (1977b)] is forced to imagine the interviewer, the physical setting, and a host of other situational details which might encourage or inhibit the relevant behavioral options. If these imagined details seemingly would encourage one to sign the release, then the subject is more likely to assume that he personally would sign, that a similar decision would be a common response among his peers, and that signing the release would reflect little about the distinguishing dispositions of any particular actor. By contrast, if the details imagined by the subject would inhibit signing of the release, the subject is more likely to assume that he personally would refuse, that his peers typically would do likewise, and that signing of the release would reveal much about the personal dispositions of the relevant actor.

In questionnaire studies this resolution of ambiguities in descriptions of situations and behaviors may seem a troublesome artifact. However, the same factor becomes an important source of bias in everyday social judgments and inferences where attributers may often respond to accounts of situations or actions that are vague and frequently secondhand. The intuitive psychologist constantly is confronted with statements like "Sally hardly ever dates short men" or "John refused to pay the painter's bill when he saw the paint job." In such circumstances he is forced to resolve ambiguities or uncertainties in the statement. Such resolutions in turn will exert parallel effects upon his assumptions about his own behavior, his impressions about consensus, and his inferences about the dispositions of those whose behavior has been loosely categorized or described.

The false consensus effect demonstrated in Ross *et al.* (1977b), it should be reemphasized, was not restricted to circumstances where raters relied upon ambiguous secondhand descriptions. However, even when attributers actually experience or have fully adequate descriptions of a choice situation, ambiguities remain which inevitably will be resolved differently by different subjects. Thus, subjects who anticipated and feared the ridicule of peers for wearing the "EAT AT JOE'S" sign and regarded the experimenter's wishes and expectations as trivial were likely to refuse to wear the sign, to assume similar refusals by their peers, and to draw strong inferences about the traits of any subject who chose to wear the sign. Opposite priorities, of course, would have produced opposite personal choices and opposite social estimates and inferences.

The false consensus bias, in summary, both reflects and creates distortions in the attribution process. It results from nonrandom sampling and retrieval of evidence and from idiosyncratic interpretation of situational factors and forces. In turn, it biases judgments about deviance and deviates, helps lead actors and observers to divergent perceptions of behavior, and, more generally, promotes variance and error in the interpretation of social phenomena.

C. INADEQUATE ALLOWANCES FOR THE ROLE-BIASED NATURE OF SOCIAL DATA

Interpersonal encounters provide an important informational basis for the intuitive psychologist's self-evaluations and social judgments. Often, however, the course of such encounters is shaped and constrained by the formal and informal roles that the various actors must play. More specifically, social roles typically confer unequal control over the style, content, and duration of an encounter; such control, in turn, facilitates displays of knowledge, skill, wit, or sensitivity, while permitting the concealment of deficiencies. Accurate social judgment, accordingly, depends upon the intuitive psychologist's ability to make adequate allowances and adjustments for such role-conferred advantages and disadvantages in self-perception.

In a recent paper, however, Ross, Amabile, and Steinmetz (1977a) have proposed that social perceivers may typically *fail* to make these "necessary" adjustments and, consequently, may draw inaccurate social inferences about role-advantaged and role-disadvantaged actors. In one sense the proposal of Ross *et al.* is simply a special case of the fundamental attribution error described in Section II,A: The fundamental error is a tendency to underestimate the impact of situational determinants and overestimate the degree to which actions and outcomes reflect the actor's dispositions. The special case proposed by Ross *et al.* deals with the intuitive scientist's underestimation of the effects of roles upon success in self-presentation. In another sense, the proposal of Ross *et al.* contends that the intuitive psychologist is insufficiently sensitive to the biased nature of the data provided by role-constrained encounters and, perhaps, insufficiently sensitive to the problem of sampling bias in general.

The particular roles dealt with in the empirical demonstration reported by Ross *et al.* (1977a) were those of "questioner" and "contestant" in a general knowledge quiz game. The questioner's role obliged the subject to compose a set of challenging general knowledge questions from his or her own store of information, to pose the questions to a contestant, and to provide accurate feedback after each response. Both of these participants (and, in subsequent reenactments, observers as well) were then required to rate the questioner's and the contestant's general knowledge.

The arbitrary assignment and fulfillment of these roles, it should be apparent, forced participants and observers alike to deal with nonrepresentative and highly biased displays of the questioners' knowledge relative to that of contestants. Indeed, the nature of the role-conferred advantages and disadvantages in self-presentation were neither subtle nor disguised. Questioners were allowed and encouraged to display their own wealth of general knowledge by posing difficult and esoteric questions to which their role guaranteed that they would know the answers. The contestant's role, by contrast, prevented any such selective self-serving displays and more displays of ignorance virtually inevitable.

The quiz game contrived by Ross *et al.*, in a sense, provided a particularly stringent test of the intuitive psychologist's proposed insensitivity to role-conferred self-presentation advantages and to corresponding biases in the data samples upon which social judgments frequently are based. For instance, the random nature of the assignment to advantageous and disadvantageous roles was salient and uncontestable. Furthermore, subjects were fully aware of the specific obligations, prerogatives, and limitations associated with each role. In short, subjects seemingly enjoyed an ideal perspective to overcome the proposed source of bias. Nevertheless, the unequal "contest" between questioners and contestants led to consistently biased and erroneous impressions (Table II). As predicted, questioners rated their own general knowledge higher than that of the contestants; moreover, this false impression was shared by the contestants themselves and by uninvolved observers of the encounter.

The narrower as well as the broader implications of the demonstrations of Ross *et al.* should not be overlooked. Indeed, the encounter between advantaged questioners and disadvantaged contestants has obvious parallels within academic settings. Teachers consistently enjoy the prerogative of questioners, and students typically suffer the handicaps of answerers (although some students leap at opportunities to reverse these roles). Consider, as a particularly dramatic in-

TABLE II
EFFECTS OF QUESTIONER–CONTESTANT ROLE UPON
SUBJECTS' PERCEPTIONS OF THEIR OWN AND THEIR
PARTNER'S KNOWLEDGE[a]

Subjects' role	Rating of self[b]	Rating of partner[b]	Self–partner difference
Questioner	54.84	51.66	+3.18
Contestant	40.24	65.16	−24.91

[a]Summarized from Ross et al. (1977a).
[b]Higher number indicates belief that the person rated is relatively high in general knowledge (1 = minimum; 100 = maximum).

stance, the role-constrained encounters that characterize the typical dissertation "orals." The candidate is required to field questions from the idiosyncratic and occasionally esoteric areas of each examiner's interest and expertise. In contrast to the examiners, the candidate has relatively little time for reflection and relatively little power to define or limit the domains of inquiry. In light of the present demonstrations, it might be anticipated (correctly so, in this author's experience) that the typical candidate leaves the ordeal feeling more relief than pride, whereas his or her examiners depart with increased respect for each others' insight and scholarship. Such evaluations, of course, may often be warranted. It is worth entertaining the possibility, however, that an alternative procedure for the oral examination, one in which the candidate first posed questions for his examiners and then corrected *their* errors and omissions, would yield more elated candidates and less smug examiners.

There are, of course, countless other contexts in which formal or informal social roles may constrain interpersonal encounters and, in so doing, bias both the data available to the intuitive psychologist and the interpersonal judgments that follow from such data. Thus the employer may dwell upon his personal triumphs, avocations, and areas of knowledge and may avoid mention of his failures, whereas his employee enjoys no such freedom. The physician, likewise, is relatively free to assume with his patient whichever role—stern parent, sympathetic friend, or detached scientist—he wishes. Similarly, the more dominant partner in a personal relationship can disproportionately dictate the rules and arenas for self-presentation and that partner's choice is likely to be self-serving.

If subsequent research confirms the generality of the present thesis, the implications may be all too clear for our understanding of social structures and of the forces that impede social change. Individuals who enjoy positions of power by accident of birth, favorable political treatment, or even their own efforts also tend to enjoy advantages in self-presentation. Such individuals, and

especially their disadvantaged underlings, may greatly underestimate the extent
to which the seemingly positive attributes of the powerful simply reflect the
advantages of social control. Indeed, this distortion in social judgment threatens
to provide a particularly insidious brake upon social mobility whereby the
disadvantaged and powerless overestimate the capabilities of the powerful, who
in turn inappropriately deem their own caste well suited to the task of leadership.

D. OVERLOOKING THE INFORMATIONAL VALUE OF NONOCCURRENCES

The astute Sherlock Holmes directs our attention to a rather subtle but
potentially interesting and important shortcoming of the intuitive scientist. In
the relevant episode (described in "The Silver Blaze" in *The Memoirs of
Sherlock Holmes* by Arthur Conan Doyle) the great detective invites the faithful
Dr. Watson to consider "the curious incident of the dog in the night-time."
Watson, the conventional behaviorist, remarks correctly that "The dog did
nothing in the night-time." Holmes, the inspired behaviorist, triumphantly
observes, "That was the curious incident." For the premier practitioner of the
science of deduction this *nonincident* or *nonoccurrence* furnishes the key to
subsequent interpretations and inferences. (Specifically, Holmes recognizes that
a barking dog would have provided no evidence but a silent one proved the
intruder in question to be someone well known to the dog.)

The intuitive psychologist, it can more generally be postulated, is like Dr.
Watson, a rather conventional behaviorist. He attends to actions or occurrences
in forming inferences but neglects to consider the information conveyed when
particular responses or events do *not* occur. The author can cite no research
directly relevant to the postulated "behaviorist" bias. One source of indirect
evidence, however, is provided by findings concerning subjects' use of the
observations in a fourfold, presence–absence table. Specifically, Smedslund
(1963), Ward and Jenkins (1965), Wason and Johnson-Laird (1972), and others
report that only the "present–present" cell strongly influences subjects' inferences regarding covariation (for example, the covariation of diseases and symptoms). Logically, of course, frequency in this cell is no more relevant to the
assessment of covariation than are frequencies in any of the other three cells
(including the absent–absent cell, which, if our general contention is apt, should
prove particularly difficult for subjects to use appropriately in forming impressions of covariation and causal inferences).

Although more directly pertinent research data may be lacking, there are a
number of common social experiences which become more explicable in the
light of our present speculations. Consider for example the following, rather
common episode: Jack meets a new acquaintance, Jill, and after some personal
interaction with her, he forms the vague impression that she does not like him.

Such impressions are rarely unfounded. Nevertheless, if Jack searches his memory for specific actions or responses by Jill that reveal her dislike, he will likely be frustrated in his search since, under normal circumstances, acquaintances do not express dislike in overt words or deeds. Thus, if Jack relies upon the sample of evidence he retrieves from memory, he may well conclude that his impression is incorrect and unjustified by the evidence; alternatively, he may cling to his impression but resort to "intuition" or "sixth sense" in order to justify it. If the peerless Mr. Holmes were available for consultation, he doubtless could end Jack's attributional dilemma by focusing his attention on what Jill did *not* do. Jack might well note that Jill did *not* deliberately prolong encounters, did *not* furnish positive nonverbal feedback, and, in general, did *not* show any of the responses that normally signal liking or interest.

In the encounter just described Jack has not been totally oblivious to the information conveyed by Jill's nonresponses—he has correctly discerned her sentiments; he has merely failed to process the information in a manner which facilitates accurate causal inferences or overt verbal expression. In other instances the attributer might even fail to detect or to store the relevant information and might entirely misjudge the sentiments of his acquaintance. The general contention is simply that nonoccurrences are rarely as salient or as cognitively "available" to the potential attributer as are occurrences. As a consequence, recognition, storage, retrieval, and interpretation all become less likely.

The difference between an occurrence and a nonoccurrence can, of course, sometimes be one of semantics. The absence of eye contact can be coded by the potential attributer as the presence of gaze avoidance (e.g., Ellsworth & Ross, 1975). The absence of sexual responsiveness similarly can be coded and interpreted as the presence of frigidity. These seemingly moot semantic distinctions, however, can have nontrivial consequences for the intuitive psychologist. Indeed, if present speculations are warranted, it should be possible to demonstrate that particular absences of response are more noted, more remembered, and more likely deemed as relevant by the attributer when he is provided with positive or active category labels to apply to such absences.

III. Attributional Biases in the Psychology of Prediction

Implicit expectations and explicit predictions are important products of the intuitive psychologist's collection, coding, storage, retrieval, and interpretation of social data. Often, such expectations and predictions are also crucial mediators of social responses. The attribution theorist, as we have noted earlier, has reason to be concerned with intuitive prediction not only because of its obvious connection to widely studied attributional processes, but also because of its unique potential for revealing the degree of attributional accuracy and the direction of particular biases. Nevertheless, it has not been attribution researchers but rather two cognitive psychologists, Daniel Kahneman and Amos Tversky, who recently have stirred social psychology's interest in prediction.[5]

A. THREE HEURISTICS GOVERNING INTUITIVE PREDICTION AND JUDGMENT

In a very impressive series of papers (Kahneman & Tversky, 1972, 1973; Tversky & Kahneman, 1971, 1973, 1974) these investigators have demonstrated that intuitive predictions and judgments made by typical social observers (and often those made by trained social scientists as well) deviate markedly from the dictates of conventional statistical models. Instead, such predictions seem to reflect the operation of a limited number of "heuristics," or informal decision-making criteria. Among these heuristics are "availability" (Kahneman & Tversky, 1973), "adjustment" (Tversky & Kahneman, 1974), and "representativeness" (Kahneman & Tversky, 1972, 1973). Each heuristic leads the intuitive psychologist to particular errors or biases in subjective estimates and predictions, and each is relevant to the concerns of this chapter.

Use of the *availability* heuristic leads the intuitive psychologist's estimates of the frequency or probability of events to reflect the ease of imagining or remembering those events. Since availability is often poorly correlated with frequency or probability, systematic errors and biases in judgment inevitably result. Thus subjects who heard lists of well-known personalities of both sexes subsequently overestimated the representation of that sex whose members were more famous. The false consensus bias, described earlier, and Chapman and Chapman's (1967, 1969) classic demonstrations of "illusory correlation" in clinical judgment, also seem to reflect the operation of the availability heuristic. Finally, we shall cite the role of availability in our subsequent discussions of impression perseverance and the effects of explanation upon expectation.

Use of the *adjustment* heuristic leads one to make estimates and predictions by "adjusting" either some salient initial value or the result of some partial computation procedure. Such adjustments, however, are rarely sufficient, and the result is typically an "anchoring effect." In one study (Tversky & Kahneman, 1974), for example, subjects were asked to adjust an arbitrary initial estimate of the percentage of African countries in the United Nations. Those starting with anchors of 10% or 65% produced adjusted estimates of 25% and

[5] Unfortunately, the scope of the present chapter forces us to neglect earlier contributions dealing with subjective prediction, expectation, and discrepancies between logical and "psychological" judgment (e.g., Alberoni, 1962; Edwards, 1968; Peterson & Beach, 1967; Slovic & Lichtenstein, 1971; Wheeler & Beach, 1968). Much of this research is acknowledged and described in Kaheman and Tversky's papers and in a recent review by Fischhoff (1976).

45%, respectively. Tversky and Kahneman argue convincingly that overestimation of likelihood for conjunctive events (i.e., the likelihood of A *and* B *and* C *all* occurring) and underestimation for disjunctive events (i.e., the likelihood of at least *one* of A *or* B *or* C occurring) are further results of the intuitive statistician's failure to adequately adjust preliminary or partially computed estimates.

Use of the *representativeness* heuristic is easier to illustrate than to define. It is reflected in the intuitive statistician's tendency to predict that outcome which appears most representative of salient features of the evidence while ignoring conventional statistical criteria such as the reliability, validity, and amount of available evidence, or the prior baseline probabilities associated with the relevant outcomes.

A use of the representativeness heuristic that is particularly striking and pertinent to present concerns is reflected in the intuitive scientist's tendency to give too much weight to *predictor* variables and too little weight to central tendencies in the population distribution of the variable to be *predicted*. Indeed, a sample prediction problem may help the reader to recognize his or her own susceptibility to this bias: *I (the present author) have a friend who is a professor. He likes to write poetry, is rather shy, and is slight of stature. Which of the following is his field: (a) Chinese Studies, or (b) psychology?* The reader who has guessed Chinese Studies, or even seriously entertained the possibility, has fallen victim to the bias described so compellingly by Kahneman and Tversky. Let the unconvinced reader first consider his prediction in light of the number of psychology professors relative to the number of Chinese Studies professors in the overall population. Then let him further consider the more restricted population of the present author's likely friends. Surely *no* psychologist's implicit personality theory about the relationship among avocation, shyness, stature, and academic discipline is sufficiently strong to warrant overlooking such "baseline" considerations.

Errors in parametric prediction problems similarly reflect the use of the representativeness heuristic. Most obvious, perhaps, is the layman's shortcomings in dealing with problems of regression. People expect and predict behaviors and outcomes on variable Y to be as "distinctive" or deviant from the norm as the predictor variable X, and they are surprised and often disturbed by the phenomenon of "regression to the mean."[6] In fact, they are prone to invent spurious explanations for events that, in reality, are simple regression phenomena. Kahneman and Tversky (1973) describe a relevant anecdote: Israeli flight instructors, urged to make use of positive reinforcement, expressed skepticism. In their experience, they argued, praise of exceptionally good performance typically "led

---

[6] Nonregressive prediction is, in a sense, a special case of the intuitive statistician's inattentiveness to "baselines" or population distributions for the variable to be predicted. A regressive prediction minimizes error relative to a nonregressive one simply because the former is closer to more observations in the population than is the latter.

to" *diminished* performance on the next trial, while criticism of exceptionally poor performance typically "produced" an immediate *improvement* in performance. On the basis of such firsthand experience, in fact, the instructors concluded that, contrary to accepted psychological doctrine, punishment is more effective than reward.

B. USE OF CONCRETE INSTANCES VS. ABSTRACT BASELINES

The relevance of Kahneman and Tversky's work to the general concerns of attribution theory has recently begun to be appreciated (cf. Fischhoff, 1976). Nisbett and Borgida (1975), for example, were quick to note that the weak effects of base rate information on category prediction are analogous to the weak effects of consensus information on attributional judgments (e.g., Cooper, Jones, & Tuller, 1972; McArthur, 1972, 1976; A. G. Miller, Gillen, Schenker, & Radlove, 1973). Pursuing the implications of this observation, Nisbett and Borgida demonstrated that intuitive behavioral predictions, like category predictions, may be relatively impervious to consensus or baseline information. Specifically, subjects were given accurate baseline information about the behavior of previous participants in experiments involving such responses as altruistic. intervention and willingness to receive electric shock. As the investigators anticipated, this authentic baseline information did not influence subjects' guesses about the behavior of particular participants in the original experiment. Similarly, this information did not influence subjects' attributions about the causes of such behavior, or their predictions about what their own behavior might be.

Nisbett and Borgida's research design also considered the opposite prediction task, that of estimating overall base rates for behavior on the basis of knowledge provided about the responses of particular individuals. The results were dramatic and consistent with yet another bias described by Tversky and Kahneman (1971). Nisbett and Borgida's subjects' previously demonstrated "unwillingness to deduce the particular from the general was matched only by their *willingness* to infer the general from the particular" (p. 939). Thus, given information that two subjects had behaved in an extreme and counterintuitive fashion (e.g., by taking the maximum possible shock level in a pain threshold experiment), raters predicted that such extreme behavior was *modal* for subjects as a whole.

In attempting to account for these seemingly contradictory but equally nonrational prediction biases, Nisbett, Borgida, Crandall, and Reed (1976) have contrasted the *concreteness* and vividness of specific cases with the pallid *abstract* character of statistical baselines. To illustrate, they invited their readers to participate in the following "thought experiment":

> Let us suppose that you wish to buy a new car and have decided that on grounds of economy and longevity you want to purchase one of those solid, stalwart, middleclass Swedish cars—either a Volvo or a Saab. As a prudent and sensible

buyer, you go to *Consumer Reports*, which informs you that the consensus of their experts is that the Volvo is mechanically superior, and the consensus of the readership is that the Volvo has the better repair record. Armed with this information, you decide to go and strike a bargain with the Volvo dealer before the week is out. In the interim, however, you go to a cocktail party where you announce this intention to an acquaintance. He reacts with disbelief and alarm: "A Volvo! You've got to be kidding. My brother-in-law had a Volvo. First, the fancy fuel injection computer thing went out. 250 bucks. Next he started having trouble with the rearend. Had to replace it. Then the transmission and the clutch. Finally sold it in 3 years for junk." [p. 129]

The logical status of this information, Nisbett *et al.* remind the reader, is that the frequency-of-repair record should be shifted by an iota or two on a few dimensions. As they contend, however, the reader's thought experiment is likely to suggest a more dramatic result. The implications of this thought experiment are also borne out in more formal empirical demonstrations. In a series of experiments Borgida and Nisbett (1977) gave undergraduate subjects course-evaluation information and invited them to state their own choices for future enrollment. Some students received summaries of the evaluations of previous course enrollees; others received the information through face-to-face contact with a small number of individuals. As anticipated by the investigators, abstract data-summary information had little impact on course choices, whereas concrete information had a substantial impact.

C. SOURCES OF NONCONSERVATIVE (NONREGRESSIVE) PREDICTION

Demonstrations of man's apparent failings as an intuitive statistician promise to capture the attention of attribution theorists. In attempting to clarify the implications of seminal research in this area by Kahneman and Tversky and by others (cf. Fischhoff, 1976), it is important to distinguish between two different sources of bias or error in judgment. Ross *et al.* (1976a) have termed these, respectively, shortcomings in intuitive *psychological theory* and shortcomings in informal *statistical methodology*. The former are misconceptions about the nature of objects and events in the domain of psychological inquiry; the latter are faulty applications of knowledge or information about that domain in making estimates, inferences, and predictions.

Ross, Amabile, and their associates have emphasized this distinction in a series of studies dealing with the intuitive psychologist—statistician's tendency to be "nonconservative" (i.e., nonregressive) in bivariate prediction tasks. In these studies (Amabile, 1975; Ross *et al.*, 1976a) the investigators made use of "authentic" data distributions derived from preliminary studies, student records, and self-report questionnaires. The use of such authentic data, of course, permitted direct assessment of the degree of accuracy and the direction of error in the subjects' predictions and estimates.

Amabile (1975) and Ross *et al.* (1976a) had little difficulty in replicating the basic phenomenon described by Kahneman and Tversky (1972, 1973). Subjects' predictions about the behavior, characteristics, and outcomes of their peers were clearly nonregressive and, by conventional statistical criteria, insufficiently "conservative." For bivariate distributions in which population or large sample correlations were in the range of $r = 0$ to $r = +.30$, subjects made predictions of one variable based on knowledge of the other variable that would have been justified only by correlations in the range of $r = +.60$ to $r = +1.00$.

As anticipated, two distinct sources of error were shown to underlie such nonregressive prediction tendencies. First, it was clear that the intuitive scientists in these studies typically held incorrect assumptions about the strength of the relationship among the observable characteristics and behaviors under consideration. Subjects were required to specify the degree of relationship they believed to exist between particular variables through a variety of "matching tasks" using scatterplots, bivariate charts of numbers, and figures portraying different degrees of covariation between simple physical properties. Using such procedures, subjects consistently overestimated the relevant correlation coefficients and, in so doing, consistently overestimated the degree of cross-situational consistency existing in the relevant behavioral measures and outcomes. This source of bias, accordingly, can be termed *correlation error*. In a sense, it reflects the intuitive psychologist's unwarranted adherence to simple broad "trait theories" of the sort that receive so little support in the systematic investigations of personality theorists (cf. Mischel, 1968, 1969, 1973).

A second source of bias reported by the investigators reflects the intuitive scientist's failure not as a psychologist but as a statistician. This bias, which we may term *regression error*, was reflected in predictions of variable Y from knowledge of variable X that were even less regressive than could be justified by the subjects' already-inflated estimates of population correlation. An example from the results reported by Amabile (1975) will help to illustrate the two different sources of nonconservative prediction. In one problem subjects dealt with the relationship between verbal Scholastic Aptitude Test (SAT) scores and subsequent GPA measures for Stanford freshmen. Through examination of a large sample of academic records the investigators estimated the relevant population correlation coefficient (Pearson r) to be $+.20$. The subjects' estimate for this relationship, indicated by their choice of appropriately labeled scatterplots, was a correlation coefficient of $+.60$ (i.e., correlation error). The subjects' predictions of GPAs from knowledge of SAT scores and vice versa, however, would have been justified by a population correlation not of $+.60$ but of $+.94$ (i.e., regression error). This pattern of results was replicated using a wide variety of authentic data matrices involving cross-situational consistency in outcomes, personal characteristics, and behaviors.

The data for individual subjects' predictions in the Ross and Amabile studies provide an interesting and more precise view of nonregressive prediction tendencies. Very few individuals rigorously and systematically applied a simple linear "prediction equation." Furthermore, it appears that subjects' departures from consistent linear prediction were governed by the strength of the relationship they believed to exist between X and Y. When the relationship was estimated to be strong, their individual predictions were well fit by a simple linear function. When the relationship was believed to be weak, subject's predictions varied widely about a best-fitting regression line. More specifically, the subjects who believed the relationship between X and Y to be relatively weak did *not* respond to extreme values of X with predictions of Y relatively close to the mean. Instead, they responded by *varying* their predictions (for example, by predicting one more extreme value of Y and one less extreme value of Y, given two identically extreme values of the predictor variable X).

The data on accuracy were also revealing. Group estimates of Y, "enlightened" by specific knowledge of X, consistently yielded a greater mean error (in terms of both absolute and square discrepancies) than would have resulted if the group had averaged across all of those estimates to produce one mean to be offered for all predictions. Similarly the vast majority of individual subjects in the various studies would have decreased the magnitude of their errors by simply repeating their average prediction for Y, never varying it on the basis of their knowledge of X. It is difficult to resist the blunt summary that, when it comes to predictions, a little knowledge (i.e., knowledge of a weakly related predictor variable) is a dangerous thing.

Before concluding our discussion of the intuitive psychologist's penchant for nonconservative prediction, a few qualifications, comments, and suggestions concerning future research directions may be in order. First, it is important to recognize that while the term *nonconservative* may be descriptive of the intuitive scientist's judgments in the contexts we have described,[7] it may not accurately describe his intent or his new view of his behavior. Indeed, he may be led to nonregressive prediction through a chain of inferences that seem impeccably conservative.

Consider, for example, a request to predict John's percentile score on a mathematics text in light of information that John scored at the ninetieth percentile in a reading test. The intuitive psychologist–statistician may begin by recognizing that academic abilities tend to be positively correlated and by reasoning that John's math score is likely to be better than average. He may then assume that, having no information about John's math score, he has no basis for predicting whether it will be higher or lower than John's reading score. From the

---

[7] There is ample evidence, in fact, that in certain judgmental contexts (those involving Bayesian probability) the intuitive psychologist is *overly* "conservative"; that is, he fails to extract sufficient information about population parameters from the data examples available to him (see Peterson & Beach, 1967; Slovic & Lichtenstein, 1971). Such conservatism, perhaps, reflects the operation both of the simple "adjustment" heuristic and of the more general "perseverance mechanisms" to be described later in this chapter.

intuitive scientist's viewpoint it may thus seem conservative to guess that the relevant scores will be equal (a judgment that would be justified, in conventional statistical terms, only by a *perfect* correlation) because such a guess seemingly represents the "middle course" between guessing either that X is greater than Y or that Y is greater than X.

A second conceptual issue involves the criterion for optimal prediction. It is entirely possible that subjects may be guided by considerations other than accuracy, or by criteria for accuracy very different from those adopted by the conventional statistician. We certainly have no a priori reason to assume that social observers are particularly concerned with minimizing average *squared* discrepancies, or even with minimizing average absolute discrepancies. Perhaps subjects are concerned with maximizing the number of "exact hits"; perhaps they are willing to increase their "average error" if it will help them to predict the few really deviant or extreme scores in the sample. Some subjects may even be concerned with criteria that are irrelevant to accuracy, for example, making their distribution of predictions reflect the range or variability of the sample scores to be predicted. Any of these nonconventional statistical goals or desiderata may characterize particular subjects or particular data domains (cf. Abelson, 1974). Indeed, one could readily suggest prediction contexts in everyday experience for which each objective would be highly appropriate.

Subsequent research could clarify these issues considerably by pursuing the following research questions: (1) What are subjects' own objectives and what are their criteria for good prediction—in the standard laboratory tasks that have been employed and in a wide range of judgment tasks outside the laboratory? (2) Do subjects recognize the costs of nonregressive prediction strategies, and do they labor under illusions about the possible benefits of such strategies? (3) What kind of feedback in a prediction paradigm, if any, could lead subjects to adopt and to generalize the use of more regressive strategies? Indeed, in what data domains, if any, may subjects already make use of such strategies, and why do they do so?

IV. Perseverance of Social Inferences and Social Theories

A. PERSEVERANCE IN SELF-PERCEPTIONS AND SOCIAL PERCEPTIONS

In the course of this chapter various biases in the sampling, processing, and interpretation of social data have been described. These biased strategies and procedures produce initial impressions about oneself or other people that typically are premature and often are erroneous. As long as they remain private and free of behavioral commitment, such first impressions may seem inconsequential, tentative in nature, and free to adjust to new input. A gradually increasing body of theory and research, however, can now be marshaled to suggest the contrary. We shall deal in detail with a pair of "debriefing" experiments reported by Ross, Lepper, and Hubbard (1975). These were designed to provide a simple and dramatic demonstration that errors in initial self-perceptions and social judgments are difficult to reverse and may survive even the complete negation of their original evidential basis (cf. also Walster, Berscheid, Abrahams, & Aronson, 1967; Valins, 1974).

The procedure in the experiments of Ross *et al.* was quite straightforward. Subjects first received continuous false feedback as they performed a novel discrimination task (i.e., distinguishing authentic suicide notes from ficticious ones). In the first experiment reported, this procedure was used to manipulate the subjects' perceptions of their own performance and ability. A second experiment further introduced observers who formed social impressions as they witnessed the false-feedback manipulation. In both experiments, after this manipulation of first impressions had been completed, the experimenter totally discredited the "evidence" upon which the actors' and/or observers' impressions had been based. Specifically, the actor (overheard in Experiment 2 by the observer) received a standard "debriefing" session in which he learned that his putative outcome had been predetermined and that his feedback had been totally unrelated to actual performance. Before dependent variable measures were introduced, in fact, every subject was led to acknowledge explicitly his understanding of the nature and purpose of the experimental deception.

Following this total discrediting of the original source of misinformation, a dependent variable questionnaire was completed dealing with the actors' performances and abilities. The evidence for postdebriefing impression perseverance was unmistakable for actors and observers alike. On virtually every measure (i.e., objective estimates of the actor's just-completed performance, estimates for performance on a future set of discrimination problems, and subjective estimates of the actor's abilities) the totally discredited initial outcome manipulation produced significant "residual" effects upon actors' and observers' assessments (see Table III).

In subsequent related experiments Ross, Lepper, and their colleagues have pursued the perseverance phenomenon using a variety of experimental settings and personal abilities. Although much of this research is still in progress, it is already apparent that the phenomenon is not restricted to the debriefing paradigm or to the suicide note task. For instance, students' erroneous impressions of their "logical problem-solving abilities" (and their academic choices in a follow-up measure 1 month later) persevered even after students learned that good or poor teaching procedures provided a totally sufficient explanation for their success or failure (Lau, Lepper, & Ross, 1976).

TABLE III
POSTDEBRIEFING PERCEPTIONS OF THE ACTOR'S PERFORMANCE AND
ABILITY[a]

Measure	Actor's own perceptions			Observer's perceptions of actors		
	Success	Failure	t	Success	Failure	t
Estimated initial number correct	18.33	12.83	5.91^e	19.00	12.42	4.43^e
Predicted future number correct	18.33	14.25	4.23^e	19.08	14.50	2.68^c
Rated ability at task	5.00	3.83	2.65^c	5.33	4.00	3.36^d
Related abilities at related tasks	4.69	4.53	<1.00	4.69	4.11	1.76^b

[a]Summarized from experiment 2 of Ross et al. (1975).
[b]$p < .10$.
[c]$p < .05$.
[d]$p < .01$.
[e]$p < .001$.

B. PERSEVERANCE MECHANISMS

1. Distortion and Autonomy

Two related mechanisms have been proposed by Ross and Lepper to account for perseverance phenomena. The first involves *distortion* in the process by which the intuitive psychologist assesses the relevance, reliability, and validity of potentially pertinent data. That is, the weight he assigns to evidence is determined, in large measure, by its consistency with his initial impressions. More specifically, he neglects the possibility that evidence seemingly consistent with his existing impressions may nevertheless be irrelevant or tainted; similarly, he too readily conceives and accepts challenges to contradictory evidence. As a result, data considered subsequent to the formation of a clear impression typically will seem to offer a large measure of support for that impression. Indeed, even a random sample of potentially relevant data "processed" in this manner may serve to strengthen rather than challenge an erroneous impression. The capacity of existing impressions and expectations to bias interpretations of social data is, of course, a well-replicated phenomenon in social psychology (e.g., Asch, 1946; Haire & Grunes, 1950; Hastorf & Cantril, 1954; Jones & Goethals, 1971; Zadny & Gerard, 1974).

The second proposed mechanism involves the *autonomy* achieved by distorted evidence. Once formed, an initial impression may not only be enhanced by the distortion of evidence, it may ultimately by *sustained* by such distortion. The social perceiver, it is contended, rarely reinterprets or reattributes impression-relevant data when the basis for his original bias in processing that data is discredited. Once coded, the evidence becomes autonomous from the coding scheme, and its impact ceases to depend upon the validity of that scheme. Thus an erroneous impression may survive the discrediting of its original evidential basis because the impression has come to enjoy the support of additional evidence that is seemingly *independent* of that now-discredited basis.

2. The Role of Explanation in Impression Perseverance

In accounting for the attributer's reluctance to abandon initial impressions, Ross *et al.* (1975) have emphasized the role of the intuitive psychologist's search for causal explanation. Individuals, they suggest do more than merely aggregate information consistent with their self-perceptions and social perceptions. They also search for antecedents that cause and account for events. These "causal schemata" play a particularly important role in impression perseverance. Once an action, outcome, or personal disposition is viewed as the consequence of known or even postulated antecedents, those antecedents will continue to *imply* the relevant consequence even when all other evidence is removed.

Consider, for example, a subject in the Ross *et al.* (1975) study who has attributed her success in discriminating suicide notes to the insights she gained from the writings of a novelist who committed suicide. Consider, similarly, an observer in that study who has attributed an actor's failure to that actor's manifestly cheerful disposition. Even after debriefing, these attributers retain a plausible basis for inferring the relevant outcome of the discrimination task. Neither participant, of course, has initially considered, or reconsidered after briefing, the many possible antecedents that might have caused and accounted for task outcomes opposite to that contrived by the experimenters.

A series of recent experiments reported by Ross, Lepper, Strack, and Steinmetz (1976c) have provided more direct evidence of the role that causal explanation can play in sustaining discredited impressions and expectations. In these experiments, subjects were presented with authentic clinical case histories. In various experimental conditions they were asked to use this case-study information to explain a significant event in the patient's later life (e.g., suicide, a hit-and-run accident, an attempt to gain elective office, or an altruistic act). In some conditions, subjects wrote their explanations believing that the event had actually occurred, only to learn afterward that the event was hypothetical and that absolutely no authentic information existed concerning the patient's later life. In other conditions, the event to be explained was presented as "merely hypothetical" from the outset. In both experimental conditions, subjects were ultimately asked to estimate the likelihood of the previously explained events and a number of other events as well. (In appropriate control conditions, subjects were given only this final prediction task.)

The results were unambiguous and compelling (Table IV). As hypothesized, the task of identifying case-history antecedents to explain an event increased the

TABLE IV

RESIDUAL EFFECTS OF "EXPLAINING" AN EVENT ON JUDGED LIKELIHOOD OF
THAT EVENT[a]

Event previously explained by subject[b]	Estimated likelihood[c] that patient will:		
	[A] Become involved in hit-and-run accident	[B] Seek election to City Council	Difference [A] − [B]
[A] Patient becomes involved in hit-and-run accident	+1.45	−2.47	+3.92
[B] Patient seeks election to City Council	−0.25	+0.66	−0.91
[C] None	−0.08	−1.55	+1.47

[a]Summarized from Ross et al. (1976c).

[b]Data are combined for subjects who explained event initially believing it to be real and for subjects who explained event knowing it to be hypothetical.

[c]More positive number indicates greater belief that the specified event is likely to have actually occurred in patient's life.

subjects' estimates of that event's likelihood. The relevant phenomenon was replicated across a variety of cases and predicted events and was demonstrated under both the "hypothetical" and "nonhypothetical" explanation conditions [see also Fischhoff (1975, 1976) and Fischhoff and Beyth (1975) for a discussion of the "certainty of hindsight knowledge," a phenomenon that may be closely related to the present demonstrations and may depend upon similar mechanisms].

C. PERSEVERANCE OF "THEORIES"

It should be apparent that the same biased attributional processes which sustain discredited individual inferences may also sustain the discredited attributional strategies that give rise to such inferences. Consider, for instance, the nonregressive or nonconservative prediction strategies discussed earlier. Why does the intuitive scientist continue to believe that correlations reflecting cross-situational consistency are strong when the evidence of his everyday experience will suggest that such correlations are weak? Why does he continue to make nonregressive predictions in a world that, presumably, better rewards more conservative strategies? The answers should be apparent from our foregoing discussion of impression perseverance. First, the intuitive observer selectively codes those data potentially relevant to the relationship between X and Y. Data points that fit his hypotheses and predictions are accepted as reliable, valid, representative, and free of error or "third-variable influences." Such data points are seen as reflective of the "real" or "paradigmatic" relationship between X and

Y. By contrast, data points that deviate markedly from the intuitive psychologist's expectations or theory are unlikely to be given great weight and tend to be dismissed as unreliable, erroneous, unrepresentative, or the product of contaminating third-variable influences.

Thus the intuitive scientist who believes that fat men are jolly, or more specifically that fatness causes jolliness, will see particular fat and jolly men as strong evidence for this theory; he will not entertain the hypothesis that an individual's jollity is mere pretense or the product of a particularly happy home life rather than obesity. By contrast, fat and morose individuals will be examined very carefully before gaining admission to that scientist's store of relevant data. He might, for instance, seek to determine whether the individual's moroseness on the day in question is atypical, or the result of a nagging cold or a disappointing day, rather than the reflection of some stable attribute. It need hardly be emphasized that even a *randomly* generated scatterplot or contingency table can yield a relatively high correlation if coded in the manner just outlined (cf. Chapman & Chapman, 1967, 1969). Indeed, the professional psychologist, like the intuitive one, can readily derive unwarranted support for almost any hypothesis if permitted to delete, post hoc, the data points that offend his thesis. Perseverant beliefs in extrasensory perception in the face of disconfirming experimental evidence may reflect such selective processing of data (see Gardner, 1975).

The autonomy enjoyed by distorted inferences may further contribute to the perseverance of nonoptimal theories and attributional strategies. The intuitive scientist detects more support for his general theory than is warranted and, having thus "coded" or summarized his findings, he is then disposed to maintain his theory in the face of subsequent logical or empirical attacks by "citing" the wealth of seemingly independent empirical support that it enjoys. It is through such means, perhaps, that the intuitive psychologist remains committed to concepts of broad, stable, heuristically valuable, personality traits and perseveres in the use of nonoptimal prediction strategies. Superstitious learning phenomena and the "partial reinforcement effect" similarly may reflect the subject's capacity to selectively attribute instances of reinforcement and nonreinforcement.

D. WHEN JUDGMENTS AND THEORIES CHANGE: OVERCOMING PERSEVERANCE MECHANISMS

An obvious question begins to emerge from our demonstrations of impression perseverance: Under what circumstances *do* erroneous or unwarranted personal judgments change? Clearly, none of us has exactly the same view of ourselves or of our fellows as he once did; personal experiences do have an impact upon such views. Therapy, education, persuasive arguments, and mass media campaigns also can alter our self-perceptions and social attitudes. Indeed, as we pointed out early in this chapter, psychology's broad view of man has changed and evolved in response to arguments and evidence presented by the field's vanguard. While a detailed examination of the requisites for such change is beyond the scope of the present discussion, a few observations may be appropriate.

First, it seems clear that neither challenges to specific bits of evidence confirming a belief (or theory) nor the addition of small amounts of contradictory evidence are likely to prove effective in producing overall change. Challenges and additions to data tend themselves to be "selectively" coded in accord with one's biased prior impressions. Such selective coding, in fact, generally is quite rational and reasonable: most of our personal impressions and beliefs *are* well founded, and confirming evidence usually *is* more valid, representative, and relevant than disconfirming evidence. But this rational selectivity in interpreting individual "bits" of evidence leads to an irrational result when a whole "batch" of evidence is considered; specifically, virtually any random sample of newly considered evidence processed in this manner will seemingly support the existing belief or theory. In the face of subsequent logical or informational challenges, furthermore, the random sample of newly "processed" data may even help to sustain the incorrect theory which dictated the processing bias. Consider, for instance, an apparently close friendship. Individual acts by either friend will be taken at face value by the other if they seem to reflect sensitivity, concern, affection, or interest. Conversely, particular acts that might seem insensitive, cold, or hostile in the eyes of some disinterested observer will *not* be taken at face value by the other—at least not without the presence of a good deal of corroborating evidence and the absence of potential alternative interpretations. Such biased attributional coding, it should be reemphasized, is not irrational. Our past experiences, and our global views of relationships, generally *do* promote more accurate attributions of specific acts and outcomes. By "rationally" giving our friends the "benefit of the doubt" in our inferences about individual acts, however, we risk irrational interpretations of larger samples of evidence. Specifically, we may be prone to overlook systematic evidence of indifference or resentment until it is overwhelming or until our peers explicitly interpret their behavior for us.

Erroneous impressions, theories, and data-processing strategies, therefore, may not be changed through mere exposure to samples of new evidence. It is not contended, of course, that new evidence can never produce change—only that new evidence will produce *less* change than would be demanded by any logical or rational information-processing model. Thus, new evidence that is strongly and consistently contrary to one's impressions or theories can, and frequently does, produce change, albeit at a slower rate than would result from an unbiased or dispassionate view of the evidence.

It seems clear that the effects of attributional distortion and autonomy can also be overcome without the brute force of consistently disconfirming data.

Dramatic religious and political conversions, for example, presumably are accomplished by other means. Specifically, these conversions seem to be the product not of new data nor attacks on old beliefs but, rather, involve assaults on whole belief systems. Typically, the target of the conversion attempt is not induced to reevaluate the evidence "objectively" or dispassionately. Instead, he is taught to make use of a new and encompassing attributional bias. Often he is also urged to reject all past beliefs and insights as the product of pernicious social, philosophical, or political forces. The attempt to induce a tabula rasa state in the individual and to provide a selective interpretation schema for both the consideration of new evidence and the reconsideration of old evidence is characteristic of strategies for ideological conversion. Insight therapies similarly attempt to overcome impression perseverance through global assaults on belief systems and through the introduction of new explanatory or inferential schemata (although the "working through" of isolated incidents and experiences responsible for perseverant feelings and perceptions is also an important aspect of many therapy regimens).

In a more limited vein, it is worth briefly considering one additional result reported by Ross *et al.* (1975). In one relevant experiment, two different types of debriefing conditions were employed. In the standard "outcome debriefing" condition, subjects were made aware that the prior success–failure manipulation

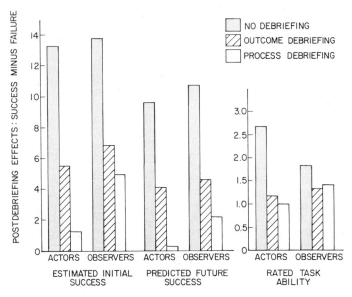

Fig. 2. Postdebriefing differences between success and failure conditions for actors and observers. Summarized from Experiment 2 of Ross *et al.* (1975). Copyright 1975 by The American Psychological Association. Reprinted by permission.

had been a total deception and that their "outcome" had been assigned without regard to their real performance and ability. In special "process debriefing" conditions, subjects also received an explicit discussion of the perseverance phenomenon and of the distortion and autonomy mechanisms which might lead them, personally, to retain inappropriate or inaccurate self-perceptions. Figure 2 presents the relevant data. While the regular debriefing procedures could not eliminate postdebriefing effects of the original outcome manipulation, the special process debriefing conditions were almost totally effective for actors (although less effective for observers). This demonstration, at the very least, suggests process debriefing is an important requirement for the ethical conduct of deception research. It also hints that personal insight concerning one's attributional biases may hasten the achievement of therapeutic goals.

V. Attributional Biases and Social Science Research

A. THE RESEARCHER'S PURSUIT OF NONOBVIOUS PREDICTIONS AND RESULTS

Among social psychologists today there is an epidemic of critical self-evaluation and debate about the current status of the field's theory, research strategy, practical contributions, and prospects for the future. In such soul-searching appraisals, the issue of "nonobviousness" has figured prominently (cf. McGuire, 1973). Researchers feel compelled to defend the nonobviousness or counter-intuitiveness of their findings lest they be ridiculed as practitioners of "bubba psychology." Furthermore, results deemed subtle and surprising by the investigator may too often seem obvious to one reader (cf. Fischhoff & Slovic, 1976), gratituitous to a second reader, and simply wrong or misconstrued to a third. The issue of nonobviousness, and its relationship to research strategy, can be reconsidered in the light of our present concern with the shortcomings of the intuitive and the professional psychologist.

It is important, first, to distinguish nonobvious empirical results from non-obvious functional relationships. Rarely does the investigator, in his pursuit of nonobviousness, postulate a direct relationship between two variables that were previously considered to be unrelated or inversely related. The nonobvious nature of most predictions in social psychology, instead, relates to the specific context in which the relationship between variables is tested. By carefully contriving the balance of forces operating in a particular setting, the investigator attempts to prove a deficiency both in the intuitive commonsense psychology of the layman and in the existing conceptual analyses of the investigator's professional peers. The demonstration will be both successful and nonobvious to the extent that those factors identified or manipulated by the investigator are more potent determinants of behavior than are other factors which would justify the "intuitive," but wrong, hypothesis. In other words, the researcher proceeds from the assumption that his professional audience is prone to some attributional bias that leads it either to ignore the relevance or to underestimate the relative magnitude of a particular set of behavioral determinants. Typically, the investigator also introduces and makes salient in his description of the research setting other potential determinants which he believes will have less impact than his professional peers expect. If the attribution biases illustrated are genuine, and the relevant determinants and experimental context are of broad significance, the research is likely to become highly visible and controversial. If the investigator has incorrectly characterized the relative weightings assigned to behavioral determinants by his peers, or has dealt with very restricted failings in such weightings, then the demonstration will be dismissed as "obvious" or "too limited in its applicability and interest." Needless to say, the research strategy of capitalizing on nonobvious predictions may depend no less on the investigator's abilities as a stage manager and mystery writer than on his ability to recognize inadequacies either in contemporary psychological theory or in the informal attribution theories of his colleagues.

Earlier in this chapter we discussed the special relevance of the fundamental attribution error that leads the intuitive psychologist to underestimate the magnitude of situational factors relative to dispositional factors or individual differences. Now the argument can be generalized to suggest that the most "classic" experiments in social psychology are nonobvious in terms of the *relative magnitude*, rather than the existence, of the situational forces they manipulate or identify. Consider Milgram's (1963) provocative demonstrations of "obedience" or Asch's (1955) studies of conformity. The importance of such research clearly does not lie in the demonstration that subjects obey authority figures or that conformity pressures excited by peers have an impact. That *would* be dull, obvious, and scientifically unproductive. Rather, they demonstrate that these variables are important *relative* to other personal and situational influences that most of us had previously thought to be far more important determinants of behavior (see Ross, Bierbrauer, & Hoffman, 1976b).

In this connection it is worth noting that these celebrated demonstrations share a very unusual characteristic—they employ no control group. Typically, of course, a control group is necessary to establish some kind of baseline from which the experimental group deviates significantly. Asch and Milgram, however, were able to let our intuitions or expectations serve as the baseline condition from which deviations could be noted. Clearly, in their classic studies, the degree of deviation from expectations was sufficiently compelling *without* statistically contrasting the experimental conditions with some control condition. It is not surprising, furthermore, that each of the classic demonstrations cited has led critics to contend that the surprising effects demonstrated were the products of factors other than those proposed by the original investigators. Indeed, such truly nonobvious demonstrations become a continuing source of inspiration and a challenge for successive generations of scientists.

B. THE INTUITIVE PSYCHOLOGIST'S ILLUSIONS AND INSIGHTS

The same attributional biases that provide the basis for nonobvious research demonstrations by misleading the professional scientist may also mislead intuitive psychologists who serve as their subjects. Nisbett and Wilson (1977) recently have described several dramatic instances of the experimental subject's inability to identify accurately the nature and magnitude of the situational features or manipulations which influence his behavior. It is noteworthy that the subject in a nonobvious demonstration or experiment is typically surprised and dismayed to learn that his behavior is so susceptible to the set of situational factors under the experimenter's control. Conforming subjects in the Asch paradigm and obedient subjects in the Milgram paradigm reportedly were shocked, embarrassed, and prone to make inappropriate inferences about themselves, both during the demonstration and afterwards when the experimenter revealed his intent. It is not surprising, moreover, that they were not easily consoled by debriefing procedures, for the experimenter could not restore what the subjects had lost—a satisfying, albeit inaccurate, implicit theory about the relative impact of specific personal and situational determinants of their own behavior.

The intuitive psychologist, shielded by perseverance mechanisms, is no less likely outside the psychological laboratory to remain ignorant of the distortions and inadequacies both in his primary assumptions and in his methods of sampling, coding, and analyzing the data of everyday experience. Sometimes the results of such ignorance are benign or even benevolent, e.g., the social observer attributes his friendships to the particular personal qualities of his friends and overlooks the role of social ecology (Festinger, Schachter, & Back, 1950). At other times, the results may be harmful to the individual or the society, as unjust and maladaptive methods of resource allocation and social control are justified and perpetuated.

The intuitive psychologist, however, cannot be totally insulated from clashes between expectations and observations, between intuitions and evidence. From such clashes he may be led to cynicism, self-doubt, or disappointment. Alternatively, he may be led to new psychological insights and a willingness to reshape his own life and the institutions of his society.

REFERENCES

Abelson, R. P. Social psychology's rational man. In G. W. Mortimore & S. I. Benn (Eds.), *The concept of rationality in the social sciences.* London: Routledge & Kegan Paul, 1974.

Alberoni, F. Contributions to the study of subjective probability. Part I. *Journal of General Psychology*, 1962, **66**, 241–264.

Amabile, T. M. Investigations in the psychology of prediction. Unpublished manuscript, Stanford University, 1975.

Arkin, R. M., & Duval, S. Focus of attention and causal attributions of actors and observers. *Journal of Experimental Social Psychology*, 1975, **11**, 427–438.

Asch, S. Forming impressions of personality. *Journal of Abnormal and Social Psychology*, 1946, **41**, 258–290.

Asch, S. *Social Psychology*. Englewood Cliffs, N.J.: Prentice-Hall, 1952.

Asch, S. Opinions and social pressures. *Scientific American*, 1955, **193**, 31–35.

Bavelas, A., Hastorf, A. H., Gross, A. E., & Kite, W. R. Experiments in the alteration of group structure. *Journal of Experimental Social Psychology*, 1965, **1**, 55–70.

Beckman, L. Effects of students' performance on teachers' and observers' attributions of causality. *Journal of Educational Psychology*, 1970, **61**, 75–82.

Bem, D. J. An experimental analysis of self-persuasion. *Journal of Experimental Social Psychology*, 1965, **1**, 199–218.

Bem, D. J. Self-perception: An alternative interpretation of cognitive dissonance phenomena. *Psychological Review*, 1967, **74**, 183–200.

Bem, D. J. Self-perception theory. In L. Berkowitz (Ed.), *Advances in experimental social psychology*. Vol. 6. New York: Academic Press, 1972.

Bem, D. J., & Allen, A. On predicting some of the people some of the time: The search for cross-situational consistencies in behavior. *Psychological Review*, 1974, **81**, 506–520.

Bierbrauer, G. Effect of set, perspective, and temporal factors in attribution. Unpublished doctoral dissertation, Stanford University, 1973.

Borgida, E., & Nisbett, R. E. The differential impact of abstract vs. concrete information on decisions. *Journal of Applied Social Psychology,* 1977, in press.

Bramel, D. A dissonance theory approach to defensive projection. *Journal of Abnormal and Social Psychology*, 1962, **64**, 121–129.

Bramel, D. Selection of a target for defensive projection. *Journal of Abnormal and Social Psychology*, 1963, **66**, 318–324.

Chapman, L., & Chapman, J. The genesis of popular but erroneous psychodiagnostic observations. *Journal of Abnormal Psychology*, 1967, **72**, 193–204.

Chapman, L., & Chapman, J. Illusory correlations as an obstacle to the use of valid psychodiagnostic signs. *Journal of Abnormal Psychology*, 1969, **74**, 271–280.

Collins, B. E. Four components of the Rotter internal-external scale: Belief in a difficult world, a just world, a predictable world, and a politically responsive world. *Journal of Personality and Social Psychology*, 1974, **29**, 381–391.

Collins, B. E., Martin, J. C., Ashmore, R. D., & Ross, L. Some dimensions of the external-internal metaphor in theories of personality. *Journal of Personality*, 1973, **41**, 471–492.

Cooper, J., Jones, E. E., & Tuller, S. M. Attribution, dissonance and the illusion of uniqueness. *Journal of Experimental Social Psychology*, 1972, **8**, 45–47.

Crandall, V. C., Katkovsky, W., & Crandall, V. G. Children's beliefs in their own control of reinforcements in intellectual-academic achievement situations. *Child Development*, 1965, **36**, 91–109.

Darley, J., & Batson, C. D. "From Jerusalem to Jericho": A study of situational and dispositional variables in helping behavior. *Journal of Personality and Social Psychology*, 1973, **27**, 100–119.

Davis, W. L., & Davis, D. E. Internal–external control and attribution of responsibility for success and failure. *Journal of Personality*, 1972, **40**, 123–136.

Deci, E. Effects of externally mediated rewards on intrinsic motivation. *Journal of Personality and Social Psychology*, 1971, **18**, 105–115.

Duncker, K. Induced motion. In W. Ellis (Ed.), *A sourcebook of Gestalt psychology*. New York: Harcourt, 1938. Pp. 161–172.

Duval, S., & Wicklund, R. A. *A theory of objective self-awareness*. New York: Academic Press, 1972.

Edlow, O., & Kiesler, C. Ease of denial and defensive projection. *Journal of Experimental Social Psychology*, 1966, **2**, 183–191.

Edwards, W. Conservatism in human information processing. In B. Kleinmuntz (Ed.), *Formal representation of human judgment*. New York: Wiley, 1968.

Ellsworth, P., & Ross, L. Intimacy in response to direct gaze. *Journal of Experimental Social Psychology*, 1975, **11**, 592–613.

Feather, N. T. Attribution of responsibility and valence of success and failure in relation to initial confidence and task performance. *Journal of Personality and Social Psychology*, 1969, **13**, 129–144.

Festinger, L., & Carlsmith, J. M. Cognitive consequences of forced compliance. *Journal of Abnormal and Social Psychology*, 1959, **58**, 203–210.

Festinger, L., Schachter, S., & Back, K. *Social pressures in informal groups: A study of human factors in housing*. New York: Harper, 1950.

Fischhoff, B. Hindsight ≠ foresight: The effect of outcome knowledge on judgment under uncertainty. *Journal of Experimental Psychology: Human Perception and Performance*, 1975, **1**, 288–299.

Fischhoff, B. Attribution theory and judgment under uncertainty. In J. Harvey, W. Ickes, & R. Kidd (Eds.), *New directions in attribution research*. Hillsdale, N.J.: Lawrence Erlbaum Associates, 1976. Pp. 419–450.

Fischhoff, B., & Beyth, R. "I knew it would happen"–remembered probabilities of once-future things. *Organizational Behavior and Human Performance*, 1975, **13**, 1–16.

Fischhoff, B., & Slovic, P. On the psychology of experimental surprises: Outcome knowledge and the journal review process. *Oregon Research Institute Research Bulletin*, 1976, **16**, No. 2.

Fitch, G. Effects of self-esteem, perceived performance, and chance on causal attributions. *Journal of Personality and Social Psychology*, 1970, **16**, 311–315.

Freize, I., & Weiner, B. Cue utilization and attributional judgments for success and failure. *Journal of Personality*, 1971, **39**, 591–606.

Gardner, M. Concerning an effort to demonstrate extrasensory perception by machine. *Scientific American*, 1975, **233**, 114–118.

Greene, D., & Lepper, M. Intrinsic motivation: How to turn play into work. *Psychology Today*, 1974, September, 49–54.

Gross, A. Evaluation of the target person in a social influence situation. Unpublished doctoral dissertation, Stanford University, 1966.

Haire, M., & Grunes, W. F. Perceptual defenses: Processes protecting an organized perception of another personality. *Human Relations*, 1950, **3**, 403–412.

Hastorf, A. H., & Cantril, H. They saw a game: A case study. *Journal of Abnormal and Social Psychology*, 1954, **49**, 129–134.

Heider, F. Social perception and phenomenal causality. *Psychological Review*, 1944, **51**, 358–373.

Heider, F. *The psychology of interpersonal relations*. New York: Wiley, 1958.

Holmes, D. S. Dimensions of projection. *Psychological Bulletin*, 1968, **69**, 248–268.

Icheiser, G. Misunderstandings in human relations: A study in false social perception. *American Journal of Sociology*, 1949, **55**, Part 2, 1–70.

Johnson, T. J., Feigenbaum R., & Weiby, M. Some determinants and consequences of the teacher's perception of causation. *Journal of Experimental Psychology*, 1964, **55**, 237–246.

Jones, E. E. How do people perceive the causes of behavior? *American Scientist*, 1976, **64**, 300–305.

Jones, E. E., & Davis, K. E. From acts to dispositions: The attribution process in person perceptions. In L. Berkowitz (Ed.), *Advances in experimental social psychology*. Vol. 2. New York: Academic Press, 1965.

Jones, E. E., Davis, K. E., & Gergen, K. J. Role playing variations and their informational value for person perception. *Journal of Abnormal and Social Psychology*, 1961, **63**, 302–310.

Jones, E. E., & DeCharms, R. Changes in social perception as a function of the personal relevance of behavior. *Sociometry*, 1957, **20**, 75–85.

Jones, E. E., & Goethals, G. R. Order effects in impression formation: Attribution context and the nature of the entity. In E. E. Jones *et al.* (Eds.), *Attribution: Perceiving the causes of behavior*. Morristown, N.J.: General Learning Press, 1971.

Jones, E. E., & Harris, V. A. The attribution of attitudes. *Journal of Experimental Social Psychology*, 1967, **3**, 1–24.

Jones, E. E., Kanouse, D. E., Kelley, H. H., Nisbett, R. E., Valins, S., & Weiner, B. *Attribution: Perceiving the causes of behavior*. Morristown, N.J.: General Learning Press, 1971.

Jones, E. E., & Nisbett, R. E. The actor and the observer: Divergent perceptions of the causes of behavior. In E. E. Jones *et al.* (Eds.), *Attribution: Perceiving the causes of behavior*. Morristown, N.J.: General Learning Press, 1971.

Kahneman, D., & Tversky, A. Subjective probability: A judgment of representativeness. *Cognitive Psychology*, 1972, **3**, 430–454.

Kahneman, D., & Tversky, A. On the psychology of prediction. *Psychological Review*, 1973, **80**, 237–251.

Katz, D., & Allport, F. *Student's attitudes*. Syracuse: Craftsman Press, 1931.

Kelley, H. H. Attribution theory in social psychology. In D. Levine (Ed.), *Nebraska symposium on motivation*. Vol. 15. Lincoln: University of Nebraska Press, 1967.

Kelley, H. H. Attribution in social interaction. In E. E. Jones *et al.* (Eds.), *Attribution: Perceiving the causes of behavior*. Morristown, N.J.: General Learning Press, 1971.

Kelley, H. H. The process of causal attribution. *American Psychologist*, 1973, **28**, 107–128.

Kelley, H. H., & Stahelski, A. The social interaction basis of cooperators' and competitors' beliefs about others. *Journal of Personality and Social Psychology*, 1970, **16**, 66–91.

Kelly, G. *The psychology of personal constructs*. New York: Norton, 1955. 2 vols.

Kelly, G. Man's construction of his alternatives. In G. Lindzey (Ed.), *Assessment of human motives*. New York: Holt, 1958.

Kruglanski, A. The endogenous-exogenous partition in attribution theory. *Psychological Review*, 1975, **82**, 387–406.

Lau, R., Lepper, M. R., & Ross, L. Persistence of inaccurate and discredited personal impressions: A field demonstration of attributional perseverance. Unpublished manuscript, Stanford University, 1976.

Lefcourt, H. M. Internal vs. external control of reinforcement revisited: Recent developments. In B. A. Maher (Ed.), *Progress in experimental personality research*. Vol. 6. New York: Academic Press, 1972.

Lemann, T. B., & Solomon, R. L. Group characteristics as revealed in sociometric patterns and personality ratings. *Sociometry*, 1952, **15**, 7–90.

Lepper, M. R., & Greene, D. Turning play into work: Effects of adult surveillance and extrinsic rewards on children's intrinsic motivation. *Journal of Personality and Social Psychology*, 1975, **31**, 479–486.

Lepper, M. R., Greene, D., & Nisbett, R. E. Undermining children's intrinsic interest with extrinsic reward: A test of the "overjustification" hypothesis. *Journal of Personality and Social Psychology*, 1973, **28**, 129–137.

McArthur, L. A. The how and what of why: Some determinants and consequences of causal attribution. *Journal of Personality and Social Psychology*, 1972, **22**, 171–193.

McArthur, L. A. The lesser influence of consensus than distinctiveness information on causal attributions: A test of the person–thing hypothesis. *Journal of Personality and Social Psychology*, 1976, **33**, 733–742.

McGuire, W. J. The yin and yang of progress in social psychology: Seven koan. *Journal of Personality and Social Psychology*, 1973, **26**, 446–456.

Milgram, S. Behavioral study of obedience. *Journal of Abnormal and Social Psychology*, 1963, **67**, 371–378.

Miller, A. G., Gillen, B., Schenker, C., & Radlove, S. Perception of obedience to authority. *Proceeding, 81st Annual Convention, American Psychological Association*, 1973, **8**, 127–128.

Miller, D. T., & Ross, M. Self-serving biases in the attribution of causality: Fact or fiction? *Psychological Bulletin*, 1975, **82**, 213–225.

Mischel, W. *Personality and assessment.* New York: Wiley, 1968.

Mischel, W. Continuity and change in personality. *American Psychologist*, 1969, **24**, 1012–1018.

Mischel, W. Towards a cognitive social learning reconceptualization of personality. *Psychological Review*, 1973, **80**, 252–283.

Mischel, W. Processes in delay of gratification. In L. Berkowitz (Ed.), *Advances in experimental social psychology*. Vol. 7. New York: Academic Press, 1974.

Mischel, W., & Ebbesen, E. B. Attention in delay of gratification. *Journal of Personality and Social Psychology*, 1970, **16**, 329–337.

Mischel, W., Ebbesen, E. B., & Zeiss, A. R. Cognitive and attentional mechanisms in delay of gratification. *Journal of Personality and Social Psychology*, 1972, **21**, 204–218.

Nisbett, R. E., & Borgida, E. Attribution and the psychology of prediction. *Journal of Personality and Social Psychology*, 1975, **32**, 932–943.

Nisbett, R. E., Borgida, E., Crandall, R., & Reed, H. Popular induction: Information is not always informative. In J. Carroll & J. Payne (Eds.), *Cognitive and social behavior*. Potomac, Md.: Lawrence Erlbaum Associates, 1976.

Nisbett, R. E., Caputo, C. G., Legant, P., & Maracek, J. Behavior as seen by the actor and as seen by the observer. *Journal of Personality and Social Psychology*, 1973, **27**, 154–164.

Nisbett, R. E., & Wilson, T. D. Telling more than we can know: Verbal reports on mental processes. *Psychological Review*, 1977, in press.

Peterson, C. R., & Beach, L. R. Man as an intuitive statistician. *Psychological Bulletin*, 1967, **68**, 29–46.

Polefka, J. The perception and evaluation of responses to social influences. Unpublished doctoral dissertation, Stanford University, 1965.

Regan, D. T., & Totten, J. Empathy and attribution: Turning observers into actors. *Journal of Personality and Social Psychology*, 1975, **32**, 850–856.

Ross, L., Amabile, T. M., Jennings, D. L., & Steinmetz, J. L. Non-conservative and non-optimal prediction strategies: Experiments on the psychology of intuitive prediction. Unpublished manuscript, Stanford University, 1976. (a)

Ross, L., Amabile, T. M., & Steinmetz, J. L. Social roles, social control, and biases in social perception processes. *Journal of Personality and Social Psychology*, 1977, in press. (a)

Ross, L. Bierbrauer, G., & Hoffman, S. The role of attribution processes in conformity and dissent: Revisiting the Asch situation. *American Psychologist*, 1976, **31**, 148–157. (b)

Ross, L., Bierbrauer, G., & Polly, S. Attribution of educational outcomes by professional and non-professional instructors. *Journal of Personality and Social Psychology*, 1974, **29**, 609–618.

Ross, L., Greene, D., & House, P. The false consensus phenomenon: An attributional bias in self perception and social perception processes. *Journal of Experimental Social Psychology*, 1977, in press. (b)

Ross, L., Lepper, M., & Hubbard, M. Perseverance in self perception and social perception: Biased attributional processes in the debriefing paradigm. *Journal of Personality and Social Psychology*, 1975, **32**, 880–892.

Ross, L., Lepper, M. R., Strack, F., & Steinmetz, J. L. The effects of real and hypothetical explanation upon future expectations. Unpublished manuscript, Stanford University, 1976. (c)

Rotter, J. B. Generalized expectancies for internal versus external control of reinforcement. *Psychological Monographs*, 1966, **80**, No. 609.

Schachter, S., & Singer, J. E. Cognitive, social and physiological determinants of emotional state. *Psychological Review*, 1962, **69**, 379–399.

Slovic, P., & Lichtenstein, S. Comparison of Bayesian and regression approaches to the study of information processing in judgment. *Organizational Behavior and Human Performance*, 1971, **6**, 649–744.

Smedslund, J. The concept of correlation in adults. *Scandinavian Journal of Psychology*, 1963, **4**, 165–173.

Smith, A. The attribution of similarity: The influence of success and failure. *Journal of Abnormal and Social Psychology*, 1960, **61**, 419–423.

Storms, M. Videotape and the attribution process: Reversing actors' and observers' points of view. *Journal of Personality and Social Psychology*, 1973, **27**, 165–175.

Strickland, L. H. Surveillance and trust. *Journal of Personality*, 1958, **26**, 200–215.

Taylor, S. E., & Fiske, S. T. Point of view and perceptions of causality. *Journal of Personality and Social Psychology*, 1975, **32**, 439–445.

Thibaut, J. W., & Riecken, H. W. Some determinants and consequences of the perception of social causality. *Journal of Personality*, 1955, **24**, 113–133.

Tversky, A., & Kahneman, D. Belief in the law of small numbers. *Psychological Bulletin*, 1971, **76**, 105–110.

Tversky, A., & Kahneman, D. Availability: A heuristic for judging frequency and probability. *Cognitive Psychology*, 1973, **5**, 207–232.

Tversky, A., & Kahneman, D. Judgment under uncertainty: Heuristics and biases. *Science*, 1974, **185**, 1124–1131.

Valins, S. Persistent effects of information about internal reactions: Ineffectiveness of debriefing. In H. London & R. E. Nisbett (Eds.), *Thought and feeling: Cognitive modification of feeling states*. Chicago: Aldine, 1974.

Wallach, H. The perception of motion. *Scientific American*, 1959, **201**, 56–60.

Walster, E. Assignment of responsibility for an accident. *Journal of Personality and Social Psychology*, 1966, **3**, 73–79.

Walster, E., Berscheid, E., Abrahams, D., & Aronson, V. Effectiveness of debriefing following deception experiments. *Journal of Personality and Social Psychology*, 1967, **6**, 371–380.

Ward, W. D., & Jenkins, H. M. The display of information and the judgment of contingency. *Canadian Journal of Psychology*, 1965, **19**, 231–241.

Wason, P. C., & Johnson-Laird, P. N. *Psychology of reasoning: Structure and content*. London: Batsford, 1972.

Weiner, B. *Achievement motivation and attribution theory*. Morristown, N.J.: General Learning Press, 1974.

Wheeler, G., & Beach, L. R. Subjective sampling distributions and conservatism. *Organizational Behavior and Human Performance*, 1968, 3, 36–46.

Wolosin, R. J., Sherman, S. J., & Till, A. Effects of cooperation and competition on responsibility attribution after success and failure. *Journal of Experimental Social Psychology*, 1973, 9, 220–235.

Zadny, J., & Gerard, H. B. Attributed intentions and informational selectivity. *Journal of Personality and Social Psychology*, 1974, 10, 34–52.

NORMATIVE INFLUENCES ON ALTRUISM[1]

Shalom H. Schwartz

UNIVERSITY OF WISCONSIN
MADISON, WISCONSIN

[1] This work was supported by NSF Grant SOC 72-05417. I am indebted to L.
Berkowitz, R. Dienstbier, H. Schuman, R. Simmons, and R. Tessler for their thoughtful
comments on an early draft of this chapter.

I. Introduction

On July 1, 1971, ACTION, a new federal agency to stimulate volunteer services, was launched. Coordinating the activities of such diverse programs as the Peace Corps, Foster Grandparent Program, and Service Corps of Retired Executives, ACTION has engaged the energies of more than 150,000 volunteers. These are but a small fraction of the millions of Americans who annually volunteer their skills and time without payment in the service of others. Nor is the spread of volunteering limited to the United States alone (*Voluntary Action News*, 1975).

This expansion of voluntarism has been accompanied by an increase in research on helping behavior documented by Wispé (1972). Tellingly, however, the prime catalyst to the acceleration of social psychological research appears to have been the public scandal of unresponsiveness to emergencies [cf. the seminal work of Latané and Darley (1970)], rather than the equally momentous if less sensational everyday acts of self-sacrifice.

True to their experimental and theoretical training, most social psychologists have defined the problem for research as the specification of situational factors that inhibit or enhance helping, and they have assumed that the potential helper is a calculating hedonist alert to the matrix of possible social and material rewards. Claims that healthy individuals make voluntary self-sacrifices without thought of personal gain are likely to be greeted with skepticism. Even volunteer kidney transplant donors are suspected of pathological motives (Fellner & Schwartz, 1971).

This prevailing approach has yielded insight into responsiveness in emergencies and other settings. But it has also impeded investigation of possible internal sources of *altruistic* motivation which may be implicated both in emergencies and in more widespread instances of helping. Altruistic motivation refers to intentions or purposes to benefit another as an expression of internal values, without regard for the network of social and material reinforcements. The common labels for what may be altruistically motivated behavior—"helping," "sharing," and especially the increasingly popular "prosocial behavior"—beg the question of the actor's intentions in favor of the observable socially defined consequences of his act, or deny altruistic purposes entirely by calling the behavior "compliance." Krebs' (1970) comment that most research has dealt with "apparent altruism" still applies.

Interestingly, the word *altruism* appears almost exclusively in titles of developmental studies and of research on children and animals. It could be that the millions of adult volunteers and the rarer responsive bystanders are not true altruists, and perhaps little additional insight into their behavior will be gained from considering how their behavior is affected by internalized values. Nonetheless, possible internal intentional processes underlying the performance of apparently altruistic behavior should be closely examined before we reach these conclusions.

The burgeoning literature on helping behavior[2] is characterized by a plethora of variables, few of them related to each other in any coherent theory. When we focus on the purposive performance of helping acts (as distinct from their learning), however, three discrete types of explanation can be discerned. In all cases the intention to help is initiated by exposure to the need of another. The explanations differ according to which process they postulate as connecting the perception of need to helping intentions: (1) arousal of emotion; (2) activation of social expectations; or (3) activation of self-expectations. The impact on helping of physical and material costs (e.g., exertion, time loss) has also been examined extensively. But costs do not explain why intentions to help are initially formed: They influence prosocial behavior by moderating the attractiveness of actions which might be carried out.

These three types of explanation are not mutually exclusive. The processes they postulate may occur simultaneously, jointly determining the occurrence and nature of prosocial behavior. This chapter is primarily concerned with self-expectations because helping is altruistic only to the extent that it is motivated by internal values. Self-expectations are experienced as feelings of moral obligation generated when perception of another's need activates the internalized structure of values and norms. I will attempt to present and integrate the research explicitly investigating this activation process or implicitly reflecting upon it.

The self-expectation process may be characterized as a normative explanation of helping based on internalized or "personal" norms. In contrast, the explanation of helping in terms of activated *social* expectations represents the more conventional conception of normative explanations which has been the target of sharp criticism (e.g., Darley & Latané, 1970; Krebs, 1970, pp. 294–295; Schwartz, 1973). Social norms consist of expectations, obligations, and sanctions currently anchored in social groups. The expectations, obligations, and sanctions which constitute personal norms, by contrast, while originating in social interaction, are currently anchored in the self (cf. Parsons, 1951, p. 36 ff.). Some aspects of social normative explanations will also be examined here, with particular attention given to how the two types of normative explanation differ. I will argue from currently available research that social norms add little to the explanation of individual differences in helping behavior provided by internalized, personal norms.

---

[2] I will try to label behavior "altruism" only in the presence of reasonable grounds for inferring the appropriate intent.

The focus on normative explanations dictates that the process of emotional arousal receive less attention, despite its importance. Since the three processes are often intertwined, however, comments on the arousal of emotion are included next. In my analysis of normative explanations I will note points where emotional arousal may provide an alternative interpretation of findings or modify supposed normative effects.

II. Types of Explanation: An Overview

A. EMOTIONAL OR EMPATHIC AROUSAL

This type of explanation postulates that perception of the need or suffering of another tends to arouse emotional distress in the observer. The arousal typically has a physiological component, and it is experienced directly without self-consciousness. The experience of this arousal is labeled *empathy*, and it is thought to derive from a learned or genetic capacity to view events from the perspective of those to whom one feels similar. In its most extreme form this explanation suggests that the source of empathetic arousal is helped in order to reduce the helper's *own* distress. Helping elicited exclusively for this purpose would be devoid of intent to benefit the other and therefore would not be altruism.

Much of the work concerned with emotional arousal as the mediator of helping has sought to identify the developmental and learning antecedents of this type of empathy. The most elaborate theoretical examination of this approach is provided by Aronfreed (1968). The Lewinian perspective on prosocial behavior developed by Hornstein (1972) also maintains that a form of arousal mediates helping—promotive tension aroused by awareness of the goal seeking of those with whom one identifies.

It is difficult to isolate the unique impact of empathic arousal on helping, since the experience of emotion can also be a source of information about the objective features of the situation (Leventhal, 1970). The stronger the empathic arousal experienced by an observer, for example, the more serious he may perceive the other's need to be, and hence the more likely he is to experience norm activation (see the next subsection). When empathy is defined as cognitive role taking rather than as direct emotional arousal (Aderman & Berkowitz, 1970), its relationship to altruism can be understood through the normative processes to be outlined shortly. The impact of emotional arousal on information processing poses an interesting point of contact for integrating empathy and normative explanations. Some of the recent research on moods and helping (e.g., Isen, 1975) explicitly grapples with the nature of this interface.

B. ACTIVATION OF SOCIAL EXPECTATIONS

In contrast to emotional arousal notions, normative explanations emphasize cognitive processing and decision making. To highlight this distinction, I have referred to the *arousal* of emotion but to the *activation* of expectations. This second type of conception holds that exposure to the need of others often leads to the activation of social expectations (norms) which define the appropriate responses in a given situation. Activation means a directing of attention to expectations sufficient to bring them into the stream of information processing. Activation does *not* necessarily bring the expectations into focal attention where the individual becomes self-consciously aware that he is considering them.

Social expectations are learned in the normal course of socialization. They are activated by explicit or subtle communications from others or by the actor's own realization that his actions may be revealed to those whose reactions will depend on whether or not he conforms to them. A crucial component of social expectations is their implicit backing by socially mediated sanctions. Sanctions may be mild, remote, and even improbable, but they are the ultimate reason why expectations motivate behavior (Blake & Davis, 1964). The expectations of particular interest for this type of explanation are those perceived to be shared by social groups and referred to as social norms. The source and presumed (though seldom questioned) justification for particular social norms is their value for preserving the integrity or enhancing the welfare of the collectivities to which the individual belongs.

Explanation of prosocial behavior in terms of activated social norms is usually predicated upon a view of the human actor as a decision maker who seeks to optimize outcomes in light of the likely social costs and benefits of actions. Perceived social expectations serve as cues to forecast the probable outcomes of given lines of behavior. Most research and theorizing based on this type of explanation attributes prosocial behavior to compliance with general social norms presumed to be widely shared: social responsibility (e.g., Berkowitz & Daniels, 1963), equity (e.g., Walster, Berscheid, & Walster, 1970), reciprocity (e.g., Wilke & Lanzetta, 1970), and the norm of giving (e.g., Leeds, 1963). Others have pointed to more specific expectations or rules (Staub, 1972) and to content-specific norms which emerge in the course of continuing relationships (Pruitt, 1972).

C. ACTIVATION OF SELF-EXPECTATIONS

This type of explanation, like the preceding one, views prosocial behavior as the outcome of decision making in which cognitive processes play an important role. It is assumed in this approach that information about another's need may lead to the activation of internalized values or norms advocating helping regardless of external reinforcements. As already noted, these self-expectations are experienced as feelings of moral obligation, and they are not necessarily considered self-consciously. Behavior is motivated by the desire to act in ways consistent with one's values so as to enhance or preserve one's sense of self-worth and avoid self-concept distress.

If general social norms recognized as prevalent in a society are also accepted as bases for self-evaluation by an individual (i.e., internalized), they too may influence behavior through the activation of self-expectations. Two widely accepted social norms that have been mentioned as generating self-expectations are equity (Walster & Piliavin, 1972) and social responsibility (Berkowitz, 1972). I have argued that the activation of more specific internalized norms intervenes between awareness of someone's need and altruistic behavior (Schwartz, 1973). Before continuing with a detailed analysis of this type of explanation, a short aside on an increasingly popular approach to understanding altruism is in order.

D. GENETIC EXPLANATIONS

Genetic explanations (e.g., Campbell, 1965, 1972; Trivers, 1971; Wilson, 1975) are primarily concerned with the question of how particular dispositions for prosocial behavior might provide a genetic advantage. They do not directly describe processes through which the perception of another's need may lead to helping intentions. The evolution of predispositions to action is of interest, not the purposes motivating the actor. Those who propose genetic explanations have a distinct preference for the term *altruism*. This is ironic, since one of their basic premises is that the behavior in question is selected genetically because it serves the long-run survival interests of the actor who performs it or at least of his group, not because it is intended to benefit others (Power, 1975). The focus of genetic explanations on the consequences rather than the purposes of behavior distinguishes them from normative explanations, points to the different senses in which the two approaches construe altruism, and suggests that they are supplementary rather than contradictory.

III. A Theory of Personal Normative Influences on Altruism: Activation, Obligation, and Defense

The theoretical process I will present to tie internalized norms to altruistic behavior consists of many steps, and the evidence is drawn from diverse sources. There is a very real danger that attention to detail will make it appear needlessly complex. I begin with a simple statement and illustration of the theory's key elements in hopes of providing a framework that will keep the formulation's complexities in perspective.

A. BASIC PROPOSITIONS

The theory is constructed of three basic propositions: an obligation proposition, an activation proposition, and a defense proposition.

1. Altruistic behavior is influenced by the intensity of moral (personal) obligation which an individual feels to take specific helping actions.
2. Feelings of moral obligation are generated in particular situations by the activation of the individual's cognitive structure of norms and values.
3. Feelings of moral obligation may be neutralized prior to overt action by defenses against the relevance or appropriateness of the obligation.

These propositions apply to the relations of internalized norms and values to any behavior motivated by feelings of moral obligation, not exclusively to altruistic behavior. Altruism is involved only when the feelings of obligation and the norms and values from which they are generated pertain to behavior which can benefit others. The propositions suggest three corollaries from which testable hypotheses can be derived:

1. Individual differences in feelings of moral obligation to perform particular actions lead to individual differences in overt behavior.
2. The impact of feelings of moral obligation on behavior is a function of conditions which influence the initial activation of the individual's cognitive structure of norms and values.
3. The impact of feelings of moral obligation on behavior is also a function of conditions which influence defense against the relevance or appropriateness of the activated obligation.

The propositions and their corollaries imply that an ordered sequence of activation, feelings of obligation, and possible defense precedes the performance of altruistic behavior. The term *personal norms* will be used to signify the self-expectations for specific action in particular situations that are constructed by the individual. Activated personal norms are experienced as feelings of moral obligation, not as intentions. How personal norms are constructed and activated will be discussed later. First, consider an example of how hypotheses based on each of the theory's three basic propositions can be generated and tested.

B. ALTRUISM IN EVERYDAY LIFE: A RESEARCH EXAMPLE[3]

People who live together in split-levels, dormitories, pads, or huts have occasion to benefit or harm each other every day. Following are two situations drawn from the daily life of college students in small housing units (circa 1966) as presented in a questionnaire.

> The girl he was going with has just broken off with one of the fellows in your house. He seems rather hurt and upset. Another fellow starts to rib him. You are tempted to rib him too. Should you? [considerateness]
>
>   *   *   *
>
> A fellow in the house needs a sport jacket for a date tonight. He has let everyone know he would like to borrow one; but he doesn't want to ask anyone directly. You have a jacket that would fit him. Should you offer your jacket to him even though he doesn't ask? [helpfulness]

Nine such situations involving considerateness, helpfulness, and reliability were presented to 118 student members of nine residential groups. To assess the personal norms available to be activated in any situation, students reported how obligated they thought they would feel to do what the central figure in the situation was considering (e.g., offer their jacket), that is, how much they would feel they ought or ought not to do it.

A week later these students indicated how likely it was that each member of their own group would do what the central figure was considering in each situation. Average peer ratings based on at least 11 raters were used as the index of behavior. General trait ratings of considerateness, helpfulness, and reliability were also obtained. Subjects experienced little difficulty in making these judgments. Because we are interested in altruism, only results for considerateness and helpfulness are presented here. Each of the six situations involving these dimensions was designed to minimize the expected value of socially mediated reinforcements, regardless of behavioral response.

The first proposition in the theory leads to the hypothesis that individual differences in the personal norms available to be activated are related to differences in altruistic behavior. Summary indices based on the considerateness and helpfulness items are presented here for simplicity. The observed correlation between the summary index of personal norms and of peer ratings of behavior was $r = .25$ $(p < .01)$. This result does support proposition 1, but the strength of the relationship is typical of what is obtained when just about any individual difference variable is used to predict behavior (Mischel, 1968, p. 78). Recall, however, that proposition 2 states that the impact which feelings of moral

---

[3] This study is more fully described in Schwartz (1968a, 1968b). Some of the data have been analyzed differently for presentation here.

obligation have on altruistic behavior depends on the activation of the individual's cognitive structure of norms and values. What evidence is there that the appropriate norms were activated when the students faced these situations?

The activation proposition and its corollary suggest that the impact of feelings of moral obligation on behavior is a function of factors which affect the initial activation of personal norms. One of the critical factors that will be identified here as influencing initial activation is the tendency to become aware of the consequences of one's behavior for others (Awareness of Consequences, AC). The more likely individuals are to perceive situations in terms of the consequences their own behavior has for others, the more likely are such individuals to attend to those of their values and norms which relate to these interpersonal consequences and hence to generate feelings of obligation expressive of these norms. The activation proposition therefore yields the following hypothesis: Norms and behavior correlate near zero among those very low in AC and increasingly more positively among groups higher in AC.

The sample was divided into quartiles on this personality variable, presumed to be conducive to norm activation. Correlations between the summary indices of personal norms and peer ratings of behavior within each quartile are presented in the first row of Table I. As predicted, the correlations increase as a function

TABLE I

CORRELATIONS BETWEEN SUMMARY INDICES OF PERSONAL NORMS AND ALTRUISTIC BEHAVIOR AS A FUNCTION OF LEVELS OF PERSONALITY CONDUCIVENESS TO THE IMPACT OF OBLIGATION ON BEHAVIOR[a]

Personality variable	Conduciveness level				Comparison: IV vs. I
	Low I	II	III	High IV	
Awareness of Consequences (AC)	.00 (27)[b]	.05 (28)	.22 (40)	.49^c (23)	$p < .05$
Responsibility Denial (RD)	.04 (27)	.17 (30)	.19 (33)	.38^c (28)	$p < .10$

Personality variable	Low I	Mod II	High III	Comparisons
Combined AC and RD	.00 (38)	.14 (41)	.54^d (39)	III vs. I $p < .01$ III vs. II $p < .025$

[a]Data reanalyzed from Schwartz (1968a, 1968b).
[b]Number of subjects upon which correlation is based appears in parentheses.
$^c p < .05$.
$^d p < .01$.

of AC. Among those highest in AC the relationship is quite substantial, and significantly greater than that for those in the lowest quartile. The data support the inference that for feelings of moral obligation to influence altruistic behavior they must first be generated in the situation by activation of personal norms.

The third proposition suggests that even when feelings of moral obligation have been generated in a situation, they may not influence behavior. When a person anticipates costs for an action that he feels obligated to perform (e.g., missing a meal to send food to Bangladesh), he may employ various defenses against this obligation, depending upon the personality and situational factors available to support such defenses. An important predisposition to defense to be identified here is Responsibility Denial (RD), the individual tendency to accept rationales for denying responsibility for the consequences of one's behavior[4]; RD presumably reflects the likelihood of deactivating or neutralizing feelings of obligation in advance of action by using the defense of denial of responsibility.

The hypothesis derivable from the defense proposition and its corollary parallels the one stemming from the activation proposition: Among those who tend to deny their responsibility, personal norms and altruistic behavior are unrelated, with an increasingly positive relationship emerging as RD decreases. Note that low scores on RD should promote the impact of personal norms on behavior. Data conforming to the trend predicted by this hypothesis appear in the second row of Table I. Personal norms and altruistic behavior are significantly correlated only in the case of those most likely to accept responsibility and hence unlikely to neutralize their feelings of obligation.

Combining the three basic theoretical propositions yields the prediction that the effect of feelings of obligation on altruistic behavior will increase as a joint function of conditions which promote initial activation and inhibit defenses. Since either failure of activation or utilization of defenses can prevent feelings of obligation from influencing behavior, little correlation is anticipated among those quite low on AC or high on RD. To test this hypothesis, the sample was trichotomized on both AC and RD. Students low on AC and high on RD and those moderate on one variable and at the nonconducive extreme on the other were grouped as *Low* on personality conduciveness to the impact of moral obligation on behavior. Those high on AC and low on RD and those moderate on one and at the conducive extreme on the other were grouped as *High* on personality conduciveness. For the remainder (*Mod*) the expectation was closer to that for the *Low* group, since either failure of activation or utilization of responsibility denial was somewhat likely.

---

[4] This variable has been called Ascription of Responsibility (AR) in past reports. By relabeling it RD I wish to emphasize that it is a defensive tendency, not a spontaneous tendency to see the self as responsible for events initially. The latter type of tendency may be important for norm activation, but no means for measuring it have been perfected yet.

Results presented in the third row of Table I clearly confirm the hypothesis. Personal norms and altruistic behavior were unrelated among those expected to experience either no activation or neutralization of feelings of obligation through denial of responsibility (*Low*). The relationship was insignificantly higher for the moderate group. But among those who the theory says are likely to experience activation and not to defend through responsibility denial (*High*), the relationship of personal norms to altruistic behavior was quite substantial and significantly greater than for both the other groups.

This illustrative study examined one factor conducive to activation (AC), one conducive to defense (RD), and one aspect of personal norms (intensity of obligation) relevant to the generation of feelings of moral obligation in decision situations. The detailed model of personal normative influences on behavior specifies numerous factors relevant to the three basic propositions in the theory, breaks the decision process into more detailed steps, and suggests feedback loops which may modify the unidirectional sequence from awareness of need to a decision regarding action. Let us turn now to a close examination of the central concept in this theory.

C. FEELINGS OF MORAL (PERSONAL) OBLIGATION AND THE INTERNALIZED NORMATIVE STRUCTURE

The most distinctive feature of the current approach is the designation of feelings of moral (personal) obligation as the motivational construct energizing altruistic behavior. I am proposing that individuals sometimes act in response to their own self-expectations, their own personal norms. What distinguishes personal norms from social norms is that the sanctions attached to personal norms are tied to the self-concept. Anticipation of or actual conformity to a self-expectation results in pride, enhanced self-esteem, security, or other favorable self-evaluations; violation or its anticipation produce guilt, self-deprecation, loss of self-esteem, or other negative self-evaluations.

There is often overlap between personal norms held by individuals and prevailing social norms. But while social norms are perceived to be shared by members of a group, personal norms typically vary from one individual to another. By calling self-expectations "norms" I emphasize the ideas that they arise or are learned from shared expectations in social interaction, that they are modified in the singular interaction history of each person, and that they represent ideals against which events are evaluated. Internalized norms are standards for behavior which are self-reinforcing.

It is all too easy to postulate the existence of an array of specific norms which have been internalized and purportedly direct behavior, especially in post hoc analyses. Social psychology abandoned a similar path when the list of instincts and drives needed to account for behavior began to proliferate, and I have no intention of returning to it. The position taken here is that each person has a unique cognitive structure of images, beliefs, evaluations, action plans, etc. This structure operates in conjunction with inputs from the external situation and from internal emotional cues to generate specific momentary feelings of moral obligation (cf. Leventhal, 1974). Specific personal norms are therefore seldom stable cognitive structures. They are reconstructions built up in situations in a manner to be suggested in the following discussion. The unique experiences and social placements of each person guarantee that each one of us will differ from others in the content of our cognitive structure and hence in the content of our personal norms, the strength of obligation we feel to conform to them, their stability, and their experiential base.

1. The Nature of the Cognitive Structure of Values and Norms

That aspect of the cognitive structure critical for altruism is the content and organization of one's values and norms. Norms "say more or less specifically what should or should not be done by particular types of actors in given circumstances. Values are standards of desirability that are more nearly independent of specific situations" (Williams, 1968, p. 284).

Values and norms are organized in vertical structures connecting values to general norms which foster their attainment and to more specific norms which articulate them in concrete situations. The value "equality," for example, may enter into norms for relationships between husband and wife, brother and brother, teacher and student, etc., as Williams notes. Moving up the vertical structure each specific norm connects with an expanding set of more abstract norms and values to which it can give expression. The norm "bystanders should swim to the aid of a drowning child," for example, may implicate more general norms prescribing aid to innocent victims and proscribing foolhardy risk taking, and such values as humanitarianism, equality, safety, and life.

Norms and values are also linked horizontally at given levels of abstraction in the sense that they contribute to the articulation of the same higher- or lower-order value or norm. The strength of horizontal structuring refers to the extent to which an action relevant to a given norm or value is perceived as having inescapable implications for others at the same level, so that they jointly influence the evaluation of the anticipated action.

The ideas of vertical and horizontal structuring apply to belief systems in general (Bem, 1970). Unique to the cognitive structure of norms and values is the idea that values are arranged in a hierarchy of importance to the self and serve as bases for self-evaluation (Rokeach, 1973). People differ in the relative importance they attach to particular values as dimensions for self-evaluation, in the particular horizontal and vertical links they perceive among norms and values, and consequently in the degree to which specific anticipated actions in a given situation are experienced as self-enhancing or self-damaging.

2. The Process of Norm Construction: A Speculative Analysis

Occasionally people have preexisting content-specific norms developed and internalized in past circumstances from which they draw their current self-expectations (Pruitt, 1972). More commonly, however, they construct specific personal norms by reference to the general norms and values they have internalized in the past. This situational construction process yields a set of one or more momentary self-expectations. It entails scanning the implications for the pre-existing structure of norms and values of performing each of the actions that seem relevant in a situation. Scanning moves up various vertical lines of increasing abstraction and across horizontal connections.

Feelings of moral obligation regarding each specific action are generated by weighing the action's impact on the norms and values to which it is related. The more important the relevant norms and values are to one's self-evaluation, the stronger are the feelings of obligation which are experienced. The size and direction of the discrepancy anticipated between the state of affairs likely to ensue from an action and the ideal state defined by an internalized norm or value also contribute to the intensity and nature of feeling. Alternative actions, evaluated simultaneously, yield different degrees of obligation because they differ in their implications for the person's structure of norms and values.

The information processing and integration involved in norm construction can occur quite quickly, and much of it probably takes place outside of awareness. The individual does not self-consciously check through all possible relevant norms and values each time, nor does he decide anew how much of his self-esteem is tied up in acting to promote particular values. It is even possible that self-conscious attention to the sources of one's feelings of obligation may diminish these feelings, as Leventhal (1975) hypothesizes it does to other feelings. Feelings of obligation are typically experienced in what Duval and Wicklund (1972) have called the state of *subjective* self-awareness. Attention is focused on events external to the individual's consciousness, especially on the need of the other, and awareness of self is limited to experiencing the self as a source of perception and action.

From Duval and Wicklund (1972) and from Kiesler, Roth, and Pallak (1974) we can infer that people are usually uncomfortable when they engage in self-conscious deliberation about the implications of an immediate future action for their self-evaluation, and they tend to avoid this deliberation. Awareness of the norm construction process may therefore be avoided, and the extent to which our behavior is influenced by feelings of moral obligation may be underestimated. This is not to assert that feelings of obligation mediate *all* responses to need not impelled by social expectations or empathy. A well-practiced instrumental reaction may be elicited directly by the appropriate stimulus without feelings of obligation (e.g., a medic treating a wounded soldier under fire).

The process of norm construction produces self-expectations experienced as *feelings* of moral obligation, rather than as coldly intellective judgments of right and wrong. The feeling component of obligation is traceable to the nature of values and norms and to the circumstances under which they are learned. The rules of physical and social reality are learned by observing regularities in nature and social relations, with occasional social intervention to draw attention to these regularities. Norms and values governing interpersonal relationships, by contrast, refer to *ideal* patterns. They are conveyed in social interaction with significant and/or powerful others who wish to convince the learner of their desirability. Socializers often use emotionally arousing promises and threats, rewards and punishments to reinforce learning. The potential for sanctions is learned along with the values, and the capacity to elicit feelings is retained even when the source of sanctions switches from the other to the self.

3. Operationalizing Personal Norms

Unless we can measure the intensity of moral obligation a person is likely to feel in a choice situation, assertions that differences in personal norms influence altruistic behavior are mere speculation. Since feelings of obligation are generated as part of the norm construction process in specific choice situations, however, measurement is difficult. It is feasible to measure the more stable elements of the cognitive structure of values and norms (e.g., the hierarchy of values), but to identify in advance the vertical and horizontal structuring that might link abstract values to specific feelings of obligation in particular situations is probably an impossible task.

One way to bypass this difficulty is to postulate that the norm construction process can be instigated simply by *asking* people how they feel they ought to behave, not only by confrontation with actual decisions to act. Questionnaire responses are undoubtedly imperfect indices of the norms constructed in the action situation because the process of scanning the cognitive structure is probably less careful and thorough when individuals react to hypothetical questions. The validity of reports of anticipated feelings of obligation depends on how well respondents project themselves into the hypothetical situation. Validity can be enhanced by drawing attention in advance to the implications of the decision to be made and by specifying the nature of the situation and actions in as much detail as possible in the norm questions.

Examples of how personal norms have been measured are presented in Table II. These items have been selected to demonstrate the variety of topics, samples, and question formats used, so that slight differences in method can be noted. Most commonly, the personal norm questions ask: "Under circumstances *X*, would you feel a moral (personal) obligation to do *Y*?" Subjects have been instructed to report what they would feel they ought or ought not to do, regardless of what others might expect of them. In studies where personal norms

TABLE II
EXAMPLES OF THE MEASUREMENT OF PERSONAL NORMS

Response categories and distributions

Question	Obligation not to donate −1	No obligation either way 0	1	2	3	4	Strong obligation to donate 5	Sample	Source
1. If a stranger to you needed a bone marrow transplant and you were a suitable donor, would you feel a moral obligation to donate bone marrow?	12%	36%	12%	13%	8%	9%	10%	State of Wisconsin clerical workers; N = 132 females	Schwartz (1973)
2. If a close relative of yours needed a heart transplant, and you were a suitable donor, would you feel a moral obligation to arrange to donate your heart to him/her upon your death?	5%	11%	3%	7%	10%	16%	49%	Madison, Wisconsin representative sample; N = 195 males and females	Schwartz & Tessler (1972)

Question	Strong obligation to refuse −3	−2	−1	No obligation either way 0	1	2	Strong obligation to agree 3	Sample	Source
3. How much of a moral obligation would you feel if the State Employment Service requested you to employ a delinquent youth with a police record?	11%	5%	5%	9%	13%	38%	19%	Private employers in Greater Tel Aviv area; N = 127 males	Schwartz (unpublished data)

continued

TABLE II (Continued)

Question	Feel some obligation not to −1	Feel no obligation either way 0	Feel slight obligation 1	Feel somewhat more obligation 2	Feel strong obligation 3	Sample	Source
4. How much personal obligation do you feel to talk to a stranger in a movie theater?	39%	52%	7%	2%	.7%	Purchasers of American Oil gas, Wisconsin; N = 303 male and female	Heberlein (1975)
5. How much personal obligation do you feel to help other people in trouble?	.7%	4%	18%	45%	33%	Same as preceding	

Question	Obligation to refuse −1	No obligation either way 0	Weak obligation to agree 1	Obligation to agree 2	Strong obligation to agree 3	Sample	Source
6. If the School for the Blind asked you to read school books to blind children a few times a week in the afternoon or evening, would you feel a moral obligation?	.4%	12%	28%	41%	19%	Hebrew University undergraduates; N = 269 male and female	Schwartz (unpublished data)
7. If the President's Office for Voluntary Services asked you to work a few hours per week as an aide in a neighborhood day care center, would you feel a moral obligation?	6%	36%	24%	25%	9%	Jerusalem housewives; N = 179 females	S. H. Schwartz & E. Geva (unpublished data)

Question	Strongly ought not to -3	-2	-1	No obligation 0	1	2	Strongly ought to 3	Sample	Source
8. If a solicitor for the School for the Blind came to your door and requested a 1 lira contribution, would you feel a moral obligation?	.6%	2%	5%			29%	64%		Same as preceding
9. Assume someone favoring welfare increases asked . . . indicate whether you would feel a personal obligation to . . . give some free time to a civic organization helping welfare recipients in need.	9%	5%	5%	29%	23%	16%	13%	Madison, Wisconsin representative sample; N = 382 females	S. H. Schwartz & J. Fleishman (unpublished data)
10. Assume someone favoring reinstating the death penalty asked . . . indicate whether you would feel a personal obligation to . . . sign a petition to be published in the newspaper, supporting the death penalty.	42%	6%	4%	36%	6%	3%	3%	Same as preceding	

237

are to be related to subsequent behavior, the question about feelings of obligation toward the critical behavior is embedded among such distractors as irrelevant norms and controversial political or social attitude items.

Response scales always include the positive anchor point of "strong obligation to do Y," and a zero point of "no obligation either way." This latter
alternative enables people to assert that they do not view the particular decision
in terms of obligation. Such a response is taken to signify that people would
generate no feelings of moral obligation from scanning their normative structure
in this situation, so that their behavior would not be influenced by personal
norms. Depending on the study and the nature of the issue, one to three scale
points on the negative side of zero have been used to tap feelings of obligation
not to perform the behavior.

The distributions shown in Table II are representative of those obtained in
different studies. There is substantial variance in responses to most questions,
implying heterogeneity in the feelings of obligation likely to be generated in
each sample. Instances in which fewer than 1% of the respondents use an
extreme category may represent errors or perhaps extraordinary individuals. An
interview rather than a questionnaire methodology might eliminate such unusual
responses, but probably at the cost of promoting self-presentation biases and
losing real outliers.

On questions concerned with helping and altruism the whole range of
positive responses has been elicited. Feelings of obligation to oppose requests or
not to perform actions have also been expressed. Information from other parts
of the surveys suggests two types of reasons why people experience opposition
as morally obligated rather than as the absence of obligation. First, an action
may be perceived as endangering or undermining values to which the person is
committed (e.g., life, integrity of the human body, individualism, freedom from
government control). Second, even people who favor an action may believe they
have stronger conflicting obligations to avoid risks inherent in the action which
are potentially detrimental to themselves and their own dependents (e.g., maintaining one's health and income-producing potential to support one's family).

Use of the category signifying no feelings of obligation either way ranged
from 52% to 2%. This category was employed by substantial numbers even on
issues where others responded with strong feelings (e.g., Q10). Individuals
apparently differ not only in the strength and direction of their moral obligations but also in whether they see self-expectations as important to a decision at
all. Note that on questions where many felt no obligation either way others
sometimes tended toward feeling positive obligations (Q7, Q9) and sometimes
toward obligations in opposition (Q4, Q10).

Interestingly, two of the questions which elicited large proportions of "no
obligation" responses (Q1, Q7) entail substantial and disruptive self-sacrifices for
strangers. This may indicate that not only do people feel *more* obligation to

members of ingroups, but they often define relations with strangers as not involving obligation at all. In response to a set of questions regarding heart, kidney, and bone marrow transplants either to a stranger or to a close relative, subjects chose "no obligation either way" more than three times as often for strangers as for relatives.

The two questions on which almost everyone responded with some degree of obligation (Q8, Q5) deserve comment primarily to highlight the differences between them. The practice of soliciting small sums door to door for blind children is well established in Jerusalem, and the School for the Blind is known for its valuable work. Given the detail in the question, respondents undoubtedly projected themselves into the decision situation successfully. The fact that so few reported they would feel no obligation probably reflects accurately what their feelings would be. The act was not demanding and conjured up no conflicting obligation. Moreover, a legitimate appeal for helpless victims by a volunteer apparently acting out of his own sense of obligation is well calculated to activate anyone's feelings of obligation. In this sample, 65% of those contacted actually contributed later.

The question on helping "other people in trouble," in contrast, is so nonspecific that respondents had no definite situation to imagine and no basis for determining the implications of actions for their values and norms. Responses to this type of question may therefore not be a product of norm construction, not a reflection of feelings which might motivate behavior, but an index of the respondents' guesses about the socially appropriate level of obligation. Having learned their social lessons, they knew there was *some* obligation to help. Greater specificity is critical if we are to tap feelings of moral obligation in a manner that can capture the impact of personal norms on behavior.[5]

Regardless of variations, measurement of personal norms has consisted of single-item indicators using "obligation" as the operative term. Multi-item indices might improve reliability so that systematic research to this end seems worthwhile. But it will necessarily be difficult to construct nonredundant items to tap the same norm if each item must include "obligation" and specifically describe the decision situation. Perhaps measuring norms toward a set of related acts in a single behavioral domain is one way around this difficulty.

Obligation has been used to operationalize norms because this term, like norms, refers to action. The focus on action brings obligation closer to overt behavior than more strictly cognitive or evaluational attitude terms. Obligations are felt directly prior to behavior, whereas reactions such as guilt and pride are responses to action and can only be anticipated. Self-reports of obligation might therefore be more accurate. Moreover, action is motivated by the feelings which

---

[5] No criticism of the researchers who used this item is intended. They are fully aware of this point (Heberlein & Black, 1976).

precede it, like obligation, and directly experienced feelings may have a stronger impact than anticipated feelings (cf. Aronfreed, 1968).

Because *obligation* reflects past commitment, it also carries a connotation of potential sanction, the presumed source of motivation inherent in norms. The qualifiers *moral* or *personal* are added in order to inform respondents that the relevant commitments are to their own values so that they will see the self as the source of obligation and of sanctions. It is unclear which qualifier is better. "Moral" seems to suggest more distinctly that the respondent scan his internalized value system. But respondents who associate this term with a conventional morality they reject (e.g., some college students) sometimes resist using it. When accompanied by more explicit instructions, "personal" may be equally suitable.

4. Obligation and Guilt

Although Freud spoke of ego ideals as well as superego, psychoanalytic thought has followed his emphasis on guilt avoidance as the primary motive for conforming to internal obligation (Fenichel, 1945). Most social psychologists who discuss internalized control of behavior have shown the same preference (e.g., Aronfreed, 1968). Perhaps because I have studied altruistic behavior, I am impressed that people perform many self-sacrificing acts with little sign of the drivenness or duty-boundedness one typically associates with guilt avoidance. I therefore presently see no grounds for attributing more importance either to positive or to negative self-evaluations. The terms *moral obligation* or *personal obligation* have the virtue of relative neutrality with respect to the feelings implied.

Obligation clearly taps something other than guilt alone, as the following studies show. To predict blood donation by college students, Pomazal (1974) used both a personal norm question ("I personally think that I have a moral obligation to donate blood. . . .") and an item intended to tap anticipated guilt ("How *guilty* would you feel if you decided not to donate blood. . .?"). The two items were significantly related but shared only 20.5% of their variance. The personal norm question was far superior in predicting actual blood donation. The guilt item added no significant explanatory power, apparently measuring no additional component of internalized motivation important for behavior.

Heberlein and Black (1976) included five items intended to tap personal norms in a study of lead-free gasoline purchasing. Four items involved guilt or pride, one used the "personal obligation" format. All were significantly intercorrelated. Yet, the single "obligation" question predicted behavior better than any of the other items, singly or in combination. The latter explained no additional variance in behavior.

Finally, Fellner and Schwartz (1971) measured both feelings of moral obligation to donate a kidney to a family member and to a stranger, and guilt or self-criticism anticipated for refusing these requests. Guilt correlated significantly with intentions to donate in both instances. Feelings of moral obligation were substantially better predictors, however, and left no variance for guilt to explain in either instance when combined in multiple regression equations. In sum, these few studies suggest that obligation indices of internalized motivation may capture whatever impact anticipated guilt and pride have on behavior, plus something more. Further research is needed to disaggregate the components of feelings of obligation.

D. FROM THE ACTIVATION OF MORAL OBLIGATION TO ALTRUISTIC BEHAVIOR: A PROCESSUAL MODEL

The full theoretical model will now be expounded. The model spells out a process moving from the initial perception of need through the activation of the normative structure and the generation of feelings of moral obligation to the eventual overt response. Many variables, both situational and individual, influence the progress of this process. These variables will be identified, and findings from studies which examine their influence on helping will be integrated into the overall model. I begin by outlining steps in the theorized sequential process.[6]

I. *Activation steps: perception of need and responsibility*
   1. Awareness of a person in a state of need
   2. Perception that there are actions which could relieve the need
   3. Recognition of own ability to provide relief
   4. Apprehension of some responsibility to become involved
II. *Obligation step: norm construction and generation of feelings of moral obligation*
   5. Activation of preexisting or situationally constructed personal norms
III. *Defense steps: assessment, evaluation, and reassessment of potential responses*
   6. Assessment of costs and evaluation of probable outcomes
   (The next two steps may be skipped if a particular response clearly optimizes the balance of costs evaluated in step 6. If not, there will be one or more iterations through steps 7 and 8.)
   7. Reassessment and redefinition of the situation by denial of:
      a. state of need (its reality, seriousness)
      b. responsibility to respond
      c. suitability of norms activated thus far and/or others
   8. Iterations of earlier steps in light of reassessments
IV. *Response step*
   9. Action or inaction response

Like other cognitive decision-making models, this one does not presume that self-conscious awareness of another's need characterizes any of the steps (cf. Boneau, 1974). Moreover, mistakes or distortions in perception and evaluation often make resulting decisions appear quite irrational even from the viewpoint of

[6] An earlier version of this outline and a more detailed examination of some aspects of steps 1–4 appears in Schwartz (1975).

the actor. Decisions which involve consideration of personal norms are irrational in the sense that they do not optimize external reinforcements for action.

Most studies investigate influences on helping which affect only a single step in the sequence. I am therefore constrained to present evidence on one step at a time. Since the steps may not simply add to one another, studies which examine factors presumed to have an impact on two or more steps are especially important. In order to draw upon relevant research in which personal norms were not measured, I will assume along with most of the researchers that their subjects were committed to appropriate values and norms in the situations examined. This assumption is probably reasonable for studies which involve obvious and legitimate need. Studies in which feelings of moral obligation were explicitly measured or manipulated, however, are the ones particularly critical for evaluating the claim that activated personal norms influence altruism.

1. Awareness of Others' Need

For our purposes others' need is defined as any actual or potential deficiency of a required, desired, or normally possessed resource. The needy party may be an individual, group, or more abstract entity such as a social class. The perception of need stimulates cognitive operations because perceived states of need are discrepant from the person's preexisting cognitive representations of the other's normal or expected states (Reykowski, 1974). Simple awareness of need constitutes a threshold for initiating all three explanatory processes for helping—emotional arousal, and activation of social expectations and of self-expectations.

The variables which influence initial awareness of need are the prominence of the need in the environment, its clarity, and individual receptivity to need cues. The necessity of *prominence* sufficient to attract notice is self-evident. In fact, failure by subjects to notice the need which was intended to elicit their reactions has been viewed as a nuisance factor in some helping studies, justifying elimination of these subjects (e.g., Staub & Baer, 1974). Prominence could be viewed, however, as a topic for investigation itself. *Clarity* regarding the nature of need (Clark & Word, 1972, 1974), as well as definitions of its reality implied or conveyed in the responses of others (Darley, Teger, & Lewis, 1973; Latané & Darley, 1970), have been found to influence bystander intervention dramatically in emergencies.

Individual receptivity to need cues may depend on both trait and state characteristics. I have described above, for example, how the trait variable, Awareness of Consequences (AC), mediated the impact of personal norms on altruistic behavior. AC was also correlated directly with the altruism index in that study ($r = .27, p < .01$). Berkowitz (1972) found that inducing a state of self-concern reduced his subjects' helpfulness, perhaps because self-preoccupation interfered with attention to the needs of others. Stimulus overload may also reduce helping by lowering attentiveness to external stimuli including need cues (cf. Sherrod & Downs, 1974).

Once beyond the threshhold of awareness, the impact of the other's need on helping depends on its seriousness (intensity). Degree of seriousness may influence many aspects of the perceived outcomes of action or inaction: moral costs (and benefits), social costs, arousal, outcomes for the recipient, and material or psychological costs to the actor (Schwartz, 1975; Staub, 1974). Two examples of seriousness effects will suffice. Experimenters who asked women in supermarkets for a dime to help purchase a food item were more successful when holding a high-need (milk) than a low-need (frozen cookie dough) item (Bickman & Kamzan, 1973). The frequently replicated finding that female victims of dangerous emergencies elicit more help than males (e.g., West, Whitney, & Schnedler, 1975) is at least partly attributable to the perception of females as more needy.

In the preceding studies, and even more so in other instances of seriousness effects [e.g., more help for the victim of a bad heart than a bad knee; Staub & Baer (1974)], several mediating processes probably worked together. The following field experiment was designed to examine the effects of awareness and seriousness of need on helping as mediated primarily through personal norm activation. A low-keyed appeal to perform a simple behavior, delivered impersonally by a stranger, was utilized to minimize mediation of helping by arousal, social expectations, and variation in perceived material and nonmoral psychological costs of action.[7]

Based on the idea that AC taps the *spontaneous* tendency to attend to possible consequences of one's behavior for the welfare of others, I hypothesized that AC is positively related to helping under low prominence and seriousness of the others' need in the stimulus environment. The higher one's AC score, the more likely one is to experience activation of personal norms under low prominence of need. When need cues are spelled out fully, on the other hand, everyone is likely to be aware of consequences for others. Hence AC was hypothesized to have no impact on helping under high seriousness. High seriousness was expected to elicit more help overall because the greater the intensity of need the greater the information conveyed which could activate the normative structure and prevent defenses.

a. Method. The AC scale consists of six short story—completion items described to respondents as "a test of your understanding of the way people go about making the choices they do." Each story stub depicts a central character confronted with a situation in which the welfare of others may be affected by his decisions. The others' need and the potential consequences for them are not spelled out. Respondents are asked to describe the inner dialogue engaged in by the central characters as they decide what to do. Responses are coded on a 5-point scale for the extent to which the needs of others are mentioned as part of the decision making, regardless of actual decisions reached. A score of 0

[7] For greater detail, see Schwartz (1974).

indicates no awareness of others' needs; a score of 4 indicates awareness of detailed needs, adopting the perspective of others, and reflecting on the consequences of actions from their viewpoint.

The following is an example of a story stub:

> Dick was happy he could drive home a little faster than usual because traffic was light at this hour. He had promised his wife he'd be early, so they could make it during the visiting hours at the hospital to see her father tonight. As he turns to exit from the highway, Dick sees a car some 50 yards ahead of him suddenly veer off the road into a ditch and turn over. As he approaches the place where the other car left the road, what thoughts and feelings are running through Dick's mind?

Seventy college girls who had earlier completed the AC scale received a phone call asking them to pledge time to staff a bake sale booth to raise funds for Head Start. The caller was a student who supposedly picked their names out of the directory. High seriousness of need was generated by pointing out that if college girls did the selling, mothers of the Head Start children could stay home with their children. Pledges were accepted only from girls who insisted they would show up.

b. Results. An average of almost twice as much time was pledged under high as under low seriousness ($p < .01$). AC had its expected positive effect on helping under low seriousness, and no effect under high seriousness. The results (Fig. 1), however, reveal an interesting and unexpected pattern. The impact of seriousness appeared among those low and moderate in AC, but disappeared and even reversed among those highest in AC, yielding a significant interaction ($p < .02$).

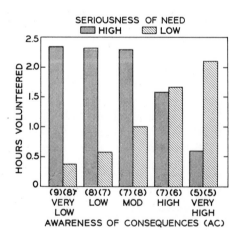

Fig. 1. Hours pledged for bake sale as a function of seriousness of need and awareness of consequences. Means are adjusted for the linear effects of ascription of responsibility. Numbers in parentheses are sample sizes.

c. Discussion. Personal norms favoring aid to Head Start undoubtedly prevailed on the University of Wisconsin campus at this time. The confirmations of the hypotheses support the idea that awareness of need, whether fostered by trait receptivity or situational prominence, leads to helping by activating these norms. As hypothesized, the positive AC effect on helping was limited to the condition where other's need was not sharply drawn to the potential helpers' attention. This accords with a view of AC as a *spontaneous* tendency to note consequences, and explains why AC was unrelated to bystander intervention in a clear emergency where serious need was prominent (Schwartz & Clausen, 1970).

Subjects high on AC who were exposed to the high-seriousness manipulation did not respond as the activation process predicts. They should have been most aware of need, yet their helping was quite low. I will discuss this unexpected finding in a later section (IV) on boomerang effects, which also considers two of our other studies.

2. Perception That There Are Actions Which Could Relieve Others' Need

Even an apparently straightforward need often subsumes a potential multiplicity of needs. Ambiguity may refer not to whether a need exists but to which of many potential needs are present. If we hear that a friend is suffering from an incurable disease, we may think first that he needs a miracle cure. Further thought will disclose needs for sympathy, validation of human worth, settling of affairs, etc. Those who stop with their first perception may become depressed and wish they could do something. They will not move toward activation of personal norms, because they detect no real actions that could relieve the need they identify.

Step 2 alone merely involves the recognition that there are some actions which can be taken. The clumsy performances of many adults upon meeting an acquaintance who recently lost a dear one, for example, betray a failure to recognize needs to which responses could be made. When activation goes beyond this step, the nature of the specific actions which the person views as potentially useful becomes critical. These actions eventually determine which norms and values in the cognitive structure become implicated, the content to which personal norms constructed by norm construction are addressed, and the feelings of moral obligation the person will experience.

3. Recognition of Own Ability to Provide Relief

Activation will be aborted even when need-meeting actions are recognized unless the person sees himself as capable and responsible to take one or more of these actions. The meager research evidence supporting the intuitively obvious notion that amount of helping varies with actual or with self-perceived ability to perform helping actions is reviewed elsewhere (Schwartz, 1975). One additional study merits mention because it shows how ability modifies the impact of seriousness of another's need on helping. Coeds informed that their responses could help a victim of electric shock responded more quickly the greater the victim's suffering. Those informed that their responses could not help tended to engage in more activities designed to "blot out" the victim's suffering as the suffering increased, but did not respond more quickly (Baron, 1970).

Denial of ability is an important technique for neutralizing feelings of moral obligation after they have arisen. But *initial* recognition of ability is required for personal norm activation to occur in the first place. Ability may also influence helping through increasing the probability of success and reducing the physical and social costs anticipated for action.

4. Apprehension of Some Responsibility to Become Involved

The final step in the activation phase is to sense some responsibility to become involved with the needy party. Responsibility refers to a sense of connection or relatedness with the person in need. Defined in this manner, responsibility is not the same analytically as the feelings of obligation to act generated in the next phase. Feelings of obligation are directed toward the performance of specific acts; their strength is a function both of the connection with the needy (responsibility) and of the implications of the act for self-evaluation.

Ongoing *role relationships* trigger responsibility virtually automatically. In less structured social contacts, the following five conditions promote the emergence of a sense of responsibility.

First, if a person recognizes his own ability to perform a useful action, even a *chance encounter* with evidence of another's need may suffice to elicit responsibility. Pedestrians who happen to find wallets, documents, and contributions belonging to strangers, for example, readily mail them to their owners or to other concerned parties (Hornstein, 1972; Schwartz & Ames, 1977). Some relatedness is apparently generated even by the presumed chance contact involved in giving another the correct time. Such a manipulation increased helping in a study where the other's books were later stolen (Howard & Crano, 1974).

Being *causally* connected to another's need is a second means of establishing responsibility. Theorizing about harm-doer responses to their victims postulates that harmful acts are seen as establishing a relationship with the victim (i.e., responsibility) which fosters activation of internalized equity-based norms (e.g., Walster & Piliavin, 1972).

a. Helping in an emergency. In a recent study of helping in an emergency (Schwartz & Ben David, 1976), we examined the combined effects of causal responsibility for need and of self-perceived ability to relieve it (step 3). Earlier research has indicated that manipulations of ability may improve mood or increase overall feelings of competence. Such changes might influence helping by reducing anticipated material costs of action and increasing empathic inclinations and readiness to attend to need. In order to permit a stronger inference that the process which mediates ability effects is norm activation, an ability was selected for manipulation in this study which seemed unlikely to affect mood or feelings of competence: the ability to work with rats.

(1) Method. Seventy-two male Israeli undergraduates participated in a biofeedback study involving training rats by administering shocks. All were informed, based on purported physiological and self-report measures, that "your attitude toward rats is like most people's." Three levels of ability were created by adding either "you are able to work with rats if you have to" (Able), or "when it comes to dealing with rats you are not comfortable and may even find sometimes that you can't touch them at all" (Unable), or nothing further (Control). Later, during the training procedure, a loud crash was heard from the adjacent room, followed by the female experimenter's scream of fright at the rat's escape. Her (recorded) cry varied one unaccented Hebrew syllable to manipulate three levels of causal responsibility: "What did you do?!" (High: subject causally responsible; but note there was no tone of accusation); "What did I do?!" (Low: experimenter responsible, not subject); "What happened?!" (Moderate: chance and perhaps subject responsible). She concluded, "Oh, I'm scared; it bites," making no direct appeal for help.

(2) Results. The speed and frequency of bystander attempts to help revealed main effects for ability and for causal responsibility ($p < .01$ for each), and no interaction. Responses were approximately twice as fast under high as under low responsibility (64 vs. 126 seconds) and in the able as against the unable condition (60 vs. 130 seconds), with intermediate speed for both control and moderate responsibility conditions (105 seconds).

(3) Discussion. Causal responsibility influenced helping as expected, probably through activating both self-expectations and social expectations. Since the experimenter knew how able the subject supposedly was, the ability effect might also be attributed to the subjects' estimation of how easily they could deflect the social sanctions for failing to act. Measures of self-perceived ability and of perceptions that others would accept ability as justifying refusal to have contact with a rat were obtained prior to the emergency. A path analysis using these as intervening variables revealed that both self-perceived ability and public defense mediated the effects of the ability manipulation.

A third way to induce a sense of responsibility is to make a person *accountable* for what happens to another. Such responsibility may be built into a role by letting a person know he is "responsible" (e.g., Tilker, 1970) or assigned on a particular occasion by putting someone "in charge" (e.g., Staub, 1970, 1971). What must be close to the minimum conditions for establishing accountability are reported by Moriarty (1975). A female confederate seated herself at the subject's table in an Automat. When she said "Excuse me . . . may

I leave this here for a few minutes?," pointed to her suitcase and then went to the food dispensers, every subject acted to stop a thief who approached a few minutes later. By contrast, only one of eight subjects intervened when the confederate had only asked, "do you have a light?"

A fourth basis for responsibility is the possession of such *distinctive suitability* to respond as especially appropriate skills, knowledge, or physical characteristics, or the relative exclusiveness of one's availability (e.g., lone vs. multiple bystanders to emergencies). Suitability of various sorts influences helping through implying special relatedness and hence activating personal norms. It may also influence helping through alternative processes which do not involve mediation by feelings of moral obligation: decreasing anticipated costs of action because of more likely success, increasing mood or self-esteem, and increasing the expectation of social sanctions for inaction.

b. *Distinctive suitability, responsibility, and salience of consequences.* Distinctive suitability was manipulated in the following study in a manner intended to vary salience of personal responsibility in the situation while holding other potential mediators of suitability constant across conditions. Salience of consequences—the spelling out of need in the situation—was also varied, permitting joint examination of variables postulated to effect movement through steps 1 and 4 of the model. A third variable, odds that commitment to action would lead to actual self-sacrifice, was included to investigate the impact of varying the probability of incurring costs.[8]

(1) Method. While relaxing in a Red Cross canteen after giving blood, people were interviewed individually by a medical sociologist. After obtaining background information, the interviewer described in detail the reasons for bone marrow transplanting, the procedures involved for donor and recipient, and problems of obtaining adequate matches. All were told about a dying young female patient in need of a bone marrow transplant for whom there was no matching family donor. At this point, subjects were randomly assigned to one of 12 conditions in a 3 × 2 × 2 design.

Salience of consequences was varied across three levels by spelling out in greater detail the harm which would ensue from failure to perform a successful transplant: Low—no further information added; Moderate—added that she is a mother; High—added "And of course losing their mother will be a tragedy for her kids, what with the emotional shock and the hardship of growing up without her." An assertion that either one in 25 or one in 1,000 members of the general population could provide an adequate match manipulated odds. To induce high personal responsibility through distinctive suitability, half the subjects were told: "[We] are turning to people like you who are giving blood today rather than to the general public, because your blood is available so we can get the tests

---

[8] For greater detail, see Schwartz (1970).

started right away and we know you meet the minimal health standards." The remaining subjects were informed: "[We] are turning to the general public. We are running ads for potential donors in newspapers across the state; and we are also asking people at blood centers around Wisconsin. . . ."

Commitment to being a bone marrow donor was measured on a 4-point scale from 0 (unwilling to have a sample of blood tested for matching) to 3 (willing to join a national pool of potential bone marrow donors for future call). Before ending the interview all volunteers learned that substances they ingested earlier precluded accurate tests on the available blood sample.

(2) Results. Fully 59% volunteered to join the national pool of donors! Commitment was greater under high than under low salience of responsibility ($p < .02$). Odds had no overall effect on volunteering but interacted with salience of consequences in an unexpected manner. The predicted increase in volunteering as consequences were made more salient appeared under 1/1000 odds ($p < .05$). For 1/25 odds, however, volunteering increased from low to moderate salience of consequences, but boomeranged to its lowest level when consequences were most salient. Salience of consequences and of responsibility did not interact.

(3) Discussion. Those whose distinctive suitability consisted of being part of a limited group whose blood samples were already available committed themselves significantly more than those given to believe that appeals were being made at numerous blood centers and in the public media. This manipulation of distinctiveness provided no apparent grounds for subjects to perceive themselves as more or less socially pressured, efficacious, competent, worthwhile as human beings, etc. An inference that differences in volunteering were mediated by differences in personal responsibility therefore seems reasonable.

Salience of consequences (step 1 in the model) and of responsibility combined additively to produce more volunteering. Manipulation checks revealed correct perception of the two salience manipulations; but no difference in anticipated costs was associated with the odds manipulation. This latter may account for why odds did not have the predicted effect on volunteering. Nonetheless, odds must have influenced perceptions in some way, since they interacted significantly with salience of consequences. I will discuss the unanticipated boomerang in volunteering under 1/25 odds and high salience of consequences later, together with reversals in other studies.

A final basis for responsibility is exposure to a direct *appeal.* Implicit in any appeal is the focusing of responsibility by the solicitor of help upon the person addressed. In addition to inducing responsibility, of course, appeals may promote helping by drawing attention to the existence of a need, overcoming ambiguity regarding its reality, and pointing to social expectations for behavior.

The various conditions promoting responsibility are undoubtedly not equally potent. Differences in potency beyond a threshold level probably matter less for the initial awakening of responsibility than for later responsibility denial (step 7). Studies in which different bases of responsibility induction are manipulated simultaneously would clarify their relative potency under particular conditions.

One additional condition which promotes responsibility is *dependency*. Numerous studies have shown that effort expended to help another increases as a function of the needy person's dependency (e.g., Berkowitz & Daniels, 1963; Berkowitz, Klanderman, & Harris, 1964). Dependency has been operationalized as the extent to which the potential helper's actions determine the other's outcomes. As such, it combines need, ability, and responsibility. The greater the other's dependency, the more salient and serious the other's need, the more able one is to relieve it, and the more suitable and distinctive one is as the source of aid. Thus dependency is a complex variable which may influence the decision process in each one of the activation steps and may later inhibit some defenses.

Because conditions which can generate a sense of responsibility often point to social expectations for action, they may induce compliance to social norms in order to avoid the costs inherent in social sanctions, without the experience of feelings of moral obligation. When socially mediated costs are substantial, the whole process of personal norm activation may be short-circuited as irrelevant to reaching a decision.

5. Activation of Preexisting or Situationally Constructed Personal Norms

Movement through steps 1–4 activates the cognitive structure of norms and values and initiates the obligation phase. Feelings of moral obligation are now generated by reference to preexisting norms, or more often by the process of situational norm construction described earlier (Section III,C). I have postulated that the feelings of moral obligation generated when norms are constructed in the situation have a causal impact on altruistic behavior. Support for this causal link depends upon evidence that altruism covaries with personal norms measured at the individual level, under conditions conducive to norm activation. Most of the evidence that factors presumed to foster norm activation are related to helping, cited in the discussion of steps 1–4, is consistent both with mediation by personal norms and with other mediating processes (i.e., emotional arousal, activation of social norms).

Personal norms, measured at the individual level, have been correlated with altruistic behavior in the six studies listed in Table III. All the correlations were significant, but their varying strength invites comment. Most striking is the correlation of .59 for buying lead-free gasoline (study 1), an action intended largely to reduce general air pollution in 1973. Two elements which influenced this correlation shed doubt on the direction of causation: the behavior index was partly composed of a self-report, and buying behavior was recurrent so that some instances had preceded norm assessment. The other very high correlation

TABLE III
CORRELATIONS BETWEEN PERSONAL NORMS AND ALTRUISTIC BEHAVIOR

Study No.	Nature of norm and behavior	Correlation
1	Buying lead-free gasoline (Heberlein & Black, 1976)	.59[a]
2	Donating blood in a campus blood drive (Pomazal, 1974)	.43[a]
3	Pledging to take class notes and send them to students serving in the Israeli army (Rothstein, 1974)	.26[c]
4	Considerateness and helpfulness in everyday peer interactions (Schwartz, 1968a, 1968b)	.25[b]
5	Volunteering to be a bone marrow transplant donor (Schwartz, 1973)	.24[b]
6	Volunteering to tutor blind children (S. H. Schwartz, unpublished data)	.26[b]

[a] $p < .001$.
[b] $p < .01$.
[c] $p < .05$.

(study 2) may be due in part to a related phenomenon. Many subjects may already have decided whether to donate blood before responding to the norm questionnaire. Norms were assessed just a few days before blood was actually collected, after subjects had been exposed to a campus-wide campaign.

These characteristics of the two studies with strong correlations undermine any firm inference that norms caused behavior. Norms may have been inferred from behavior, or both may have been caused by other factors (Schwartz & Tessler, 1972). Based on this reasoning one would also expect a strong correlation in the study of recurrent everyday considerateness and helpfulness (study 4). Perhaps the use of peer ratings rather than actual observations of behavior weakened the norm–behavior relationship in that study.

Normative explanations used in the absence of personal norm measurement or in cases of recurrent similar behaviors are vulnerable to the criticism that associations of behavior with norms may reflect the post hoc invocation of norms as explanations or justifications for behavior (Darley & Latané, 1970; Krebs, 1970). The problem of inferring causality with recurrent behaviors also plagues attempts to determine whether cultural differences in norms and values cause group differences in behavior, are caused by them, or reflect some other causal process.

Causal inference is less problematic for the remaining studies in Table III. These studies selected unusual and nonrecurrent instances of altruistic behavior; they measured personal norms prior to behavior; and they used separate auspices and a substantial time interval between norm and behavior measurement to deter respondents from connecting the two. As a further precaution, Rothstein (1974) included an index of possibly related past behavior in her prediction equation for helping Israeli soldiers (study 3), with no effect on the norm-behavior correlation (partial $r = .26$).

Correlations in studies 3–6 were in the range typical for attitude type variables (cf. Wicker, 1969). This is not unexpected according to our theoretical model, since we have yet to consider how these correlations were modified by conditions conducive to norm activation and defense. The importance of such modification was demonstrated in the discussion of study 4 in Section III,B: Recall that under personality conditions maximizing the possibility of norm activation, the correlation between norms and behavior was shown to be .54. Data from studies 5 and 6, on the modification of norm–behavior relations in the defense phase of the model, will be examined shortly.

Since personal norms are commonly constructed anew in each situation, the feelings of moral obligation measured in a questionnaire are virtually certain to differ somewhat from those experienced at the time of behavioral decision. Measured norm–behavior correlations are therefore likely to underestimate the actual correspondence between behavior and the norms constructed in the action situation. The magnitude of the discrepancy between the norms constructed in response to a questionnaire and in the action situation is likely to depend on the stability of the underlying structure of values and general norms scanned during the construction process. Norm–behavior correlations should be higher for norms constructed by reference to stable than to unstable structures of values and general norms. This derivation from the theoretical model was tested in a study of Hebrew University undergraduates.

   a. Method. During the first few weeks of the semester (T1), first-year students individually completed questionnaires containing personal norm questions regarding eight altruistic actions embedded among various demographic, personality, and political items. Approximately 3 months later (T2), part of this sample ($N = 141$) completed the questionnaire again, purportedly to check how the first few months of university affect attitudes. Students received a letter from the director of the School for the Blind some 2 months later, requesting that they give a few hours each week to read to blind school children. Responses were made by returning a postcard containing five levels of commitment, scored from 1 (refusal, or failure to answer even after a follow-up letter) to 5 (specifying a definite number of times per week, giving days and hours).

   The best available indicator of the general structure of values and norms relevant to altruism was the set of responses to all eight personal norms. A stability index was constructed by taking the absolute differences between each person's feelings of obligation for each action at T1 and T2 and summing these differences across the eight norms. The sample was dichotomized on overall norm stability and the personal norms for tutoring blind children measured at T1 and T2 were correlated with subsequent behavior. For purposes of control, one group completed the questionnaire only at T1, another only at T2, and another received the appeal but no questionnaires. These groups did not differ in behavior from the group used here for the stability analysis, which completed the questionnaire twice.

b. Results. For those showing little norm change between T1 and T2, the correlation between the key norm (tutoring blind children) and behavior was higher than for those whose normative structure was less stable: $r = .35 > r = .10$, $p < .07$, for the key norm measured at T2; $r = .23 > r = .04$, n.s., for the key norm from T1. This finding did not depend upon change in the key norm itself. When the sample was split on change vs. no change in the key norm alone, correlations between norms and behavior were very similar in the two sub-samples, both for T1 and T2. Limited ranges of variation did not account for these findings.

c. Discussion. The results, while weak, generally confirm the hypothesis that measured personal norms are better predictors of altruism to the extent that they are constructed by reference to more stable cognitive structures. The fact that stability had a moderating effect when indexed by the sum of change across eight norms, but not when indexed by change in the key norm alone, suggests that it is instability in the larger structure which matters.

Since change cumulates in the normative structure with the passage of time, personal norms should correlate more highly with behavior the less the time elapsed between norm assessment and behavioral decision. In line with this hypothesis, the personal norm for tutoring blind children was a better predictor when measured closer in time to behavior: $r = .26$ at T2 $> r = .13$ at T1, $p < .05$ for dependent samples.

Another source of information on stability effects may be tapped by noting that cognitive value structures probably become more stable reference points for constructing personal norms as children mature. Hence the correlation between norms and behavior would be expected to increase with age through childhood. Data supporting this proposition are found in a study by Henshel (1971), who measured honesty values and observed cheating behavior among school girls. Neither honesty values nor cheating increased with grade; but the correlation between them increased significantly and systematically from $r = -.02$ among fourth graders to $-.78$ in the seventh grade.

6. Assessment of Costs and Evaluation of Probable Outcomes

Once feelings of moral obligation to perform particular actions have been generated, the defense phase begins. In assessing outcomes of actions, four types of costs (and benefits) may be considered: social, physical, psychological, and moral costs. I have described these types elsewhere (Schwartz, 1975, p. 127) and others have suggested similar categories (e.g., Janis, 1959; Piliavin & Piliavin, 1975). The critical point is that, other things being equal, the impact of personal norms on behavior is a function of the magnitude of moral costs and benefits anticipated for actions which conform to or violate these norms.

Findings reported for the studies in which personal norms were related to altruistic behavior are evidence for this point. These correlations presumably reflect a process in which persons facing behavioral choices experience antici- pated moral costs roughly proportional to those measured by the reported strength of their feelings of obligation in personal norm questionnaires, and these anticipated costs motivate overt behavior. Since moral costs and benefits are experienced as changes in self-evaluation, their magnitude is likely to depend upon how central or important the attributes reflected upon by a given behavior are to a person's overall self-evaluation (cf. Miller, 1963). A similar view is implied in Bem's (1972) suggestion that people monitor their behavior more closely and self-consciously in domains which are particularly important for their self-image. This hypothesis received support in the following test.

In the study of altruism in everyday life considered in Section III,B, students ranked how central and important they felt their status on each of seven attributes (eg., flexibility, independence, helpfulness) was for their overall self-evaluation. Self-rankings of the centrality of considerateness correlated sig- nificantly with behavior for each of the single considerateness situations and for the summary index of considerateness behavior ($r = .23$, $p < .01$). Rankings of the centrality of helpfulness for self-evaluation were also significantly correlated with helpful behavior in three of four specific situations and for the summary index ($r = .22$, $p < .01$).

The intensity of anticipated moral costs should logically reflect the com- bined (multiplicative) impact of the centrality of the behavioral domain and of the strength of moral obligation felt to perform a behavior. While people tend to feel more strongly obligated to perform behaviors related to ego-central domains, centrality and strength of obligation are not the same. For nine incidents we studied the correlations between the centrality rank of the relevant domain and the strength of personal norm ranged from $r = .10$ to $r = .34$ ($\bar{r} = .18$). When a behavioral domain is of peripheral importance to the self, the moral costs of violating a personal norm should be relatively weak. When the domain is central, personal norms should foreshadow moral costs better and hence be related more closely to behavior.

This hypothesis was also tested with data from the study of altruism in everyday life. The sample was dichotomized at the median for the centrality rank given to helpfulness. Within each subsample individuals' personal norms (i.e., self-reported sense of moral obligation) to help were correlated with peer ratings of their helpfulness. A similar analysis was performed for considerateness.

For both types of behavior the correlations between the respective summary indices of personal norms and of behavior were higher among those who ranked the relevant attributes as more central to their self-evaluation than among those who ranked it less central. The correlation difference was significant for considerateness ($r = .32 > r = .04, p < .05$), though not for helpfulness ($r = .21 > r = .09$, n.s.). Thus centrality of the behavioral domain moderated the norm—behavior relation as predicted.

Nonmoral costs play a critical role in deflecting the impact of personal norms on behavior. The anticipation of nonmoral costs for a morally desirable line of behavior stimulates people to defend against their feelings of moral obligation. The influence of nonmoral costs on helping has been analyzed theoretically by Piliavin and Piliavin (1975) and received some empirical support (e.g., Gross, Wallston, & Piliavin, 1975; Wagner & Wheeler, 1969). Lerner (1975) has suggested a fascinating example of a nonmoral psychological cost of altruism: By aiding those in need one acknowledges the existence of injustice. This is costly because it threatens the belief that one's own good fortune is deserved.

7. Reassessment and Redefinition of the Situation through Defensive Denial

Since individuals attach conditional probabilities to the possible outcomes of actions based on past experience (Boneau, 1974), the process in step 6 yields an assessment and evaluation of the balance of anticipated costs and benefits associated with responses. In situations where no personal norms have been activated (i.e., the person feels no obligation either way regarding potential acts), or where activated norms generate only weak feelings of obligation, behavior follows from the balance of nonmoral costs. Where moral and nonmoral costs support the same helping responses, action can occur without reassessment. When anticipated costs favoring and opposing action are both high or are practically balanced, reassessment of the decision situation may ensue in search of means to reduce costs of modify their balance.

Conflict is experienced when anticipated moral costs for an action are high and opposed by nonmoral costs: Compliance with activated personal norms can satisfy feelings of moral obligation only at the risk of incurring substantial social, physical, and/or psychological costs. One way to escape this conflict is to neutralize the feelings of obligation, to deactivate the norms by redefining the situation. Three general modes of neutralization are inherent in the model presented here. Activation requires awareness of need and some sense of responsibility. Norm construction requires recognition of the implications of actions for values and general norms of importance to self-evaluation. Hence reassessment can lead to deactivation by denying the state of need (its reality, seriousness), by denying responsibility, or by viewing different actions or different implications of action as appropriate.

a. Denial of the state of need. All factors which make need more salient initially make it more difficult to deny need subsequent to norm activation. The relative ambiguity of the need cues themselves and the interpretation of these cues given by others or implied by their actions, for example, undoubtedly influenced helping through need denial in several bystander studies (Darley *et al.,* 1973; Piliavin & Piliavin, 1975). It is not feasible, unfortunately, to estimate how much of the reduction in responsiveness induced by ambiguity and social interpretations of cues is due to initial failure to perceive need and how much to denial of need when faced with the costs of helping.

It is also possible to neutralize feelings of moral obligation by *increasing* the perceived seriousness of need and reinterpreting the situation as beyond hope. Debates over the ethics of extraordinary efforts to sustain terminal patients revolve upon the question of whether the moral obligation to help ends when hope of relieving need is abandoned. In a less spectacular vein, partial neutralization of the obligations felt to help the homeless, maimed, starving, and otherwise "underprivileged" groups portrayed in the media is achieved by concluding that any actions one might take are futile faced with such overwhelming need. This type of defense works against the requirements for norm activation specified in steps 2 (relief possible) and 3 (own ability) of the model.

The finding that conditions conducive to need denial reduce helping is consistent both with an intervening process of neutralizing the moral costs of (in)action and with alternative explanations. The nonresponse of other bystanders to an emergency increases social costs of action (e.g., appearing foolish) and reduces social costs of inaction (e.g., anticipated condemnation), for example, at the same time it implies that need is not serious. Clear-cut investigation of norm neutralization through need denial requires studies in which the association between measured personal norms and behavior is compared under conditions varying in conduciveness to denial of need. Emergencies of the type commonly studied are inappropriate for such research; the personal norms likely to be constructed to guide behavior in emergencies do not vary sufficiently across individuals.

b. Denial of responsibility to respond. Conditions which make the connection between the potential actor and the needy party more salient initially (see step 4) are likely to make denial of responsibility more difficult. Research on the phenomenon labeled "diffusion of responsibility" postulates that situations are reassessed in order to deny or reduce responsibility to act, thereby neutralizing felt obligation. In studies of emergencies, diffusion has been found to be a function of the number of other bystanders, their apparent medical competence, their physical separation from the victim, and their age (see review in Piliavin & Piliavin, 1975).

The interpretation of diffusion effects as due to denial of responsibility after norm activation is corroborated by findings from a study by Schwartz and

Clausen (1970). Female bystanders to a nervous seizure helped less as a function both of the number and competence of other bystanders. When the sample was dichotomized on the personality tendency toward responsibility denial (RD), however, it was only among those who tended to accept rationales for denying responsibility that these effects were observed.

Outside of emergency settings there is little research directly interpretable as reflecting denial of responsibility effects. Difficulty in denying responsibility probably accounted for part of the increment in volunteering to donate bone marrow caused by the salience of responsibility manipulation in Schwartz (1970), discussed earlier (Section III,D,4). In another relevant study, passersby were confronted by a student who requested a nickel for five pennies as he stepped from a phone booth (Ernest & Cooper, 1973). Eye contact was maintained with all passersby, establishing personal connection and responsibility. Helping was an inverse function of spatial distance, perhaps reflecting relative difficulty of denying responsibility. Studies like these two, which expose the potential helper to social contact, necessarily confound variation in social costs with moral costs. To reduce this confounding more *impersonal* methods for manipulating need and responsibility are required. First, however, consider the evidence for individual differences in denial of responsibility.

Responsibility denial (RD)[9] is the individual tendency to deny that one is responsible for the consequences of action and hence to neutralize moral obligation. RD is measured by agreement with or rejection of a set of 28 items which mention or allude to actions with interpersonal consequences and provide rationales for ascribing (some) responsibility for the actions and/or their consequences away from the actor (Schwartz, 1968b, 1973). Acceptance of the rationales is coded as indicating a tendency to deny responsibility. Agreement or disagreement with each item is expressed on a 4-point scale. The following sample items are coded for acceptance of the rationales.

_A_ When a person is nasty to me, I feel very little responsibility to treat him well.

_A_ I wouldn't feel badly about giving offense to someone if my intentions had been good.

_D_ Being upset or preoccupied does not excuse a person for doing anything he would ordinarily avoid.

_D_ Professional obligations can never justify neglecting the welfare of others.

Factor analyses of responses in various samples reveal clusters of rationales including overriding pressures, prior harm done, intentionality, and job obligations.

[9] As explained in footnote 4, this variable was formerly labeled Ascription of Responsibility.

When most people in a population hold positive personal norms toward an action, as they do with helping behaviors, RD should correlate negatively with that action because high RD scores signify a tendency to neutralize personal norms.

RD scores have been related significantly to: bystander responses to a seizure victim (Schwartz & Clausen, 1970), to an experimenter frightened by an escaped rat (Schwartz & Ben David, 1976), and to moaning and groaning from an adjoining room (Staub, 1974); everyday considerateness and helpfulness (Schwartz, 1968b); refraining from littering on a busy street (Heberlein, 1971); volunteering to donate bone marrow [data from study reported in Schwartz (1973)] ; pledging time to raise money for Head Start (Schwartz, 1974). As might be expected, RD was more strongly associated with helping in nonemergency studies, where the opportunity to deny responsibility was not constrained by the conspicuous dependency of a victim upon quick reactions. The correlation with helping was strongest in the Head Start study ($r = -.48, p < .001$).

From the viewpoint of the theoretical model exposited here, the particular importance of RD is as a moderator of the impact of personal norms on behavior: Responsibility denial can be used to deactivate personal norms. Support for the operation of RD as a moderator was found in the study of everyday peer relations among college students described earlier (Section III,B): Personal norms were significantly related to altruistic behavior only among those lowest on RD. This relationship can be attributed neither to the committing effects of answering the norm questions nor to responsiveness to demand characteristics for consistency, since the behavior was measured by peer ratings and referred to an earlier time. The conclusiveness of the findings is weakened, however, because the behavior was not observed directly and because it was recurrent. The latter problem suggests an alternative explanation for the interaction between RD and personal norms in their impact on behavior. The interaction could conceivably have been produced because the students inferred their norms from their behavior, and those who tended to deny responsibility also misperceived their past behavior more. The following study was designed to overcome these weaknesses and to provide a test of the alternative explanation.[10]

(1) Method. A random sample of 253 female clerical workers for the State of Wisconsin was mailed a questionnaire ostensibly as part of a national survey on public attitudes toward organ transplantation by a New York hospital. Embedded in the questionnaire were the RD scale and an item to tap the personal norm constructed toward donating bone marrow for a stranger (see Table II, question 1). Three months later an appeal to join a pool of potential bone marrow donors was received by 132 of those who had completed the questionnaire. The appeal letter, from a renowned Wisconsin transplant special-

---

[10] For greater detail, see Schwartz (1973).

ist, described the reasons for, problems with, and procedures involved in marrow transplants. It mentioned no association with the preceding survey.

Volunteers were asked to provide local doctors with blood samples for analysis in a central laboratory, so that their marrow characteristics could be filed in a national listing of donors for future call. Responses were indicated on a card providing four alternatives of increasing commitment: 1, not interested; 2, send information; 3, probably interested, have doctor phone to discuss; 4, interested, call for appointment. Those who failed to respond after two reminders were scored as a stronger refusal (0).

(2) Results. The sample was trichotomized on RD and correlations between personal norms and behavior were computed within each RD subsample. These correlations are shown in the first row of Table IV. The variances for behavior and norms did not differ across RD subsamples. The expected increment in correlations between personal norms and altruistic behavior as responsibility denial decreased was evident. For those most likely to neutralize any feelings of moral obligation (high RD), norms and behavior were unrelated. For those least likely to deactivate personal norms through responsibility denial (low RD), the association was substantial and significantly higher. Even stronger results were found when the data were analyzed using a more clear-cut behavioral distinction, the dichotomy between rejecting further contacts (0, 1) vs. requesting them (2, 3, 4).

(3) Discussion. The findings of this study reinforce the argument that personal normative influences on altruism are indeed causal. The conditions for a

TABLE IV
CORRELATIONS BETWEEN PERSONAL NORMS AND ALTRUISTIC BEHAVIOR AS
MODERATED BY RESPONSIBILITY DENIAL (RD)

		RD levels			
Norm and behavior	Sample	I High	II Moderate	III Low	Comparison: III vs. I
Donating bone marrow for a stranger (Schwartz, 1973)	132 female Wisconsin clerical workers	.01 (42)[a]	.27 (49)	.44[c] (41)	$p < .05$
Reading to blind school children	141 Hebrew University undergraduates	−.13 (52)	.34[b] (49)	.72[d] (40)	$p < .001$

[a]Number of persons on which correlation is based is given in parentheses.
[b]$p < .05$.
[c]$p < .01$.
[d]$p < .001$.

normative impact were specified in advance, personal norms were measured before behavior and were logically independent of meaningful inferences based on past behavior, and behavior itself was directly observed. These findings, together with those from the study of everyday altruism among college students provide evidence that responsibility denial mediates the impact of personal norms on altruism for momentous as well as routine decisions, and among samples of very different composition.

The next study sought to replicate these findings in a different cultural setting and addressed itself to yet another alternative explanation for the interaction between RD and personal norms. Might RD tap something that reflects the accuracy with which personal norms are reported by subjects? Perhaps those low in RD are more careful and thorough in responding to norm questions than those who readily deny their responsibility, so that the answers given are better predictors of the norms that low-RD subjects construct in the decision situation. Neither of the earlier studies provided evidence supporting this speculation, nor could they be used to refute it.

One index of the accuracy of personal norm reports might be their consistency or stability over time. People who thoroughly scan their normative structure before responding to norm questions should show greater stability in the feelings of obligation they report than those who answer less carefully. We have seen that overall stability of the normative structure did moderate the associations between personal norms and behavior in the study of Hebrew University students described earlier (Section III,D,5). Thus, if RD and stability were correlated highly, *quality* of reported norms rather than deactivation of norms in the action situation might account for RD's moderating effect on the norm–behavior relationship.

A Hebrew version of the RD scale was included in the questionnaire completed twice by the Hebrew University undergraduates. Contrary to the alternative explanation under consideration, the correlation between this scale and the index of overall norm stability was −.16 for RD measured both at T1 and T2; nor was RD correlated with consistency in the key norm toward reading to blind children.

On the other hand, RD did moderate the norm–behavior relationship in this study. Correlations between volunteering and personal norm within subsamples formed by trichotomizing on RD, using data from T2, are shown in the second row of Table IV. The correlation of .72 among those unlikely to deny responsibility is quite striking and significantly greater than within either the moderate or high RD subsamples. Similar though weaker results, as expected, are found using data from T1.

Taken together, these studies eliminate alternative explanations and support the notion that personal norms influence altruistic behavior so long as they are not deactivated by responsibility denial. The effect has shown robustness across samples, cultures, and types of behavior. Only one study has been inconsistent with the others in finding no interaction between RD and personal norms in their effect on behavior, namely, Heberlein and Black's (1974) study of the purchase of lead-free gasoline. Perhaps this failure has to do with problems noted regarding that study: The behavior index was partly a self-report and, more importantly, norms were measured subsequent to recurrent behavior. To the extent that the norm—behavior association in that study was due to inferring norms or developing them from past behavior, there is no reason that RD should moderate it.

We return now to situational influences on denial of moral obligation. The theoretical model suggests that the norm—behavior relationship should be stronger under high salience both of need and of responsibility in an appeal, since these conditions render denial of need and responsibility more difficult. Furthermore, to the extent that positive norms are activated, the impact of situational variations on denial should lead to greater volunteering among those in high-salience than in low-salience conditions.

To test these hypotheses, the appeal for bone marrow donors in the study of Wisconsin clerical workers described earlier contained manipulations of salience of need and salience of responsibility in a 2 × 2 design. The appeal was made in an impersonal mass mailing rather than through direct social contact in order to minimize possible social costs of refusal. Any salience effects might therefore be attributed more confidently to activation of moral rather than social obligation.

(1) Method. Women were assigned to conditions so as to match experimental groups on the distribution of RD, personal norms, age, and attitudes toward transplants. Salience of the need for potential donors was manipulated by projecting an imminent major breakthrough in marrow transplant techniques that would make this the only procedure offering hope for curing leukemia-related diseases (High) vs. noting that this procedure was one of many on which research was continuing in hopes of an eventual breakthrough (Low). Responsibility was manipulated by emphasizing that every volunteer makes a unique contribution because each transplant requires a donor with different characteristics: It was noted that those being contacted were thought more likely than the general public to meet necessary physical and mental health standards (High); or it was suggested that people should consider such barriers to their volunteering as their health and their conflicting obligations and should be certain they were in a position to undertake such a responsibility (Low).

(2) Results. Personal norms were significantly and positively correlated with behavior in three of the four conditions. In the cell hypothesized to produce the highest norm—behavior correspondence (high salience of both situational variables), however, the correlation was close to zero, and it was considerably weaker than in the other three cells combined ($r = .01 < \bar{r} = .34, p < .09$, two-tailed)! The hypothesis was therefore not only rejected, but there was a trend toward a reversal of the expected effect. This reversal was also reflected in the effect of salience of responsibility among those with positive norms: Volun-

teering was significantly greater under low than under high salience of responsibility [$F(1,65)$ = 4.29, $p < .05$]. There was no effect for salience of need and no interaction between the manipulated variables. As expected, neither manipulation influenced the behavior of those whose norms opposed donating or who did not view the question normatively.

(3) Discussion. Behavior was indeed influenced by the salience of need and responsibility in the situation, but not in the manner predicted. Instead it seems that the impact of personal norms on behavior was neutralized under just those conditions in which denial was expected to be most difficult, under high salience of need and of responsibility. In contrast, the correlations suggest that activated personal norms had an impact in the remaining conditions. Moreover, among those with positive norms, increasing salience of responsibility led to a reduction in volunteering, another boomerang effect. These findings will be discussed in a special section (IV) dealing with this and earlier boomerang effects.

c. Shifting the suitability of norms perceived. This third mode of neutralizing feelings of moral obligation is facilitated by the tentativeness of meaning inherent in ongoing interaction (Garfinkel, 1967). The meanings and implications of behavior typically emerge and change as events unfold, producing retroactive reinterpretations. As a result, defensive redefinitions which make different actions and hence norms seem appropriate can be viewed as natural and legitimate.

Since situations often pose a multiplicity of possible needs, people may be responsive even if they shift their focus to needs which activate norms prescribing behavior with lesser nonmoral costs. Actions responsive to alternate needs are suggested by habitual patterns of response, enduring or momentary aspirations, or expectations voiced by others. Personal norms which conflict with the obligation to respond to the original focal need may be activated when outcomes point to more than one consequence of action. Some seminarians in a study by Darley and Batson (1973), for example, failed to aid a man slumped in a doorway because they felt a stronger obligation to help the experimenter who was dependent on them to hurry.

Step 7 has described three general modes of defense against feelings of moral obligation. Although each mode might alone suffice to neutralize norms, they are probably often used in concert, because circumstances seldom permit complete denial of need or responsibility, and alternate norms may not entirely supersede initially activated norms.

8. Iterations of Earlier Steps in Light of Reassessments

Depending on how the situation is redefined, the person may return to any of the earlier steps in the model. Needs, possible actions, ability, responsibility, obligation (i.e., steps 1–5), all may be perceived differently. This leads to reconsideration of response options and reevaluation of their probable outcomes. Iterations continue and may delay action until a distinctly best option emerges. An exaggerated form of iteration is exemplified by one group of potential family kidney donors described by Simmons, Klein, and Thornton (1973). These people repeatedly postponed committing themselves to a decision whether to donate, drifting until events either precluded donation or locked them into it.

Rapid intensification of the other's need, as in emergencies, tends to curtail iterations because the moral (and often nonmoral) costs of inaction increase with the passage of time. Iterations will also be cut short, and a less favorable balance of costs accepted, when anticipated nonmoral costs to the self grow with delay (e.g., the chance that one's miserliness will be revealed publicly). When response is delayed, on the other hand, pressure for inaction mounts, because the implication of subsequent compliance with an altruistic norm is that the correct assessment of the situation demanded responsiveness all along. Perhaps this is why so few bystanders who failed to intervene within the first 2 minutes in various emergency studies intervened subsequently.

With the many methods for avoiding the moral costs of violating personal norms, one might wonder why people ever act on their feelings of moral obligation when nonmoral costs are high. Apparently self-deception regarding need, responsibility, and the implications of actions for one's values is not always easy. It is sometimes easier to deflect social costs attendant upon violating others' expectations, because others are prone to collude with the actor to accept reasonable public accounts (Goffman, 1959). Moreover, until relief comes, information about the persistence or growth of need continues to be processed. Even physical escape from need cues leaves a residue of cognitive representations which may be difficult to ignore.

9. Action or Inaction Response

The decision to act according to one or another plan or to refrain from action constitutes the endpoint of a single cycle through the model. Both actions and inaction have impacts which may change the situation and/or the person's perception of it, so that a new cycle through the model is initiated. New needs may become salient, for example, or the level of connectivity with the needy may be altered. Moreover, the reinforcements elicited in response to an action can change the person's structure of values and norms. While this model of how personal norms influence altruism can be used to describe the process for reaching a single decision, it applies equally to social behavior viewed as a chain of sequential interdependent decisions, if attention is given to feedback.

IV. Boomerang Effects on Altruism

In three of the studies described above, decreased helping was produced by increments in conditions which, according to the model of norm activation, should foster feelings of moral obligation to help. I have referred to these findings as *boomerang effects,* because both theory and empirical evidence suggest that increments in these conditions ordinarily promote helping. Unless an explanation consistent with the theory can be generated for these findings, they would appear to raise serious problems. Such an explanation is offered here.

The special danger of altruistic behavior is exploitation. In the absence of compensating social or material gains for self-sacrifice, and without the protection of reciprocity, equity, or law, the altruist may be drawn into an extensive sequence of demands. Worse yet, altruists may discover that the needs to which they responded were not genuine, that they were created or portrayed to gain resources which the needy party could have sought through his own efforts. Needs whose sources are perceived to be under the intentional control of the dependent other (e.g., laziness), rather than caused by external conditions (e.g., bad luck), are especially suspect as illegitimate and therefore less likely to elicit help (Berkowitz, 1969; Schopler & Matthews, 1965).

Trust in the purity of need may also be undermined by actions implying undue pressure or manipulativeness on the part of the person seeking help. Hence conditions conducive to generating feelings of moral obligation will promote altruistic behavior only so long as they do not also induce suspicions that someone may be trying intentionally to manipulate one's perceptions of a situation in order to elicit emotions, images, values, or associations calculated to generate strong feelings of personal obligation.

If the critical threshold of pressure is traversed, feelings of moral obligation will be reduced and altruistic helping will decrease because: (1) the reality or seriousness of need may be denied; (2) the desire to retain one's behavioral freedom by resisting pressure [i.e., reactance (Brehm, 1966)] may be stimulated; and (3) external pressure may be experienced as replacing internalized motivation.[11] This last point is uniquely important for an approach which emphasizes the role of internalized norms and values as motivators of altruism. When an appeal is overdone so that people perceive themselves coerced toward the altruistic alternative, they feel deprived of the self-satisfactions which are available when they act in response to their internalized moral obligations.

It remains to examine whether this reasoning can explain every one of the boomerang effects observed above. Recall first the surprising finding in the experiment in which blood donors were asked to volunteer to become bone marrow transplant donors (Section III,D,4): Among those told that one in 25 members of the general population could provide an adequate match, volunteer-

---

[11] It is no coincidence that the latter two reasons will also be mentioned in connection with the direct activation of social norms, since high pressure appeals may be experienced as invocations of social obligation.

ing increased from low to moderate salience of consequences, but boomeranged to its lowest level when consequences were most salient. By way of contrast, the predicted monotonic increase in volunteering with increasing salience of consequences was found under 1/1000 odds of matching.

The explanation proposed here requires that the unique combination of high salience of consequences and 1/25 odds be viewed as implying greater manipulativeness and illegitimate pressure than the other conditions. Strong external pressure to comply was probably experienced under high consequences, because the manipulation referred to the possible tragic death of the young mother and stressed the emotional shock and hardship for her kids of growing up without her. This play upon emotion may have seemed legitimate and reasonable when it was obviously crucial to test everyone possible because there was only a 1/1000 chance of finding a compatible donor. But under 1/25 odds the chances of finding a compatible donor must have seemed quite good, even if some people refused to undergo testing. The emotional intensity and pathos of the appeal may therefore have been viewed as manipulative pressuring.

The reasoning proposed above suggests that in this condition: (1) denial of need and responsibility was facilitated by the belief that another donor would be found; (2) the usual motivation to neutralize feelings of moral obligation due to high nonmoral costs was supplemented by reactance; and (3) the perception of inept overpressuring by the solicitor undermined the self-satisfactions available for volunteering out of self-generated obligation.

A second boomerang effect was observed in the study of pledging time to run a bake sale booth to raise money for Head Start (Section III,D,1). As predicted, substantially more time was pledged under high seriousness of need than under low, and volunteering increased monotonically with the spontaneous tendency to attend to possible impacts of one's behavior on the need of others (AC) under low seriousness. Under high seriousness, however, those highest in AC showed unexpectedly little volunteering (significantly less than those with low and moderate AC scores), although *they* should have been most aware of the other's need.

Only those very high in AC appear to have responded negatively to having their attention drawn to the possible interpersonal consequences of their behavior. Perhaps this was because those highest in AC recognized these consequences spontaneously themselves. The seriousness manipulation, explicitly emphasizing detailed need, may therefore have appeared more blatant, unwarranted, and manipulative to them, generating reactance and denial of moral obligation.

Support for this interpretation is derived from an extension of this study (Reavy, 1976) in which Canadian students were asked to run a craft sale for mentally retarded adults. Reavy noted that two-sided appeals are unlikely to elicit reactance. She then reasoned that if it was reactance against the pressure of a high-salience appeal which produced the boomerang among those high in AC, the boomerang would be eliminated by a two-sided appeal that acknowledged other viewpoints. As in my Head Start study, Reavy found that a one-sided appeal elicited less volunteering under high than under low situational salience of need among those high in AC. With a two-sided appeal, however, increasing salience of need significantly increased volunteering among those high in AC, presumably because they were not inhibited by reactance.

This interpretation of the AC findings illustrates how an individual difference may interact with characteristics of an appeal to cause a boomerang against helping. A field experiment by Kriss, Indenbaum, and Tesch (1974) illustrates how a different interaction, one involving subject and victim status, can produce a similar boomerang.

In this study, the wrong telephone number technique was used to solicit aid in calling a garage to report that a motorist was stranded on the highway. Status of subject was varied by the cost of homes in the neighborhood (high vs. low), and status of caller (high, ambiguous, low) was manipulated by reference to the type of car he was driving. Three types of appeal were used, characterized by the researchers as a simple request ("Would you please call my garage for me?"), a negative appeal (". . . think how you would feel if you were in a similar position and you weren't helped. . . ."), and a positive appeal ("If you help me, I'd appreciate it and you'd know that you helped someone out of a really tough spot. . . .").

The positive appeal and simple requests elicited more frequent help than the negative appeal, as predicted. Unexpectedly, appeal type did not influence helping in the *same status* conditions. The authors attribute the appeal effect to the arousal of positive vs. negative feelings. But this does not explain why the negative appeal failed to reduce helping in the same status conditions. A more adequate interpretation of these results can be derived from the argument I have been making. Note that the negative appeal implies an obligation based on similarity. This implication had no legitimate basis in the opposite status and ambiguous conditions. Hence it was probably perceived as manipulative and externally pressuring, eliciting denial and reactance and undermining altruistic motivation. In the same status conditions, by contrast, the negative appeal was less likely to set off these processes: Subjects were indeed similar to the caller, could identify with him, and might therefore generate an internalized sense of obligation in response to his plight.

The final boomerang effect requiring explanation occurred in the study of female clerical workers who received a mailed appeal to join a national pool of potential bone marrow donors (Section III,D,7). Salience of need and of responsibility were manipulated in the appeal in a 2×2 design. Theoretically these salience manipulations enhance altruism because they promote norm activation and inhibit denial of need or responsibility. Hence positive effects on volunteering were expected for both manipulations, especially for subjects with pre-measured norms favorable to being a bone marrow donor. Contrary to theory and to findings in other studies, there was significantly less volunteering under high than under low salience of responsibility among those with favorable norms, and an insignificant negative trend for salience of need. Even more startling were the correlation findings suggesting that personal norms influenced volunteering in all the conditions ($\bar{r} = .34, p < .01$) *except* the one hypothesized to promote this influence most strongly—the high-high cell ($r = .006$).

An explanation of these boomerang effects within the framework of the theoretical model and of the analysis proposed in this section must show: (1) that personal norms might have been activated and not neutralized even at the low levels of both salience manipulations in this study; (2) that some elements of the high salience of responsibility manipulation were likely to be perceived as unduly pressuring or manipulative; and (3) that this latter perception was particularly likely among those whose own personal norms favored becoming a marrow donor, when salience of need was also high. The following post hoc examination of the study can only show that these are *reasonable* assumptions, of course, not that they are correct.

A rationale for the first assumption is straightforward. Sufficient need to activate personal norms and inhibit their neutralization was almost surely suggested by the very fact that a renowned transplant physician chose to make an appeal. This was reinforced by such phrases included in the low salience of need condition as "aiding us in our medical work" and "we must go forward." As regards responsibility, even in the low-salience condition people were told that "everyone who is able is needed," and responsibility was focused by receipt of the personally addressed letter.

The remaining two assumptions are supported by responses of 100 college students who read one of the four appeals and rated them on several dimensions as significantly more "manipulative" than the low salience of responsibility appeal ($\bar{x} = 15.2 > 9.8, p < .01$), and as somewhat more "pressuring" ($p < .10$) and "illegitimate" ($p < .10$). The highest ratings on all three dimensions were given to the high-high appeal (e.g., for manipulativeness, $\bar{x} = 17.4$). Moreover, students' own personal norms were significantly positively correlated with their ratings of the appeal's manipulativeness only for the high-high appeal ($r = .45, p < .05$). To the extent that the women who constituted the original sample perceived the manipulativeness of the appeals in the way these students did, the women's volunteering responses fit the explanation for boomerang effects I have offered here.

Interestingly, positive personal norms, like high AC, appear to predispose people to feel manipulated when exposed to appeals that emphasize information or views which they would ordinarily notice and accept on their own. Dienst-bier[12] has suggested that this is because those most likely to perceive their obligation and to respond after minimal pressure are denied the opportunity to feel good about their altruism if they perceive themselves virtually forced into the altruistic alternative. Those least likely to spontaneously engage in altruism, on the other hand, need more external push to construct altruistic norms, so that the danger of overkill reducing personal satisfaction is not as great for them. This basis for boomerang effects is especially intriguing and deserving of explicit investigation. Studies are now needed in which specific boomerang effects are predicted in advance.

V. Social Normative Influences on Helping

People comply with social norms either to maximize socially mediated external reinforcements or, if the norms have been internalized, to maintain or enhance self-evaluation. Compliance with social norms can occur whenever a person recognizes that interested groups expect and will sanction particular acts. Social norms may supplement the influence of personal norms on behavior, but they may also counterbalance this influence if the two are opposed. When social norms are internalized they become personal norms, so that our processual model for the influence of moral obligation on altruism would then apply to them.

The interests of researchers into helping have been directed primarily to the general social norms of reciprocity, equity, parity, and social responsibility. Assuming broad acceptance or knowledge of these norms in the population, researchers have sought to identify the specific situational conditions which foster their activation. Research on conditions for eliciting the norms of social responsibility and reciprocity such as degree of dependency and past help received (e.g., Berkowitz & Daniels, 1963; Wilke & Lanzetta, 1970) exemplifies this concern. General social norms tend to be such vague guides for behavior in concrete situations, however, that it is difficult to know whether they have caused a particular action. Further, since measurement of the prevalence of numerous potentially relevant norms is not obtained, it is possible that various combinations of unidentified norms have influenced behavior. Most important, there are many explanations for why these eliciting conditions might influence helping other than the presumed activation of social norms. Increments in the salience of dependency, for example, might cause empathic arousal, shifts in mood, and redefinitions of costs.

[12] Personal communication, January 5, 1976, commenting on an earlier version of this chapter.

Studies which consider group differences in the endorsement of social norms which have potential importance for helping and also studies which examine the conditions conducive to activating these social norms have been reviewed perceptively by Berkowitz (1972), Staub (1972), and Lerner (1974). My remarks are therefore limited to two questions raised by findings involving social norms which might seem problematic for the theory of personal normative influences on helping: How do verbalizations which draw direct attention to social norms affect helping? In what ways do the perceived expectations of others influence helping above and beyond self-expectations?

A. DIRECT ACTIVATION OF SOCIAL NORMS

One might expect that verbalizations by others which raise the salience of socially prevalent helping norms would increase a person's helping behavior. These verbalizations might activate general internalized norms directly, skipping past the initial steps needed for activation according to our model. Contrary to this expectation, direct verbalizations reminding people of the value of helping (e.g., telling children "it is good to give," and promoting and rewarding women's expressions of helpful ideals) failed to increase childrens' or women's helping behavior in several studies (Berkowitz, 1972; Bryan, 1972).

Why should directing attention to general helping norms have no impact on helping? In answering this question we must note that the studies which manipulated salience of social norms were specifically designed to minimize the threat of external punishment or the promise of external rewards for behavior. The impact of the verbal exhortations therefore depended primarily on their capacity to activate feelings of moral obligation. But these exhortations made neither the consequences for the needy person nor the responsibility for him salient in the ways described in steps 1–4 of our model. They emphasized how one ought to behave, without pointing to aspects of the situation that might lead individuals to experience norm activation through their *own* perceptions.

By directing attention to the general social norms themselves rather than to norm-activating conditions, such verbalizations may block the activation of personal norms or lead the actor to feel deprived of freedom of choice and hence of responsibility and self-satisfactions. Social articulation of a norm may create a perception of social pressure to act which elicits reactance, especially in the absence of attention to those elements in the situation which lead to the spontaneous activation of personal norms.

According to this reasoning, direct appeals for help which emphasize social obligation make responsiveness contingent primarily upon social sanctions. Emphasis on the need of the victim, on the other hand, activates personal norms and fosters responses based upon feelings of moral obligation. In two relevant field experiments, Langer and Abelson (1972) examined the effect on helping of a "target-oriented" vs. a "victim-oriented" appeal. The former emphasized the subject's duty to help (i.e., social obligation), whereas the latter focused on the victim's plight (i.e., conditions for personal norm activation). A favor was requested which was either legitimate or illegitimate. Among those who received the victim-oriented appeal, substantially more helped when the favor was legitimate than illegitimate. This supports the idea that helping is enhanced by feelings of moral obligation and that these feelings are neutralized when a request is illegitimate. The rate of helping by those exposed to the target-oriented appeal was intermediate, and was unaffected by the legitimacy manipulation. This outcome can be viewed as reflecting compliance due primarily to anticipated social sanctions rather than to feelings of moral obligation, so that the legitimacy of the appeal was unimportant.

I have argued that it is the pressure of social obligation implied in verbalizations of social norms which prevents them from activating internalized obligation and thereby fostering helping. Drawing attention to social ideals without any social pressure should therefore enhance helping. A study by Darley and Batson (1973) might be cited in opposition to this argument. Seminary students who were sent from one building to another to deliver a talk either on "nonhelping relevant topics" (norm not salient), or on the parable of the Good Samaritan which they had just read (norm salient), passed a shabbily dressed man slumped in a doorway. Thus the social ideal of helping was presumably made salient in a manner implying no external pressure for behavior. Nonetheless, helping was not significantly affected by the salience manipulation.

This finding is probably not problematic, however, for two reasons. First, the salience manipulation was weak: Students in the putative *low*-salience condition were preparing to talk on how seminary graduates might best minister to others, a topic also likely to direct some attention to helping ideals. Second, despite the weakness of the salience manipulation, those who had read the parable helped substantially more frequently than those who had not (53% vs. 29%) and had helping scores almost twice as high ($p < .07$, one-tailed). These comparisons were not significant at the conventional .05 level, with only 34 degrees of freedom, but, as Greenwald (1975) has shown, the findings are more favorable to the hypothesis of a moderate effect for norm activation than to the hypothesis of no effect.

B. JOINT INFLUENCE OF SELF-EXPECTATIONS AND PERCEIVED SOCIAL EXPECTATIONS

What people feel they ought to do themselves sometimes differs from what they perceive others expect of them. Social expectations may therefore exert influence on helping above and beyond that of self-expectations. Items asking what people perceive that others feel they ought to do were included in several of the studies in which personal norms were measured. The types of perceived social norms tapped included: peer expectations for interpersonal considerateness and helpfulness (Schwartz, 1968a, 1968b); best friend's expectations towards purchasing lead-free gasoline (Heberlein & Black, 1974); expectations of "the people whose opinions you value most" for joining a bone marrow donor pool (data from Schwartz, 1973); expectations held by "those whose opinions of you are important to you" toward aiding soldiers with university course work (Rothstein, 1974); what a variety of potential referents (parents, close friends, minister, doctor, etc.) "think I should do" regarding donating blood (Pomazal, 1974).

In every case the single-item personal norm index was more strongly correlated with helping than social norm items, and perceived social norms failed to add significantly to the variance in helping accounted for by personal norms. This finding cannot be attributed to an identity between measures of personal and perceived social norms: Variance shared by the two indices ranged from 3% to 43% in the various studies, with a median of 16%.

Why did perceived social expectations have no unique effect on helping despite their divergence from personal norms? Note that in each study the social expectations measured were those of important referent others (e.g., roommates, best friends, people whose opinions were valued most). The views of such referent others would most likely have been built into the personal norms already held by the individual or constructed in the situation. Hence any influence they might have on behavior through generating feelings of moral obligation would be captured by the personal norms. Discrepancies in expectations which remain despite extensive contact with important others probably reflect the particular expectations of others that have been rejected as an internalized basis for self-evaluation.

Social norms still influence behavior through the mechanism of external social sanctions, of course. If referent others are likely to witness and sanction the behavior in question, their expectations may have an effect; but their sanctions may be discounted in advance when the actor believes he can maintain his established relationships. Hence the social norms of primary interest for adding to the prediction of behavior by personal norms are those held by others *(a)* whose perspective the individual does not adopt as his own; *(b)* who have not influenced the formation of his own norms; and *(c)* who are seen as likely to sanction him for action.

In the absence of studies on *norms* relevant to these speculations, consider a study of student *attitudes* toward the legalization of marijuana and their behavior of voting in a mock election on legalization (Acock & DeFleur, 1972). Perceived peer attitude added significantly to the explanation of variance in voting provided by own attitude, whereas perceived family attitude did not. [13] The incremental effect of peer attitude took the form of substantially less voting for legalization among those whose own attitude favored legalization if they perceived that their peers were opposed or even neutral. For these students, their peers apparently were not referents; but they were a potential source of sanctions, because informal discussion about how people had voted was likely to occur. Family attitudes probably had no effect either because they were already built into own attitudes or because it was improbable that family members would find out about the behavior and sanction it.

Research on how personal and perceived social norms combine to influence helping is just beginning. To clarify the theorizing proposed here requires studies in which both types of norms are measured, and in which the norms of others who stand in different types of relationship to the focal individual are considered (e.g., referents and nonreferents, sources of various sanctions and nonsanctioners).

VI. Is There An Altruistic Personality?

The approach of this chapter to personality variables is distinctive in its emphasis on two types of individual differences as mediators of altruism: differences in the cognitive structure of values and norms which are expressed in measured personal norms, and differences in personality tendencies which affect norm activation and defense such as AC and RD. The influence of these individual differences on behavior has been portrayed as systematic and predictable but quite complex, involving interactions with each other and with specifiable variations in decision situations. Both parsimony and conceptual simplicity would be gained were these differences found to reflect an underlying general propensity to altruism across situations.

Data from numerous studies cited earlier, however, argue against the existence of such a general propensity. In the two studies where both AC and RD scores were obtained, these personality tendencies were virtually independent ($r = -.07$, $r = -.08$), although both correlated with altruism and moderated the effects of personal norms and situational variables as predicted (Schwartz, 1968b, 1974). Nor do these personality tendencies appear to be indicators of some general internalized altruistic values or norms. AC showed no significant correlations with nine single measures of personal norms nor with a composite index of norms. RD has been correlated with 40 different personal norms regarding altruistic behavior and with five composite indices based on sets of

---

[13] This discussion follows the reanalysis of the original data presented in Susmilch, Elliott, and Schwartz (1975).

norms in eight different studies. Only 3 of 60 separate correlations were significant at the .05 level or better. Parsimony to the contrary, personal norms, AC, and RD are apparently quite distinct determinants of altruism.

Staub (1972) has raised the possibility that RD may reflect a desire to appear socially responsible, a sensitivity to potential social consequences, implying that RD correlations with helping are due to avoidance of social costs rather than to neutralization of personal norms. This interpretation of RD effects must be rejected on two grounds. First, it fails to explain RD's demonstrated function as a moderator of the impact of personal norms on behavior. Second, it implies that RD is related to measures of socially desirable response. In fact, the correlations of RD with the Crowne and Marlowe (1964) social desirability scale in two studies were −.01 and .07. Nor was RD correlated significantly with reports of any of 19 different perceived social expectations in four studies.

Few studies of helping other than those involving personal norms, RD, and AC have shown consistent predicted associations between individual difference variables and altruistic behavior. The data impel one to conclude that the effects of person variables on helping depend upon the precise mesh between the nature of the situation, the person, and the help required. [See Gergen, Gergen, and Meter (1972) for a similar conclusion.] While explicitly recognizing this, Staub (1974) has nonetheless argued that individuals are characterized by a general prosocial orientation. He measured this presumed orientation with a composite score based on a factor analysis of nine personality scales, including RD, which he thought might relate to helping. This is not strictly an *altruistic* disposition; it includes such qualities as ambition and manipulativeness.

Close examination of the data Staub presents (Staub, 1974, pp. 327–333), as well as a reanalysis using multiple regression methods,[14] suggest that in his study too the impact of personality variables on helping depended upon the particular situational conditions and the help required. Use of the composite glossed over these differences and reduced predictive power as compared with regressions based on just two or three significant predictors. Working with a composite score that purports to represent a general altruistic personality orientation may well obscure the nature and meaning of the relationships between personality and behavior.

VII. Conclusions and Future Directions

Central to the theoretical model I have presented is the idea that altruistic behavior is causally influenced by feelings of moral obligation to act on one's personally held norms. Research supporting this central tenet of the model has

---

[14] Ervin Staub graciously provided the data to perform the reanalyses.

demonstrated associations between personal norms and behavior, rather than causal relations. I have argued that these associations are at least partly causal, however, because: (1) the associations appear primarily in the presence of personality conditions conducive to norm activation and are absent when personality conditions are conducive to deactivation; and (2) attributes of personal norms (e.g., centrality, stability, intensity) relate to altruism singly and in combination in ways predicted when we assume the causal impact of anticipated moral costs on behavior.

A third critical link in this argument would be forged by studies showing that variations in situational conditions conducive to activation of moral obligation also influence the relationship between personal norms and behavior. There is ample evidence that variables which foster movement through the activation process, according to the theoretical model, are themselves related to altruistic behavior (e.g., seriousness of need, uniqueness of responsibility). What remains to be determined is whether the impact of these variables on altruism is mediated by personal norms.

Evidence relevant to the sequential nature of the steps in the theoretical model is sparse. Both the distinctiveness and ordering of the postulated steps rests largely on logical rather than empirical grounds. The role of feedback among the steps, with new input of information from later redefinitions or overt actions in a chain of decisions, also merits investigation.

It is worth noting that study of how personal norms are related to altruism is part of a larger enterprise, the investigation of attitude—behavior relations in general. Personal norms are a subtype of attitudinal variable, i.e., evaluations of acts in terms of their moral worth to the self. Techniques developed to discover whether the impact of personal norms on altruism is causal might profitably be imported into general attitude—behavior research. Reasoning like that employed to identify personality and situational moderators of the impact of personal norms on altruism might be used to track down the elusive moderators of other attitudinal variables. Characteristics of personal norms and the normative structure which influence their impact (e.g., centrality, stability) might also suggest characteristics of attitudes which warrant consideration. Equally important, the extensive research on attitude—behavior relations may yield leads for understanding the workings of personal norms.

Next steps in developing the theory will have to address three issues given cursory treatment here. First, how do emotional arousal and feelings of moral obligation jointly influence altruism? Under what conditions and in what ways do they enhance or blunt each other's effects? How might emotional arousal modify the perception and processing of need-relevant information, for example? And how might rapidity of onset and deterioration in need cues affect shifting between empathic and morally mediated responsiveness?

Second, how do perceived social norms and personal norms complement or supplement each other in their impact on altruistic behavior? Under what conditions do social norms have *any* influence? And do these effects ever interact with those of personal norms? Finally, how, if at all, do personal norms mediate boomerang effects on helping? What are the differences between conditions which elicit feelings of moral obligation and those which induce a sense of undue pressure or manipulation? Speculations and hypotheses regarding some of these questions, offered in my discussion of past research, may suggest directions for approaching these three issues.

Experimental social psychologists, with their chariness toward individual differences, have conducted most of the research on prosocial behavior. Attention to internalized norms and values has consequently been restricted, and normative explanations have received short shrift (Darley & Latané, 1970; Krebs, 1970). I hope that the theory and research presented here will strengthen the credibility of normative approaches. Altruism—in contrast to the more inclusive "prosocial behavior"—implies purposes based in the person's value system. Hence altruism cannot be understood fully in the absence of studies which consider individual differences in values and norms as they interact with situational variables.

REFERENCES

Acock, A. C., & DeFleur, M. L. A configurational approach to contingent consistency in the attitude–behavior relationship. *American Sociological Review,* 1972, 37, 714–726.

Aderman, D., & Berkowitz, L. Observational set, empathy, and helping. *Journal of Personality and Social Psychology,* 1970, 14, 141–168.

Aronfreed, J. *Conduct and conscience: The socialization of internalized control over behavior.* New York: Academic Press, 1968.

Baron, R. A. Magnitude of model's apparent pain and ability to aid the model as determinants of observer reaction time. *Psychonomic Science,* 1970, 21, 196–197.

Bem, D. *Beliefs, attitudes and human affairs.* Belmont, Calif.: Brooks/Cole, 1970.

Bem, D. Constructing cross-situational consistencies in behavior: Some thoughts on Alker's critique of Mischel. *Journal of Personality,* 1972, 40, 17–26.

Berkowitz, L. Resistance to improper dependency relationships. *Journal of Experimental Social Psychology,* 1969, 5, 283–294.

Berkowitz, L. Social norms, feelings, and other factors affecting helping and altruism. In L. Berkowitz (Ed.), *Advances in experimental social psychology.* Vol. 6. New York: Academic Press, 1972. Pp. 63–108.

Berkowitz, L., & Daniels, L. R. Responsibility and dependency. *Journal of Abnormal and Social Psychology,* 1963, 66, 429–436.

Berkowitz, L., Klanderman, S. B., & Harris, R. Effects of experimenter awareness and sex of subject and experimenter on reactions to dependency relationships. *Sociometry,* 1964, 27, 327–337.

Bickman, L., & Kamzan, L. The effect of race and need on helping behavior. *Journal of Social Psychology,* 1973, 89, 73–77.

Blake, J., & Davis, K. Norms, values and sanctions. In R. E. L. Faris (Ed.), *Handbook of modern sociology.* Chicago: Rand McNally, 1964. Pp. 456–484.

Boneau, C. A. Paradigm regained? Cognitive behaviorism restated. *American Psychologist,* 1974, **29**, 297–309.

Brehm, J. W. *A theory of psychological reactance.* New York: Academic Press, 1966.

Bryan, J. H. Why children help: A review. *Journal of Social Issues,* 1972, **28**, 87–104.

Campbell, D. T. Ethnocentric and other altruistic motives. In D. Levine (Ed.), *Nebraska symposium on motivation.* Vol. 13. Lincoln: University of Nebraska Press, 1965. Pp. 283–312.

Campbell, D. T. On the genetics of altruism and the counter-hedonic components in human culture. *Journal of Social Issues,* 1972, **28**, 21–37.

Clark, R. D., III, & Word, L. E. Why don't bystanders help? Because of ambiguity? *Journal of Personality and Social Psychology,* 1972, **24**, 392–400.

Clark, R. D., III, & Word, L. E. Where is the apathetic bystander? Situational characteristics of the emergency. *Journal of Personality and Social Psychology,* 1974, **29**, 279–288.

Crowne, D. P., & Marlowe, D. *The approval motive: Studies in evaluative dependence.* New York: Wiley, 1964.

Darley, J. M., & Batson, C. D. "From Jerusalem to Jericho": A study of situational and dispositional variables in helping behavior. *Journal of Personality and Social Psychology,* 1973, **27**, 100–108.

Darley, J. M., & Latané, B. Norms and normative behavior: Field studies of social interdependence. In J. Macaulay & L. Berkowitz (Eds.), *Altruism and helping behavior.* New York: Academic Press, 1970. Pp. 83–102.

Darley, J. M., Teger, A. I., & Lewis, L. D. Do groups always inhibit individuals' responses to potential emergencies? *Journal of Personality and Social Psychology,* 1973, **26**, 395–399.

Duval, S., & Wicklund, R. A. *A theory of objective self awareness.* New York: Academic Press, 1972.

Ernest, R. C., & Cooper, R. "Hey mister, do you have any change?": Two real world studies of proxemic effects on compliance with a mundane request. Unpublished manuscript, Loyola University, Chicago, 1973.

Fellner, C. H., & Schwartz, S. H. Altruism in disrepute: Medical vs. public attitudes toward the living organ donor. *New England Journal of Medicine,* 1971, **284**, 582–585.

Fenichel, O. *The psychoanalytic theory of neurosis.* New York: Norton, 1945.

Garfinkel, H. *Studies in ethnomethodology.* Englewood Cliffs, N.J.: Prentice-Hall, 1967.

Gergen, K. J., Gergen, M., & Meter, K. Individual orientations to prosocial behavior. *Journal of Social Issues,* 1972, **28**, 105–130.

Goffman, E. *The presentation of self in everyday life.* New York: Doubleday, 1959.

Greenwald, A. Does the Good Samaritan parable increase helping? A comment on Darley and Batson's no effect conclusion. *Journal of Personality and Social Psychology,* 1975, **32**, 578–583.

Gross, A. E., Wallston, B. S., & Piliavin, I. M. Beneficiary attractiveness and costs as determinants of responses to routine requests for help. *Sociometry,* 1975, **38**, 131–140.

Heberlein, T. A. Moral norms, threatened sanctions and littering behavior. Unpublished doctoral dissertation, University of Wisconsin, Madison, 1971.

Heberlein, T. A. Social norms and environmental quality. Paper presented at the annual meeting of the American Association for the Advancement of Science, New York, January 1975.

Heberlein, T. A., & Black, J. S. The land ethic in action: Personal norms, beliefs and the purchase of lead-free gasoline. Paper presented at the annual meeting of the Rural Sociology Society, Montreal, August 1974.

Heberlein, T. A., & Black, J. S. Attitudinal specificity and the prediction of behavior in a field setting. *Journal of Personality and Social Psychology,* 1976, **33**, 474–479.

Henshel, A. M. The relationship between values and behavior: A developmental hypothesis. *Child Development,* 1971, **42**, 1997–2007.

Hornstein, H. Promotive tension: The basis of prosocial behavior from a Lewinian perspective. *Journal of Social Issues,* 1972, **28**, 191–218.

Howard, W., & Crano, W. D. Effects of sex, conversation, location, and size of observer group on bystander intervention in a high risk situation. *Sociometry,* 1974, **37**, 491–507.

Isen, A. Positive affect, accessibility of cognitions, and helping. Paper presented at the meeting of the Eastern Psychological Association, New York, April 1975.

Janis, I. L. Motivational factors in the resolution of decisional conflict. In M. R. Jones (Ed.), *Nebraska symposium on motivation.* Vol. 7. Lincoln: University of Nebraska Press, 1959. Pp. 198–231.

Kiesler, C. A., Roth, T. S., & Pallak, M. S. Avoidance and reinterpretation of commitment and its implications. *Journal of Personality and Social Psychology,* 1974, **30**, 705–715.

Krebs, D. L. Altruism–An examination of the concept and a review of the literature. *Psychological Bulletin,* 1970, **73**, 258–302.

Kriss, M., Indenbaum, E., & Tesch, F. Message type and status of interactants as determinants of telephone helping behavior. *Journal of Personality and Social Psychology,* 1974, **30**, 856–859.

Langer, E. J., & Abelson, R. P. The semantics of asking a favor: How to succeed in getting help without really dying. *Journal of Personality and Social Psychology,* 1972, **24**, 26–32.

Latané, B., & Darley, J. M. *The unresponsive bystander: Why doesn't he help?* New York: Appleton, 1970.

Leeds, R. Altruism and the norm of giving. *Merrill-Palmer Quarterly,* 1963, **9**, 229–240.

Lerner, M. J. Social psychology of justice and interpersonal attraction. In T. Houston (Ed.), *Perspectives on interpersonal attraction.* New York: Academic Press, 1974. Pp. 331–351.

Lerner, M. J. The justice motive: Some hypotheses as to its origins and forms. Unpublished manuscript, University of Waterloo, 1975.

Leventhal, H. Findings and theory in the study of fear communication. In L. Berkowitz (Ed.), *Advances in experimental social psychology.* Vol. 5. New York: Academic Press, 1970.

Leventhal, H. Attitudes: Their nature, growth, and change. In C. Nemeth (Ed.), *Social psychology classic and contemporary integrations.* Chicago: Rand McNally, 1974. Pp. 52–126.

Leventhal, H. A perceptual motor theory of emotion. Unpublished manuscript, University of Wisconsin, 1975.

Miller, D. The study of social relationships. In S. Koch (Ed.), *Psychology: A study of a science.* Vol. 5. New York: McGraw-Hill, 1963. Pp. 639–737.

Mischel, W. *Personality and assessment.* New York: Wiley, 1968.

Moriarty, T. Crime, commitment, and the responsive bystander: Two field experiments. *Journal of Personality and Social Psychology,* 1975, **31**, 370–376.

Parsons, T. *The social system.* Glencoe, Ill.: Free Press, 1951.

Piliavin, J. A., & Piliavin, I. M. Good samaritan–Why does he help? Unpublished manuscript, University of Wisconsin, 1975.

Pomazal, R. J. Attitudes, normative beliefs, and altruism: Help for helping behavior. Unpublished doctoral dissertation, University of Illinois, 1974.

Power, H. W. Mountain bluebirds: Experimental evidence against altruism. *Science,* 1975, **189,** 142–143.

Pruitt, D. G. Methods for resolving differences of interest: A theoretical analysis. *Journal of Social Issues,* 1972, **28,** 133–154.

Reavy, P. Factors that arouse and inhibit reactance in dependency situations. Unpublished manuscript, University of Waterloo, 1976.

Reykowski, J. Position of self-structure in a cognitive system and prosocial orientation. Paper presented at a conference on Mechanisms of Prosocial Behavior, Nieborow, Poland, November 1974.

Rokeach, M. *The nature of human values.* New York: Free Press, 1973.

Rothstein, H. R. Attitudes and behavior: The effects of perceived payoffs and facilitating intrapersonal conditions. Unpublished master's thesis, Hebrew University, Jerusalem, 1974.

Schopler, J., & Matthews, M. W. The influence of the perceived causal locus of partner's dependence on the use of interpersonal power. *Journal of Personality and Social Psychology,* 1965, **2,** 609–612.

Schwartz, S. H. Awareness of consequences and the influence of moral norms on interpersonal behavior. *Sociometry,* 1968, **31,** 355–369. (a)

Schwartz, S. H. Words, deeds, and the perception of consequences and responsibility in action situations. *Journal of Personality and Social Psychology,* 1968, **10,** 232–242. (b)

Schwartz, S. H. Elicitation of moral obligation and self-sacrificing behavior. *Journal of Personality and Social Psychology,* 1970, **15,** 283–293.

Schwartz, S. H. Normative explanations of helping behavior: A critique, proposal, and empirical test. *Journal of Experimental and Social Psychology,* 1973, **9,** 349–364.

Schwartz, S. H. Awareness of interpersonal consequences, responsibility denial and volunteering. *Journal of Personality and Social Psychology,* 1974, **30,** 57–63.

Schwartz, S. H. The justice of need and the activation of humanitarian norms. *Journal of Social Issues,* 1975, **31,** 111–136.

Schwartz, S. H., & Ames, R. Positive and negative referent others as sources of influence. *Sociometry,* 1977, **40,** in press.

Schwartz, S. H., & Ben David, A. Responsibility and helping in an emergency: Effects of blame, ability and denial of responsibility. *Sociometry,* 1976, **39,** 406–415.

Schwartz, S. H., & Clausen, G. T. Responsibility, norms, and helping in an emergency. *Journal of Personality and Social Psychology,* 1970, **16,** 299–310.

Schwartz, S. H., & Tessler, R. C. A test of a model for reducing measured attitude–behavior discrepancies. *Journal of Personality and Social Psychology,* 1972, **24,** 225–236.

Sherrod, D. R., & Downs, R. Environmental determinants of altruism: The effects of stimulus overload and perceived control on helping. *Journal of Experimental Social Psychology,* 1974, **10,** 468–479.

Simmons, R. G., Klein, S. D., & Thornton, K. Family decision-making and the selection of a kidney transplant donor. *Journal of Comparative Family Studies,* 1973, **4,** 88–115.

Staub, E. A child in distress: The effects of focusing responsibility on children on their attempts to help. *Developmental Psychology,* 1970, **2,** 152–153.

Staub, E. Helping a person in distress: The influence of implicit and explicit "rules" of conduct on children and adults. *Journal of Personality and Social Psychology,* 1971, **17,** 137–144.

Staub, E. Instigation to goodness: The role of social norms and interpersonal influence. *Journal of Social Issues,* 1972, **28,** 131–150.

Staub, E. Helping a distressed person: Social, personality and stimulus determinants. In L. Berkowitz (Ed.), *Advances in experimental social psychology.* Vol. 7. New York: Academic Press, 1974. Pp. 294–341.

Staub, E., & Baer, R. S., Jr. Stimulus characteristics of a sufferer and difficulty of escape as determinants of helping. *Journal of Personality and Social Psychology,* 1974, **30,** 279–284.

Susmilch, C., Elliott, G., & Schwartz, S. J. Contingent consistency and the attitude-behavior relationship: A comment. *American Sociological Review,* 1975, **40,** 682–686.

Tilker, H. A. Socially responsible behavior as a function of observer responsibility and victim feedback. *Journal of Personality and Social Psychology,* 1970, **14,** 95–100.

Trivers, R. L. The evolution of reciprocal altruism. *Quarterly Review of Biology,* 1971, **46,** 35–57.

Voluntary Action News, 1975, **6.** National Center for Voluntary Action, Washington, D.C.

Wagner, C., & Wheeler, L. Model, need and cost effects in helping behavior. *Journal of Personality and Social Psychology,* 1969, **12,** 111–116.

Walster, E., Berscheid, E., & Walster, G. W. The exploited: Justice or justification? In J. Macaulay & L. Berkowitz (Eds.), *Altruism and helping behavior.* New York: Academic Press, 1970. Pp. 179–204.

Walster, E., & Piliavin, J. A. Equity and the innocent bystander. *Journal of Social Issues,* 1972, **28,** 165–189.

West, S. G., Whitney, G., & Schnedler, R. Helping a motorist in distress: The effects of sex, race, and neighborhood. *Journal of Personality and Social Psychology,* 1975, **31,** 691–698.

Wicker, A. W. Attitudes vs. actions: The relationship of verbal and overt behavioral responses to attitude objects. *Journal of Social Issues,* 1969, **25,** 41–78.

Wilke, H., & Lanzetta, J. T. The obligation to help: The effects of amount of prior help on subsequent helping behavior. *Journal of Experimental Social Psychology,* 1970, **6,** 488–493.

Williams, R. M., Jr. Values. I. The concept of values. In D. L. Sills (Ed.), *International encyclopedia of the social sciences.* Vol. 16. New York: Crowell-Collier, 1968. Pp. 283–287.

Wilson, E. O. *Sociobiology: The new synthesis.* Cambridge, Mass.: Belknap Press, 1975.

Wispé, L. Positive forms of social behavior. *Journal of Social Issues,* 1972, **28,** 1–20.

A DISCUSSION OF THE DOMAIN AND METHODS OF SOCIAL PSYCHOLOGY: TWO PAPERS BY ROM HARRÉ AND BARRY R. SCHLENKER

Leonard Berkowitz

In his 1973 book with P. F. Secord, *The Explanation of Social Behaviour*, Rom Harré, lecturer in the philosophy of science at Oxford University, strongly criticizes much of the thinking governing contemporary research in experimental social psychology. The book's argument reflects many of the misgivings others have also expressed. But in addition to questioning our now conventional assumptions and methods, Harré and Secord also offer what they regard as a superior alternative. Here is how they summarize their views in the 1973 text:

> Regularities in human behaviour may be explained according to several different schemata. Two extremes are: (1) the person acting as an agent directing his own behaviour, and (2) the person as an object responding to the push and pull of forces exerted by the environment.... This book ... will emphasize self-directed and self-monitored behaviour, because it has been generally neglected in the behavioural sciences, because this is the prototype of behaviour in ordinary daily living, and because we believe it to be the main factor in the production of specifically social behaviour....
>
> If we follow the paradigm of non-positivist science, explaining behavioural phenomena involves identifying the generative "mechanisms" that give rise to the behaviour. The discovery and identification of these "mechanisms" we call *ethogeny*. We believe that the main process involved in them is self-direction according to the meaning ascribed to the situation. At the heart of the explanation of social behaviour is the identification of the meanings that underlie it. Part of the approach to discovering them involves the obtaining of *accounts*—the actor's own statements about why he performed the acts in question, what social meanings he gave to the actions of himself and others. These must be collected and analysed, often leading to the discovery of the rules that underlie the behaviour.... An important tool in obtaining these meanings is ordinary language, which is well adapted for explaining a pattern of social interaction in terms of reasons and rules.... (pp. 8–10)

In the following paper Dr. Harré continues and extends his advocacy of the ethogenic approach. He shows how the procedures he favors can be employed in the investigation of a wide variety of problems.

281

But is there nothing to be said in behalf of traditional experimental social psychology? Barry R. Schlenker, of the University of Florida, takes up the defense in his paper, answering some of the ethogenic criticisms and pointing up several of the difficulties confronting this approach.

I am confident that we can all benefit from this debate, whether we side with the conventional experimentalists or support the critics now attacking the ramparts of traditional experimental social psychology.

THE ETHOGENIC APPROACH:
THEORY AND PRACTICE

R. Harré

LINACRE COLLEGE
OXFORD UNIVERSITY
OXFORD, ENGLAND
AND STATE UNIVERSITY OF NEW YORK
BINGHAMTON, NEW YORK

I. Theoretical Introduction

A central preoccupation of the ethogenic approach is to establish a fruitful connection between microsociology and social psychology, and in particular to base social psychology on an adequate and explicit microsociology. It is vital to utilize the extremely good microsociology that has been developed by the symbolic interactionists and ethnomethodologists in the construction of a social psychology which takes its problems from that kind of microsociology and not from amateur or intuitive conceptions of the structure and meaning of social interactions. And since the main psychological technique in ethogenics is the analysis of the speech of participants in social life, we can employ the very detailed and often extremely subtle analyses of ordinary language made by the Oxford School of philosophers and others in the linguistic tradition in the course of which are revealed the theories implicit in ordinary speech. These two developments, the one in microsociology and the other in language analysis, contribute an enormous but previously untapped resource which we ought to be able to put to use.

A. INTELLIGIBILITY AND WARRANTABILITY OF ACTIONS: MICROSOCIOLOGICAL ANALYSIS

I shall try to show how the link between microsociology and linguistic analysis is actually established, and why we believe that account analysis is an enormously fruitful empirical method. Indeed, this method has already proved to be important in developing an adequate social psychology based upon an empirical technique which escapes the lethal criticisms that have been leveled against "experimental" methods and the use of statistical procedures.

Account analysis is neither very fancy nor strange. It is the analysis of both the social force and explanatory content of the speech produced by social actors as a guide to the structure of the cognitive resources required for the genesis of intelligible and warrantable social action by those actors. Intelligible action is social action in which the item in question (something, let us say, like a handshake) is intelligible if we view it as part of an ongoing structure, a structure which we recognize as having a certain social force and in which we see the handshake as having a particular and proper place. Regarding it as part of that structure makes it intelligible. If it is to be warranted it must be at the right place in that structure for an item of that kind. Appearing just *there*, it usually requires no further justification. Intelligibility and warrantability are two quite distinct properties of social actions, and both may come under critical scrutiny.

Let us first consider intelligibility. I may not know what you are doing when you take hold of my hand. I might be very puzzled as to what the gesture means, not knowing in what structured sequence of actions it occurs. It might be part of a betting ritual, or an opening move in a karate encounter, or part of various other action sequences. It is obviously of great practical importance to understand its meaning in this sense. The second property, warrantability, can also be problematic. A handshake can be in the right ceremony but in the wrong place, appearing, say, with appropriate other items but in the "wrong" order. Any piece of social action must have both properties if it is not to generate unease, doubt, and uncertainty, undesirable perlocutionary consequences. But much more seriously, such an action is liable to fail as an illocutionary performance, that is, as the action required to generate the socially appropriate act. [The distinction between (a) the *perlocutionary* force and consequences of a social action and (b) its *illocutionary* force and consequences is basic to sociolinguistics but may be unfamiliar to social psychologists. The perlocutionary consequences of, say, a promise, are the changes brought about in the world by its fulfillment. The illocutionary consequences include the commitment to the fulfillment of the promiser. We owe the distinction to Austin (1965).]

The structure responsible for the presence of the two desirable properties, intelligibility and warrantability, is discerned in action sequences by microsociological analysis. This analysis is based on an analog to the linguistic studies of semantics and syntax, the former relevant to intelligibility and the latter to warrantability. The outcome is a set of sociologists' generalizations as to the structure of the sequence on the basis of which we may, as social *psychologists*, propose hypotheses as to the cognitive resources of people who work together to generate, as a mutual product, the pattern of action by means of which the social act they take to be required of them in that setting is performed.

B. ACCOUNTING: PSYCHOLOGICAL ANALYSIS

The ethogenic method is based upon the assumption that the very same cognitive resources can be employed in another task, namely, the explication and justification of the manifested patterns of action in speech. Thus, the bases of successful action by socially competent people are revealed in two distinct forms and are available to two different modes of empirical studies.

In the analysis of the second mode of representation, speech, we must distinguish the speech we use when we are talking descriptively about the prescriptions of our own culture—contributing to our own ethnography, so to speak—from the speech we use to justify some action of ours to others within the culture, the kind of speech that has come to be called accounting. It may be that both call on the same material, but one is in the scientific mode and the other is a kind of social action. It is part of an argument, the conclusion of which, however informally implied, is that what we did made sense and was right at that place and that time, that is, the action is intelligible and warrantable. Saying, "I'm terribly sorry, I didn't mean to bump into you" is a simple case of the explication of social meaning, locating the bump outside any planned sequence, neutralizing it by making it intelligible in such a way that if it is not warrantable at least it is not offensive in that situation.

In sum, speech relevant to action is geared to two different tasks. One task is a conscious bit of sociology on its own account, a contribution to the local ethnography, whereas the other is part of the local social techniques for elucidating and making meaningful (or meaningless) something which has appeared "out of place" in the social order. Thus, accounting may involve justificatory reference to some rule for an action whose meaning is in doubt, or it may achieve explication merely by the elucidation of meaning.

C. TYPES OF SCIENCES: PARAMETRIC VS. STRUCTURAL

The most fundamental methodological point which distinguishes ethogenic from traditional social psychology turns on the sort of science we take psychology to be. There are two quite different kinds of scientific investigation in the natural and social sciences: those I shall call *parametric* and those I shall term *structural*.

1. Parametric Sciences

In a parametric study it is assumed that the properties referred to by the variables which describe the system are not internally related, that is, that they can be varied separately while retaining their identity. The gas law $PV = RT$, relating pressure, volume, and temperature, is a relation between parameters such that one can hold constant any one parameter and vary the others, and the property represented by that parameter will remain unaffected by the abstraction. As far as pressure, volume, and temperature are concerned, a gas is not a structure of internally related properties. On the other hand, an element of an internally related structure ceases to be that element if detached from the structure. In a parametric process the elements interact causally but retain their identity and do not change in type if detached from the structure. Pressure remains pressure however temperature and volume may vary. In a structured entity the component parts derive their meaning from the other details to which they are internally related. A handshake is not the same action when embedded in a betting routine as when part of a greeting. The frequency of meeting someone is not a social item at all if detached from a particular social milieu from which it can gain significance as a meaningful feature of interaction.

2. Structural Sciences

We can readily think of a number of structural sciences. One notable example is molecular genetics, where we explain the anatomical structure of an organism by reference to the structure of the deoxyribonucleic acid (DNA).

Anatomical structure is the structured product and DNA is the structured template—and the one is a replication of the other, since at the end of the process the template still remains in existence. Yet another example is to be found in reactions in organic chemistry where one structure can be transformed into another, e.g., phenol into C_6H_5OCl. The phenol is not destroyed in the transformation; it is not broken up and reconstituted, and yet it does not exist as a separate entity after the reaction. In both of these cases the structure of the product is somehow represented in the template as a preformed structure (as the benzene ring in the phenol). The scientific explanation of the anatomical structure of an organism is in terms of the preformed structure of the DNA. One of the social sciences has already taken a structural turn, and that, of course, is linguistics. This discipline instructs us to think in terms of preformed structures which are transformed into the product structure by the following of rewrite rules. But the process by which the preformed structure is produced is something quite different from the process by which the preformed structure is transformed into something manifest and visible, namely, a spoken or written sentence.

But there are other structural sciences, such as crystallography, where though the product is a structure, say, a diamond, the process by which it is produced is neither replication nor transformation. A diamond is a tetrahedral crystal because the four valencies of carbon atoms are arranged on the vertices of a tetrahedron. But diamonds are neither transformations nor replications of that structure; they are simply an assemblage of myriads of structured objects which go together in only one way. A diamond occurring by nature has no particular overall structure, although it will always have a tetrahedral form because of the structure of its components.

My contention is that we should analyze the diachronic structure of social interaction not in parametric terms, nor yet in the manner of the crystallographer, but rather in the way molecular geneticists or structural linguistics approach their problems. That is, we should treat social interaction as a social product, and then try to discern in the people involved in the interaction the template or representation of this structure that led to this product.

3. Pseudostructural Studies

I want to distinguish this very sharply from another kind of process by which nonrandomness is generated in social behavior. This is the kind of order revealed in some speech studies, e.g., Duncan's (1972) investigation of the way in which people take turns in a conversation. Two people, A and B, acting in concert, are found to produce an orderly sequence of utterances having the form ABABAB. . . . That is, the conversation involves regular turn taking. This is a highly structured product. Argyle and others (e.g., see Argyle & Dean, 1965) have shown that the structure of such a sequence is not the product of "formal

causality," i.e., template following. There is no template for the whole conversation which leads to the structure ABABAB. Rather, B's speech-turn is produced
by an atomistic property of the speech unit of A, something which happened at
its end, a kind of pause, eye-lock, etc., which sets B going; B as speaker, in turn,
does the same thing which sets a speech by A going, and so on. That kind of
structure is produced by successive efficient causality. Such structures are rare in
speech patterning. Much more typical is the pattern demonstrated in the work of
Schegloff and Sacks (1973). A discourse analysis of a whole conversation reveals
an overall structure generated, we must suppose, from a preformed template.
For example, when two people are talking they do not end their interaction by
just stopping. There is a preclosing sequence, e.g., "O.K., well . . . ," which
allows the warrantable introduction of the closing sequence; the first "Goodbye" suspends the transition relevance of the second so that the first speaker
does not have to follow the second "Goodbye" with another speech, but can
break off. The conversation has an overarching structure which is not generated
bit by bit by successive atomistic efficient causes. The preclosing comes when it
does because the conversation is divided into topics, and the preclosing comes at
the end of a topic as part of the overall structure of a proper conversation. Once
the preclosing has occurred we can warrantably insert the pair of "Goodbyes."
In dealing with this type of structured interaction our hypothesis will be that a
conversation structure is the representation in manifest form of a preformed
template represented in this case by the conventions for generating whole
conversations. On the other hand, turn taking, the ABABAB structure, is
indefinitely extensible, and has no closure as an overall structure. Its form
derives from properties of each component speech taken atomistically. It is more
like a diamond than an anatomical structure.

D. SOCIAL PSYCHOLOGY AS A STRUCTURAL SCIENCE

How to tackle structural analyses scientifically? I will draw upon a version of
the competence/performance distinction employed by the generative gram-
marians to explain the central methodological idea. Generally speaking, the
competence/performance distinction argues that if anyone is to be capable of
performing in a certain way, he must have some internal property (for example,
some kind of knowledge) and by virtue of this property is competent in that
area of action and is able to perform in appropriate ways. There are problems
with the application of this distinction in linguistics. For one, competence is a
peculiarly elusive notion which has not been well articulated and should perhaps
be replaced by the deeper idea of the power/nature description. There is also
uncertainty about the way in which linguistic knowledge is represented in an
individual. If linguistic knowledge is said to exist only because we have induced
people to speak and we then judge speech for various desirable properties, there

is no nonlinguistic way of deciding whether that attribution is correct. Moreover, whatever one has to say about knowledge of language has to be said linguistically. The rather peculiar and paradoxical situation thus arises that the underlying semantic structure which leads by rewrite and transformation to the actual piece of speech is to be somehow preformed in a nonlinguistic medium so that it can then be given linguistic clothing by the base rules and so be made ready to be transformed into speech.

Happily, in the field of social psychology we are in a rather better situation. We have at least the theoretical possibility of availing ourselves of two different manifestations of the knowledge that we can assign to a person on the basis of his demonstrated ability (say, competently to introduce somebody to somebody else). We can propose hypotheses on the basis of his performance, and we can also analyze the kind of speech that occurs in accounting for and justifying certain related kinds of social action. Our studies show that account analysis yields much the same sort of hypotheses about a person's cognitive content and organization as does the analysis of action sequences in microsociology. Microsociological analyses could reveal product structures from which we would then derive hypotheses about a person's cognitive capacity to generate the template structures which lie behind the production of the manifest or product structure. Thus, in analyzing the incorporation of strangers into a group, e.g., a party, we will want to say that host, sponsor, and stranger somehow each contain a replica of the structure of the ceremony of incorporation. It is by the transformation of that template into the medium of action that they produce the actual action sequence. Competent people "contain" template structures. We will not necessarily find the template structures explicitly represented in accounts, say, as consciously attended rules, because most people do not know explicitly how they introduce people. Instead, the cognitive resources will show tacit representation of template structure, for instance, in the range of judgments about the propriety and impropriety of a given form of conduct. If we find these tacit or explicit representations, we will have the material for a structural explanation of the person's skill.

What sort of template structures might we find? It is important to distinguish between those preformed notions that are employed only on one occasion and those template structures that we can employ over and over again. And furthermore we must differentiate between those templates that we have to follow exactly if we are to achieve our intention and those which are merely strategic guides. Finally, two different kinds of preformation of template structures must be distinguished: those which express the local ethnography and are a permanent part of our cognitive resources, and those which are improvised for particular occasions. An improvisation would, of course, have to be in terms of shared cognitive resources, particularly readings of meanings, otherwise what *you* did would not be intelligible and warrantable as a public performance to *us*.

An adequate theory of social meaning is a very complex matter (Harré, 1975a), but all we need for the purposes of this paper is the idea that an action is the social meaning of a speech or gesture as read off by a knowledgeable and intelligent interactor.

It seems natural to use the word *rule* for preformed, mandatory templates of the structure of action sequences, particularly when these can be given linguistic form as written sentences or spoken utterances. On the other hand, the word *plan* will be kept for the templates of action that are improvised within our local range of intelligibility, sometimes having mandatory force, sometimes being merely advisory. Plans may be represented in quite concrete objects, such as notes for a speech or a builder's blueprint.

So far we have identified the problems addressed by ethogenic social psychology only in a rather formal way. On the one hand, there is the analytic problem of discovering the structure of the products of mutual social action. There is also the genetic problem of discovering the corresponding template, its structure, and the form of representation it has in each human being competent in that social milieu. The necessity to allow for individual representation raises the problem of idiography, that is, how far our individual representations of the templates are like one another. I shall return to this point in a later section.

Finally, we should notice that we have not yet identified a source for the conceptual apparatus with which we will be conducting the microsociological investigation and the analysis of accounts. It will turn out that the source of the analytical scheme is, in the first instance, the accounts themselves.

II. Social Action as Problem Solving

The great Japanese novelist Yukio Mishima once pointed out that we have to show both to ourselves and to others that we have "willed." There seem to be two aspects to such an achievement. For one, a social actor has to achieve recognition by the others around him that he is indeed a social actor. Some categories of people, for example, children, can find this recognition hard to achieve. Then, too, he has also to make what he says and does intelligible, meaningful to the others present, those whom his action and speech affect and who realize that he was the author of them. Each of these aspects supports the other. To recognize him as an actor is to see his actions as informed by his intentions and he, as actor, realizing them in actions. To recognize his speech and movements as meaningful, that is, as actions, is to see them as informed by his intentions. I shall take for granted in this paper that an adequate theory of the meaning of social actions is available. Such a theory deals with the beliefs of the others about the actor's intentions (Grice, 1957) and also recognizes the structured sequences of public actions and the individual semantic fields to which each person's contribution to the action is related (de Saussure,

1974). These aspects of meaning can be welded into a unified theory (Harré, 1975a).

A. ACHIEVEMENT OF INTELLIGIBILITY IN ACTION

1. Standardized Solutions

In accordance with the unified theory of the meaning of social actions, the problems of intelligibility are solved as a continuous day-to-day achievement by the use of two main techniques. We attain intelligibility most readily if we draw upon standardized solutions to the specific social problems with which our social and physical environment presents us. These solutions involve a standardized, integrated personal style appropriate to each type of problem situation. There is a local typology of personas available to draw upon. We recognize, by reference to cues not yet fully investigated, stylistic unities of action and the appropriate heraldic regalia of such as policeman, nurse, bank clerk, leftish ecologically oriented mother of two, and so on. Simmons and McCall (1966) have proposed, but as yet not published, a detailed study of these organized styles, their etiology, and the processes by which they come to be widely enough known to be a social resource for the achievement of intelligibility. Style and regalia associated with specific role places in football fan groups have been closely studied by Marsh (1976).

The solutions to standard problem situations that are available under each persona are also socialized in a standardized form in a social locality. The use of ritual and ceremonial forms for the production of an action sequence appropriate to some recognized social task guarantees the intelligibility and effectiveness of what has been done. The ritualization of apology, for example, allows each of us to maintain our dignity as actors when one of us inadvertently bursts into the other's space and time (Goffman, 1972).

2. Improvised Solutions

Wide though the scope of these ritualized ceremonies may be in solving socially problematic situations, there is a penumbra of uncertainty remaining. Empirical studies (e.g., Williams, 1976) are beginning to show that the improvisation of a solution draws upon the same repertoire of actions which serve as components, that is, as parts of the "vocabulary" of standardized solutions available in a local culture.

B. ACHIEVEMENT OF INTELLIGIBILITY BY ACCOUNTING

Human beings have a further resource for achieving the intelligibility required of their actions, namely, accounting. This is speech which precedes, accompanies, and follows action and which is produced to ensure the twin goals of intelligibility and warrantability, that is, meaningfulness and propriety. We

R. HARRÉ

shall be looking at accounting in detail in Section III. For the moment, we need only notice that empirical studies have shown that accounts involve, among other items, statements of rules, implicit or explicit exposition of meanings, and stories and anecdotes, the social meaning of which may need some interpretation (Helling, 1976). Accounts may draw on the rhetoric of causality but are not to be taken as unproblematic, introspective causal explanations. Rather, accounts reveal the sources of the structural properties of action in the resources of individuals, and allow us to develop hypotheses of ideal social competence for a given society against which the actual resources of any individual can be matched. Whatever one may think about the merits of introspective investigations of alleged cognitive causal processes is quite irrelevant to account analysis; our research is not aimed at that goal. Indeed, the ethogenic movement holds that the study of the efficient causes of human action is not possible, at least in the immediate future, because the causes of action may be quite idiosyncratic. The commonalities of social life are structures which preexist action and speech as templates and upon which meaning depends, and it is to the study of these that accounting theory is directed.

C. THE SOURCES OF SOCIAL PROBLEMS

If we regard the day-to-day social world as a cooperative achievement, what sort of achievement is it? The ethogenic theory views it as the successful and continuous attainment of solutions to a myriad of problems of action and understanding, modulating from one set of conventions to another. Clear-cut gaps seldom develop in the flow of interaction. We modulate smoothly through sequences like attending a meeting, breaking up, walking down the corridor, and having a drink in the bar. In the course of these sequences the very same topics may be under discussion, but action proceeds according to distinctly different sociality, that is, of ways of maintaining a socially coherent and continuously interacting group.

Theoretically, we can draw a distinction between (*a*) socially *constructive* solutions that bring people together into a fragment of the orderly, meaningful action sequences which constitute social life and (*b*) socially *maintaining* solutions whereby threats to existing orderliness are dealt with in a ritual fashion. In detailing the importance of the socially maintaining solutions, I am not implicitly claiming anything about whether existing forms of order should be maintained; only that as a matter of fact they are preserved. Those who wish to change the social order had best know how it is achieved.

Problems come into being from three sources:

1. *Contingencies in the physical environment the social meaning of which requires interpretation*: The first and most obvious contingency is the presence of human beings or other social animals (like dogs). This presence, though its

significance may be problematic, would pose no problem if the physical environment did not have features which force propinquity and interaction. These qualities could be spatial, such as the narrowness of a path or corridor, or might involve contingencies such as shortage of meat or depletion of resources, that require the setting up of an agreed practice for sharing or conservation.

2. *Contingencies in the social environment*: The appropriateness of a solution will depend upon the state of the other people, e.g., their attitudes (hostile or friendly), their projects, and their traditions of response to the situation—such as their formalized obligations of hospitality or politeness.

3. *Contingencies in the actor*: There are fluctuations of attitudes, projects, and so on in the actor's makeup which are among the conditions which create the problematic character of the situation. If the actor were not determined to ascend by the narrow path, the descending goatherd would not constitute a problem.

D. TYPES OF SOCIAL PROBLEMS

Out of these contingencies arise three distinct types of problems:

(*a*) With what category of person are we dealing?
(*b*) What are his current attitudes?
(*c*) How am I to secure agreement to the practical details of the solution I propose while remaining within the boundaries of the social?

E. TYPES OF SOLUTION: SOCIAL VS. NONSOCIAL

Of all the ways open to the actor at this point we must distinguish the social from the nonsocial as basic categories of solution. Clearly, to knock down or shoot the descending goatherd and throw him off the path is not a social solution, just as lashing out when someone bumps into one in a crowded public place is not a social solution to the problem of maintaining a social space. Compare these with greeting the goatherd, squeezing back against the rock wall, and ushering him past with a smile, or dealing with the bump by taking the blame oneself and opening with "I'm very sorry" and getting the return, "No, no, my fault," achieving (as Goffman calls it) the maintenance of civility. The distinction between these categories is intuitively obvious, but we must look more closely into the differentia.

1. Initial Role Casting

Each category of solution depends upon an initial ontological casting of the interactor by the actor. The nonsocial solution clearly involves treating the goatherd as being in the same category as an awkwardly placed boulder, a thinglike impediment to be merely disposed of. To attempt the social solution involves an attribution of cognitive status and of autonomy to the interactor, that is, he is cast as a person, and in that category is expected to behave as such. Social psychologists have yet to address the problem of how personhood is achieved against the ever-present threat of being cast as a thing. The study of alter-casting is beginning but so far has been sociologically naive.

2. Techniques of Effective Action

Further, each type of solution draws upon a technique of effective action. The nonsocial solution depends upon the techniques involving physical causality and requires the actor to have knowledge of elementary natural science. The social solution calls upon techniques of revealing intentions through speech and action, as well as the recognition of the force of speech-acts such as pleas and apologies upon which their effectiveness depends. And the actor's knowledge must include (as an ethnography) representations of the general form of these achievements, e.g., the rule for achieving polite ushering. Remember that much of this knowledge may be tacit or reduced to habit and known explicitly only to Machiavellians, those capable, for example, of controlling and utilizing the eyebrow flash and the gaze interaction, treating the discoveries of Eibl-Eibesfeldt (1972) and Argyle and Dean (1965) as material for formulating explicit rules of behavior.

These distinctions of ontological status and action technique are not new. They are central distinctions of Immanuel Kant's theory of human interaction by which he identifies moral action. And they are also implicit in everyday practice. For example, we occasionally cast a doubtful dog into the role of social actor by treating him as such, assigning him to that category by such civil attributions as "There's a *good dog*" or "Down *boy*."

The three problems of the social actor are solved by the technique of civility. The upshot of greeting is the casting of the other into the role of a person, requiring intelligibility and warrantability to be sustained in *his* action sequences. The second problem is solved by the demeanor of the other person, his formalized style of self-presentation, which ought to reflect and respond to the way the actor has opened the encounter with a civil greeting. How far problems of the second type can be solved independently of local cultural conventions is unknown. Finally, a solution to the technical problem is achieved by the mutual production of a standardized (or improvised) ritual action sequence, which provides a conventional solution to the problem of preserving the dignity of each individual as a person, and characterized by a style expressive of civility.

Sometimes the local solution to the technical aspect of a social problem is itself covertly social. For example, it may reflect the social relations between people. As an illustration, we have "killing the pig" as described in *Lark Rise to Candleford*, where each member of the community had a right to a certain part of the pig depending upon his or her social place, so the division of meat was not regulated by reference to the dietetic needs of various members of the community but by their social standing (Thompson, 1945).

3. Example of a Standardized Action Sequence as Problem Solving

I have already touched on the standardization of the form of some action sequences available for social problem solving. These generally occur either when the act to be performed is socially important (consider, for instance, name-giving rituals such as baptisms) or when the problem situation occurs very frequently, such as when a stranger is present in a social gathering. An introduction of a stranger by a sponsor to a host can be seen as a device to solve in standardized form the following problems:

(*a*) What is the stranger's name?
(*b*) What is his relative status?
(*c*) Can he be "one of us"?

These questions are answered in one way or another in the course of our familiar introduction rituals. Detailed studies have shown the complexity of even such commonplace action sequences as the introduction (Harré & De Waele, 1976) and that several kinds of knowledge and several different levels of self-management are required for their successful accomplishment. Analysis suggests that the linguistic distinction between semantics and syntax can be used in the exposition of the form of these sequences. That is, there are questions about the meaning of component elements of the ritual (semantics) as well as uncertainties about the sequential structure or syntax of the sequence. Both the semantics of elements of the ritual and the syntactic structure determine its overall significance. For instance, the syntactical property of relative order of speech by host, sponsor, and stranger reflects and expresses the relative status each allows the other. Initially, unless the host is manifestly more socially important than the stranger, the stranger has notional high status reflected in, among other features, the ordering of speech. However, in the course of the introduction, if a microsequence occurs in which status uncertainty is resolved, there may be a formal recognition of his inferior standing. This is reflected and expressed in his losing temporal precedence in speech and action. The introduction of a stranger thus involves both the creation and the maintenance of social orderliness. It extends orderliness to include the stranger, and it serves to maintain the existing order surrounding the host by minimizing the threat the stranger, as unknown, may pose for him.

4. Agonistic vs. Cooperative Rituals

Action sequences are standardized in form when the outcome or act performed involves the coordinated interests of the parties to it and when the outcome is problematic, not as to its form but as to who remains in sole possession of the good achieved. For example, a formalized resolution of a status uncertainty involves a nonproblematic and shared conception of status. But since, logically, only one of, say, a pair of contestants can occupy the upper position, the determination of which person achieves this status is problematic. Those action sequences, or components of action sequences, that accomplish the resolution of such problems *within a framework of orderliness*, I shall call *agonistic sequences*.

F. NONSTANDARD ACTION SEQUENCES

1. Types of Nonstandard Rituals

The idea of a nonstandard action sequence can be applied at two levels of generality. There are sequences which are nonstandard relative to the social techniques available to anyone in the community but which nevertheless are the standard sequences for some isolated group of people. The private rituals of individual families are nonstandard in this sense. There are also sequences that are nonstandard in that they are improvised for a particular occasion, for the solution of a problem for which a ritual solution does not exist in the local ethnography. Examples of improvisation can be seen at semiformal social gatherings. As a case in point, no one knows how to find out by ritual means what are the connections of the various people present at a party given to launch the very first book of a new publishing house. So a solution to the problem has to be improvised within the community's traditions of civility. These traditions tend to preclude the direct question, "What is your part in this enterprise?" Successful improvisation may lead to immediate standardization, as the outsider guest passes from person to person at the new publisher's soirée.

It is worth noticing that the improvisations of nonstandard solutions may still open out into an "agonistic abyss" even though they are within traditions of civility. The improvisations may bring the standard components under challenge. This may even extend to pretended incomprehension of another's words. When even the intelligibility of speech is conventionally denied, the possibility of improvising a civil encounter is gone. Some unfortunate people may forever feel as if they are on the edge of an agonistic abyss. There are people who, for one reason or another, find it very difficult to make themselves understood, either through the peculiar character of the content of their speech and actions, or more germane to this present discussion, because they do not use language or action in the standard ways. Improvisation, unless in the hands of genius, cannot extend to the basic semantic system.

2. Negotiation of Situations and Persons

Finally, I would like to emphasize the role of interactive social processes as essential preliminaries in the improvisation of a solution to a socially defined problem. Standard solutions work because they are applied in recognized situations and involve recognized styles of presentation of the person, i.e., personas appropriate to those situations. With situation and persona settled, action can proceed smoothly to the accomplishment of the act, be it friendly or hostile. Correspondingly but problematically, a nonstandard solution requires a definition of the solution and a negotiation of social identities or personas. These proceedings may have standard forms, but again they may be improvised for the occasion, opening up once again the possibility of an indefinitely prolonged challenge to the successful completion of the act. Some people regularly open proceedings with a stranger by adopting a probing, challenging, testing kind of stance, the effect of which is to force the other either into a display of coolness or counterprovocation or into a demeaning display of annoyance, fear, aggression, and so on. These encounters are not well documented and could do with much more detailed study.

G. ACTIONS AS MEANINGS

It is vitally important to the understanding of ethogenic theory to realize that action sequences are defined at the level of meanings. Linguists distinguish between the meaning structure of a form of speech and its "substance," the vehicle by which the utterance is achieved as a public object. The substance of speech can be sound sequences, sign sequences for the deaf and dumb, or marks on paper. Some constraints on meaning derive from properties of the substance, but they are minimal. Ethogenic analysis of social action is indifferent in general to the substance of action, recognizing both speech and gesture, posture and style, or mode of action as possible vehicles of meaning. However, the posing of developmental questions as to the origins, both personal and cultural, of social skills cannot ignore this distinction. An action sequence may contain elements embodied in various substances, e.g., speech, gesture, or postures. Speech, as part of the action, that is, with respect to its illocutionary force, comes under the same analytical scheme as gesture and is subject to assessment for warrantability in terms of the same criteria. We shall have occasion in Section III to distinguish speech as part of the action from speech as commentary upon the action, and to investigate the interplay of the two roles.

H. THE GENESIS OF ACTION SEQUENCES: RULES AND PLANS

So far we have looked at action sequences from only one point of view, that of the microsociologist, questioning neither their mode of genesis nor their relation to larger structural properties of society. Ethogenics proposes the study of the genesis of rituals according to the structure–template methodology sketched in Section I. The schema for study of the genesis of action sequences takes the following dogmatic form:

The potent preformed templates or formal causes of the structure or pattern of standard action sequences are to be called *rules*. They must preexist the action and must be known, though not necessarily explicitly, to all for whom the action pattern is socially potent as a ceremony accomplishing an act. Our hypothesis is that in general the rules are learned, that is, preexist individuals, and exceptions would have to be proven.

The potent templates or formal causes of nonstandard action patterns we preemptively propose to call *plans*. They may be modulated to rules through such processes as Miller, Galatner, and Pribram (1960, p. 29) hypothesized in their TOTE (test–operate–test–exit) hierarchies; they must preexist the action but perhaps as part of the resources of only one of the interactors, who has the problem of making his actions intelligible and warrantable to the others not privy to his plan. Plans are constructed; they are among the achievements of individuals.

The cognitive resources which are the basis of social competence are revealed as representations in some medium of:

(*a*) knowledge of the local rule system, the immediate resource for competent social performance;

(*b*) knowledge of the general principles of action, laws of nature, etc., the resource for the competent formation of plans, for testing them by imaginative rehearsal, for negotiating them with others in the course of the action.

These resources can be hypothetically attributed to people on the basis of their observed success in encounters, that is, as social actors, because success constitutes an overt proof of competence. But how do we proceed to test the correctness of these hypothetical attributions? This takes us to account analysis.

III. Account Analysis

In accounting we so produce speech as to generate a meaning interpretation linked with a theoretical explanation of the action sequences that we perform and the acts we thereby accomplish. We shall have occasion to distinguish the interpretations and theories that are implicit in the speech accompanying the action from explicit interpretation and explanation in speech. We shall credit the cognitive achievement of accounting to both implicit and explicit interpretation and explanation, provided of course that the implications are understood, although that understanding may be no more explicit than the accounting and is shown only in the smooth, unbroken, unchallenged flow of meaning and the achievement of sociality.

To forestall a common misinterpretation to which accounting theory is particularly prone, I want to emphasize again that an account is not to be interpreted as an introspective causal explanation, although some accounts, *inter alia*, do have that character. Accounts are generated by ordinary people in the ordinary course of social action (and this is encouraged by ethogenically oriented social psychologists) primarily to make actions intelligible and warrantable by interpreting them as proper parts of the structure of interaction sequences. Accounting could be glossed as part of the technique to achieve *verstehen* (Weberian understandings of what people are about).

Broadly speaking, accounting seems to involve the performance of two main tasks: the explication of action, and the justification of action. Satisfactory performances of the tasks may be linked one with the other.

A. ACCOUNTING AS EXPLICATION OF MEANING

1. Explicit Explications

Explication as accounting may be explicit or implicit. A common form of explicit explication is the simple, "Sorry, I didn't mean to . . . ." This makes available an interpretation which suspends meaning altogether and hence suspends the question of warrantability. Less common, but more committing is the formula, "Well, what I meant was . . . ." It is of considerable importance to grasp the fact that the production of an account can do no more than make available a justification or explication. Mere production of the account cannot ensure that the interpretation offered will be accepted. This brings out the negotiable quality of the meanings and explanations that are going to survive in public space, so to speak, as mutual achievements.

2. Implicit Explications

Implicit accounting is more complex. We have already had occasion to notice the sociological distinction between *actions*, the meaningful components of action sequences identified through their meanings, and *acts*, the social upshot of the performance of a particular pattern sequence. Thumbing one's nose is an action, the resulting insult is an act; saying "Guilty" is an action, the resulting verdict is an act; and so on.

From the ethogenic view, actions are the meanings of behavior and speeches and as such are readings of the various vehicles by which they are conveyed. As readings they are products of interpretation and can be influenced by the interpretations made available in accounting. In a certain sense, then, actions can be generated by the form a description takes.

Broadly speaking, the descriptive vocabulary available to a speaker intent on accounting allows three stages of description, in two of which meaning is imposed.

"He bumped into her" describes body contact in such a way that it has no meaning. The explanation of the contact calls upon neither private intention nor shared social convention. Another example: "Her fourth finger went through a ring held by him."

"He pushed her" is a redescription by which the contact becomes invested with the possibility of meaning as an action. The meaning is realized when we know its place in some fragment of social life. The explanation of the happening as now described calls for intentions and perhaps social conventions as well. Another example: "He put a ring on her fourth finger."

"He tried to murder her" is a further redescription in which the action is seen as the commission of a socially defined act—attempted murder—that is, attempted unlawful killing. Another example: "He married her." In the second example, the act has meaning in itself and has its own social potency in an obvious way. We should not overlook that the former action, glossed as murder, is also socially potent, leading to commitment by the state and its officers to accomplish the man's arrest, trial, and conviction, all of which are themselves social acts at the second level of meaning. Clearly, the social psychological investigation of the potency of actions as acts to produce all kinds of effects through society must take its start from the interpretation of the meaning-giving act, implicit accounting.

The effect of successive reinterpretation is profound. We can perhaps grasp the theoretical possibilities by supposing that even when we proceed to interpretations of acts, as we usually do, we have reached them by the successive interpretations I have just separated logically. First, there is a change in relational structures as we go from behavior and speech to act. Behaviors are related, probably through physiological mechanisms, and these relations may be largely irrelevant to their social significance. Actions are related in semantic fields and syntactically into action patterns, but require knowledge of the act and its local conventions to be fully disambiguated for meaning. Acts relate to the social structure at large. Not only are the behaviors, actions, and acts in nonisomorphic relational structures, but the relational structure of the people involved is different under each stage of the attribution of meaning. If they are merely behaving, they are related by physical causality. When they are in this mode, a speech made by one of them may be too piercing but it cannot be insulting. Further, we would also say that if people are performing the *action* of getting married, they are performing the ceremony together, are required to understand one another, and relate to each other within the terms of the role system for that ceremony. On the other hand, when they are performing the *act* of getting married they are generating a fragment of the relatively permanent social order, a fragment which involves the anticipation of the future as well as requiring another ceremonial act to annul, change, or undo.

B. ACCOUNTING AS JUSTIFICATION OF ACTION

Transition from one descriptive system to another involves transition from one justificatory and warranting system to another. The rules specifying the variety of actions are usually person centered and culturally specific and are what we would treat as social conventions. It is a social convention that defines the action of giving of a ring as part of the act of marriage. Acts on the other hand come up for judgment under moral and legal rules.

1. Warranting by Self-Recategorization

The techniques of warranting by redescription, that is, justifying, deserve careful analysis. They involve subtle relations between the presentation of the person and the presentation of his actions and acts. The primary move may be recategorization of himself. A person may produce an account in which he identifies himself in the form of his description as a mere thing, an object. The events he is accounting are correspondingly described in the mere-happenings vocabulary, translated neither into actions nor acts. There may be explicit attention in such accounting to causality; he claims as a thing to be subject to physical causality, a form of determination which involves both efficient and material causes and which repudiates the normal assumptions of self-management. The prime linguistic mode for achieving such recategorization separates the speaker into an "I" and a "me," the former an astonished spectator of the behavior of the latter. This implies the breaking of control of the "I" over the "me," and by categorizing the "me" as a thing, suggests either a physical causality of its behavior or, at best, an automatism since the putative action is treated as a mere effect of happening within the "me." Transcripts of defendants' evidence in murder trials is a rich source of examples of the use of this technique: "I blacked out, but when I came to I found myself with the knife in my hand and I saw him lying on the floor." Should the court, as listener, accept the implication, the actions of the speaker (I) as murderer could be classified not as an act of murder, but as mere behavior, the effects of automatic processes within the "me." As behavior they escape the issue of their warrantability.

2. Warranting by Action–Act Recategorization

However, the preservation of dignity and selfhood is incompatible with the primary mode of recategorization, and this mode occurs most often in moral emergencies. More common, and indeed an everyday technique, is the recategorization of what the actor did. The original impetus to the study of this technique came from Austin's famous distinction between excuses and justifications, in the context of warranting an action (Austin, 1961). Again we will see an interplay between the categorization of the behavior and the claim to a special status or

situation for the person. Austin proposed that we treat as excuses those speeches
in which we admit the moral quality of the act, allowing it to be offensive,
insulting, and the like, but disclaim freedom of action. There is a corresponding
technique of modest disclaimer of virtue when we accept praise for the products
of our activity but disclaim primary responsibility as the agent of the production: "I'm only the representative of a team, you know. . . ." An excuse
addresses the warrantability of what has occurred in such formulas as "I'm
terribly sorry I'm late. I got caught in the rush-hour traffic." The first phase of
the excuse serves the joint task of apology and admission that lateness is an
offense, whereas the second phase disclaims agenthood vis-à-vis that occurrence.
A more thorough study of the structure of apology rituals can be found in Harré
(1977) and Goffman (1972).

A justification, on the other hand, denies the moral quality of the act and
claims free agenthood. This often takes the general form, "I did it, but it was not
wrong (obscure, cruel, etc.)." An extreme form of justification is to be found
in the speech of a participant in ethogenic studies who, when chided with being
late, turned on the critic and made a slashing attack on the institution of
punctuality, arguing that it was not a matter of respect between persons but a
neurotic symptom.

Austin's investigations were both incomplete and purely conceptual. Backman (1976) has recently carried out an empirical study of the speech produced
by people set to warrant their actions. He found that justifications formed a
complex category in need of subdivisions. An extremely common form involves
the use of the technique he calls *conventionalization.* From the point of view of
accounting, conventionalization is a redescription of the act. The action is
conserved, "Oh yes, I took the money," but the description of this action as the
act of theft is rebutted, "but I was only borrowing it. . . ." Utilizing the Gricean
conditions for intelligibility, the speaker proceeds to "I intended to put it back
next week. . . ." Finally, there is the technique of *normalizing,* again revealed in
Backman's study. This technique may apply to action or act and involves the
claim that what the actor did is normal or commonplace and hence does not in
general come up for special accounting. Normalizing can be achieved either in
terms of frequency ("It happens all the time") or generality ("Everybody does
it"). Normalizing conserves the standing of the actor as agent and the imputed
quality of the act but repudiates the demand for an account as justification.

C. CONTENT ANALYSIS OF ACCOUNTS: ASSUMPTIONS

So far we have followed Austin and Backman in examining accounts as to
their social function. The next step is to proceed to the analysis of the content
of accounts, in search of the cognitive resources available to an individual as a
member of a community. Account analysis starts always with the particular and

the local. It begins idiographically and proceeds only in the second stage to claim a limited generality for the structures it reveals. We assume that there is a commonality in the use and understanding of ordinary language between analyst and accounter but recognize this as an assumption that may be questionable in specific cases (as an example, analyst and accounter may not use the same range of grammatical forms in giving instances of the category of rule). In general, however, unless commonality is assumed as a working hypothesis, analysis cannot begin.

1. Attributing Cognitive Resources: The Local Ethnography

The analysis of the accounts of individuals reveals the cognitive groundings of their individual social competence, and from these a hypothetical grounding for an ideal competence in that milieu can be abstracted. I shall refer to the former as *cognitive resources* and to the latter as the *local ethnography*. The capacity for achievement, in the ethnomethodologist's sense, is rooted in the individual's cognitive resources, insofar as these are representations of the local ethnography. Looked at from the point of view of the person producing it, an account has the status of a sociopsychological theory being made available as an explanation of the accounted actions and acts. But merely making the account available is no guarantee that it will be accepted by the listener. This brings up an interesting class of social events, the negotiation of accounts (Harré & Secord, 1972). These negotiations are action sequences in the course of which accounting acts are performed, e.g., acts of excuse and justification which are themselves accountable. Our problem as social psychologists is to reveal a match between *(a)* our imputations of cognitive resources to an individual on the basis of what we, by reference to *our* accounting system, take to be the structure and meaning of his performances and *(b)* those resources as indicated in his account. Difficulties abound, particularly those posed by self-deception, false consciousness, and unconscious motives. We shall return to a partial resolution of these difficulties later.

The step from the local ethnography to a universal human action-centered system cannot be made at this time.

1. The nomothetic transition from individual to local society is problematic enough and not yet clearly established. I am certainly not prepared to propose that the formal structural properties of the cognitive resources of the individuals we have studied so far should be taken as universal, even within contemporary Western society. We are still smarting under the consequences of the absurd assumption that sophomore psychology students are typical human beings. The greater power of the new empirical methods in ethogenics ought not to tempt us to make the same mistake again. The empirical work reported here is to be understood as strictly of *local* significance.

2. Furthermore, as Gergen (1973) has pointed out in a paper of considerable significance, what little evidence exists concerning the temporal stability of social formations and practices, personality types, etc., points to their remarkably ephemeral character. We are quite unjustified in supposing that the forms of microsocial action, and even perhaps the way individuals are related to these forms, that is, their social psychology, are constant over time. All the evidence we have, slender though it is, suggests that social forms and individual cognitions of these forms are highly unstable and in rapid flux. We expect stability and are alarmed and outraged by social change, but contrary to our social mythology, social forms have a very short life. I believe that this has always been true. Where detailed records exist, as in the cases of ancient Greece or pre-Columbian America, a picture of rapid change emerges. Indirect indicators point to the same conclusion: the flux and reflux of fashion in clothes, hairstyles, furniture, and so on were apparently as rapid in pharaonic Egypt as they have been in western Europe.

The fact that certain artifacts, particularly tools and utensils, have a long and unbroken history in a region shows nothing about the accompanying social forms. Few major changes in basic artifacts occurred between 1300 and 1750 in western Europe, a period which saw enormous social and linguistic changes in the area.

The anthropological study of "primitive" people outside Europe reveals the forms of life current when they were examined. Linguists have long since abandoned the idea that such "primitive" societies have preserved earlier forms of language. We should abandon the corresponding assumption in other societies. I propose to start with the assumption then that human social practices are unstable. Since these so-called primitive societies lack any kind of historical record, we must take their rhetoric of "ancient ways" with considerable scepticism.

It may yet turn out that social science can present us only with a method for understanding each social formation, its practices, and the relation of competent people to it, one by one, and that no social universals may be revealed. But at present we have neither an adequate cross-cultural social psychology by which we can proceed from idiographic to nomothetic assertions nor an adequate theory of social change. Marxist theory is too localized and Darwinian theory as yet too biological for either to serve as the basis for a diachronic theory of society. Perhaps some development which fuses these limited but powerful theories into some kind of synthesis will serve.

D. CONTENT ANALYSIS OF ACCOUNTS: COMPONENTS

1. Semantic System

Accounts reveal the social semantic system of individuals. As we have seen, that system involves social knowledge, for example, of situations and the action sequences proper to them. But accounting is not only a method for revealing the meanings of one's actions but also for warranting or justifying them. The cognitive resources required for successfully warranting an action overlap the resources required for explanation of meanings, since a knowledge of the situations that are regarded as socially distinct in the culture and of the form of action sequences appropriate in those situations is required for both. Two further items are revealed by account analysis. The public presentation of the self as the distinct persona occurs in the way the action sequences required for the performance of social acts are carried out, that is, in their style. Distinct situations call for distinct styles of performance, and hence present the self under distinct personas. Few people seem to have explicit knowledge of the style of actions that are required in distinct situations, even though they are perfectly adequate performers at the stylistic level. Nevertheless, they do know at the "knowledge-how" level. This knowledge can be revealed indirectly by picking up the basis of critical judgments of style in accounts as well as by assembling explicit fragments of tacit knowledge by forcing a participant to contemplate actions and style he previously took for granted as natural (Argyle & Little, 1972). E. Rosser, however, has shown that some adolescents have very detailed and explicit knowledge of style and its relation to impression management (Rosser & Harré, 1977).

2. Rehearsal and Intuitions of Propriety

Account analysis reveals a further structure-linked resource. The TOTE hierarchies, discussed by Miller, Galanter, and Pribram (1960), are run, for certain important bits of social action, in advance of the realization of the action sequence in real life. The TOTE hierarchies of social life are partly pretests run in the imagination. Competence is acquired through rehearsal (De Waele & Harré 1974; Marks & Gelder, 1967). Judgment of our actions by other people is replaced in these rehearsals by an imagined judgment of an imagined other, which realizes a store of intuitions of proper and improper actions, not as rules but as the imagined approval or disapproval of some specific person. At present our knowledge of these resources grows out of studies of violent school children (Marsh, Rosser, & Harré, 1977), murderers, and rubber fetishists—a rather atypical profile of human beings. In each case, the representation by the actor of his knowledge of how his actions will be judged has been as a representation of the imagined responses of a concrete individual, his mother, the dominant member of a peer group, his wife, etc. Which individual's reactions are imagined is highly situation specific. Mischel (1975) has proposed that the clash of these empirical findings with the theoretical concept of "generalized other" proposed by G. H. Mead for a similar role could be resolved by the hypothesis, as yet untested, that "ordinary" people utilize a generalized arbiter of action for each and every situation in the course of imaginative rehearsal, that is, do not have the reactions of a specific person in mind when they consider how their actions will be viewed by others. This is an interesting idea, but as yet one cannot say whether it is correct.

3. Rule Systems

Control and rehearsal of action in situations is represented in accounts by normative material one could summarily call "the rules." Again, empirical studies of accounting reveal the situation-specific character of rule systems. A recent study of the rules adverted to by pupils in a secondary school where traditional "order" has broken down (Harré & Rosser, 1975) revealed a twelve-fold system, based upon twelve distinguishable situations, in each of which a different rule system operated. Some of these situations were fantasy worlds. "College" represented a fantasy educational institution in marked contrast to the real institution the pupils knew and recognized as "school," and "marriage" presented a fantasy homelife sharply removed from "home." Interestingly, the system of rules, arbiters, and so on revealed in the accounts clustering around "school" as a distinct social situation were almost perfect analogs of the system for "home." In a certain sense these situations, though treated as distinct, were socially identical.

There is some evidence that there may be deficits in an individual's cognitive resources. It seems likely that the capacity to recognize situations as socially distinct may be well developed without a corresponding development of knowledge of the appropriate style of self-presentation or of the rules for successful action. The deficit of style may be the more damaging to competence because its implicit character makes it less readily available to contemplation and correction by self-monitoring and self-control.

The structure revealed by the analysis of accounts represents an ideal social competence for that society, that is, represents the local ethnography in ideal form. The central ethogenic hypothesis is that this structure also represents the ideal cognitive resources of individuals competent in that society and, coupled with known deficits, the actual resources of real individuals. The structure of social action is matched by the templates of social action, that is, the cognitive resources upon which competence is based.

E. CONTENT ANALYSIS: FINE STRUCTURE

A further step, however, is required, since account analysis provides the units of cognitive resources without explicitly identifying their fine structure and nterrelations. Fortunately, Kelly's (1955) techniques provide a method by which those fine structures can be revealed. Suppose that we identify "school" as a distinct social situation in the accountings of a young person. "School" is a complex concept and has a fine structure involving (at least) the teachers, the curriculum, the ordered time units of the day, the socially distinct physical spaces (e.g., classrooms, corridors, teacher's room, boiler house, yard, gym). By building up repertory grids based upon polar constructs, elicited for triads in each set of elements, the fine structure of *that* young person's concept of school can be discovered. For example, three teachers may yield the construct "strong—weak" as a criterion by which two of the triad differ from the third. And applying this to all the teachers, we form the first row of the grid.

If we imagine the material elicited in accounts as arranged in a matrix of four columns—situations, personas, arbiters, and rule system—each row represents the resources deployed in a given type of situation and each cell is to be elaborated by the use of a Kelly grid. Mischel (1964) has shown how this is to be treated as an elucidation of rules, thus subsuming Kelly's constructs under a generally ethogenic conceptual system.

Accounting, like social action itself, is an intellectual skill that can be done well or ill and is subject to improvement. I would like to toss in here two thoughts I cannot elaborate at this time. If rough passages in social action are smoothed over by accounting, then lack of skill in accounting is sure to lead to a troubled life for the individual with that deficit. He stumbles from one minor crisis to another. Perhaps one of psychiatry's functions is to provide powerful accounting material as well as a measure of improved skill in using it. It may be that psychiatry could be a more potent technique if its practitioners made more deliberate efforts to amplify both resources for and skill at accounting. My second passing thought concerns how we might rescue some of the research done under the old "experimentalist" paradigm. Some of this classical social psychology might be salvaged if we look upon the products (the theories) as accounting systems. Perhaps cognitive dissonance studies, for example, reveal not implausible causal mechanisms but a resource people have for resolving the social problem of accounting for their actions when they find that these contradict their beliefs. Forced compliance could be understood as creating the occasion for accounting.

F. ACCOUNTING AS PART OF ACTION

But not all accounting is offered as retrospective explanation in the attempt to make actions intelligible and warrantable that would otherwise be anomic or bizarre. In real life, accounting becomes a social technique in its own right, not a mere ancillary of action. I would like to illustrate this with some examples taken from empirical studies of accounting speech.

1. Accounting in Advance of the Action

My first category is "accounting in advance of the action." Marks and Gelder (1967) have shown that fetishists may prepare their perverse action in advance by developing an account that makes their action intelligible and warrantable under some explanatory scheme *other than* fetishism. These people often provide in advance a context of interpretation in which the action has a predetermined and commonplace meaning and is warrantable under the rule system for that kind of situation. For instance, a rubber fetishist, in preparing to don his gear each Saturday, devotes much of his talk during the preceding week to developing a definition of his dressing up as "keeping clean while unstopping the drains." He may even include some actual drain cleaning to sharpen the situational definition and ground the warranting in empirical reality.

2. Preemptive Accounting

Another form of accounting in advance of the action is preemptive accounting. This occurs in agonistic situations and involves B using a form of expression which traps A, the interlocutor, so that all accountings open to him are personally discreditable. An example revealed in empirical study of talk is the "Do you mind?" maneuver. Here is how one instance proceeds:

1. A is asked by B to do something (x) and forgets to do it.
2. B (much later): "Do you mind doing x?"

As preemptive accounting this works in the following way:

Implication 1. A had an ulterior motive for not doing x, that is, he "minded."

Implication 2. The query offers A the mock possibility of saying he does mind doing x, suggesting that even if A did not have a covert reason for doing x he might have. The mere contemplation of a covert reason for not doing x may be denigrating to the social relationship between A and B.

So A is trapped. If he takes the question literally and says he does (or doesn't) mind, he is discreditable, for either he has a covert reason or he did not but might have had. If he challenges the literal meaning then he is discreditable, for that challenge is itself a denigration of B. He thereby suggests that B did indeed set up a "Do you mind?" trap for A.

Again, there are cases where action occurs in advance of the accounting but is aimed at predetermining the form that that accounting can take. A simple example from empirical study of talk is the case of a woman who repeatedly found reasons for not accompanying her husband to the theater or restaurants; after accumulating evidence for an accounting of her continued remaining at home discreditable to her husband, she then voices the accusation, "You never take me out!" I have chosen an example of an agonistic relationship, but the preempting of accounting also occurs in nonagonistic contexts, as when someone does something exciting or dangerous while keeping in mind the subsequent anecdote he will tell his friends. In all these cases the form either of the action or of the account is preempted by an initial move which constrains the possible accountings or actions.

3. Nonverbal Accounting

Accountings need not necessarily be achieved by verbal means. The desirable sought-after properties of intelligibility and warrantability can also be attained in various nonverbal ways. Empirical studies reveal the following:

a. Situational discounting. An action which would be accounted as discreditable, offensive (unwarranted), or meaningless in one kind of situation is transformed by a nonverbal directing of attention to the *umwelt,* with respect to which the action under enquiry acquires meaning and propriety. For instance, bodily contact which would be offensive in an open context is accounted by the putative offender glancing about to indicate the press of the crowd, and shrugging his shoulders to indicate his helplessness in the situation. This sequence of action can be seen in underground trains (subways), football crowds, and other tightly packed places.

b. Body gloss. Goffman has drawn attention to the phenomenon of body gloss, using an exaggerated form of the usual gestural accompaniment of an action to make a public action intelligible and warrantable. For example, a person making a sudden turnabout in a public place accompanies the change of trajectory by an exaggerated form of the "I've just remembered" gesture, often a finger flick followed by a sharp downward movement of the hand. Situational discounting of this sort can be seen from a vantage point in otherwise deserted plazas.

G. SUMMARY

What, then, can be discovered by the use of ethogenic analysis?

1. The range of skills necessary for someone to be a competent actor in interaction with other competent actors, relative to a local theory of sociality, may be systematically revealed and tested. A theory of sociality is essential to identifying social skills, since it is in terms of that theory that action sequences and routines are recognized as having social force. Ethogenic analysis, combining microsociology and the study of accounts, leads us to the idea that the skills which we recognize as necessary to action, are fundamentally intellectual skills coordinate with the skills of competent language users.

2. The employment of a skill by a competent social actor depends upon his having available to him certain cognitive resources necessary both to possessing the skill and to making successful use of it. These cognitive resources are revealed, just as skills are revealed, by the joint use of microsociological analysis and the study of accounts.

The ethogenic method, then, is best considered as a successor to both microsociology and social psychology. An essential feature of the method is that it lessens the artificial division between these studies of human society.

IV. Developmental Social Psychology

The methods of analysis and preliminary results outlined in the first three sections have been concerned with adult, or near-adult, skills and knowledge. Since the skills and knowledge revealed by ethogenic studies must have been acquired, a range of developmental questions naturally arises. In this section I want to report on progress so far in the study of children's ethogenics. My aims are to indicate the current status of research in this area and also perhaps stimulate others to investigate these matters further.

A. GENERAL FRAMEWORK OF THE STUDY

The work that has so far been done reveals two important features of children's social life.

1. The milieu in which the skills revealed in adult ethogenics are acquired seems primarily to be a social world that exists only among children and is not much penetrated either by adult understanding or action. This world comes into existence when children are organizing and creating social reality among themselves. It is the world of playground games and the like.

2. The child's social worlds seem to develop in the following sequence:

   a. *The world of social symbiosis.* Children up to about 5 years of age seem very largely to live in a world which has two prominent features: (i) The separation of the child as an independent social being from associated adults is not fully achieved (Newson & Shotter, 1974). (ii) The dynamics of thought and action in the world of social symbiosis seem largely to depend upon sentiments, particularly those identified by Bowlby (1969), namely, the sentiments associated with attachment and loss.

   b. *The independent precursor world.* Between the ages of 6 and 11 children create for themselves a social reality in which convention and ceremonial are the dominant modes of action. The studies I shall be reporting in Section IV,B have attempted to penetrate this world.

   c. *The transition world.* From the ages of 12 to 17, our studies have revealed a progressive change in the content of the techniques and routines by which social reality is created and managed. Broadly speaking, two characteristics emerge. (i) Social skills, particularly those involving the ceremonial control of action, are supplemented by formal sanctions of various kinds. The power of words alone declines although it never wholly disappears, gradually becoming absorbed in the contractual arrangements characteristic of adult ceremonial action. (ii) There is a corresponding development of the dramaturgical aspects of social life, particularly those concerned with the presentation of selves. Our studies show a progressive decline in capacity as the transition progresses, so that, in general, one is inclined to say that young adults are less competent in this matter than adolescents.

B. RESEARCH AREAS

   Research is presently engaged in three areas.
   1. The development of skills in persona presentation and control seems to be facilitated by nicknaming. So far as we can tell this phenomenon has not previously been systematically studied. Our research so far has revealed two major features (Harré, 1975b, 1976).
   a. Slotting. at least in the independent precursor world of British children there seems to exist a standard set of nicknames which appear very frequently and have distinctive social properties. These are names such as Fatty, Piggy, Beanpole, Fleabag, Titch, Thinker, and Tombstone, and variants. It became apparent that the occupancy of a "slot" designated by one of these names was not entirely explicable in terms of physical characteristics alone. The fattest individual in the group is often not the one called Fatty. These names seem to designate a socially important range of characters apparently needed for the smooth social functioning of the group. For example, Porky tends to be characterized by certain physical peculiarities such as, perhaps, wearing spectacles and being physically incompetent. But he is also the archetypal henchman and has a wide range of technological skills, such as the ability to manufacture stinkbombs. Titch, although small, is licensed to be waspishly witty at the expense of the other members. There also seems to be a prominent element of scapegoating in the way these names single out not individuals but characteristics for approbrium. Fatty bears the weight of the sin of greed for all the group, as does Fleabag the sin of squalor. Thinker and Tombstone represent the intellect under different aspects, and so on (Harré, 1975b).
   b. Setting boundaries. A second prime function of nicknaming seems to be that of identifying the boundary between the people and nonpeople in a group. Our studies show that while three-quarters of the children in large school classes have nicknames, the inner core have several nicknames, one of which is known only to the members of the inner group. The remaining members are marked off as nonpersons by some aspect of naming. Two characteristic forms of this have been seen. In one, the people have nicknames and the nonpeople are called by their official names. In the other cases, the people have their official names and the nonpeople have obscene or derogatory names. It is our impression that in

those cases where the nonpeople have been noticed to the extent of being given obscene names their situation is less anomic than in the first case.

2. Our second project involves the pursuit of the formalized techniques of the creation and maintenance of social reality that were first revealed in detail by the work of Opie and Opie (1959). Our studies have indicated that not only ?re there formalized ways of maintaining property, creating moments of truce, determining the order of turns, and the like, but there is also a widespread ceremonial or formalized set of devices by which formalized risks are taken and character is achieved in the Goffman sense. We call these *hazarding*. They range from the whispering of rude words in class to the performance of ritualized dangerous acts such as ritual stealing from the school dining room.

3. Studies of the spatiotemporal conceptions of the independent precursor world revealed a previously unreported phenomenon—that certain important institutions, such as the school, were conceived according to institutional models provided by literary or televisual sources. A florid example recently uncovered was the use of a television serial about the Colditz Castle prison camp as a resource for naming the parts of the school, the exits and entrances after escape routes from the Castle, the teachers after the guards and staff of the prison. The film *Planet of the Apes* has also been drawn upon. We are presently engaged in the difficult task of attempting to give a historical dimension to this matter by investigating the devices used for similar purposes among Victorian children.

The upshot of these studies will, we hope, be a clearly defined account of the practices in the course of which the skills that create the adult world are acquired. The most striking conclusion that we can already come to is that these developments take place almost without benefit of interaction with adults. This is a surprising observation, and we have yet to elaborate all its consequences.

V.   Further Research Dimensions

Looking into the world of children is only one aspect of our studies. Since the whole of the study is explicitly situated in local milieu in both space and time, two further dimensions are required:

Ethogenic studies of other cultures are necessary, and we are presently engaged in a systematic attempt at comparative ethogenics of the Japanese (Morsbach, 1976), that is, a study of how their accounting practices relate to their social activities. There are very great difficulties in carrying out such research, centering on what has been called the problem of "the translation of cultures." Morsbach's recent study of a prominent feature of Japanese adult social life and the difficulty of "translating" it into European terms illustrates this point clearly. However, provided we take a thoroughgoing ethogenic view, our aim can be no more than the juxtaposition of completely formulated understandings in terms of the sociological and psychological concepts of the local folk. The possibility of formulating concepts from which a universal human sociopsychology can be developed remains, in my view, highly problematic. The issue of the origin of contemporary practices in adult skills cannot be addressed wholly in terms of developmental ethogenics. I have already mentioned the beginnings of a historical project to look into the evolution of uses of changing resources for conceptualizing an institution that are available to children from their life situation, in books or television programs, or whatever. The origin of contemporary practices should be made the basis of a historical ethogenics which, drawing upon Darwinian metaphors, would look at the historical sources of a practice, the variability and mutation of human conduct, and the selection of variants by historical (social and economic) conditions. It is my view that such a study must make a clear distinction between mutation conditions (those leading to variations in practices and conduct) and selection conditions (those leading to the survival, promulgation, etc., of some variant of practice). But these are matters which are still very much open to further investigation.

REFERENCES

Argyle, M., & Dean, J. Eye-contact, distance and affiliation, *Sociometry*, 1965, **28**, 289–304.

Argyle, M., & Little, B. R. Do personality traits apply to social behaviour? *J. for the Theory of Social Behaviour*, 1972, **2**, 1–35.

Austin, J. L. A plea for excuses. In J. O. Urmson & G. J. Warnock (Eds.), *Philosophical papers*. London & New York: Oxford University Press (Clarendon), 1961. Pp. 123–152.

Austin, J. L., and Urmson, J. O. (Eds.), *How to do things with words*. London & New York: Oxford University Press, 1965.

Backman, C. W. Exploration in psycho-ethics, the warranting of judgements. In R. Harré (Ed.), *Life sentences*. New York: Wiley, 1976. Pp. 98–108.

Bowlby, J. *Attachment and loss*. Vol. 1. London: Hogarth Press, 1969.

de Saussure, F. *A course of general linguistics*. London: Collins, 1974.

De Waele, J.-P., & Harré, R. Towards a criminological file model. *Proceedings of the Institute of Criminology*, Genova 1974.

Duncan, S. D. Some signals and rules for taking speaking turns in conversations. *Journal of Personality and Social Psychology*, 1972, **23**, 283–292.

Eibl-Eibesfeldt, I. Similarities and differences between cultures in expressive movements. In R. A. Hinde (Ed.), *Non-verbal communication*. London & New York: Cambridge University Press, 1972. Pp. 297–312.

Gergen, K. Social psychology as history. *Journal of Personality and Social Psychology*, 1973, **26**, 309–320.

Goffman, E. *Relations in public*. London: Allen Lane, Penguin Books, 1972. Pp. 124–225.

Grice, H. P. Meaning. *Philosophical Review*, 1957, **66**, 377–388.

Harré, R. Are we justified in treating actions as meanings? In T. Borbé (Ed.), *Proceedings of the Wiener Symposium über-Semiotik*. Munich: Fink-Verlag, 1975. (a)

Harré, R. The origins of social competence in a pluralist society. *Oxford Review of Education*, 1975, **1**, 151–158. (b)

Harré, R. Living up to a name. In R. Harré (Ed.), *Personality.* Oxford: Blackwell, 1976, in press. Ch. 3.

Harré, R. Architectonic man: On the structuring of lived experience. In S. M. Lyman & R. Brown, (Eds.), *Structure, history and consciousness.* Cambridge University Press, 1977, in press.

Harré, R., De Waele, J.-P. The ritual for incorporation of a stranger. In *Life sentences.* R. Harré (Ed.), New York: Wiley, 1976. Pp. 76–86.

Harré, R., & Rosser, E. The rules of disorder. *Times Educational Supplement,* July 25, 1975, p. 11.

Harré, R., & Secord, P. F. *The explanation of social behaviour.* Oxford: Blackwell, 1972; and New York: Littlefield, Adams, 1973.

Helling, I. Autobiography as self-presentation. In R. Harré (Ed.), *Life sentences.* New York: Wiley, 1976. Pp. 42–48.

Kelly, G. A. *The psychology of personal constructs.* Vol. 1. New York: Norton, 1955.

Marks, I. M., & Gelder, M. G. Transvestism and fetishism. *British Journal of Psychiatry,* 1967, **113,** 711–729.

Marsh, P. Careers for boys; nutters, hooligans and hard cases. *New Society,* 1976, **36,** 346–348.

Marsh, P., Rosser, E., & Harré, R. *The rules of disorder.* London: Routledge & Kegan Paul, 1977, in press.

Miller, G. A., Galanter, E., & Pribram, K. H. *Plans and the structure of behavior.* New York: Holt-Dryden, 1960.

Mischel, T. Personal constructs, rules and the logic of clinical activity. *Psychological Review,* 1964, **71,** 180–192.

Mischel, T. Psychological explanations and their vicissitudes, Parts III and IV. In W. J. Arnold (Eds.), *Nebraska symposium on motivation.* Vol. 23. Lincoln: University of Nebraska Press, 1975.

Morsbach, H. Some Japanese–Western linguistic differences concerning dependency needs: The case of "amae." In R. Harré (Ed.), *Life sentences.* New York: Wiley, 1976. Pp. 129–145.

Newson, J., & Shotter, J. How babies communicate. *New Society,* 1974, **29,** 345–347.

Opie, I., & Opie, P. *The lore and language of schoolchildren.* London & New York: Oxford University Press (Clarendon), 1959.

Rosser, E., & Harré, R. Knowledge of personal style. *Journal for the Theory of Social Behaviour,* 1977, 7, in press.

Schegloff, E., & Sacks, H. Opening up closings. *Semiotica,* 1973, 8, 289–327.

Simmons, J. L., & McCall, G. J. *Identities and interactions.* Glencoe, Ill.: Free Press, 1966.

Thompson, S. *Lark Rise to Candleford.* Oxford University Press, London, 1945.

Williams, M. Presenting oneself in talk: The disclosure of occupation. In R. Harré, (Ed.), *Life sentences.* New York: Wiley, 1976. Pp. 37–41.

ON THE ETHOGENIC APPROACH: ETIQUETTE AND REVOLUTION[1]

Barry R. Schlenker

UNIVERSITY OF FLORIDA
GAINESVILLE, FLORIDA

I. Introduction

Doldrums have recently settled on the field of social psychology. Some claim that "contemporary social psychology" (and social science in general) has failed—its perspective, theories, and methods are deficient (for some of these views, see Armistead, 1974; Buss, 1975; Chapanis, 1967; Gadlin & Ingle, 1975; Hendrick, 1974; McGuire, 1973; Moscovici, 1972). The despair is sufficiently serious to cause a questioning of whether social psychology is a science in any meaningful sense of the term (e.g., Cronbach, 1975; Gergen, 1973; Greenwald, 1974; Hendrick, 1974). Elms (1975) has described the situation as a "crisis of confidence" precipitated by unfulfilled promises of relevance and disappoint-

[1] The present paper was facilitated by the support of the Organizational Effectiveness Research Program, Office of Naval Research (Code 452), under Contract No. N00014-75-C-0901; NR 170-797. Thanks are extended to Marvin E. Shaw, Donelson R. Forsyth, and Howard Goldman for their helpful comments on an initial draft.

ment at the theoretical fruits of our research labors. Many feel that the discipline is ill beyond the point of healing by standard medicines and must be placed under the knife of radical surgical techniques to rid us of a decaying mass of ideas that is robbing us of our vitality.

Few of the voices that have been raised in attack have offered constructive recommendations; they have instead been content to point out assumed difficulties and hope that others can find solutions. This background makes Harré's (1974, and in this volume; see also Harré & Secord, 1973) work all the more important. He offers what appears to be a coherent alternative that is undoubtedly welcomed by many.

In brief, Harré urges us to treat people as human beings rather than as rats, computers, or whatever. To explain behavior, we must understand the nature of people. An anthropomorphic model of man is elaborated by rejecting parametric interpretations of social behavior (i.e., those that consist of describing functional relationships between variables) and substituting structural interpretations. These structures are derived from microsociological analyses of life as theater, as in Goffman's (1959, 1967) insights into interaction rituals and the dramaturgical aspects of social behavior.[2] The role of experimentation as currently conceived is abandoned, and ethnomethodological techniques are urged. Harré and Secord (1973) also reject what they view as the philosophical core of contemporary social psychology: an emphasis on logical positivism, a Humean conception of cause, and a mechanistic model of man.[3] This surgery will undoubtedly be viewed by some as a radical alteration of the face of the discipline, though each aspect considered separately has had its advocates for years.

Some of what Harré says should be applauded, some tolerated, and some seriously questioned. Given a choice between the ethogenic approach and "contemporary social psychology" (frequently described by critics as trivial,

---

[2] It seems that every theorist prefers to believe that his or her model is more humanistic than the models of others. Thus, advocates of the ethogenic approach contend that the study of interaction rituals is superior to alternatives because it treats people as people, not as mere pawns of external variables or as computers or whatever. Every such analogy, of course, has its critics. Margaret Trudeau, wife of the prime minister of Canada, rebelled against the social conventions and rituals that govern her life: "If you rely completely on protocol . . . you can become a robot. . . . You don't have to be a human being, you don't have to be kind, you don't have to be spontaneous, you don't have to be warm" (Not a robot, 1976). It's not clear that any single analogy can ultimately be viewed as superior to others in terms of its being more humanistic, since humanism is often in the eye of the beholder.

[3] The emphasis on logical positivism and a mechanistic model are straw men that are consistently employed by critics. As Shaw (1974, p. 97) noted, these positions would certainly be personally rejected by most social psychologists, though they might be "willing to attribute this to others." Space does not permit an adequate discussion of the relevant changes that have taken place since the 1940s.

constipated, and overly conservative, even by scientific standards), I would choose the latter, though there are advantages and liabilities in each. Happily, however, one should not feel compelled to make a choice between them; the best can be selected from what each has to offer.

Contemporary social psychology does indeed have its problems: the mathematical techniques which would allow it to deal with many of its problems do not exist [Kemeny (1959) notes that the types of mathematics that would be most relevant and useful to social scientists have yet to be developed]; its theories are often less than rigorous and elegant (cf. Harris, 1974); its methods are often applied to trivial problems (naturally, the other person's research and not one's own always lands epithets such as "trivial"); and our awe at the scientific method makes us misunderstand its simplicity and attempt to follow "rules" that those in other disciplines would never consider (cf. Feigl, 1970; Feyerabend, 1970; Kemeny, 1959; Schlenker, 1976). But even with such problems, I do not see the decaying flesh of the straw man that is described by most critics.[4]

II. Objections to the Ethogenic Approach

To avoid a dull eclecticism, I will concentrate my comments on aspects of the ethogenic approach that appear most faulty. In particular, these aspects to include: *(a)* the nature of rules and rule following; *(b)* parametric vs. structural interpretations; *(c)* the universality issue; and *(d)* experimentation vs. ethnomethodology.

A. RULES AND RULE FOLLOWING

A key to the ethogenic vision of a new social psychology is the role played by plans and rules, particularly the latter. These critical concepts appear to accomplish two objectives: (1) they allow a shift in focus from parametric to structural interpretations; and (2) they provide answers for perplexing questions about motivation (plans are directive but not energizing; it is assumed that plans are always executed, and they guide actions in accordance with their structure). Rules presumably are a social counterpart to plans, forming the major explanatory core of the ethogenic approach. However, the terms rule and rule following are used in a commonsense way. Despite implications to the contrary (Harré, in

---

[4] Writing in our bicentennial year, I have overpowering feelings of being a Tory in the midst of the new revolutionaries. But then I content myself with the thought that not all revolutions are wise, useful, or successful, as the histories of many South American banana republics can attest.

this volume), "rules" are not analogous to the highly successful concept of "plans." Using the terms *rules* and *rule following* in the manner prescribed would greatly limit the scope of social psychology and make the anthropomorphic model largely immune to empirical challenge. Examine each of these points.

Miller, Galanter, and Pribram (1960) described a plan as a hierarchically organized structure, like a computer program, that guides action. Feedback loops and reality testing provide constant interaction between the person and the environment. In this usage, the concept of a plan has had a great deal of success in the area of cognitive psychology (Neisser, 1967). Carson (1969) employed "plans" as a key element of his integration of personality and social psychology. Plans have some of the characteristics that McGuire (1973, p. 450) called for when he stated that social psychology must employ "theoretical models of the cognitive and social systems in their true multivariate complexity, involving a great deal of parallel processing, bidirectional relationships, and feedback circuits." The concept also provides a fine meld between parametric and structural interpretations. The computer analogy provides the structure, and parametric interpretations can be formulated to describe how information affects strategies and action.

Harré (in this volume) implies that rules are the social counterparts of the highly successful concept of plans. Like plans, rules guide action and serve as structure. Unlike plans, rules are social, are known to all interactants, are guides for "standard action sequences," and preexist individuals. Thus, rules supposedly are social guides for action that explain the forms that social behavior takes; they form templates. When examined closely, though, the analogy between rules and plans is sorely strained and usefulness of the template idea must be questioned.

As used by Harré, rules are simply conventions, customs, norms, social habits, and/or interaction rituals that exist in specific situations for a particular subgroup within a particular society. They do not serve an executive, universal guiding function as do plans. If they did, it would make no sense to talk of breaking the rules. That would be like saying that a computer ran without a program or "disobeyed" the program submitted to it. It is one thing for a plan to be disrupted by external circumstances; it is quite another for it to be "broken." Thus, rules amount to being external, social conventions that people agree should be followed and generally follow themselves.

The task of the ethogenic social psychologist is to elucidate these social prescriptions for interaction patterns. Garfinkel (1972, p. 357) described the task as gaining "common sense knowledge of social structures," that is, we should compile the "socially-sanctioned-facts-of-life-in-society-that-any-bona-fide-member-of-the-society-knows." Goffman (1967, p. 2) is explicit about how the individual fits into the approach: "I assume the proper study of interaction is not the individual and his psychology, but rather the syntactical relations among the acts of different persons mutually present to one another." The individual's knowledge, plans, strategies, needs, and so on are ignored in favor of the ritual itself. Since "people follow rules," the cataloging of social conventions becomes the form of social explanation. Ethnomethodology is employed to question people about the conventions that they followed, since the desired datum is the person's account of the appropriate behavior patterns for that time and place.

If we pursue the above recommendations, social psychology would certainly be given a radical face-lift. Somehow prescriptions for behavior become transformed into explanations of behavior. Social psychologists would become the "scientific" counterparts of Emily Post. With efficient detective methods, we could compile books of etiquette that describe the appropriate interaction rituals and conventions that particular groups employ [recognizing full well that these are not meant to be universal, general explanations for behavior since they are limited to the local conditions (see Harré, in this volume)].

Several problems become apparent:

First, the lack of universality of the products of such an approach is distressing, and more shall be said about the issue shortly.

Second, the ethogenic approach seems partial and fragmentary in its explanatory prowess. For example, the most fascinating sociological discussions of accounting and social motivation (e.g., Mills, 1940; Scott & Lyman, 1968) begin after an action has taken place and that action has been recognized by the actor and/or the audience as a faux pas or something which breaks conventions. But sociologists have always given minimal attention to why the action that caused the social dilemma occurred in the first place. Some such incidents are accidental, in which case one could say that the person was trying to follow rules but slipped. However, on many occasions the social dilemma is the by-product of an intentional action. A person may lie for self-gain, or get involved in one-upmanship at the expense of another's "face" in the interaction. Or consider the antisocial character who, after a faux pas, stares his audience down without apology and demands, "What are you going to do about it?" These flagrant abuses of conventional interaction rituals are not easily explained by a rule-following model and hence have received scant attention by microsociologists. When do people choose not to follow social rules? What happens when social rules give competing directions? Why do people sometimes "obey" and sometimes disregard conventions? When gathering accounts, how do we separate self-deception and lying from actual perceptions of the situation? Until such questions are answered, or at least systematically addressed, the rule-following approach will contain major liabilities as a viable explanatory system.

Third, the domain of social psychology is severely restricted. One way to deal with incidents in which social rules are broken is to define them as outside the range of events that social psychology has to explain. This is what Harré seems to have done. According to Harré's usage, social psychology has as its scope of inquiry the structured conventions and rituals that are "standardized" in a particular setting. For example, he notes that if one lashes out at a person who bumped into one in a crowded place, the "solution" would not be social. To qualify as social, the person must exhibit the "maintenance of civility." Why does the frustrated card player throw over the table after a loss rather than follow more appropriate social conventions? It seems that this question is outside the range of social psychology, since it is a "nonsocial" event that fails to maintain civility. Excluding such a wide variety of actions and events from the domain of social psychology should certainly frustrate social psychologists who are interested in, say, aggression, power, and other such topics.

Fourth, the "rules" (i.e., laws, hypotheses, propositions) that social scientists employ to explain behavior may or may not be the same rules that individuals use to account for their own behaviors in social settings. This distinction has produced a major criticism by philosophers of the anthropomorphic model of man. Such a model derives from logical and conceptual considerations of everyday language and accounts (Hampshire, 1960; Strawson, 1959). Clearly, ordinary language may or may not be useful in explaining behavior—both in terms of precision and the value of the concepts involved. But, beyond this, the model uses everyday language as a *criterion* for judging the adequacy of explanations, thereby making the model itself incapable of alteration. Mackinnon (1975, p. 72) chides Harré for placing "*a priori* restrictions limiting psychologists to the prescientific model of man implicit in ordinary language as the ultimate standard to use in judging the acceptability of any proposed revisions or replacements. . . ." Mackinnon continues, "The fundamental conceptualization of man implicit in ordinary language would on this account become logically immune to replacement or substantial revision." Oddly, with many philosophers concerned with the inadequacies of everyday language (e.g., Kaplan, 1964; Kemeny, 1959; Nagel, 1961), it is quite a change to have one employ such language as a major aspect of explanation.

The hypotheses, propositions, and laws that social scientists use in their theories should describe how people do behave, not how they would behave if their actions constituted an acceptable ritual. It is certainly not the case that we must assume that people follow scientific laws any more than we should assume that they follow social rules (Schlenker, 1974). All that general hypotheses do is to describe regular relationships that occur between two or more variables; the laws derive from people's behaviors, not vice versa. These hypotheses could incorporate the aspects of interaction rituals that Harré discusses, but they should also do more. They should indicate when rules are followed and when they are not. They could describe how social conventions affect plans, rather than assuming that social rules are somehow a social counterpart to plans.

Parametric explanations could be employed to relate how particular conditions affect the selection of, modification of, and adherence to particular interaction rituals. Simply to state that social rules act as templates guiding actions raises numerous questions that must be considered before the ethogenic approach can emerge as a serious alternative.

B. PARAMETRIC VS. STRUCTURAL INVESTIGATIONS

Harré (in this volume) calls the distinction between parametric and structural investigations the "most fundamental methodological point which distinguishes ethogenic from traditional social psychology." It is therefore worth attention. It seems implied that (1) structural investigation is a mutually exclusive alternative to parametric investigation; (2) an anthropomorphic, rule-following perspective that views people as agents demands a structural investigatory base and not a deterministic, parametric one; and (3) ethnomethodology replaces experimentation as the major research technique. Fault can be found with each of these implications.

One can reasonably argue that many contemporary parametric analyses of social behavior include ambiguous, invalid, or nonheuristic parameters. But it is unreasonable to argue a priori that parametric interpretations of social behavior are untenable. One major charge against parametric analyses is that interactions are often obtained between supposedly independent parameters. The occurrence of interactions themselves, though, does not mean that a situation cannot be described by parametric means. Anderson (1974) has had success not only with additive parametric models of social processes but with multiplicative ones as well (a multiplicative relationship between variables will emerge as an interaction in an analysis of variance procedure).

A humanistic, nonpositivistic view of man does not necessitate the adoption of a structural interpretation nor the abandonment of a parametric one. Ossorio (1973), for example, champions a man-as-agent, nonpositivistic perspective and has presented an insightful parametric analysis of the concept of behavior. He states that the parameters of behavior include identity, motivation, cognition, competence, performance, achievement, personal characteristics, and significance. These are the fundamental "ways in which one particular behavior can be the same or different from another particular behavior as such" (Ossorio, 1973, p. 125). Here the focus is upon the psychological and social parameters that pertain to behavior and not the structure of it, and such an analysis is certainly needed. The point, of course, is that a humanistic view of people does not preclude a parametric interpretation nor make a structural one superior.

Parametric interpretations should not be confused with either "causal" or "mechanistic" explanations. To state that we can describe regularities between antecedent conditions (such as information in the environment, or internal states) and meaningful units of behavior does not imply acceptance of fatalistic determinism, nor does it abrogate "free will" (cf. Kaplan, 1964; Nagel, 1961; O'Conner, 1971; Schlenker, 1974). Internal variables can enter into parametric interpretations just as easily as can external variables; and most recent work in social psychology takes into account self-monitoring, self-regulation, internal processes, and so on (e.g., Bandura, 1974; Carson, 1969; Mischel, 1973). Further, to state that behavior is affected by environmental variables, for instance, that attitude similarity is linearly related to interpersonal attraction under a wide range of conditions (cf. Byrne, 1971), does not imply that the other's attitudes "compelled" liking to occur. It would in fact be "irrational" if a person's actions were not affected by external information in a somewhat consistent fashion. Thus, we can describe a relationship between external conditions (i.e., the attitude statements of another) and interpersonal attraction without assuming that people are the pawns of either mysterious external forces or scientific laws. It is actually quite a shame that the word *cause,* such a useful little word in everyday discourse, found a home in social science after being kicked out of natural science. Few social scientists understand it. Bertrand Russell (1965, p. 185) put it well when he stated that "the law of causality, as usually stated by philosophers, is false, and is not employed in science. . . . Instead of stating that one event A is always followed by another event B, [scientific laws actually state] functional relations between certain events at certain times, which we call determinants, and other events at earlier or later times or at the same time." Notice that teleological explanations and causal explanations are indistinguishable in this statement. Functional relations (in the mathematical sense) simply offer summary descriptions of regularities that are observed. Further, the term *mechanism* means many different things to different people (cf. Nagel, 1961). To some, it means reducing higher-order processes to biochemical events; to others, it means explaining behavior in terms of external events, minimizing internal factors, and employing S–R or S–O–R analogies. Harré (see Harré & Secord, 1973, p. 27) offers the latter interpretation. Clearly, though, there is nothing about parametric interpretations that demands either of these views of mechanism.

There is another level at which structure can be discussed and related to parametric interpretations. Whenever we examine behavior, we are imposing some type of structure. To make a decision about what to use as a unit of analysis in an experiment presupposes a decision about a meaningful structure. Should the unit of analysis in a speech experiment be an uttered word, sentence, paragraph, or what? In attitude research one does not measure the muscular movements, glandular secretions, etc., that are the components of an attitude statement; instead, the entire structured action is employed as the unit of analysis. In conflict research, gaming studies frequently use the joint responses of two or more individuals as a single unit of analysis when making predictions about cooperation. In all of these cases, the structured unit that is being examined plays a role in a parametric interpretation of a particular process. Given the integral relationship between parametric and structural conditions, it seems futile to suggest that structural interpretation should supercede parametric interpretation, or vice versa.

Parametric and structural interpretations are not mutually exclusive, and it is unfortunate that Harré implies that they are. As an example, dissonance studies are reexamined with the comment that it might be possible to achieve the "rescue of some of the work done under the old 'experimentalist' paradigm" (Harré, in this volume). He continues, "Perhaps cognitive dissonance studies . . . reveal not implausible causal mechanisms but a resource people have for resolving the social problem of accounting for their actions when they find these contradict their beliefs." The latter hypothesis can be examined using the "old 'experimentalist' paradigm," and the use of this particular example is perplexing. The hypothesis relates two variables: accounting (i.e., excusing, justifying, etc.) for one's actions as a function of having engaged in counterattitudinal behavior. Note that it is not necessary to state that counterattitudinal actions "cause" accounts in the sense that the former compels the latter into existence. But it can be said that they covary and are functionally related. One could examine the amount of embarrassment, degree and kind of excuses and justifications employed, etc., following different types of counterattitudinal actions. Such a combination of parametric and structural interpretation is not new in the counterattitudinal behavior literature (e.g., Alexander & Knight, 1969; Bramel, 1968; Riess & Schlenker, 1977; Schlenker, 1975b; Schlenker & Schlenker, 1975; Tedeschi, Schlenker, & Bonoma, 1971). One can conceptualize warranting in both structural and parametric ways.

The relationship between structural and parametric interpretation is also evidenced in the nature of scientific theories. The traditional description of scientific theory is that it has three components: (1) internal principles, or an abstract calculus that specifies the basic entities, processes, and laws that govern them; (2) a set of bridge principles or rules of correspondence that link the internal principles of the theory to phenomena explained by the theory; and (3) a "model for the abstract calculus," that is, something that is iconic and allows a conceptualizable or visualizable structure (Hempel, 1970; Nagel, 1961). If the internal principles are viewed as largely parametric whereas the model is structural, we again find that they are inextricable.

It is conceded that the previous discussions of the structure in units of analysis and scientific theories is pushing Harré's description of structural interpretation quite far, perhaps past the point where any resemblance remains. Harré focuses on structure as a template and suggests that we probe to illuminate the structure created by rules and conventions. I have tried to show that we constantly deal with structured, meaningful units, in both our theories and experiments. It is more fruitful to consider all types of structure, as well as ways to fit structure into parametric analyses, than it is to focus on only one type.

C. INVARIANCE AND UNIVERSALITY

There is a major difference between Harré's structural interpretation and that successfully used in genetics, linguistics, cognitive psychology, and perception. Harré (in this volume) draws the pessimistic conclusion that universal concepts, patterns, and sequences probably cannot be developed in social psychology. In this he echoes Gergen's (1973) thesis that social psychology must content itself with being the study of contemporary history. Such a conclusion must follow from the way that the domain of social psychology has been defined—since we should study local customs and rituals, we must expect that these change over time and locality.

Yet each of the other structural models that Harré (1974, and in this volume; see also Harré & Secord, 1973) mentions as examples has a much loftier aspiration. Chomsky (1965) has noted that minor grammatical surface rules vary across cultures. But Chomsky's goal has been to specify the deep structure of language; he aims to describe the universal rules that transcend local dialects and customs. Similarly, in his theory of perception, Gibson (1966, p. 242) finds that "the informative variables of optical structure are invariant under changes in the intensity of illumination and changes in the station-point of the observer." Miller *et al.* (1960) have proffered their TOTE (test—operate—test—exit) units, the building blocks of plans, as the successor to the concept of reflex arc; the intent is to build a model that possesses the requisite universality. In every other usage of a structural interpretation the intent is to proffer universal, invariant characteristics. It seems strange to propose a particular type of interpretation, praising its usage in other areas, and then to omit a major characteristic of the interpretation as it has been employed in those other areas. By the definition of its domain (i.e., the templates formed by local conventions), a structural interpretation as advanced by Harré excludes any possibility of finding universals. This is a serious fault, since invariant relationships are cornerstones of scientific explanations (Kaplan, 1964; Nagel, 1961; Schlenker, 1974, 1976). Since it cannot accomplish one of the major objectives of scientific explanations, providing highly general statements about its domain of discourse, its pragmatic appeal is quite low.

D. ETHNOMETHODOLOGY AND EXPERIMENTATION

Arguments in support of the *superiority* of ethnomethodology (Garfinkel, 1967; Psathas, 1968), a type of participant-observer study of people's activities and accounts under everyday conditions, over other research techniques such as experimentation have always seemed less than convincing. When in the hands of skilled and careful researchers, ethnomethodological studies can yield important insights for social psychologists, just as can any heuristic technique that plunges the researcher into the subject matter. If nothing else, the "candid camera" type of investigation that is often used is fascinating to behold and quite entertaining. Such studies can be used to obtain descriptions of how people perceive the rules, meanings, and relationships relevant to a particular situation, and to show how people react when caught in social dilemmas. The apparent external validity of such studies is an advantage; one does not have the problem of generalizing from an often contrived laboratory setting to a natural environment.[5] For these reasons, the technique has appealed to sociologists.

Ethnomethodological studies do have problems that counterbalance some of their advantages. They lack the control, precision, and intersubjective reliability of experiments. A reader is often at the mercy of the researcher, trusting that subjective interpretations of ongoing events are reasonably accurate. At least on "Candid Camera" Alan Funt allows the viewers to see the subjects' actual behaviors and draw their own conclusions. Experimenter effects are not confined to "experiments." Ethnomethodologists can easily affect the accounts and activities of the participants in their studies. One is also never sure of the degree to which accounts are colored by "self-deception and lying," a consideration Harré views as "problematic" and is never able to successfully resolve. Finally, it has always been my impression that ethnomethodological studies produce interesting ideas that should be subjected to further refinement and systematic testing.

Experimentation is denigrated because it is aimed at establishing the effects that particular conditions have on selected behaviors and, of course, this reeks of a "causal" analysis of action. However, as previously shown, there is no reason to assume causality, only functional relationships between variables. We can experimentally examine how accounts are influenced by particular types of social dilemmas occurring under particular conditions. Experimentation is extremely valuable since it is the most valid technique for examining how selected variables are related.

Everything is, of course, not perfect. Experimentation as currently conducted in social psychology has its faults. Many experiments are designed to serve as demonstrations that a particular behavior occurs rather than as tests of carefully considered hypotheses. Human behavior is complex, and practically every conceivable behavior has occurred under one or another set of conditions. Yet many experiments do nothing more than demonstrate that a particular result does indeed occur. Such studies, as McGuire (1973) noted, do little more

---

[5] Generalizations are made on the basis of corroborated theories, not data alone, a point that is often overlooked in discussions of external and ecological validity (see Schlenker & Bonoma, 1976).

than test the ingenuity of an experimenter. In no way is a hypothesis subjected to a test. When a test proves negative, many experimenters would reject the test as inadequate and investigate a different area rather than reject an original hypothesis or systematically explore other ways to set up a test in which the hypothesis, rather than experiment, would be rejected. Instead of conducting such demonstrations, social psychologists should become familiar with the systematic methods of strong inference as described by Platt (1964). In strong inference, alternative hypotheses are delineated and experiments are designed to pit one alternative against another; decision trees are spelled out in advance to guide further work, which is contingent upon the outcomes of experiments. Simply, social psychologists have been less than diligent in specifying the conditions under which they would be willing to abandon a pet hypothesis (one's own hypothesis, not that of a colleague). Unless such systematic proce- dures are employed, there is no way to separate the wheat from the chaff, and science cannot progress (Lakatos, 1970; Popper, 1965).[6] Unfortunately, a pro- gram of research in social psychology frequently amounts to doing about three to five marginally related experiments on one topic.

The scientific method is not so dogmatic that it demands the exclusive use of one perspective, type of explanation, or type of research technique. Field studies can accomplish objectives that are not possible in controlled laboratory situa- tions, and vice versa. Some disciplines, such as astronomy, advanced without the aid of experimentation. Research techniques should always be selected to fit the nature of the appropriate problem or question. Never should a technique be used in a way that follows Kaplan's (1964) law of the instrument: Give a small boy a hammer and he'll find that everything in sight needs pounding. Controlled laboratory experimentation has been the hammer that social psychologists have swung at the world. A problem has not yet been uncovered that is insignificant enough to escape from under the experimental microscope. Even with these faults, though, experimentation is a powerful technique that should be applied when appropriate. If forced to make a choice, I would prefer to rely exclusively

---

[6] Greenwald (1975) has proposed a distinction between operational disconfirmability, in which disconfirming data will throw doubt on the operations but not the hypotheses of an experiment, and conceptual disconfirmability, in which disconfirming data threatens the hypothesis. Greenwald suggests that major theories in social psychology, e.g., dissonance and self-perception theory, possess the former but not the latter types of disconfirmability; hence our theories are not touched by our data. However, this distinction may not be highly fruitful. In any discipline, the results of one or a very few tests can always be attributed to improper operationalizations, measurement errors, faulty auxiliary hypotheses, and so on (cf. Hempel, 1966). But when a series of studies, each of which provides slightly different operations and circumstances, all disconfirm a particular hypothesis, the hypothesis itself is certainly called into question. Research programs, not individual studies, are what compete for a claim to truth (Lakatos, 1970).

on experimentation rather than on ethnomethodology. But again, no such choice is necessary. All research techniques have something to offer.

III. Interface

The ethogenic approach should be seriously studied and considered by social psychologists. The stress on structural interpretation is a needed ballast to counter the emphasis that has been placed on parametric interpretation. Many aspects of the ethogenic approach are reminiscent of Heider's (1958) heuristic analysis of "naive psychology." The dramaturgical analogy, the study of the syntactical nature of interaction rituals, accounting, and other microsociological ideas have greatly enriched the social sciences. Some of my own work on social influence has drawn heavily from this perspective (e.g., Schlenker, 1975a, 1975c; Tedeschi et al., 1971), so I am more than sympathetic to it. But just as there are strengths in the ethogenic approach, so there are weaknesses. In the present paper, I have focused on areas of disagreement and moot aspects of Harré's approach. Debate usually advances knowledge far better than does backslapping.

As Kemeny (1959, p. 172) has remarked, "Science should never be hampered by philosophical prejudices as to what type of explanation it should use."[7] This comment applies to both sides of the controversy. We must be willing not only to tolerate but to explore fully various alternative perspectives and research programs. However, just because some individuals find one approach advantageous does not mean that others will share their enthusiasm—any other state of affairs would be intolerably boring.

REFERENCES

Alexander, C. N., Jr., & Knight, P. Situated identities and social psychological experimentation. Sociometry, 1971, 34, 65–82.
Anderson, N. H. Cognitive algebra: Integration theory applied to social attribution. In L. Berkowitz (Ed.), Advances in experimental social psychology. Vol. 7. New York: Academic Press, 1974.
Armistead, N. (Ed.). Reconstructing social psychology. Baltimore: Penguin, 1974.
Bandura, A. Behavior theory and models of man. American Psychologist, 1974, 29, 859–869.

[7] There is a temptation to infer from Harré's discussions that philosophers are univocal regarding many of his key points. If only psychologists possessed the conceptual skill of philosophers, they would be compelled to arrive at the logically necessary conclusions that he describes. This, however, is far from correct. Harré's (1970, 1972) views of the philosophy of science in general and the nature of social science in particular have not been greeted by philosophers with open arms. For example, Mackinnon (1975, p. 73) has stated, "The real problem here is not one of refuting Harré but one of finding some way of salvaging what is valid and potentially valuable in his treatment of scientific explanation."

Bramel, D. Dissonance, expectation, and the self. In R. P. Abelson *et al.* (Eds.), *Theories of cognitive consistency: A sourcebook*. Chicago: Rand McNally, 1968.

Buss, A. R. The emerging field of the sociology of psychological knowledge. *American Psychologist*, 1975, **30**, 988–1002.

Byrne, D. *The attraction paradigm*. New York: Academic Press, 1971.

Carson, R. C. *Interaction concepts of personality*. Chicago: Aldine, 1969.

Chapanis, A. The relevance of laboratory studies to practical situations. *Ergonomics*, 1967, **10**, 557–577.

Chomsky, N. *Aspects of the theory of syntax*. Cambridge, Mass.: MIT Press, 1965.

Cronbach, L. J. Beyond the two disciplines of scientific psychology. *American Psychologist*, 1975, **30**, 116–127.

Elms, A. C. The crisis of confidence in social psychology. *American Psychologist*, 1975, **30**, 967–976.

Feigl, H. The "orthodox" view of theories: Remarks in defense as well as critique. In M. Radner & S. Winokur (Eds.), *Analyses of theories and methods of physics and psychology*. Minneapolis: University of Minnesota Press, 1970.

Feyerabend, P. K. Against method: Outline of an anarchistic theory of knowledge. In M. Radner & S. Winokur (Eds.), *Analyses of theories and methods of physics and psychology*. Minneapolis: University of Minnesota Press, 1970.

Gadlin, H., & Ingle, G. Through the one-way mirror: The limits of experimental self-reflection. *American Psychologist*, 1975, **30**, 1003–1009.

Garfinkel, H. *Studies in ethnomethodology*. Englewood Cliffs, N.J.: Prentice-Hall, 1967.

Garfinkel, H. Common sense knowledge of social structures: The documentary method of interpretation. In J. G. Manis & B. N. Meltzer (Eds.), *Symbolic interaction*. (2nd ed.) Boston: Allyn & Bacon, 1972.

Gergen, K. J. Social psychology as history. *Journal of Personality and Social Psychology*, 1973, **26**, 309–320.

Gibson, J. J. *The senses considered as perceptual systems*. Boston: Houghton, 1966.

Goffman, E. *The presentation of self in everyday life*. Garden City, N.Y.: Doubleday, 1959.

Goffman, E. *Interaction rituals*. Garden City, N.Y.: Doubleday, 1967.

Goffman, E. *Relations in public*. New York: Harper, 1971.

Greenwald, A. G. Transhistorical lawfulness of behavior: A comment on the papers of Gergen and Schlenker. Mimeographed manuscript, Ohio State University, 1974.

Greenwald, A. G. On the inconclusiveness of "crucial" cognitive tests of dissonance versus self-perception theories. *Journal of Experimental Social Psychology*, 1975, **11**, 490–499.

Hampshire, S. *Thought and action*. New York: Viking Press, 1960.

Harré, R. *The principles of scientific thinking*. Chicago: University of Chicago Press, 1970.

Harré, R. *The philosophies of science*. London & New York: Oxford University Press, 1972.

Harré, R. Blueprint for a new science. In N. Armistead (Ed.), *Reconstructing social psychology*. Baltimore: Penguin Books, 1974.

Harré, R., & Secord, P. *The explanation of social behavior*. Totowa, N.J.: Littlefield, Adams, 1973.

Harris, R. J. Two comments on the uncertain connection between theory and data in social psychology. Mimeographed manuscript, Ohio State University, 1974.

Heider, F. *The psychology of interpersonal relations*. New York: Wiley, 1958.

Hempel, C. G. *Philosophy of natural science*. Englewood Cliffs, N.J.: Prentice-Hall, 1966.

Hempel, C. G. On the "standard conception" of scientific theories. In M. Radner & S. Winokur (Eds.), *Analyses of theories and methods of physics and psychology*. Minneapolis: University of Minnesota Press, 1970.

Hendrick, C. Social psychology and history: An analysis of the defense of traditional science. Mimeographed manuscript, Kent State University, 1974.

Kaplan, A. *The conduct of inquiry: Methodology for behavioral science.* San Francisco: Chandler, 1964.

Kemeny, J. G. *A philosopher looks at science.* New York: Van Nostrand, 1959.

Lakatos, I. Falsification and the methodology of scientific research programmes. In I. Lakatos & A. Musgrave (Eds.), *Criticism and the growth of knowledge.* London & New York: Cambridge University Press, 1970.

Mackinnon, E. A reinterpretation of Harré's Copernican revolution. *Philosophy of Science,* 1975, **42**, 67–79.

McGuire, W. J. The yin and yang of progress in social psychology. *Journal of Personality and Social Psychology,* 1973, **26**, 446–456.

Miller, G. A., Galanter, E., & Pribram, K. H. *Plans and the structure of behavior.* New York: Holt, 1960.

Mills, C. W. Situated actions and vocabularies of motive. *American Sociological Review,* 1940, **5**, 904–913.

Mischel, W. Toward a cognitive social learning reconceptualization of personality. *Psychological Review,* 1973, **80**, 252–283.

Moscovici, S. Society and theory in social psychology. In J. Israel & H. Tajfel (Eds.), *The context of social psychology.* New York: Academic Press, 1972.

Nagel, E. *The structure of science: Problems in the logic of scientific explanation.* New York: Harcourt, 1961.

Neisser, U. *Cognitive psychology.* New York: Appleton, 1967.

Not a robot. *Gainesville Sun,* Feb. 4, 1976.

O'Connor, D. J. *Free will.* Garden City, N.Y.: Doubleday, 1971.

Ossorio, P. G. Never smile at a crocodile. *Journal for the Theory of Social Behavior,* 1973, **3**, 121–140.

Platt, J. R. Strong inference. *Science,* 1964, **146**, 347–353.

Popper, K. R. *The logic of scientific discovery.* New York: Harper, 1965.

Psathas, G. Ethnomethods and phenomenology. *Social Research,* 1968, **35**, 500–520.

Riess, M., & Schlenker, B. R. Attitude change and responsibility avoidance as modes of dilemma resolution in forced compliance settings. *Journal of Personality and Social Psychology,* 1977, in press.

Russell, B. *On the philosophy of science.* New York: Bobbs-Merrill, 1965.

Schlenker, B. R. Social psychology and science. *Journal of Personality and Social Psychology,* 1974, **29**, 1–15.

Schlenker, B. R. Group members' attributions of responsibility for prior group performance. *Representative Research in Social Psychology,* 1975, **6**, 96–108. (a)

Schlenker, B. R. Liking for a group following an initiation: Impression management or dissonance reduction? *Sociometry,* 1975, **38**, 99–118. (b)

Schlenker, B. R. Self-presentation: Managing the impression of consistency when reality interferes with self-enhancement. *Journal of Personality and Social Psychology,* 1975, **32**, 1030–1037. (c)

Schlenker, B. R. Social psychology and science: Another look. *Personality and Social Psychology Bulletin,* 1976, **2**, 384–390.

Schlenker, B. R., & Bonoma, T. V. Fun and games: The validity of games for the study of conflict. Mimeographed manuscript, University of Florida, 1976.

Schlenker, B. R., & Schlenker, P. A. Reactions following counterattitudinal behavior which produces positive consequences. *Journal of Personality and Social Psychology,* 1975, **31**, 962–971.

Scott, M. B., & Lyman, S. Accounts. *American Sociological Review*, 1968, **33**, 46–62.

Shaw, M. E. New science or non-science? *Contemporary Psychology*, 1974, **19**, 96–97.

Strawson, P. F. *Individuals*. London: Methuen, 1959.

Tedeschi, J. T., Schlenker, B. R., & Bonoma, T. V. Cognitive dissonance: Private ratiocination or public spectacle? *American Psychologist*, 1971, **26**, 685–695.

AUTOMATISMS AND AUTONOMIES: IN REPLY TO PROFESSOR SCHLENKER

R. Harré

Professor Schlenker's sympathetic criticism of my account of some aspects of the ethogenic approach allows me the opportunity to elaborate certain aspects of the theory to remove some misunderstandings which are apparent in his remarks. He raises four main issues: the status of rules in psychological explanation, the nature of the explanation of structure, the issue of universals, and the role of correlational studies. I shall say something about each of these in turn.

First, let me address the question of *rules*:

(*a*) Clearly, I have not been able to get across to Professor Schlenker the relation we believe obtains between plans and rules. It is not that rules are the social member of the pair; rather they are concerned with the explanation of the genesis of standardized or formal behavior and are involved in its accounting. The distinction between plans and rules is related to that between improvised and standardized action sequences; both are social. At this level of analysis, plans and rules stand in contrast to one another in that plans are constructed for an occasion whereas rules are drawn from a common and learned cultural stock.

(*b*) However, it is a central tenet of ethogenics that action and accounting draw upon common cognitive resources so that the genesis of plans must draw upon the resources which would be deployed in accounting for the actions done in accordance with them. Hence, improvisation, if it is to be meaningful, must draw upon second-order rules for the genesis of orderly and intelligible action.

The emphasis on rule following derives not just from its practical success in ethogenic research, but from a powerful tradition in philosophy exemplified particularly by Wittgenstein, Winch, and Peters, all of whom have emphasized the role of rules in human intellection. In its use in social psychology, the concept of a rule functions both literally and metaphorically, and it is the metaphorical aspect that Professor Schlenker seems to have missed. We have argued (Harré, 1973, 1976a; Harré & Secord, 1972) that rule following is to be considered as the source of a paramorphic model for the understanding of the genesis of action, so that it plays the role both of a literal explanation and of a model of a causal mechanism.

The description of the ethogenic method in this volume presumed an acquaintance with other parts of the literature, particularly my paper "Some Remarks on 'Rule' as a Scientific Concept" (Harré, 1973), where the distinction between principles, conventions, and maxims was drawn and related to S. Toulmin's sevenfold classification that relates rules in a precise way to the modes of action for whose formal order they are deemed to be responsible. The categories of rules reveal differences in possible universality, a point to which I shall return.

Second, I suspect that some of Schlenker's difficulties with a wholehearted acceptance of the ethogenic method derive from his not deploying a traditional but crucial philosophical distinction between formal and efficient causality, that is, between those items which are deemed to be responsible for the form or structure of a product and those items which are deemed to be responsible for its coming into existence. Rules are representations of the formal causes of action, and it by no means follows that either a rule or a plan is necessarily carried out. Plans are abandoned and changed, and rules are broken. Both are representations of *possible* futures. Following Piaget (1971), Secord and I generally assumed that a rule or a plan was a potent or powerful entity which would have the same general character as the commonsense idea of an intention, which is both the driving force behind the genesis of action and the template responsible for its structure. We now think that this Piagetian notion is too simple. It needs to be elaborated in two ways. Some plans and rules no doubt are potent in the Piagetian sense, but it is still necessary to investigate the occasions of their release into action. In other cases, the passivity of the rule requires us to contemplate the possibility of a stimulus. I am very far from thinking, however, that the investigation of releasing conditions or stimuli is clearly and unambiguously located in the science of psychology. There is some reason to think that at least for some classes of social behavior, for example, quarreling or smoking, the efficient causes are likely to prove to be physiological. *At the present time* it seems to me profitable to pursue the understanding of formal causes; then, on the basis of an adequate understanding of *what* it is that is generated in social interaction, we can turn later to the much more difficult question of the stimulus for releasing conditions [see my "Friendship as an Accomplishment" (Harré, 1976b)].

Third, on the matter of universals, Schlenker is, I believe, wholly mistaken if I understand him aright. He seems to be arguing that we should begin with the assumption that there are universals and, on the basis of that assumption, so structure our research program that they are the immediate yield. I believe this to be a serious error in method and that the revelation of universals may be quite as difficult in social psychology as it was in chemistry. As I have argued (Harré, 1973), there are a variety of possible loci for universals in social matters, both at the act level, e.g., the preservation and support of selves, and at the action level, e.g., the syntactical structure of greeting sequences. However, whether there are universals or not is a matter for empirical investigation and cannot be assumed a priori. It may be that in the end, after detailed and thorough ethogenic studies of local cultures, and their methodology for generating and maintaining sociality, comparative studies may show that there are indeed universals. But they are the last things we are likely to reveal, and it would be a serious mistake to begin our investigations with universals as our prime targets. In this matter we follow linguistics in its post-Chomskian phase, in which while universals are not excluded, they are nevertheless relegated to the later stages of a scientific investigation.

Finally, I should like to say a word about the relation of correlational studies to ethogenic studies. Of course we must try to find correlations between types of occasions and types of social action, and indeed the emphasis in ethogenics on situational identification and the specificity of rules to situations is an example of an inherently correlational aspect of the study. But correlations are not science. The accusations that Secord and I leveled against psychologists, i.e., that they often follow uncritically the unsatisfactory logical empiricist or positivist philosophy of science, seem to be particularly relevant to this issue. I suspect that Schlenker's citation of Kemeny, for example, is illustrative of a lingering positivism even in his more liberal mode of thought. Correlations in nonpositivistic science are the occasions for the investigation of the causal mechanisms responsible for those correlations, the discovery of which would be a contribution to science. Correlational studies remain at the level of natural history. It does not follow from this that they are not an important ingredient. To pursue preliminary correlational studies is not at all the same thing in my view as to try to do social psychology according to the parametric methodology. In that methodology it is supposed that treatments externally imposed produce action, and that is what we strenuously deny. It is, perhaps, a somewhat subtle matter to get this straight. It is our belief that social action is generated by a number of different kinds of processes which can be assembled on a spectrum: at one end are *automatisms* such as the adjustments by which we keep our distance and orientation in conversations, whereas at the other end are what I have recently come to call *autonomies* (Harré, 1976c), cases where action is generated by fully conscious and carefully planned self-control. There are intermediate cases which Secord and I dubbed "enigmatic" and upon the methodology of which our argument ultimately turned. Parametric method, with the use of dependent and independent variables, is appropriate to the investigation of autonomism. The ethogenic method, with its emphasis upon rules, plans, and meanings, is particularly appropriate to the study of autonomies. It is our argument that the less

self-conscious forms of human action are better studied as if they were autonomies than as if they were automatisms, and the success of our researches so far
encourages me to think that we are right.

REFERENCES

Harré, R. Some remarks on "rule" as a scientific concept. In T. Mischel (Ed.), *Understand-
ing other persons*. Oxford: Blackwell, 1973.
Harré, R. The constructive role of models. In L. Collins (Ed.), *The use of models in the
social sciences*. London: Tavistock, 1976, Pp. 25–43.
Harré, R. Friendship as an accomplishment. In S. Duck (Ed.), *Theory and practice in
interpersonal attraction*. New York: Academic Press, 1976. (b)
Harré, R. When actions and words speak together. *Times Higher Educational Supplement*.
April 9, 1976, p. 15. (c)
Harré, R., & Secord, P. F. *The explanation of social behaviour*. Oxford: Blackwell, 1972.
Piaget, J. *Structuralism*. London: Routledge & Kegan Paul, 1971. Ch. IV.

SUBJECT INDEX

CONTENTS OF OTHER VOLUMES